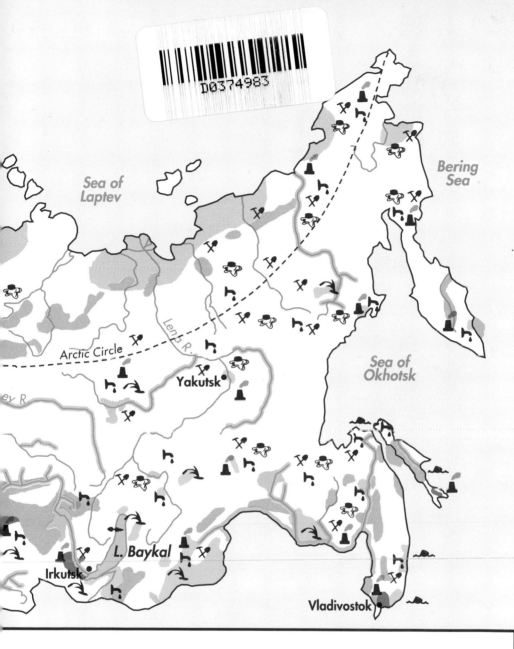

Sea of Laptev

Bering Sea

Lena R.

Arctic Circle

ev R

Yakutsk

Sea of Okhotsk

L. Baykal

Irkutsk

Vladivostok

Air Pollution		Multiple Pollutant Danger	
Groundwater Depletion or Contamination		Characteristic Pollutants	
Pollution of Seas		Soil Erosion	
Depletion of Fish Resources		Deforestation	
Soil Salination, Depletion, or Contaminatinon		Acid Rain	
Disruption of Permafrost Soil Conditions		Water Pollution	
Disruption of Land or Depletion of Subsoil			

ECOCIDE IN THE USSR

ECOCIDE
IN THE USSR,

Health and Nature Under Siege

MURRAY FESHBACH

AND

ALFRED FRIENDLY, JR.

Foreword by Lester Brown

BasicBooks
A Division of HarperCollinsPublishers

To Our Families

Epigraph on p. v from Nikolai Kluyev, "Destruction: A cycle of poems," translated from *Ogonyok* by Richard McKane, © Index on Censorship, 1991.

Excerpt from "150,000,000" by Vladimir Mayakovsky, translated by Joanne Turnbull with the assistance of Nikolai Formozov, in Andrei Sinyavsky, *Soviet Civilization: A Cultural History.* Copyright © 1988 by Albin Michel, S.A. Translation copyright © 1990 by Arcade Publishing. By permission of Little, Brown and Company, in association with Arcade Publishing.

Excerpt from Iurii Shcherbak, *Chernobyl: A Documentary Story,* translated by Ian Press, © 1989, reprinted by permission of Macmillan Press Ltd.

Excerpt from Robert G. Kaiser, *Why Gorbachev Happened: His Triumphs and His Failure,* © Simon & Schuster, New York, 1991, reprinted with permission.

The map that appears as the end papers is based on a consolidation of two maps prepared by the Institute of Geography, USSR Academy of Sciences. The first map appeared in Serge Berg, "Désastre en URSS," *GEO* 134 (April 1990): 30–31, entitled "First Map of a Gigantic Pollution." The title of the second map, hand-drawn and unpublished, is "Karta naiboleye ostrykh ekologicheskikh situatsii"("A Map of the Most Acute Ecological Situations"). The map was prepared by a team of geographers under Dr. B.I. Kochuburov in the Laboratory of Complex Geographic Forecasts. We are indebted to the Office of the Geographer, U.S. Dept. of State for a copy of this latter map.

Library of Congress Cataloging-in-Publication Data

Feshbach, Murray, 1929–
    Ecocide in the USSR : health and nature under siege / by Murray Feshbach and Alfred Friendly, Jr.
        p.   cm.
    Includes bibliographical references and index.
    ISBN 0–456–01664–2 : $24.00
    1. Enviromental health—Soviet Union.   I. Friendly, Alfred, 1938– . II. Title.
RA566.5.S65F47   1992
615.9'02'0947—dc20   91–55456 CIP

Designed by Ellen Levine

92 93 94 95 CC/RRD 9 8 7 6 5 4 3 2

The news we received was bitter
the rippling waves of the Aral sea in dead ooze,
the storks rare in the Ukraine,
the feather grass drooping in Mozdok,
and in the bright Sarov desert
the wheels of machines squealing underground.
Black clouds brought us further news;
the blue Volga is getting shallow,
evil men in Kerzhents are burning
the green pine fortresses,
the Suzdal wheat fields bring forth
lichen and stubble.
The cranes call to us
as they're forced to fly in for remains.
The nesting finches' feathers fall out
and they're plagued by ravening aphids,
the furry bees have only
the big veteran mushrooms to buzz at.
The news was black:
that there was no home land left . . .

—NIKOLAI KLUYEV

"Destruction: a cycle of poems,"
written before his arrest in 1934
Richard McKane, translator

CONTENTS

CONTENTS

FOREWORD

EACH YEAR WHEN we do our *State of the World* report at the Worldwatch Institute, we, in effect, give the earth an annual physical examination. The results of this annual checkup are not reassuring. Each year, the world's forests are smaller, the deserts are larger, the topsoil on cropland is thinner, the stratospheric ozone is more depleted, the concentration of greenhouse gases in the atmosphere rises and the number of plant and animal species with which we share the earth diminishes. And air pollution has reached health-threatening levels in hundreds of cities.

Already the physical degradation of the earth is damaging human health, slowing the growth in world food output and contributing to a reversal in economic progress in dozens of Third World countries. Human health is affected by environmental degradation in every society, though the precise causes and effects vary widely. By the age of ten, thousands of children living in southern California's Los Angeles basin have respiratory systems that are permanently impaired by polluted air; cancer rates have climbed dramatically in Czechoslovakia over the last few decades; in Australia, skin cancer has reached near-epidemic proportions.

We have long known from these and thousands of other examples that we cannot separate our health from that of the earth itself—but no one has documented this link for any country in as much detail as Murray Feshbach and Alfred Friendly have for the Soviet Union. Just when you think the litany of soaring cancer rates, chronic respiratory ailments and birth deformities can't go any further, the next chapter unfolds yet another case of callous disregard for the environment devastating human health. Those who now think that environmental deterioration is a greater threat to our future security than military aggression will find much here to support that notion.

My own personal exposure to these issues in the Soviet Union, particularly a recent visit to the Aral Sea basin, illustrates the dimensions of Soviet health deterioration. In the basin, a closed system with no drainage to the outside, insecticides and herbicides sprayed on irrigated cotton fields percolate downward, reaching dangerous concentrations as they accumulate in the underground water supply. As most tap water comes from wells, the people who live there drink a cocktail of diluted chemicals, some of which are known carcinogens. Not surprisingly, the local medical literature is filled with stories of birth deformities, increased liver and kidney disease, chronic gastritis, rising infant mortality and soaring cancer rates. For example, in Karakalpak, a small, ethnically defined autonomous republic within Uzbekistan along the south shore of the Aral Sea, the esophageal cancer rate is seven times higher than in the rest of the country.

In the Bozataus region of Karakalpak, an area simultaneously plagued with a lack of sewage treatment facilities, inadequate maternal and child health care and rising levels of pesticides and herbicides in drinking water, 110 of every 1,000 infants die before their first birthday. This compares with an average of 109 in Africa, 95 in India, and 37 in China. Although the Asian republics were part of the Soviet Union, their vital statistics are increasingly those of a poor Third World country.

Staggering though the health damage described by Feshbach and Friendly is, their estimates may be conservative. Dr. Vladimir Chernousenko, the nuclear physicist who was appointed scientific supervisor of the emergency cleanup of Chernobyl, estimates in a forthcoming book, *Chernobyl: Insight from the Inside*, that the cleanup alone, with the associated exposure to radiation, has claimed between five thousand and seven thousand lives to date. All of those initially involved in the cleanup who were exposed for one hour or more to the intense radiation from the demolished plant are now dead. He estimates that at least 20 million Soviet citizens have been exposed to excessive levels of nuclear radiation. The ultimate loss of life in the Soviet Union and elsewhere from Chernobyl may eventually be measured in the tens of thousands.

Ecocide in the USSR demonstrates that the production quotas of socialism can be at least as environmentally destructive as the profit motives of capitalism. In capitalist market economies it is assumed that people are naturally greedy, and this is taken into account in establishing the framework of rules within which the economy operates. Socialism assumes an inherent lack of greed and hence fails to guard against its potentially destructive consequences.

In the wake of the failed coup in August, the various republics face a staggering array of problems, including how to clean up the environment. As Feshbach and Friendly demonstrate, these newly independent republics find themselves in a situation where the problems are so grave that economic recovery depends on environmental cleanup and, hence, a restructuring of the economy. The same grass-roots movements and initiatives that caused the coup to fail can also generate the initiatives to reverse environmental degradation. But it is difficult to overstate the economic and environmental dimensions of the challenge now facing the republic governments.

This book contains a rich collection of data on the health effects of environmental degradation in what was, until recently, the world's third most populous country. It provides a window on the future of other countries if environmental degradation is not taken seriously.

This information-rich volume is the product of two men who have devoted much of their lives to studying the Soviet Union. Feshbach has been analyzing social trends in the Soviet Union for much of his career, initially as chief of the Soviet branch in the Foreign Demographic Analysis Division of the Department of Commerce and more recently, as a research professor at Georgetown University. Friendly covered Soviet affairs for several years as a Moscow correspondent for *Newsweek* magazine. The combined research and writing skills of the two have produced a remarkably useful book, a case where one plus one equals far more than two.

Lester R. Brown
Worldwatch Institute

PREFACE

As it broke down, the Soviet Union opened up. Our book, while an examination of some of the factors and forces responsible for the political and economic collapse, is in many ways a product of the information revolution that preceded and propelled the disintegration. We have tried to use layman's language both to describe the disastrous consequences of health and environmental policies on the Soviet people and to document the protests against those policies that gathered mounting force in the Gorbachev years. The story is drawn in the main from Soviet sources which, but for *glasnost,* would have been inaccessible. We owe a major debt to the journalists, scientists and citizen-activists who compiled the public record on ecological and health conditions in the USSR and who, in a number of cases, explained their work and their findings to us in person.

The core of the book, however, is scholarly research, the work of a professional lifetime spent ferreting out and analyzing the grudging flow of often suspect Soviet data about labor, fertility, mortality, education, migration, welfare and military manpower. Those studies by Dr. Feshbach led to significant discoveries: the rising rates of infant mortality in the 1970s and the official effort to conceal the facts; the high birth rates of Muslims in Central Asia that, along with their low mobility, foreshadowed labor and ethnic imbalances as likely sources of social, economic, military and political tensions. The 1978 publication of a courageous *samizdat* work on environmental abuse—*The Destruction of Nature,* written by Ze'ev Wolfson under the pseudonym of Boris

Komarov[1]—dictated a new dimension of research by revealing the harm that pollution was doing to economic and human health.

The various strands of scholarship first came together in *Economics of Health and Environment in the USSR*,[2] a comprehensive analysis Dr. Feshbach did for the Office of Net Assessment of the Department of Defense, where, as director, Andrew Marshall has been a steady source of support. Among those who read that study, Dr. Harley Balzer, director of the Russian Area Studies Program of Georgetown University, and Steve Fraser, senior editor of BasicBooks, were both firm in their belief that the findings needed to be put before an audience broader than the community of academic and official specialists in Soviet affairs. Harley, in particular, was the catalyst for our collaboration and a perceptive critic of its product.

To the extent that our use of the English language is reasonably clear and occasionally graceful, we owe profound thanks to the editorial acumen of our uncommon, common friend, Peggy Nalle, who read, marked and guided the rewriting of the first draft of the manuscript. Other gentle readers—Muriel Feshbach; Strobe Talbott; Mary Bingham; Edmund Pellegrino, M.D.; Michael Ryan, Ph.D. and Maria Cherkasova, Ph.D.—have saved us from a variety of errors and lapses. As research assistants, Ann Rubin, Elizabeth O'Shea, Margot Jacobs, Shawn Dorman and Scott DiGruttolo served as keen-eyed guides through the mountains of technical and other literature we have tried to explore. Less formally, Dina Kaminskaya, Gary Litman, Vladimir Litwak, Larisa Silnitskaya and Konstantin Simis in Washington, Yevgeniya Albats and Marina Konovalova in Moscow, Nikolai Babushkin in Krasnoyarsk and Timur Isatayev in Alma-Ata culled, clipped and kept us in touch with a range of Soviet publications on ecological and medical issues. Having utilized much literature in translation, we are also deeply indebted to the anonymous linguists of the Foreign Broadcast Information Service (FBIS) and the Joint Publications Research Service (JPRS), as well as to the American taxpayers who finance their invaluable work.

For supporting some of our travels to the USSR, especially a 1990 reporting trip on population, health and environmental issues that took us to Moscow together and Friendly on to Volgograd, Odessa and Yaroslavl, we owe special thanks to the International Research and Exchanges Board (IREX). For hospitality in the Soviet Union on that occasion and advice on understanding the changes in progress, we are grateful as well to Rosemary Forsythe of the U. S. Embassy and to the Ambassador of Italy and Mrs. Ferdinando Salleo. Our thanks are also due to Professor Ronald Liebowitz and his fellow geographers at Middlebury College for their assistance in preparing the maps used to guide readers to locales mentioned in various chapters.

Seeking a broad readership, we have used simplified spellings of Russian names (Grigory, Vassily, Yevgeny and Norilsk, for example) in the text and put the scholarly transliterations (Grigoriy, Vasiliy, Yevgeniy, Noril'sk) of the Cyrillic alphabet on maps and in the source notes at the end of the book. The place names are those in use as of mid-August 1991 when, for example, Belarus was Belorussia, St. Petersburg was Leningrad and Yekaterinburg was Sverdlovsk.

The book is a cautionary tale. It is full of depressing, often deeply distressing evidence of man's inhumanity to man and to nature, of the terrible price in human health and natural wealth exacted from the Soviet people by leaders and a system that put first things last. The bleakness of the story, however, is partly redeemed by the other evidence we found of a social and civil awakening, of popular movements to defend the environment against further abuse and to put the subjects of history in charge, at last, of their own destiny. It is hard to be optimistic about the speed or even the likely success of that effort in a setting as ravaged and an economy as battered as the Soviet Union is in the fall of 1991. It is possible, nonetheless, to harbor the hope that a turning point has been reached and passed and that a nation that has endured so much avoidable tragedy in its history is still capable of making for itself a humane future.

Something of that hope animated the sweeping thirty-one-point Declaration of Human Rights and Freedoms adopted by the Soviet parliament as it disbanded on September 5, 1991. The resolution is an almost Jeffersonian set of pledges of individual liberty that also spells out social guarantees of work, pay, welfare, public housing and education. Articles 28 and 29 of the Declaration proclaim a right to "health protection," including free medical care, and a double entitlement to "a favorable natural environment" and to "compensation for damage to . . . health or property" caused by "ecological violations."

Those will be hard and expensive promises to keep. Neglecting them, however, has brought calamity. We hope our portrait of that disaster and its causes may prove useful to people in what was once the Soviet Union, to those who seek to assist them to recover and to others who want to avoid such errors in their own countries and on the planet that is our common home.

Murray Feshbach
Alfred Friendly, Jr.

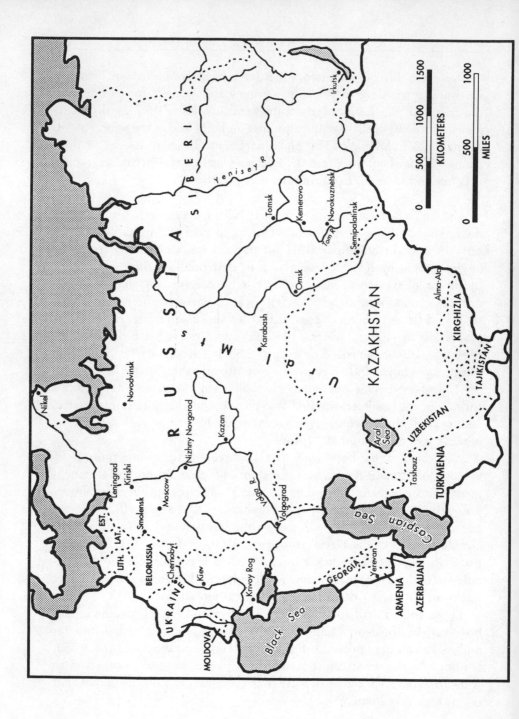

CHAPTER 1

Facing Facts

WHEN HISTORIANS FINALLY conduct an autopsy on the Soviet Union and Soviet Communism, they may reach the verdict of death by ecocide. For the modern era, indeed for any event except the mysterious collapse of the Mayan empire, it would be a unique but not an implausible conclusion. No other great industrial civilization so systematically and so long poisoned its land, air, water and people. None so loudly proclaiming its efforts to improve public health and protect nature so degraded both. And no advanced society faced such a bleak political and economic reckoning with so few resources to invest toward recovery.

In land area, the Soviet Union was the largest country in the world. In population in 1990 it ranked third, after China and India. For decades it was the leading producer of oil and steel, the owner of a quarter of the planet's forest reserves and an equal portion of its fresh water. Yet it beggared itself by endangering the health of its population—especially its children and its labor force—the productivity of its soil and the purity of its air and water.

These threats, in turn, endanger prospects for economic recovery, even if sweeping systemic reforms take hold in the successor states. Aside from the time required to remedy decades of environmental abuse, the costs of cleaning up could drain staggering sums from all the resources needed to rebuild housing, hospitals, roads, power plants and water systems and to modernize industry and agriculture.

The investments that former Soviets must make to combine ecological restoration with economic recovery can only be estimated. They will

1

have to be enormous. Ideally, to compensate for the long-term and continuing abuse of two essential resources, nature and human health, between 1990 and 2015, the new nations would have to allocate funds amounting to many times the value of total 1990 USSR gross national product (GNP). While outlays of such magnitude appear crippling, even unattainable, properly directed investments could make economies more efficient and the people stronger. In the absence of such remedial action, environmental neglect will continue to put added strain on the debilitated medical care system.

Disease that victims traced, rightly or wrongly, to pollution put an extra element of indignation into Gorbachev era politics. Activism produced loud, sometimes unrealistic demands for immediate ecological cures. Protest that originated in environmental disputes quickly widened in many cases to fan ethnic tensions and complicate politicians' efforts to hold the component parts of the Soviet Union under central rule.

Together, environmental and medical failures not only deflated pretensions about the social merits of the Soviet system; they also reflected an accumulating social breakdown. A few examples of the ways in which Soviets have laid siege to their environment and, in consequence, undermined their health and well-being only begin to suggest the scope of the crisis.

• To make up for the inefficiency of their farming practices, Soviets resorted to the massive but untutored use of toxic agricultural chemicals. They even spread tons of DDT long after other nations banned it, so much for so long that 25 million acres of cropland are still overloaded with the poison. In some areas marked by pesticide abuse, the infant mortality rate runs twice as high as in cleaner, nearby regions. Nitrates and other dangerous substances appear in produce and in more than 40 percent of baby food at levels high enough to touch off medical and consumer alarm.

A drive to raise Central Asia's cotton output through extensive irrigation and intense application of pesticides and defoliants dried up and contaminated the rivers that used to sustain the Aral Sea, once larger than Lake Huron. As its volume shrank by two-thirds, storms carried the toxic salts from its exposed bed to fertile fields more than one thousand miles away. So much contamination by chemical wastes has been dumped into the drinking water supply that mothers in the Aral region cannot breast-feed their babies without running the risk of poisoning them.

• Industrial growth, pursued at reckless speed, without effective measurement of economic or social costs, has put 70 million out of 190 million Soviets living in 103 cities in danger of respiratory and other

2

life-shortening diseases from air that carries five and more times the allowed limit of pollutants. Almost three-fourths of the nation's surface water is polluted; one-fourth is completely untreated. By themselves, the two giant ministries of energy and metallurgy account for half the air pollution. Untreated, waterborne agricultural, industrial and human wastes together threaten to kill the Sea of Azov, the Black Sea and the Caspian and have turned giant rivers, including the Volga, the Dniepr and the Don, into open sewers.

• Inefficiency in extracting fuel and generating electricity has brought the USSR to the brink of a severe energy crisis, intensified by post-Chernobyl protests strong enough to stall and even to cut back the growth of nuclear power. Oil production has plummeted, and hard-currency sales of oil and gas—the bulk of Soviet export earnings—dropped by over one-third in just three years. Meanwhile, the costs of the 1986 reactor explosion have kept climbing: Beyond a 9-billion-ruble cleanup bill, economic losses could mount to 200 billion rubles. Similarly, the number of fatalities inside the USSR, officially put at thirty-one, almost certainly reached four thousand in excess deaths by mid-1991 and may go ten times as high before 2036.

• Environmental decay, as a menace to human health, has combined with a breakdown in medical care and with dietary deficiencies to reduce the country's military strength. In 1990 fewer than half of Soviet draft-age men were fit for duty, while a steep rise in the proportion of young non-Slavs—mostly Muslims from Central Asia—threatens in coming years to upset the ethnic balance in the ranks. The Red Army is both polluter and victim of pollution. The physical and political fallout from its nuclear-weapons testing grounds has been so intense that, since 1989, only very limited experiments have been permitted at what had been the most active site in Kazakhstan. Radioactive wastes allegedly of military origin also have generated fear and protest near White Sea ports used by the Soviet fleet and commercial ships.

• Doctors, most of them honest and caring but many of them incompetents who bribed their way into medical schools, are severely handicapped by the low level of sanitation even in operating rooms and by the chronic and worsening shortage of supplies of reliable instruments and medicines. Fear of infection from unsterilized needles and unsafe vaccines has driven parents to put off immunizing their children. One result was a 1990 outbreak in Moscow of more than seven hundred cases of diphtheria, a disease that strikes one or two Americans at most a year. While a few surgeons were forced on occasion to substitute safety razors for scalpels in performing appendectomies, two out of five young graduates of medical schools entered service unable to read an electrocardiagram, and half the working pediatricians (in one group of four hundred tested in Kazakhstan) proved completely ignorant about the properties of sixteen widely used drugs.

SHORTENED LIVES, NEEDLESS DEATHS

By failing to invest effectively in health care and environmental protection, the rulers of the USSR brought the average life expectancy of its citizens down to the level of average life expectancy in Paraguay. From 66.1 years in 1964–65, life expectancy for Soviet men dropped to 62.3 years in 1980–81, making only a small recovery to 63.8 years in 1989.[1] Fifty-year-old males could expect in 1985 to die earlier than men who reached the half-century mark in 1939.[2]

Claimed illness kept nearly 4 million Soviet workers from their jobs on an average day in 1989.* That absenteeism cost the system over 7 billion rubles a year in sick pay and an estimated 20 billion rubles in lost production.[3] Using 900 billion rubles as the likely sum of Soviet GNP in 1990 (100 billion rubles less than the official figure that Soviet authorities themselves acknowledge is inflated), the losses due to ill health could be calculated at about 3 percent of the economy's total output.

After bringing the death rate of children in their first year of life down from 80.7 per thousand in 1950 to 22.9 in 1971,[4] the USSR—alone among industrialized nations—saw infant mortality, as officially calculated, rise again to 25.4 per thousand in 1987, roughly the same level as in Malaysia, Yugoslavia, East Harlem and Washington, D.C. Even though the reported toll dropped to 22.3 infant deaths per thousand births in 1989, the actual infant mortality rate in the USSR was more likely to be as much as 33 per thousand, a frequency comparable to that of China and Sri Lanka.

In counting deaths in the first year of life, as in many areas of demographic, economic and environmental reporting, Soviet statistics cannot be trusted. In the late 1980s their accuracy began to improve, but the road to reliability is long and far from fully traveled. Part of the reason lay with the Soviet practice, contrary to international standards, of counting many premature, underweight babies as miscarriages rather than live births. Additionally, record keepers falsified data to make it seem that infants died after, instead of before, their first birthday.

---

*In the United States, according to Bureau of Labor Statistics data for 1989, an average of 287,000 workers a day stayed off the job on account of illness or injury.

4

Deaths in the first year of life have been deliberately underreported by as much as 86 percent in some parts of Central Asia and even by half in the Russian Republic.[5] Given the prevalence of such conduct in the very regions where infant mortality and birth rates were the highest in the USSR, it is justified—perhaps even conservative—to scale official data upward by 50 percent—from 22 deaths per thousand live births to 33 deaths per thousand.

In another measure of deteriorating public health in the USSR, the incidence of intestinal and respiratory infections increased by 18 and 30 percent, respectively, from 1980 to 1987.[6] In 1988, when 1.8 million cases of severe intestinal infection were recorded, delegates to the Nineteenth Communist Party Conference in Moscow learned that 53 percent of all Soviet schoolchildren were considered to be in poor health.[7] Health researchers found that not only were two out of every five young men reporting for compulsory military duty unfit to serve, but also that only 20 to 25 percent of high school graduates could be termed truly healthy.[8]

Pressing the case in late 1990 for a 500-day program of sweeping economic change and social reorganization, leading economists said that every fourth adult and every sixth child in the USSR was chronically ill. With that reform program shelved and no substitute agreed on, a senior officer on the Red Army's General Staff reported in mid-1991 that "no more than 48 out of every 100 persons can be drafted today."[9]

Inadequate diet; pervasive alcoholism; cramped living conditions; dirty, noisy and dangerous workplaces and poor sanitation are all among the causes of the Soviet health crisis. They are simultaneously ingredients and symptoms of the backwardness that plagued both the Russian Empire and the Soviet Union. While Lenin's successors had claimed and even achieved marked progress in medical care and environmental protection, performance never matched propaganda. The shortfall has spelled not just policy failure but human suffering as well.

The gap opened with the most basic elements of medical and social infrastructure. At the end of 1990, for instance, it was reported that in a nation where one-third of the population still lived outside cities, almost half of all rural hospitals and polyclinics had no sewer connections. Eighty percent had no hot water, and in nearly three-quarters, between six and fifteen patients were crowded into wards that should have held just four beds.[10]

In part, the inadequacies of rural medical facilities are a reflection of the perennial backwardness of the countryside. In the republics of Azerbaijan, Uzbekistan and Turkmenistan, with over 30 million mostly Muslim inhabitants, between 44 and 48 percent of the townships lacked sewer systems.[11] But neglect extended to urban health care as well. In Moscow, the showcase capital, the medical care system ranked "as one of the most backward" in the country, the new Soviet health minister reported in early 1987. Of thirty-three maternity homes, only twelve "are up to modern requirements and public health standards," he said. In the ten preceding years, he noted, the city's hospitals had not added a single bed for infectious diseases.[12]

Even if basic hygiene were adequate, equipment, medicines and doctors are not. In a country where, as in the United States, cardiovascular disease is the leading cause of death, there were only 130 angiogram devices in operation in 1988, and only 60 of them were of recent manufacture.[13] X-ray machines could only be found in half of all hospitals and polyclinics, and only 2 percent of such institutions had the machinery to do ultrasound diagnosis.[14]

Kazakhstan alone started the year 1988 with a shortage of 6,200 maternity ward beds. Of the beds available, 13,600 were in buildings classified as dangerous. The republic's children's hospitals fell 14,000 beds behind their needs and were forced to house 16,000 pediatric cases in substandard facilities.[15]

Such neglect and the hypocrisy that had long kept it hidden infuriated even Soviet officials far from the scene. In an impassioned speech to the Nineteenth Communist Party Conference in Moscow on June 28, 1988, then Minister of Health Yevgeny Chazov told of a Siberian railroad station, a prestige project, built of aluminum and marble while the local hospital "is housed in a barracks-like building without any conveniences."

He continued:

> In Moscow a hospital for Patriotic [World] War [II] invalids took 11 years to build. . . . Think how many high-flown words were said about Kazakhstan. . . . But, comrades, how could these words be accepted by the 60,000 inhabitants of the republic with tuberculosis—a disease we were in such a hurry to say we had eliminated. They had seen a public bath and health center built in marble in the center of Alma-Ata at a cost of 15 million rubles. Perhaps this public bath was necessary; perhaps this center was needed. But you should see the conditions in which patients . . . are treated in the tuberculosis institute close by.[16]

Medical equipment was in such short supply, Chazov also disclosed, that hospital openings were being delayed for the lack of "approximately 1,000 operating tables, 5,000 surgical lamps, and 100,000 bactericidal lamps."[17] As for medicines, a perennial shortage of specialty drugs turned into an acute and general one between 1985 and 1989 as domestic demand rose in value by 33 percent and output by only 28 percent.[18]

Some Soviet capacity, moreover, went into making obsolete or even dangerous products such as pyramidon, almost universally banned as carcinogenic.[19] Politburo members learned late in 1989 that the Soviet pharmaceutical industry was supplying only 30 percent of needed cardiovascular medicines, 43 percent of cancer medications and just 15 percent of hormones and insulin.[20]

Such shortages produced some remarkable examples of official thinking. Facing an AIDS scare that boosted demand for disposable syringes and single-use needles to 5 billion more than Soviet factories could hope to turn out in 1990, Medical Industry Minister Valery A. Bykov proposed a curious remedy. "Now we produce 30 million multiple-use syringes a year, but we need at least 50 million," he told an *Izvestiya* interviewer. "I think we can solve the problem by making it possible for each family to have its own syringe, like a thermometer."[21]

Even with a full medicine cabinet at home, an ordinary Soviet family still has to cope with the shortage of qualified medical personnel. Taking over as minister of health in February 1987, Chazov instituted a reportedly lenient recertification process as a first step toward raising competence levels. After about one-third of the USSR's 1.3 million physicians were tested, 320,000 doctors were allowed to continue in practice, 1,000 were dismissed and some 30,000 more were given only temporary licenses.[22]

Many who should have lost their licenses continue to practice. For example, a 1989 report on obstetricians-gynecologists in the Tashauz *oblast* (region) of Turkmenistan revealed that because 70 percent of them lacked surgical skills, half of their patients who underwent surgery died as a result. "Moreover, . . . the medical documentation on deceased pregnant women, recently confined women and gynecology patients makes it clear that two out of every three deaths could have been prevented."[23] Such tragedies were hardly surprising in a republic where maternal and pediatric health researchers found that one-fourth of all rural midwives and one-third of all rural pediatricians did not meet even rudimentary professional requirements.[24]

Nor is incompetence limited to Central Asia. In the Ukraine, according to a September 1988 disclosure, the asphyxia, pneumonia, respiratory-disorder syndrome and very premature birth that ranked as the principal causes of deaths among newborns were "directly related to the inadequate skills" of the medical personnel in attendance.[25]

"The level of education and qualification among doctors is plummeting," Andrei Sakharov's widow, herself a former pediatrician, told an

American audience in 1990. "We practice almost no modern heart surgery . . . [and according to a recent Health Ministry report] of the 800 heart [bypass] operations performed in the USSR over the last several years, a high proportion were unsuccessful."[26]

VICIOUS SYNERGY: POLLUTION AND DISEASE

While many of the systemic failings of Soviet medicine can be remedied, the public health structure stands in need of a complete overhaul if it is to deal effectively with pollution-related diseases. Better training, better pay, better facilities, better sanitation and better organization of health care priorities could all, over time, bring significant improvements. Unfamiliar environmental threats, however, present new demands that are hard to measure with certainty and impossible to handle by medical means alone.

In most cases, even in Western countries, scientists lack the data to correlate disease and environmental abuse definitively. Soviet environmental monitoring, moreover, is as primitive as Soviet health statistics are suspect. Although experts counted "tens of thousands" of harmful substances in manufacturing use in the USSR, the Ministry of Health set upper limits for only 413 dangerous atmospheric compounds and 691 such substances in surface waters.

Soviet inspection services in 1991 were equipped to check for just 52 air pollutants and 7 that endangered water quality.[27] A Russian Republic system of environmental fees and fines, initiated in 1991, covered only 210 air pollutants and 129 discharges into water.[28] Given those limitations, raw data nevertheless painted an alarming picture.

Soviets have found, for instance, that in sixty-eight cities where air pollution is regularly measured at ten or more times above permissible maximums,* the rate of illness among the 40 million residents—almost one-seventh of the entire population of the USSR and nearly one-fifth of all city dwellers—was higher than the national average by factors of 1.5, 2, and even more.[29] From another study comparing health in two groups of five cities each, Soviet researchers determined that cancer, blood and liver diseases as well as other "serious disorders" occurred three to four times more frequently where air and water pollution were acute.[30]

Aleksei Yablokov, a zoologist who became one of the USSR's most

*For definitions of maximum permissible concentrations of various substances, see tables 10a, b, c and d in the appendix.

8

passionate and best-informed environmental advocates, cited two cases that he said documented pollution's effect on health:

> In the [Urals] city of Karabash (Chelyabinsk region), where harmful emissions from the smokestacks of the copper-smelting combine reach nine tons per capita per year, half the youngsters of draft age cannot be called up for army service because of the state of their health. In the Krasnodar district [of the northern Caucasus] there are rice-growing areas where the intensive use of pesticides has had such an effect on health that not a single young man could be accepted for military duty. In some farming villages of that district cancer is the only cause of death![31]

Although the ties between environmental abuse and illness remain inevitably more presumptive than proven, there is little question about the extent of pollution itself. Few industrialized areas of the Soviet Union are environmentally risk-free, and some form of severe ecological condition obtains in 16 percent of the country's land area, where one-fifth of the population lives.[32]

According to data presented to Soviet prosecutors late in 1990, the life expectancy of Moscow residents—ten years below what it had been in 1970—ranked the metropolis "70th among the world's 90 largest cities." Congenitally deformed children were being born in the Soviet capital "one and a half times more often" on average than in the USSR as a whole. With infant mortality rates running "two-to-three times higher" in Moscow than in other republic capitals, as of 1989, "more inhabitants . . . died than were born."[33]

The testimony presented tied the demographic disaster directly to the fact that three-quarters of "Moscow's plants and factories do not have the resources to control environmental pollution. As a result the ground is saturated with zinc, lead, molybdenum and chromium, and specialists have warned in all seriousness" that children playing in sandboxes risk grave illnesses. A typical "Catch-22" situation arose when city authorities tried to close down an environmentally offensive rubber-goods manufacturer. They found that the plant made hoses essential for the assembly line of a huge automotive works from which, in turn, the municipal budget derived crucial funds.[34]

Such trade-offs are not new to Western environmental policymakers, but Soviets are only beginning to confront and be confounded by them. The delay has had major consequences. "The [Russian] republic is in catastrophic condition," the chairman of the Russian Federation Committee on Nature Protection told his agency's first meeting in April 1989. Not only are five regions—the Urals, East and West Siberia, Central and

North Russia—"on the brink of ecological disaster," but, where air quality was monitored, "it is theoretically impossible to live in every seventh city."

> There is 20 times as much nitrous oxide as the norm in the air of Gorky [now Nizhny-Novgorod], Smolensk and Omsk; 33 times as much sulfur dioxide as the norm in Nikel; 183 times as much methyl mercaptan as the norm in Volzhsky, 289 times in Arkhangelsk, 478 times in Novodvinsk; the benzopyrene content in Novokuznetsk's air is 598 times above the maximum permissible.[35]

The air in Novokuznetsk, in fact, ranked only as the fifth most polluted in the USSR.* During 1990 stationary sources alone put 889,000 tons of harmful emissions a year into the city's atmosphere.[37] Close to Novokuznetsk in the southeastern corner of Western Siberia, the city of Kemerovo is also an environmental death trap for its 565,000 inhabitants. A coal-mining town since it was founded in the 1830s and a burgeoning industrial center since Stalin's first Five-Year Plan began in 1929, the city has become a smoky inferno of chemical, metallurgical and mining enterprises.

Of Kemerovo's 109 large factories, 66 are sited in residential neighborhoods. Along with fertilizers, paints, plastics and farm and mining equipment, Kemerovo industries annually produce nine times the maximum permissible levels of sulfur dioxide, seven times the allowed limits of hydrogen sulfide and almost four times more solid phenols, nitrous oxides and carbon monoxide than Soviet rules set as safe.[38]

One result was that residents in 1989 were two to three times as likely to suffer from blood diseases, chronic bronchitis and disorders of the endocrine system as Soviet citizens on average. From birth to the age of fourteen, Kemerovo children had almost half again the rate of respiratory illness as the national average and nearly three times the incidence of kidney and urinary tract infections. In one heavily polluted district of the city, retardation among children was 2.1 times more frequent than in a cleaner neighborhood on the opposite bank of the Tom River, itself an industrial sewer carrying thirty-four times the maximum permissible level of formaldehyde and forty-two times that set for oil products.[39]

The Kemerovo statistic on child retardation echoed a national one:

---

*The worst air was in the Siberian city of Norilsk, above the Arctic Circle. The area's 267,000 residents were subjected to 2,368,700 tons of industrial atmospheric pollutants in 1990. By contrast, São Paulo, Brazil's largest city, home to 9.7 million people, was considered severely polluted because its factories emitted 350,000 tons of soot and smoke annually. Per capita, Norilsk's pollution rate was 222 times São Paulo's.[36]

From 1975 to 1990 the rate at which women gave birth to retarded children—nearly 2 million by 1991—increased more than twice as fast in the USSR's big cities as in the countryside.[40] "There is no worse ecological situation on the planet than ours in the USSR," judged Dr. Grigory Matveyevich Barenboim, a leading independent environmental analyst. "Pyotr Chadayev said 150 years ago that it was Russia's fate to serve as an example to the world of how not to live. I would say that we have become both an environmental testing ground for the whole world and an ecological threat to the entire planet."[41]

CHERNOBYL: THE
GLASNOST FALLOUT

If there is any bright spot in this sketch of a nation on the edge of ecological and human disaster, it is in the awareness that Soviet citizens and leaders, such as Dr. Barenboim, show of the gravity of their crisis. That consciousness can lead to change; it is at least the beginning of wisdom.

After decades of suppressing the truth with slogans and secrecy, Soviet authorities began to acknowledge the facts of their health and environmental breakdown only after the Chernobyl nuclear accident in 1986. Beginning three years after that disaster, a torrent of revelations fed the alarm and, among some, a sense of despair. A society long given to the use of self-descriptive superlatives came to see itself not as the world's best but as the most polluted, most incapacitated.

There is typical excess in that image. The Soviet Union remains a land of vast natural resources, of strong, talented and resilient people. It is, however, a crippled giant. Its self-inflicted social and ecological wounds, compounding and compounded by its economic and political failures, sapped Soviet military strength and undermined Moscow's pretense to global influence. Forced to turn inward to recuperate and rebuild, the USSR, well into the twenty-first century, must also find ways to turn outward for help.

Its needs for medical technology and training and for environmental protection and cleanup equipment and expertise will be enormous, ranging from the simplest pharmaceutical supplies—vitamins and condoms, for instance—to the most sophisticated oil-drilling and pollution-control machinery. At the beginning of the 1990s, however, Soviet planners were barely in a position to define their problems or set their goals in quantitative terms. Moreover, their society was only starting to come to grips with the politics and culture that, in exalting collective power

11

for over seventy years, had disdained individual well-being and that, in promising to subdue nature, had laid it waste. The first steps toward recovering human and ecological health had to be psychological.

Facing facts that had been so long denied or camouflaged was the essential start of the therapy. "For seventy years we were taught never to think for ourselves," Dr. Barenboim observed. "That's the explanation for our ecological catastrophe. Like the mammoth hunters, we still think of nature as something to fight."[42]

Appropriately, it took a catastrophe to blast the truth into the open. The two barely separated explosions that rocked Unit Number 4 of the V. I. Lenin Chernobyl Nuclear Power Station, seventy-two miles north of the Ukrainian capital of Kiev, at 1:23 A.M. on Saturday, April 26, 1986, poured more radioactive material into the atmosphere than had been released in the atomic bombings of Hiroshima and Nagasaki.[43] In the days that followed, a mile-high plume of radioactive gas and particles dispersed some of its 30 million curies as far north as Sweden, west into Germany, Poland and Austria, and as far south as Greece and Yugoslavia. Another 20 million curies dropped onto some 50,000 square miles of the Ukraine, Belorussia and western Russia, poisoning soil and water, even in the heavily populated Leningrad region, where it lodged.[44]

The extent of the fallout, however, was hidden from most residents of the affected areas. The first maps to show where radiation had contaminated the Ukraine and Belorussia were not published until March 1989, and for four Russian Soviet Federated Socialist Republic (RSFSR) *oblasts,* only in February 1990.[45] A similarly classified map, reportedly showing 1,500 Leningrad city sites where radioactive wastes or nuclear production posed a danger to health, became an election issue in the late winter of 1990 in a city already so alarmed that it had put 1,200 people to work with dosimeters to check produce headed for its stores and markets. New civic leaders, many of them victors at the polls, charged Party bosses with concealing the danger and the fact that only thirty of the hot spots had been rendered harmless.[46]

Although Academician Valery Legasov, the senior scientist on the first Soviet government commission sent to Chernobyl, compared the blowup's historical consequences to those of the eruption of Mt. Vesuvius,[47] the parallel was inexact. Volcanic ash buried Pompeii and Herculaneum for seventeen centuries. Chernobyl's fallout, by contrast, helped to melt away much—but far from all—of the secrecy that authorities had long used to hide a vast range of health and environmental dangers.

Old habits die hard, and the obsession with concealing ugly realities is an ingrained Russian trait. It long antedates the 1917 Revolution. Writing from the court of Czar Nicholas I in 1839 after a severe storm in the middle of an imperial celebration had killed somewhere between thirty and fifteen hundred people, a French nobleman observed: "We shall never ascertain the exact circumstances of the event. Every accident here is treated as an affair of state: it is God who has failed in his duty to the emperor. . . . A silence more frightful than the evil itself, everywhere reigns. . . . Russia is a nation of mutes."[48]

Nearly a century and a half later, secrecy was still so much the rule* that Moscow authorities did not admit to outsiders that a nuclear accident had occurred at Chernobyl until April 28, more than forty-eight hours after the explosions. Even then the disclosure—forced by Swedish scientists whose instruments first picked up the burst of radioactivity from the plant—was limited to a terse announcement of accidental reactor damage.

Initially and falsely, Soviets were told that "the radiation situation in the power station and the surrounding area is stabilized."[49] Not until a May 6 press conference in Moscow and a May 14 television address by Soviet Party leader Mikhail Gorbachev, in which he angrily blamed the West for using the accident "as a jumping-off point for an unrestrained anti-Soviet campaign," did the extent of the danger even begin to emerge.[50]

Gorbachev had come to power in March 1985 as an unknown political quantity to most Soviets and outsiders. Despite his pledges to be a reformer, his first steps toward *perestroika,* or restructuring, seemed limited to reinstating a tough campaign against alcoholism and to restating the primacy of the Communist Party—suitably pruned of deadwood—in Soviet life. In early speeches, however, Gorbachev also proclaimed a commitment to the concept of *glasnost,* a kind of openness that Lenin, in 1918, had endorsed as a technique for the press to use in "stimulating the masses into taking part themselves in solving the problems closest to them."[51] Before the 1917 Revolution, *glasnost* was a primarily juridical term relating to legal reforms of 1864 that had made trials open to the public.

Dropped from the Soviet lexicon under Stalin, the word reappeared only at the end of 1965 as a rallying cry for a few dissenters demanding access to the political trial of writers Andrei Sinyavsky and Yuli Daniel.

---

*In its original form, the State Secrets Act of 1947 prohibited publication of all economic and social data, let alone information about sensitive military or political topics. Not until nine years after the law was promulgated and three years after the death of Joseph Stalin was the first postwar statistical handbook issued, and even then much of its contents—like many ordinary Soviet documents, such as city maps—was falsified.

As human rights protests spread during the 1970s, Andrei Sakharov and others called for *glasnost* as part of a broader attack on all official secrecy.

Even though the Twenty-seventh Party Congress confirmed *glasnost* as official policy in March 1986, the purpose seemed more to legitimize inquiry into the political sins of Gorbachev's predecessors than to license a genuinely free and informed discussion of contemporary Soviet ills. The Chernobyl disaster a month later, however, put the regime's sincerity about *glasnost* to the test and contributed significantly to breaking the censors' hold on public information.

The explosion deeply shocked the new Kremlin leadership. A "well-informed official" told Robert Kaiser, a veteran American observer of Soviet politics and society, that "eventually . . . Gorbachev realized that he had been misled by local officials." As Kaiser imagined the moment,

> There must have been great anger and frustration around the tables where Gorbachev and his colleagues met for honest discussion. Chernobyl was a scary and tragic accident, but it was also a painful reminder of the huge mess that was—and is—the Soviet economy. . . .
>
> This was the first of many occasions when Gorbachev would be faced with an unexpected event that challenged his plans. His reaction was—it turned out—characteristic. He took the Chernobyl disaster as a prod to move farther and faster.[52]

FROM SUBJECTS TO ACTIVISTS

Glasnost accelerated as a result. First to be sanctioned were reports of accidents, then the writings of long-banned authors and, by 1989, denunciations of Stalin and Stalinism. The torrent of uncensored speech in turn fed a social awakening. Under the pressure of the Chernobyl catastrophe and perhaps without estimating all the political consequences, Gorbachev allowed his subjects to see the truth about their society and, especially, its maladies. Combined with the policy of democratization Gorbachev initiated, moreover, *glasnost* tacitly encouraged Soviets, individually and in groups, to respond to the facts so long hidden from them.

The resulting surge of civic activism had a Topsy-like quality; it just grew. While environmental protest spread first and, in some cases, fastest, it was still scattered in the fall of 1987, more a novelty than a movement. Moreover, until the creation of an environmental protection agency for the USSR in 1988, officialdom provided the protesters neither an advocate nor a forum to which to appeal.

Even so, environmentalists could count some victories. A massive letter-writing and petition campaign in 1986, sparked by published appeals from nationally known scientists and writers, won a high-level decision to shelve plans to divert the northward flow of several major Siberian rivers south to the parched cotton and rice fields of Central Asia.* The Kremlin decision followed close on the Chernobyl disaster and seemed a tribute to Gorbachev's June 1986 orders to Party functionaries (*apparatchiks*) "to adopt a new style of working with" Soviet intellectuals. "It is time to stop ordering [them] about."[54]

In the fall of 1986 a broad public outcry in Latvia—street rallies and tens of thousands of letters—targeted plans to build a dam and hydroelectric plant on the Daugava River in the southeastern part of that Baltic republic.[55] When Latvia's Council of Ministers and, in November 1987, its Soviet counterpart ruled against the project, the young poets, artists and musicians who had led the fight felt that "we had won our first great victory."[56]

Equally successful but on a smaller scale, some 8,000 angry residents of the Siberian city of Irkutsk rallied on November 26, 1987, in the city's Constitution Square to protest piping untreated factory wastes into the river that supplied the city its drinking water. In response to more than 100,000 signed petitions, the pipeline was cancelled.[57] In Kirishi, a small city some sixty-five miles southeast of Leningrad, 12,000 of the 60,000 residents, led by a twenty-six-year-old postman, staged a demonstration on June 1, 1987, to demand the closing of a protein and vitamin concentrate plant they blamed for the town's soaring rate of bronchitis and asthma. The thirteen-year-old factory shut down but resumed its production of the additive for livestock feed early in August, supposedly cleaner but still bitterly contested.[58]

Except for the issue of diverting the Siberian rivers and the fight over the Kirishi animal-fodder additive factory, the early protests generally drew only local press attention. Even without national publicity, however, environmental agitation rolled through the Soviet Union. On June 5, 1987, a rally in the Volga River city of Kazan brought together some of the 70,000 residents who had petitioned against plans to build a

---

*The diversion had been proposed in part as a remedy for the disaster caused by massive and massively mismanaged irrigation schemes in Uzbekistan and neighboring republics. From 1960 to 1989 the flow of river water into the Aral Sea had been cut from forty cubic kilometers a year to five, lowering its volume by 66 percent. A parallel buildup of pesticides and herbicides in drinking water so affected health in the region that "the incidence of typhoid fever has risen almost 30 times . . . and child mortality is more than 50 per 1,000 births."[53] (See chapter 4.)

biochemical plant in a park area. On October 17 some 2,000 protesters appeared outside the Nairit chemical complex on the outskirts of the Armenian capital of Yerevan to demand an end to air pollution so thick that it regularly hid the 16,496-foot heights of Mount Ararat thirty miles away.[59]

PROTEST BY THE VOLGA

That same month the wave of ecological activism reached the lower Volga, to a city that traders founded as Tsaritsyn in 1589, that gained lasting fame as Stalingrad in 1942–43 and that boomed under the name of Volgograd after 1961. The first to respond to the new mix of freedom and anxiety were a group of women among the 5,000 employees of the Fiftieth Anniversary of the October Revolution oil refinery. For some time, these women and their friends in the southern reaches of the city had been giving birth to an alarming number of severely deformed and retarded children. By late 1987 they had concluded that chemical pollution in the heavily industrialized Krasnoarmeisky (Red Army) district *(rayon)* where they lived and worked was to blame.

They may well have been right. Aside from the refinery, the district housed a major aluminum factory and two large chemical complexes. In adjacent *rayony* stood another chemical installation and a mill, similar to the one in Kirishi, for converting paraffin distillates of petroleum into vitamin-enhanced supplements for animal feed. The 180,000 district residents had also heard that they were to get an unwelcome new neighbor: a plant to manufacture the pesticide Basudin, which inaccurate rumors identified as containing the very chemicals that leaked at Union Carbide's Bhopal, India, factory, killing over 2,500 people in December 1984.

The Krasnoarmeisky women were scared, angry and determined "to start a fight against the chemical factories," declared Galina Maksimovna Borovina, the head of the women's council at the refinery. That, in brief, was the appeal she put to Alfred Aleksandrovich Pavlenko, the bald, intense, garrulous film and theater director who ran the refinery's cultural center. Both in their early fifties, Pavlenko and Borovina were friends of long-standing. Her husband, the refinery's former general director, was a devout Communist who, in retirement, enjoyed arguing politics with Pavlenko, an outspoken nonconformist. Pollution and its consequences was one of the few issues on which the two families agreed.[60]

Over the years since the 1960 completion of the giant Volgograd

Hydroelectric Station north of the city, they had seen progress turn to blight. The farmland between the Volga River to the east and a line of low hills on the west had filled up with people, prefabricated high-rise apartment buildings, high-voltage power lines and industrial smokestacks. Sprawling more than forty miles north to south along the river's right bank, much of Volgograd had come to look like a vertical Levittown set in the midst of a giant New Jersey petrochemical complex. Where Catherine the Great had put German-speaking settlers in the late eighteenth century to till the soil and stand guard against incursions by Tatars from the eastern steppes, where Soviet heroism had turned the tide of World War II in Europe and left 90 percent of the city in ruins, unchecked industrial development, a new kind of enemy, was killing the lower Volga and the land along it.

Pollution was also, it seemed, killing children. Borovina and Pavlenko did not know the dimensions of the health crisis building around them. Even two years into the era of *glasnost,* accurate statistics on rates and causes of death and disease were still guarded as a state secret. Doctors in Volgograd itself, however, knew that during the 1980s they were delivering significantly higher numbers of sick newborns than before. Parents, maternity clinic personnel and statisticians at the Ministry of Health's local Institute of Professional Pathology, a "closed" center connected with the chemical industry, knew bits and pieces of what was happening. But in 1987 such phenomena—far from unique to Volgograd—were neither discussed in public nor explained.

Even in the fall of 1990, Dr. Vladimir Vinoshkin, a forty-year-old cardiologist at City Hospital Number Three in the center of Volgograd, could tell a visitor what had been happening but not why. "In the last ten years," he said, "there has been a significant increase in births of babies without eyes, babies without skin, babies with severe developmental defects and with lowered immunity to all sorts of illness. We are seeing more pneumonia and bronchial asthma too, lots of skin allergies, and even more heart disease among men under forty. We send fifteen to twenty patients a year to Moscow for bypass operations, but between two and three hundred need them and just have to wait.

"Maybe alcoholism is responsible in part, but pollution must play a role. All we see are the consequences. We don't know the origins. We don't have the scientific information or expertise. They tell us what's emitted into the air, but we don't know what it really means for people's health."[61] The "consequences" in the Krasnoarmeisky district went beyond birth defects. There, the incidence of bronchitis, asthma and allergic reactions was two and a half times the rate for the Volgograd *oblast* as a whole.[62]

Overall in the Soviet Union, children living near aluminum factories such as the one in the Krasnoarmeisky district were seven times more likely to come down with rickets than youngsters in cleaner surroundings.[63] Downwind from such a factory at Tursun-Zade on the border of Uzbekistan and Tajikistan, "the children never smile," Dr. Barenboim had observed. "Their teeth have all rotted out."[64] In the Krasnoarmeisky neighborhood of the "Kaustik" and "Khimprom" enterprises, where hydrogen chloride emissions were especially high, residents who died of cardiovascular diseases were, on average, seven and a half years younger than those who died of the same causes but lived in the relatively cleaner air of central Volgograd.[65]

"Relatively" is an important qualifier. In 1989 Volgograd ranked twenty-second among Soviet cities in population but fourteenth in terms of the quantity of harmful emissions measured in its atmosphere.[66] Over one-third of the 39,000 stationary sources of air pollution in the entire *oblast*—and more than half of those inside the city limits—lacked purification equipment.[67] In the industrial center of Volzhsky, north of the city and on the eastern bank of the Volga, a single petrochemical enterprise, Orgsyntez, was blamed for causing "systematic and extreme" levels of air pollution. Because it failed to control its emissions, an official report said, concentrations of methyl mercaptan occasionally rose "hundreds of times" above the legal limit.[68]

Nor was dirty air the only environmental hazard in Volgograd. "A Niagara of untreated waste" flows into the Volga all along its 2,293-mile length, and not far upstream from the Krasnoarmeisky district, the huge Red October metallurgical plant is only one of the industries that burden the river with petroleum products one hundred times above the permitted limits.[69]

ONTO THE STREETS

When Galina Borovina went to Alfred Pavlenko to enlist him in her battle against chemical pollution, neither they nor any of their neighbors had more than an intuitive sense of these environmental hazards. What they did have was a few acquaintances they could trust to share their alarm and to join them in a new venture for Soviet citizens: the organization of an "informal" association, unofficial in its sponsorship and outlook. Called the Ecology Club, theirs was among the earliest Soviet environmental associations. It was registered on December 4, 1987, with local authorities as a legal entity. Within a few months it had several hundred members.

The club's first venture was polite—and futile. A published appeal to Party leader Mikhail Gorbachev and government head Nikolai Ryzhkov under the title "Which Way Are You Looking?" received no acknowledgment. More successfully, but without publicity, club leaders went to local Communist Party officials with data obtained from sympathetic insiders to show that the waste-water emissions from the caustic soda factory were turning a small lake in the district into a toxic cesspool.

That complaint did win a reduction in the factory's output of liquid poison, but the victory was small, reversible and only marginal to the main goal of ending all chemical pollution. As new members joined the Ecology Club, its leaders determined to make it a real social force in the district. Like so many other aggrieved Soviets at the time, newly freed of old fears of repression, they moved to confront the political establishment with a public show of strength. "The idea," Pavlenko recalled, "was to shake up the system."[70]

The time for their first sally was set for noon, February 23, 1988. The place, a small plaza in front of the boxy, glass-fronted, five-story Jubilee movie theater. Postcards appeared in Krasnoarmeisky district mailboxes to announce the meeting and urge citizens to attend. To the organizers' surprise, some three thousand showed up. "It was a bolt from the blue," Pavlenko said. "There had never been anything like it in the *oblast* before."[71]

Unprecedented, the assembly was also somewhat unfocused. No one had thought to install loudspeakers, and some in the crowd had to strain to hear Nikolai Perepyolkin, the Ecology Club's first chairman, read out a list of ecological grievances. The applause was warm—especially for the demand that construction be stopped on the factory being built to produce a multipurpose pesticide called Basudin—but it did not unite the audience behind any further course of action.

The act and fact of speaking out was almost catharsis enough. At least, it might have been if local authorities had not perceived the rally as a threat and moved to quash it. The attempt backfired. A second secretary from the district Party committee shouldered his way up the dozen shallow steps from the esplanade to the platform where the clump of Ecology Club activists stood. Equipped with a battery-powered bullhorn, he interrupted the speakers to declare that the meeting had gone on long enough and that the crowd should disband.

"He tried to bully us, and that is what turned it into a demonstration," remembered Vladimir Polosukhin, a slight, fair-haired computer programmer, who had seen "the most awful destruction of nature" with his own eyes as an astronomy student touring the eastern shore of the Caspian Sea in 1984. "On all our maps, the Bay of Kara Bogaz Gol was blue; it was water, but I drove across it in a truck, and it was nothing but dry seabed," Polosukhin said. "It made me understand how bad things had gotten in Central Asia."[72]

The story of the Kara Bogaz Gol, as it happened, was told in detail only a few months after the Volgograd demonstration. A wide-ranging indictment of Soviet water policies that gave the first public warning of the disasters facing the Aral Sea region, Leningrad's Neva River and other bodies of water was printed in the popular literary journal *Novy Mir* in July 1988. The article pioneered Soviet environmental journalism. The author reported how water planners built a dike in 1980 across the narrow inlet that separated the Bay of Kara Bogaz from the Caspian Sea. Looking for a way to start on their dream project of diverting the flow of Siberian rivers from north to south, the officials used fears of a drop in the Caspian Sea's water level—a phenomenon that proved self-correcting—to justify the dike. Within three years, the bay had dried up entirely. Mirabilite, a particularly rare form of sodium sulfate that was precipitated in its waters, disappeared as well. The dike was breached in 1984, "an indirect admission that a colossal, expensive mistake had been made,"[73] but the bay was still a sandy waste when Polosukhin saw it.

In Volgograd, married and the father of a young son, Polosukhin's ecological concern became parental anxiety. "The people I knew were people like me, people with children who were getting sick, people who were getting sick themselves." When the Ecology Club was formed, he promptly joined, and when Party *apparatchik* Vladimir Lyokin tried to break up their peaceable meeting, Polosukhin was incensed.[74]

He was not alone. A firebrand in the club, photographer Vladimir Lebedev, responded to Lyokin's call to disband by shouting to the crowd: "How much more can we take?" With spontaneous passion he called on the listeners below to march with him then and there from the Jubilee Square to the district Party committee headquarters less than a mile north, to deliver demands that the Ecology Club had formulated and to insist on a hearing and prompt action. The crowd roared its assent, and the rally, which had been on the point of breaking up only a few minutes earlier, turned into a parade of protest.

"We walked up the Prospect of the Heroes of Stalingrad in total silence," Polosukhin said in recollecting the episode thirty-two months later. "All of us knew that in the past people had been shot just for being in such a march. So there was no shouting, no slogans." And after the initial surge of enthusiasm, there was some falling off. Initially, the procession boasted between one and two thousand marchers, but about four hundred yards north, the broad boulevard narrowed to go under a ceremonial white archway and across a bridge over the Volga-Don Canal.

"A lot of people just sort of drifted off to the sides before we crossed the bridge," Polosukhin remembered. "I started out in the middle of the crowd, and by the time we got to the *raikom* [*rayon* Party committee] building, I was in the front rank."[75] Behind him in a garden where a graceful weeping willow shaded a half–life-size bronze statue of Vladimir Lenin, stood only some three hundred others, many of them KGB agents detailed to monitor the rally and its participants.

Pressed into the narrow pathways between the flower beds of the Party headquarters courtyard, the remaining demonstrators gathered their courage. Chanting *"Doloi s Basudinom!"* [Down with Basudin], they drowned out the attempts of an *apparatchik* to speak. Polosukhin pulled Vladimir Lebedev from the crowd and pushed him to the front to read aloud the list of the Ecology Club's demands. That accomplished, the protesters dispersed, unsatisfied but unharmed, to relish the outcome of their first and unplanned skirmish as agents of change.

FROM PROTEST TO POWER

Unreported in the Volgograd press, news of the incident moved by grapevine, often the fastest means of communication in the Soviet Union. When Ecology Club activists circulated a petition against the Basudin plant's construction, they had no trouble getting 30,000 signatures from the 180,000 Krasnoarmeisky residents within a few weeks. Convinced that Volgograd authorities would only ignore their demands, however, they delegated Polosukhin and two others to carry the petition to Moscow, to the offices of the Communist Party Central Committee across Red Square from the Kremlin.

In that center of Soviet political decision making, they were received by a clearly impatient Party instructor, who had previously served as a political organizer at the Khimprom factory that was one of their targets. "He told us we could have twenty minutes of his time," said Polosukhin. "We had brought an album of photos and a map of the district to show him where the pollution problems were. But I saw he just didn't get it, so when our time was nearly up, I said: 'We've brought 30,000 signatures, and if something isn't done, there will be an explosion in Volgograd that you'll hear all the way to Moscow.'

"That made him sit up and take some notice. We couldn't find any other way to get through to him. The only language those people understand is threats, threats to their power."[76]

Slowly but with gathering force in 1988 and 1989, environmental protest turned into a political threat not just in Volgograd but throughout the Soviet Union. Striking miners in the Ukraine and Siberia put environmental cleanup high on their list of political demands. Often as well, ecological issues and organizations became catalysts for broader movements against the established order. In the non-Russian republics, environmentalism and ethnic passion easily merged into a generalized anger at decisions made in Moscow and usually implemented by Russian technicians to exploit local resources—cotton in Uzbekistan or phosphorite in Estonia—at the expense of the natural habitat.

A famous Moscow circus clown portrayed himself in 1989 as an environmental activist trying to save a lone tree from a chemical plant operator. The skit ended with the tree pulling out a gun and shooting its assailant. As the clown stuffed the polluter down his own smokestack, the audience cheered.[77]

To a senior KGB official in early 1991, in contrast, ecological passion and the militants who identified themselves as "Greens" seemed dangerous. Conceding that the USSR was "at the edge of ecological crisis," he protested: "In many instances ecology movements try to claim a monopoly on truth. The most zealous 'defenders of nature' resort to open violence and the application of moral-psychological terror against workers in the nuclear energy sector. Nationalist and separatist elements also are actively exploiting environmentalist slogans."[78] He singled out tensions in Lithuania, where Soviet military action in January 1991 had led to violence, as one product of "destructive forces" protesting and eventually halting the construction of a nuclear power plant.[79]

The passage from pollution to politics was an easy one. The trend spread rapidly in 1989 and 1990 well beyond the breakaway Baltic republics but with the result that, by mid-1991, Green issues and advocates were often being submerged in broader protest movements. In Armenia and the Ukraine, as in Latvia, activists who got their civic baptism in fights against pollution emerged quickly as leaders of wider drives for cultural, economic and political independence. In Kazakhstan protest against nuclear testing at Semipalatinsk sparked wider ecological, linguistic and cultural challenges and even limited demands for sovereignty that, if pressed, could pit the Russian and Ukrainian portion of the republic's population against almost equal numbers of Muslims of Mongol origin.

"Kazakhstan was the junk heap where Russia threw its garbage," said Olzhas Suleimenov, a noted writer and organizer of the movement that called itself Nevada-Semipalatinsk as a way of linking the Soviet nuclear testing ground to the site in the United States. "Moscow decided that it could, with complete impunity, send all of its filthiest industries to the east. What's more, 93 percent of the industries here belong to the center. So we suffer, but we don't even profit. We are left deserted with a poisoned land."[80]

Suleimenov, who won a deputy's seat in the new USSR parliament in 1989, was one of hundreds of environmental protesters—Volgograd's Vladimir Polosukhin was another—whose activism led to elected office. Most acquired their mandates in local voting in 1990, almost always at the expense of Communist Party stalwarts, as part of a wider revulsion against the corrupt but entrenched political establishment that Gorbachev sought—and failed—to reform gradually from within. The electoral results signaled public impatience with the pace of change, impatience that had been rising steadily as Soviets took inventory of their health and their surroundings and found both endangered.

BEGINNINGS OF WISDOM

In the two and a half years following the Nineteenth Party Conference, Soviet health worsened, the environment deteriorated further and public frustration with the gap between proclamations and performance rose. In the spring of 1991 top medical policymakers, meeting in Moscow, were confronted with data from 1990 showing that viral hepatitis, salmonellosis, polio, diphtheria and other contagious diseases were on the rise and that acute kidney infections, especially but not uniquely, could be traced directly to disregard for sanitation in food processing.[81]

One sign of the anger such dangers aroused was a joke already popular in 1988. Rushing into a hospital emergency ward, a man demanded to see an eye doctor and an ear doctor. "Why do you need both?" an attendant asked. "Because," said the patient, "my eyes aren't seeing what my ears are hearing."

The anecdote could have been told at almost any time in the seven-plus decades of Communist rule. From Lenin onward, Soviet propaganda for both internal and external consumption had consistently made false claims of social progress. Many Soviets and many visitors accepted them uncritically. George Bernard Shaw, for one, taking leave of his hosts after a six-day visit in 1931, announced: "Tomorrow I leave this land of hope and return to our Western countries of despair."[82]

Six decades later optimists were a rare breed inside the USSR. "Russia is not a country, not a people," lamented a forty-seven-year-old Odessa physicist, "it is a thousand-year-long sickness."[83] Long characteristic of the scientific and artistic intelligentsia, such gloom has often been gainsaid by the very accomplishments of the best and brightest in the USSR.

The Odessa specialist in low-temperature physics, for instance, held patents on more than one hundred inventions, including processes that both purify water and, at significant economy in the volume used, recycle it for temperature control. He and a few Odessa University colleagues formed an institute in 1990 to apply the environment-friendly technology that they had developed under military contracts to civilian manufacturing. In October of that year a deputy defense minister formally introduced the head of the institute to a group of Soviet contractors under orders to switch from making arms to turning out 10 to 12 million new refrigerators a year.[84]

Whether or not the manufacturers hired the Odessa scientists as their consultants, they and other industrial leaders could call on a wealth of Soviet technical expertise. Most of these researchers had long been either hidden by military secrecy or ignored by managers concentrating only on central planners' orders to meet gross output targets. Even facing such obstacles, Soviet scientists showed that they were far from being technological invalids. Their laboratories produced medical breakthroughs, including a drug approved for U.S. manufacture in 1991 to regulate heart rhythms, a surgical stapling gun and a formula, purchased by Japan, for an alloy to make durable scalpels.[85] A Siberian orthopedic surgeon even won respectful international attention for a method of "stretching bones where more conventional approaches fail."[86] Having won the race into orbit but lost the one to the moon, Soviet rocketeers must also have taken some satisfaction from reported U.S. interest in acquiring one of their nuclear minireactors to power vehicles in space.[87]

Political and economic reforms that were barely beginning to take hold in August 1991 held the potential to unlock more such advances. Progress, if it resumed in a politically and economically reorganized Soviet Union, could even create a favorable setting for translating theory into practical use, the area of applied technology where the USSR has lagged farthest behind. One extensive study of high-quality patents held by various nations ranked it thirteenth in the world. Crediting the United States with more than 100,000 such patents and Japan with nearly 77,000, the report used this index of "technical vigor" to estimate Soviet patents at 400, the same number as South Korea, a nation with less than one-sixth the Soviet population.[88]

At the height of Stalinism, Moscow used to boast that Russians had been pioneers in every scientific field from electricity to radio to space. The claims of superiority in all fields were so inflated that they prompted a joke in rebuttal, naming Russia "the Motherland of Elephants." The flight of *Sputnik* in 1957 gave new impetus to the old self-confidence, but years of stagnation eroded propaganda assurances and the authority of official sloganeers. Under Mikhail Gorbachev, at last, Soviet pretensions exploded. A society looked at itself without illusions and discovered that it was profoundly, if not terminally, ill.

To undertake any effective cure, however, Soviets have to understand the practices that had put them in such danger. They have to explore and analyze their past at the same time that they try to reshape their future. Only a search backward into history can find the roots of their ailments and, if not already too late, the antidotes to total breakdown.

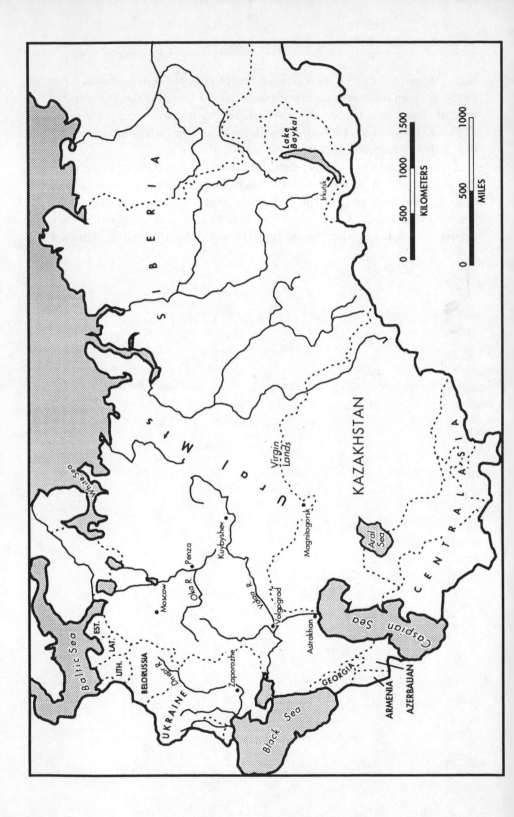

CHAPTER 2

Birth of the Future

ON THE SURFACE, the causes of the Soviet Union's ecological breakdown, the abuse of nature and of human health, appear fairly straightforward. Environmental degradation can be seen as the consequence of heedless industrialization compounded by failure to measure the social costs of exploiting limited natural resources. Similarly, it can be argued that the infirmities of the health care system originated in the priority given to economic growth over social welfare. Analyzed in such terms, the USSR looks most of all like an aggravated case of mismanagement. Only the scale of its problems and the delay in responding to them set it apart from advanced Western societies prey to similar ills.

A socialist state, however, was not supposed to make the mistakes or produce the results of capitalism. Because its values and goals were different, because its development was to be scientifically planned and because its people and government were to be liberated from the baser human impulses, it would advance only the noblest aspirations, the highest good. Mulling over a choice of slogans to inspire the Russian masses, Vladimir Lenin in 1918 settled on one, a quotation from Ovid, as his favorite: "The golden age is coming; people will live without laws or punishment, doing of their own free will what is good and just."[1]

Lenin might have done better to recall, as he did for the benefit of an American visitor in 1922, his experience as an exile in London, called on to represent workers in disputes with their employers. One such group could not at first agree on what it wanted from the negotiations. Lenin told them to leave and come back the next day with their demands precisely defined. They did. "All we want," their spokesman said, "is world revolution, and better toilets."[2]

The Bolshevik Revolution of October 1917 satisfied neither demand. Its architects, however, undertook to build a utopia, a "radiant future" of social justice and material plenty accessible to all. Generations of Soviet schoolchildren were taught to look forward to a life in which goods would be so plentiful and money so unnecessary that, in Lenin's prophecy—itself borrowed from the 300-year-old vision of an Italian philosopher, Tommaso Campanella—the toilets would be made of gold.

That promise was surreal. Worse, the utopian quest became a blinding compulsion, a "vaulting ambition" as murderous as Macbeth's, that justified destruction and deceit on a huge scale in the name of progress toward an earthly paradise. The enormity of their ambition and the certainty with which they pursued it drove the Bolsheviks to reject all tradition in politics, all convention in morals, all constraints of science. As heralds and engineers of a new age, they had not just overthrown the past but superseded its rules and limits.

In brutal lines that Lenin castigated as "hooliganism," poet Vladimir Mayakovsky in 1920 captured the ferocity of the transformation the Revolution was to work on Russia:

> *We'll destroy you,*
> *old romantic world!*
> *In place of faith*
> *in our soul we have*
> *electricity*
> *and steam.*

> *In place of misery,*
> *pocket the riches of all worlds!*
> *The old men? Kill them.*
> *And use the skulls for ashtrays![3]*

Mayakovsky, whose suicide in 1930 may have been a reaction to his own prophetic accuracy, lived only long enough to witness early examples of the Revolution's physical and spiritual brutality. The degradation of the Soviet Union's environment and the neglect of its system of medical care lay in the future. Like other assaults on human dignity and hope—mass arrests and deportations, man-made famine—the indifference to pollution and human health is a consequence of the Revolution.

Ecocide in the USSR stems from the force, not the failure, of utopian ambitions.

Initially those ambitions seemed truly humane. In public health and nature conservation, for instance, the revolutionaries' programs included pioneering efforts—and, for a time, notable progress—in controlling disease, insuring public hygiene and protecting forests and parks. Within a dozen years of their seizing power, however, Soviet Communists had changed their priorities. They retained the mania for miracles but channeled it into a drive to conquer nature and to subordinate human welfare to building an all-powerful socialist state.

Vladimir Bukovsky, a 1960s dissident activist who spent twelve of his first thirty-five years in one or another form of Soviet imprisonment, has captured the spirit of that zealotry and its costs:

> The psychological atmosphere that was created in the Soviet Union in the 1930s and 1940s pushed people to cross the limits of the possible. The slogan of the time was, "When the country commands us to be heroes, each and everyone must become a hero." And there were heroes. They were poorly fed and poorly clothed, but the pilots stormed the skies and the explorers conquered the North Pole. Practically with bare hands they dug canals, built dams, created some of the world's largest industrial complexes. Victorious proletarians marched from triumph to triumph, displaying the irresistible force of collective labor, harnessing the forces of nature, turning deserts into gardens. How could a socialist paradise be created except by performing a miracle a day? And who but a superman could enter it?
>
> Only much later did they look back and discover that the superhuman and the inhuman go hand in hand. There were a few heroes, but the rest were victims. While some burned with enthusiasm, the rest were terrified. Those magnificent dams and canals turned the rivers into stinking swamps, and those giant industrial complexes turned blooming land into desert, as if nature, the eternal enemy of the people, conspired to wreck the epic effort.[4]

That outcome was predicted. "You have replaced instinct with command," a veteran Russian socialist admonished a Lenin confidant in the early 1920s, "and you expect your command to change the nature of mankind. For this infringement of the freedom of self-determination, retribution awaits you."[5]

When that warning was written, retribution seemed not just certain but already at hand. In the midst of civil war, on the heels of terrible losses in World War I, both famine and plague were devastating the population. Already backward, Russia faced what H. G. Wells in 1920 called a "vast, irreparable breakdown. . . . Never in all history has there been so great a debacle."[6] Confirming that evaluation a year later, Leon Trotsky, head of the victorious Red Army, told the Tenth Party Congress, "We have destroyed the country in order to defeat the Whites."[7]

THE WHIP OF NECESSITY

The nation the Bolsheviks thought they had destroyed was backward even before the 1917 Revolution. Though it had made great economic advances in the last fifty years of Czarist rule, it still lagged far behind the world's other capitalist societies. In a multi-index measurement of the comparative industrial progress of the United States, Japan and nine European states, the Russian Empire ranked tenth in both 1860 and 1910.[8] At the start of World War I only about 10 percent of its population was urbanized, and just half of the eight-to-eleven-year-old children were in school.[9]

The war, in turn, cost Russia both the territory where nearly one-fifth of its industrial output was produced[10] and the lives of some 2 million soldiers and civilians. Another million died in the 1918 to 1920 civil war and 5 million more in the famine that followed it. Counting the million more who fled the Revolution and the country, by 1922 Russia had lost at least a tenth of its prewar population and a higher ratio of its young and educated men.[11] Gross industrial output in 1921 stood at less than a third of the 1913 level; steel and pig iron production had sunk from over 4 million tons each to 200,000 and 100,000 tons, respectively; electricity generated and railway tonnage were both one-fourth their prewar totals.[12]

Late in coming, Czarist industry was both highly concentrated in large enterprises and heavily dependent on the state. Where one-third of the U.S. labor force in 1910 was employed in industrial enterprises with over 500 workers, the figure for Russia was 53.5 percent. In 1890 the second largest Russian textile mill complex employed a staggering 17,000 workers.[13] Often, as well, the state was the direct or indirect employer. It owned and ran two-thirds of all the railroads, many of the mines and mineral processing plants, 60 percent of the forests, and the liquor monopoly.[14] Even at the height of the New Economic Policy (NEP) effort in the 1920s to stimulate private enterprise, "the bulk of investment capital was in the hands of the state."[15] Under Joseph Stalin, the state became the uncontested owner, planner and dispenser of all property and productive resources, all-powerful and, guided by the science of Marxism, infallible.

To a theorist of revolution, Russia's very primitiveness seemed an asset. "Under the whip of external necessity," Trotsky believed, "[a] backward culture is compelled to make leaps."[16] As leaders required to govern, though, it was Lenin and, even more so, Stalin who decreed that the "leaps" would be violent and coercive and, therefore, inevitably self-destructive. Their ambition and impatience bred a damn-the-torpedoes style of economic development and a people-be-damned style of policymaking. What had been a meddling Czarist bureaucracy became under Stalin an omnipresent tyrant, largely closed to dissent from within or advice from outside.

As Soviet rulers made the absolutist tradition their own after the free-enterprise NEP interlude, they also expanded on the Czarist legacy of centralized economic management. It fit not only their conception of planned development and their need to monopolize power but also the scale of the problems they faced and of the miracles they intended to produce. Then and now, however, the leaders denied themselves an essential ingredient of successful planning: accurate data and honest reporting. The self-defeating logic of utopian totalitarianism could tolerate only facts that served and bolstered the myth. Any others were not truths but heresies to be suppressed along with anyone incautious enough to defend them.

"Statistics," Lenin directed in 1921, "must be our practical *assistant*, and not scholastic."[17] Scholars who would not assist, he said in 1922, were "patent counterrevolutionaries . . . spies and corrupters of the student youth."[18]

SCIENCE SUBSERVIENT

From Lenin's demand for total political loyalty grew a two-pronged assault on the independence of science and scientists. On one side was suppression both of individuals, such as geneticist Nikolai Vavilov in the 1930s and physicist Andrei Sakharov in the 1970s, and of data: the embarrassingly low census count that Stalin rewrote in 1937 and the figures that could not be published in the last half of the 1970s because they showed infant mortality on the rise. The other side of the totalitarian coin was the transformation of scientists into technological serfs. As sole employer, the state set the direction for research and decided which findings fit its purposes, which could be pursued, which must be hidden.

Harnessed to political leaders hungering first for economic miracles and later for military power, Soviet science became a kind of sorcerer's apprentice. Although it started with a large reserve of remarkable talent and expanded the resources it devoted to research, the Soviet regime wasted many assets and investments on chimerical projects, such as the digging of the Belomor (White Sea) Canal under Stalin or Khrushchev's scheme to farm the Virgin Lands of northern Kazakhstan and western Siberia. The canal, actually some five hundred miles of inland waterways linking Leningrad at the head of the Baltic Sea to the port of Arkhangelsk on the south shore of the White Sea, had all the elements of other, future Soviet assaults on nature. It was a gigantic effort, forerunner of what were to be a series of "projects of the century." It was technologically primitive, dug largely by hand in order to avoid hard-currency outlays for advanced, imported equipment. Built in just eighteen months from November 1931 to May 1933 by convict labor, like the later Volga-Don canal, much of the industrial infrastructure of the Urals and the majority of the gold and platinum mining centers of northern and eastern Siberia, the canal was the first giant project supervised by the secret police. And it did not work. Although conceived as a defensive measure, a refuge for the Soviet fleet if it came under attack in the Baltic, the channels were too shallow for such ships. The pattern the canal project set in the waste of human lives, in faulty engineering and disregard for natural resources persisted for decades.

Khrushchev's vision of shifting grain production to the steppes from the fertile Ukraine, where cattle and corn were to take the place of wheat, was of a piece with Stalin's grandiose concepts. Recruiting young enthusiasts instead of convicts, he overrode local Kazakh opposition to an influx of Russian settlers and agronomists' warnings that the land, on the edge of the Central Asian desert, required irrigation and cautious crop rotation to retain its productivity. Initially, the Virgin Lands rewarded his dream—harvests in 1956 were triple what they had been in 1953. But the quick fix proved illusory. Soil erosion came on the heels of hasty plowing. "In a series of wind-storms between 1960 and 1965 some [ten] million [acres] of land were ruined in Kazakhstan, and more than [29] million [acres] were damaged. Altogether, this amounted to nearly half the Virgin Lands."[19]

Khrushchev was simply following in the heedless, hurried footsteps of his predecessor. By mid-1930 Stalin had become "completely possessed by the idea that he could achieve a miraculous transformation of the whole of Russia by a single *tour de force*," judged Isaac Deutscher, the scholar-biographer of Stalin, Lenin and Trotsky. "He seemed to live in a half-real and half-dreamy world of statistical figures and indices, of industrial orders and instructions, a world in which no target and no objective seemed to be beyond his and the party's grasp."[20] Much of his and his planners' world, however, was built on statistics that were fantasies, produced to order, not to measure reality. Stalin himself admitted that an announced 47 percent surge in industrial output in 1930 had actually been only 25 percent, and, Deutscher judged, "even this figure is doubtful."[21] Scholars have found that real industrial growth, far from quintupling during the first Five-Year Plan, rose only one and a half times.

When data did not suit propaganda, moreover, they were often simply suppressed. Thus it was not until 1990 that the results of the January 1937 census became known. The count showed a Soviet population of 162 million, a net increase of only 15 million in ten years. The total was not only far below the announced 180 million that would have supported slogans touting the "grandiose advances" of socialism; it was also 6 million short of the sum of officially registered births and deaths in the previous decade. Since disclosure would raise questions about the millions who died (and the Kazakhs who fled to China) during the forced agricultural collectivization and ensuing famine of the early 1930s, officials were ordered to keep the results secret.[22]

Nor was it enough to conceal failure. Revolutionary aspirations, justifying and driving the growth of an all-powerful political system, demanded that science and scientists serve the utopian quest in positive ways of the state's choosing. The duty of the medical profession, for example, was to insure that workers and soldiers reported for *their* duties in good health and sufficient numbers. The role of scientific researchers, similarly, was to demonstrate the superiority of Communist society by producing not just theories but tangible and unprecedented material progress.

Visiting the Soviet Union in the summer of 1931, English biologist Julian Huxley was impressed by both the scale and the novelty of a whole nation being run as a scientific experiment. He especially approved the way science was organized to achieve practical results. "Sometimes," though, he noted,

> the insistence on practical applications is not without its humorous side. Zavadovsky in the Institute of Neuro-Humoral Physiology in Moscow has considerably advanced our theoretical knowledge of the ductless glands by his experiments with thyroid extract on birds. But, *inter alia,* he has found that a certain dose of thyroid causes moulting, and so has had assigned to him a flock of one hundred geese on a State farm, on which he may experiment to see whether the feather-bed industry cannot be benefited by causing geese to moult four times a year.[23]

Huxley was a far-from-uncritical observer. Yet, like many other visitors from a Depression-wracked West in the early 1930s, he accepted the

Soviet Union on its own terms, as *sui generis,* a vast and inspiring departure from the perceived failures and inequities and decline of the capitalist world.

SOCIALISM VERSUS THE LOUSE

Especially in the area of public health, the Soviets could show impressive progress. "The achievements of the last ten years are truly remarkable," Huxley judged in 1931,

> for Russia has been raised from a famine-stricken, plague-ridden country of medieval habits to one whose health is near the general level of other European nations: and the effects of the Government's health policy are most apparent where they will have the greatest effect—among the children. If the Russian experiment succeeds, Russia in twenty years' time will have not only a very good medical service, but—what does not always follow—a very healthy population.[24]

Huxley was sharp-eyed enough to see that "most of the sanitary habits of the average Russian are very primitive," that flies, dust and typhoid were far from eradicated and that "certain important medical supplies, notably anaesthetics and rubber gloves" were scarce.[25] Those and related problems, however, could be explained as bitter legacies from an uncaring past.

Like Huxley, two experienced public health administrators, one British and one American, also saw a number of shortcomings during an extensive survey of medical care in the Soviet Union in 1932. Most broadly, they noted the shortages of personnel, the low level of doctors' training, the exclusion of "class enemies" from medical and other social services and the unbridged gap between the health care available in the cities and that in the countryside. Still, they concluded that while

> the new arrangements are far from perfect . . . other countries may well envy Soviet Russia's elaborately centralized government . . . in that it has been able to brush aside all past complexities and to initiate a nearly universal national medical service on unified lines. . . . There are some advantages in starting, as Russia has done, almost from zero point.[26]

It could be said that the starting point was less than zero. In 1898, for a population of some 116 million, Russia had only 18,000 doctors,[27] and fewer than 1 in 9 of them served in rural districts. Some provincial areas held a single physician for as many as 40,000 inhabitants.[28]

According to the first Soviet commissar of public health, crude death rates from 1904 to 1914 averaged 28.4 to 30.0 per thousand population, and infant mortality rates per thousand live births averaged 244 from 1901 to 1911. In 1914 cases of acute infectious diseases numbered nearly 12 million[29] with only 26,000 doctors available to treat the sick.[30] Another source lists only 21,747 doctors in 1913 and 27,173 *feld'shers,* or paramedics.[31] Yet a third gives the figure for doctors as 19,785.[32] Wartime medical care, in any case, was so poor that wounds and disease incapacitated 11 million of the 14 million recruits.[33] And worse was to come. With civil war still raging, a pandemic of typhus spread through and beyond European Russia. Abetted by the collapse of sanitation and intensified by famine in many places, cholera, typhus, typhoid and dysentery together killed 3 million persons between 1917 and 1923.

Such horrors would have overwhelmed the rudimentary public health services of the Czarist regime, but even they had nearly ceased to function. Mobilized to serve with the troops, Russia's doctors had died with them in such numbers that in 1921, in one Volga River province with a population of 180,000, only a single physician was available to deal with some 15,000 typhus victims.[34] Throughout Russia, nearly half the surviving doctors came down with typhus themselves, falling ill four to five times more often than the population as a whole.[35]

Since trained medical personnel could not be summoned out of thin air, the Bolsheviks added filth, fleas, ticks and lice to the enemies that they, as revolutionaries, had to overcome. "Comrades," Lenin exhorted the Seventh Congress of the Soviets late in 1919, "every attention must be given to this question—either the louse will defeat socialism or socialism will defeat the louse."[36]

That battle cry set one lasting priority for the future development of Soviet medicine: the emphasis on basic hygiene and disease prevention. It also, however, foreshadowed political control over the medical establishment. In any case, self-reliance could not dispel the combination of famine and plague. Only outside help, largely provided by the American Relief Administration (ARA), could do that job and enable the Soviet Union, by the end of 1923, to begin developing a public health system of its own.

The medical work of the ARA, in tandem with its famine relief, was literally life-saving. In addition to distributing some six tons of fifteen different kinds of disinfectants and five varieties of water-purification supplies between November 1921 and June 1923, ARA-supplied teams administered nearly 7 million doses of tetra vaccine against cholera, typhoid and paratyphoid and 1.5 million smallpox inoculations in the summer of 1922. Their work in Samara (renamed Kuibyshev until 1991) on the Volga not only cut the incidence of typhus in the region from 19 cases per 1,000 in January 1922 to 3 per *10,000* a year later; it also included treating over 12,000 patients passing through the city on trains to and from Siberia and Central Asia. In the 5,764 hospitals throughout Russia that the ARA supplied, it provided equipment ranging from 1,123 complete sets of instruments for operations and 470,000 blankets to 17,000 bedpans and 31,000 hot water bottles.[37]

"The A.R.A. Medical program," in the words of its official historian, "did not, of course, restore medical practice and health organization in Russia to its pre-war standard. It did, however, . . . stop the process of deterioration and save Russian institutions from being completely overwhelmed by the wave of disease."[38] Once the emergency was over and the Western aid-givers sent home, the Soviet rulers began to build a new medical organization on the ruins of the old.

A DUTY TO HEALTH

The Bolsheviks' strongest impulse was political, to cement their hold on power and to put medicine, along with all social services, under their full control. As early as November 1917 an angry Lenin defined the status of medical personnel as servants of the proletariat. "It is the workers that are the strength of our country," he shouted, "and it is for them that we will take power from you, the doctors, and put it in the hands of the people. Soviet medicine will not be only for the rich."[39]

One quick consequence was a 1918 decree banning physicians from taking the Hippocratic Oath. The point was to sever their allegiance to what were scorned as "bourgeois" traditions and to deprive them of any outside ethical standards against which to measure the state's demands. When the first and only Soviet physician's oath went into effect on June 1, 1971, it obliged those who took it "to work conscientiously wherever the interests of the society will require it . . . to conduct all my actions according to the principles of the Communistic morale, to always keep in mind the high calling of the Soviet physician, and the high responsibility I have to my people and to the Soviet government."[40]

Long before they were bound by that formal pledge, health care providers in the USSR were clearly constituted as a medical police whose first duty was to the state, not the individual patient. The idea of a medical police, developed by two German physicians in the eighteenth century and implemented in Prussia and the Austrian empire, had several attractions to the Bolsheviks. It not only focused medicine on the provision of public health services; it also overrode claims by medical personnel to ethical and professional autonomy at a time when the new rulers were working to absorb or disband both elitist and populist medical societies and fledgling health workers' trade unions.

An early Soviet medical historian repeated Lenin's denunciation of prerevolutionary medicine, describing it, even at its most democratic, as providing "the best care for the rich, neglect of the poor, insufficient prophylactic measures [and] superficial treatment of the workers and the peasants in order that they may be put again on the wheel of exploitation."[41] Soviet health care, by contrast, would stress prevention and—above all—be free and universal. "The health of the working masses," said Nikolai Semashko, the first commissar of health, "must be in the hands of the working man."[42] A sympathetic American physician-historian caught the thrust and declamatory rhetoric of Soviet medical thinking:

> Man has a duty to work but disease prevents him from working, from performing that duty. The state makes available to all the means of preventing and curing disease. Therefore, there is a duty to use these means, there is a duty to health. To spread disease becomes a social offense. In such a society, health . . . has become something positive, a joyful attitude toward life.[43]

Either joyfully or under compulsion to avoid the "social offense" of uncleanliness, the Soviets set out to create not only a healthy labor force but a hygienic nation. They made remarkable progress. Where there had been 142,310 nonpsychiatric hospital beds in 1913, there were 661,431 in 1941. In the same interval the number of physicians rose from 19,785 to 130,348; tuberculosis dispensaries and stations went from 43 to 1,048; beds in maternity hospitals increased from 6,824 to 141,873.[44] By 1929 the incidence of typhus was one-fifth what it had been in 1913; cases of typhoid fever and dysentery were more than halved; even the frequency of malaria, after a surge in the mid-1920s, was cut by 15 percent.[45]

That kind of success turned many Western visitor-inspectors from skeptics to admirers. There was no denying the enthusiasm that suffused the multifaceted effort to give the entire population cost-free, cradle-to-grave medical attention and to teach even the simplest people, through ubiquitous, insistent education—in home and factory, in verse and picture, with posters and lectures—to practice basic hygiene and prevent disease. "The atmosphere of this place reminds me of suffrage campaigns: discomfort and enthusiasm," journalist Dorothy Thompson wrote to her husband, Sinclair Lewis, in 1927. Recalling the city that he had drawn on as the setting for his novel *Babbitt*, she said that Moscow was "as puritan and pure as Sauk Center. There's an unquenchable social settlement house smell about it."[46]

Amateurism contributed heavily to that aroma. Veterans in the struggle for power, the Bolsheviks were novices in the art of government and the science of administration. Nikolai Semashko, who headed the People's Commissariat for Health Protection for the first twelve years after its creation in July 1918, had been a rural physician in the 1890s. From 1907 to 1917, however, he was a revolutionary in exile. His closeness to Lenin was his most important professional credential for the job of supervising the rebirth of medicine in the USSR. Working with the materials at hand, he and his colleagues set up crash six-month postgraduate courses in 1921 for medical students whose education had been hurried or interrupted by the war. Until World War II, moreover, many of those on the public health payroll—private practice having been effectively eliminated—were graduates of the workers' faculties, or *rabfaks,* as they were abbreviated.

These after-hours schools for adults with at least three years of job experience were meant to cram the equivalent of a high school education into three or four years of evening classes. Whatever the quality of such preparation, the quantity of its output was impressive. Soviet medical schools took in 10,000 *rabfak* alumni in 1931 and 21,500 the next year, close to half of their total enrollment.[47]

In the medical schools themselves—fourteen at the time of the Revolution and forty-six on its twentieth anniversary—the content of the curriculum and even the length of study underwent frequent changes. Initially entrance and licensing examinations were abolished. They were reintroduced in 1922, then dropped again in the late 1920s when students were made to work in teams of four or five from enrollment to graduation, both to compensate for shortages of textbooks and equipment and to encourage the collectivist spirit.

The diary of a Soviet medical student in 1937 recorded her first cardiology lesson and first sight of a stethoscope: "Professor Popov showed us his stethoscope and explained how it works. . . . [He] told us that in a few years every *vrach* [doctor] will have a stethoscope of her own. I wish I could have one now. It's difficult to learn about the disease without hearing their sounds."[48]*

After 1934 exams were back, and in 1945 the five-year curriculum was extended to six. By the early 1980s, when medical education lasted seven

---

*In October 1972—thirty-five years later—an American doctor treating a patient in the Siberian city of Irkutsk had to lend a nurse his stethoscope. "She holds it carefully in her palm, examining it and feeling its weight. 'With a stethoscope like this,' she says wistfully, 'I could become the best doctor in Siberia.' "[49]

years—compared to ten or twelve, including undergraduate studies, in the United States—oral exams were the rule; hands-on clinical experience was the exception and first-year courses in physics, chemistry and Latin covered subjects that undergraduates took as part of premedical training in the West.[50]

Through the decades, however, certain aspects of Soviet medicine stayed constant. As a professional field, health care drew far more women than men, paid low wages—reflecting the social status of doctors and their aides as medical police—to both sexes and got short shrift in budget allocations. Additionally, public health priorities remained fixed on preventive medicine—Lenin's louse—and public health facilities remained scarce and inferior in the countryside. Worst of all, even the many caring and competent physicians became bureaucrats muted by Party bosses, dogma and the obligation to tell no truth that would mar the image of Bolshevik triumph.

THE PLAN: AGENT OF DESTRUCTION

Secrecy, a weapon to insure passivity, choked more than medicine. It infected and distorted every decision of the Soviet regime, suppressing independent scholarship, technical advice and all other forms of expert and public feedback that might have steered the rulers away from utopian excess. No small answers would do. A giant machine needed a giant's hand, and central planning could provide it. The plan was the one instrument that fit all the requirements of ambition and ideology, of central authority and gargantuan challenge. Whether as an all-embracing, multiyear edict from Moscow or as a set of goals for the smallest unit of the economy, the plan became the master of Soviet life and growth.

The first, abortive effort at planning was a 1920 project to build one hundred electric power plants, reduced a year later to twenty-seven and then quietly shelved. One enduring by-product was a slogan, often the only one left standing in large red letters on walls and roofs in the Gorbachev era Soviet Union: "Communism is Soviet power plus electrification of the whole country."

When Lenin endorsed the original hundred-power-station version "as our second Party program"[51]—following the promises of bread, land, peace and power to the Soviets—he asserted, in effect, the primacy of Communists as economic, not just political, decision makers. That extension of authority speeded the transformation of revolutionaries into monopolists, with the secret police as their economic overseers.

For the environment, the central planning system became Franken-stein's monster. The fatal flaw was not necessarily in the idea of plan-ning but in the yardstick—gross output, *valovaya produktsiya,* or more succinctly, *val* in Russian—that Soviet planners used to set their targets and measure their progress. Without a market mechanism to determine the value of credit, goods and services, they assigned arbitrary costs and prices to capital, labor, raw material and equipment. Most damaging of all to nature, the planning system treated all natural resources—land, water, mineral deposits and forests, for example—as state property, virtually as a free good the cost of which to the user was either minimal or nil. The state, especially under Stalin, treated individuals and the mass of people with the same indifference to their innate human value and well-being. The plan and its fulfillment became engines of destruc-tion geared to consume, not to conserve, the natural wealth and human strength of the Soviet Union.

In the words of economist Marshall Goldman, the first American expert to study Soviet environmental practices,

> in order to stimulate as rapid growth as possible in an underdeveloped environment, the Russians designed an incentive system that placed maximum emphasis on increasing production. Everything else was sec-ondary. . . .
>
> Instead of serving as a referee between polluters and conservationists, government officials usually support the polluters. It is necessary to re-member that the state *is* the manufacturer, and so there is almost always an identity of interests between the factory manager and the local govern-ment official. The most important criterion for any government official who seeks promotion or recognition is how much his production has increased in his region, *not* to what extent his rivers have been cleaned.[52]

In fairness to the early Soviet planners, it must be said that they were hardly unique in their view of nature as a cornucopia to be pillaged. Not for decades would the idea of limited global resources, of "small is beautiful," be mentioned, let alone regarded as conventional wisdom anywhere. Other nations that the USSR saw as its competitors, the United States not least among them, long geared their development to the same dynamic as the Soviets, to the ancient biblical injunction to Adam to "subdue" the earth and assert "dominion" over it and "every living thing."

Also, in fairness to the victors of 1917, they did take some early steps to protect nature. Lenin, finding workers felling trees in Moscow's Sokolniki Park, barred wood cutting in all suburban forests within twenty miles of the capital. More broadly, he endorsed an ambitious project to set aside a chain of nature preserves, starting with one in the Volga River delta near Astrakhan that actually did get established in the spring of 1919, but by local initiative, not central edict. One of the Astrakhan project's advocates recorded a meeting with Lenin in January of that year: "He said that nature preservation is important not just for the Astrakhan region but for the whole republic and that he attached urgent significance to it."[53]

Despite Lenin's declared backing, however, the concept of a network of sanctuaries for research and conservation, a pioneering idea for its time, foundered under bureaucratic indifference and the pressure of development. The second preserve, also established by local authorities, came into being in 1919 near Penza on the Sura River, only to be closed along with many others in 1951.

The history of the Lazovsky nature and wildlife refuge near the Sea of Japan and the Soviet border with Manchuria is fairly typical. Created in 1935 with over 900,000 acres, it was put out of existence in 1951, was reopened in 1957 with only 420,000 acres and by 1979 had been nibbled down to 288,000. Its foresters and gamekeepers earn less than half the average Soviet wage; its researchers, not much more. Denied the power to punish poachers who hunt its rare animals—tigers, Himalayan bear, spotted and roe deer—its director is also powerless to stop local authorities from invading the preserve or its buffer zone with "roads, high-power lines, farms, weekend cottages [dachas] and fertilizer storage depots."[54]

The refuge manager's impotence mirrors common practice. A refuge near the Mongolian border lost over 100,000 acres in 1990 to a neighboring collective farm in need of more pasture for its reindeer.[55] On the banks of the Oka River, not far south of Moscow, the world's leading breeding ground for oxen known as aurochs was a tiny, twelve-acre reserve on the edge of which dachas "are growing like mushrooms." Local authorities shrugged off the director's complaints and transferred the problem to national agencies they knew lacked the authority to intervene.[56]

Even though their sanctity was in grave question, at least the number of Soviet national parks and nature reserves, including those set aside for hunting, did grow from 111 in 1975 to 183 in 1988—nearly tripling in acreage.[57] Compared to the 3 percent of U.S. land held in national parks alone, only 1 percent of the much greater Soviet territory is under such protection.[58] The oldest of the USSR's nineteen national parks came into being only in 1971,[59] ninety-nine and eighty-one years, respectively, after Yellowstone and Yosemite were set aside.

By 1930, moreover, such environmental initiatives in the USSR had not only been stripped of their "urgent significance"; they were being swamped by the rush to industrialize under the first Five-Year Plan. The Council of People's Commissars did issue a decree, under Lenin's signature, in October 1921 "On the Protection of Monuments of Nature, Gardens and Parks." Provisions to establish a strong conservation agency under that decree, however, were rejected as "premature,"[60] and the proposed high-level state committee became instead a minor department in the Ministry of Education, functioning as a policy advisory body and research sponsor with varying impact into the mid-1920s. The first Soviet environmental protection agency, also a paper kitten at the outset, did not come into being until 1988.

As a result, there was no official entity to stand up effectively for ecological concerns within the Soviet bureaucracy when the drive for development moved into high gear. Reporting on a 1930 discussion on conservation sponsored by Moscow University zoologists, the journal *Preservation of Nature (Okhrana prirody)* derided "certain university professors who still have supporters in our society" for their "academic" opposition to "any human interference" with nature. The "old theory of protecting nature for nature's own sake," the journal declared, "so sharply contradicts both our economic and scientific interests that it has no place in our country as it builds socialism."[61]

Those were fighting words, the familiar rhetoric of Bolshevik intolerance, and they led to swift action. Several distinguished zoologists were fired from their teaching jobs. The journal itself ceased publishing in 1930 as *Preservation of Nature,* reappearing the following year as *Nature and Socialist Economy.* In its first editorial, it spelled out the new line:

> The riches and forces of nature must be wisely utilized above all to fulfill the great, peaceful duties of constructing socialism. . . . Clearly all work in the field of nature preservation must be carried out with resolute class-proletarian awareness. No one has learned anything from the Great October Revolution who still believes that the unfolding socialist campaign on all fronts, the liquidation of the kulaks as a class, the powerful growth of collectivization of the peasantry do not mandate class warfare in the field of nature preservation as well.[62]

By 1935 when Trofim Lysenko, the scourge of geneticists for the next thirty years, launched his career with an attack on the "kulaks of science" that caught Stalin's attention,[63] nature's expert defenders were in full retreat, powerless to oppose either Lysenko's rise or the abuse of the earth in the name of progress. Like medical professionals before them, they were to serve the Soviet state and the class struggle dutifully, unquestioningly and, above all, silently. Stalinist planning justified itself with a forthright slogan: "We cannot expect charity from nature. We must tear it from her." Nature existed to be exploited, to be wrestled into submission. To defend it was sabotage, a hostile act against the builders of the socialist paradise.

FALSE FRONTS AND SELF-DECEPTION

They built massively, rapidly, heroically and heedlessly, more or less doubling the output of coal, electricity, oil, iron ore, pig iron and even the numbers of those employed in the labor force between 1927–28 and 1932.[64] There arose in the Urals wilderness of Magnitogorsk what was to be the USSR's leading metallurgical complex. A huge dam harnessed the waters of the Dniepr River outside Zaporozhe for Europe's largest electric power station. The world's biggest tractor factory grew on the banks of the Volga in Stalingrad. By 1941 the USSR was producing nine times more electrical power than in 1913, six and a half times more coal, three times as much steel and more than twice as much cement, pulp and paper.[65]

What was remarkable was not the environmental harm that followed and flowed from the campaign to make the Soviet Union an industrial giant. Considering the way such cities grew, there was nothing very surprising in the atmospheric emissions that made the air in Magnitogorsk, Zaporozhe and Volgograd (formerly Stalingrad), respectively, the sixth, twenty-second, and twenty-eighth most polluted in the Soviet Union in 1990.[66] Far less predictable was the survival of environmental consciousness and, at least on paper, of antipollution laws and regulations through the Stalinist years of hothouse growth.

The rules were strict. When the United States adopted its first clean air legislation in 1970, its limits on carbon monoxide, for instance, were more lenient than Soviet norms, the first in the world to define maximum permissible concentrations of various toxic substances in the atmosphere. As early as 1949 the USSR Council of Ministers issued a resolution on air pollution and created a Chief Administration for Sanitary Epidemiological Supervision to monitor its observance. But it was only in the decade after Stalin's death that all fifteen Soviet republics, led by Estonia in 1957, promulgated nature protection laws. The central government in the 1960s also decreed a variety of steps against water pollution in Lake Baikal and at Black and Baltic Sea resort areas.[67]

The regulatory effort looked impressive. It amounted, however, to another form of the old Russian practice of *pokazukha,* putting a false front over grubby reality. Prince Potemkin had done it for the Empress Catherine in the eighteenth century, erecting façades of seemingly prosperous villages for her to observe from the royal barge. A fine art in the hands of Communist propagandists, *pokazukha* shaped everything from falsified statistics to the miniparks that blossomed hastily in Moscow in June 1974 along the streets to be traveled by President Richard Nixon's motorcade.

Environmental regulation was a sham as well. The fines imposed on violators were minimal, 50 rubles for most offenses, doubling to 100 for especially serious ones.[68] At most, they constituted a minor nuisance for factory managers under pressure to fulfill their plans at all costs. And enforcement was lax; between 1963 and 1967 only twenty-nine polluters were convicted in Russian Federation courts, some of them just poachers.[69] Writing in 1972, Marshall Goldman traced the failure of the regulatory approach back to the early days of the Revolution: "[A] heavy reliance on legal restraint and good intentions . . . has generated a form of self-deception. . . . By setting unattainable goals after the 1917 Revolution when enforcement powers were too weak or lacking altogether, Lenin bred into the system of environmental control a certain contempt that persists today."[70]

The Soviet economic and political system, in any case, insured a low level of priority for environmental protection. Because natural resources, as state property, were effectively cost-free to industry, there was no way to calculate the social costs involved in degrading or wasting irreplaceable assets.

Conflicts could arise within the system between one ministry charged with maximizing fishery resources and another whose mission entailed damming rivers where fish spawned and bred. Such arguments, however, were resolved behind closed doors and usually in favor of the agency offering what was judged—without factoring in social costs—the highest economic return. Among the bureaucratic whales, the defense sector was Moby Dick. Almost as powerful were the ministries responsible for land reclamation, electric power, mining, chemical and metallurgical production and other aspects of heavy industry. These giants, especially the group known as the "metal-eaters," swallowed up the minnows that might have tried to defend Soviet ecology.

While the biggest and fiercest giant of all was the military, it was a military project—a factory built on the shores of Siberia's Lake Baikal to make aircraft tires from cellulose—that generated the first major environmental protest in Soviet history. The campaign proved futile, but it provided proof as early as 1963, after so many decades of pretense and silence, that the traditional Russian love of nature had not only survived but retained a measure of political force.

The story of Lake Baikal belongs in another chapter. (See chapter 6.) It deserves mention here because, as the first Soviet expert to write about pollution in the USSR observed in 1978: "Major ecological problems in the Soviet Union began with Baikal, but unfortunately they will not end with the lake. . . . 'The blue orb of Siberia' has become a symbol of hundreds of Russian lakes and rivers being ruined by pollution, a symbol of the smoke-filled sky suffocating forests and people, a symbol of perishing nature."[71] Ze'ev Wolfson, the author of those words, a researcher with access to unpublished official documents, had to write under the pseudonym Boris Komarov and circulate his manuscript on "perishing nature" clandestinely inside the USSR. Few there read his book, and even in the West, when it was translated, many doubted that the picture could be as bleak as he reported. In the foreword to the American edition, for instance, Goldman challenged as "unfair" Komarov's unrelentingly negative tone. "While admittedly the Soviets have a long way to go," Goldman argued, "they have at least come to recognize the problem and are beginning to seek some remedy."[72]

Nearly a decade later in 1988, the new head of the environmental protection agency Goskompriroda, shelved as "premature" in 1921, commented that the drive for serious environmental protection in the USSR was starting "30 years too late."[73] "In contrast to the economy," said chairman Nikolai Vorontsov on another occasion, "ecology requires not 10-year planning, but 50-year planning at a minimum, long-range, extraordinary decisions. But we have people who think: 'Just let me get through this quarter, and maybe the next one, too.' "[74]

That kind of thinking represented the shrunken legacy of Lenin's utopian ambitions. A few months after leaving his office as Soviet minister of health, Yevgeny Chazov compared his unfinished work to one of the labors of Hercules: cleaning the Augean stables. At best, he said, he had made only a start.[75] Like Vorontsov, who compared his budget of 20 million rubles to the $12 billion allocated to the U.S. Environmental Protection Agency, Chazov complained of having too little authority and too few resources for the task he faced.

From their separate perspectives, both Chazov and Vorontsov faced the same reality: After decades of giving little more than lip service to human and environmental health, the Soviet regime could summon no more than half measures to recover lost ground. Although public health and pollution control had figured prominently in Communist propaganda, they had always been secondary in practice to what Chazov had once sarcastically characterized as "other, higher state interests."[76] Those interests had helped in 1974 to generate a twenty-year ammonia-for-phosphate barter deal between the USSR and the Occidental Petroleum Corporation. One tangible result of the complex swap, launched in Moscow with the summit-level blessing of Leonid Brezhnev and Richard Nixon, was the construction of two huge ammonia storage tanks at what was called the "dockside factory" on the outskirts of Odessa. Each tank was built to hold 150,000 tons of the volatile substance piped from the steppes east of the Volga River.

Aside from being uncomfortably close to an artillery practice range, the facility also fed the explosive ammonia into a steady procession of tankers that, Odessans feared, sailed altogether too near the city. By May 1991 factory managers had halved the amount of ammonia held in each of the tanks and were listening to American engineers who recommended a careful survey of any structural weakness in the foundations.

"The storage is as safe as it could be based on world standards," said one of the American consultants later. "But whenever you have that much ammonia in one place, you have a problem."[77] In Odessa the problem was an incendiary political issue. Dread of a fatal explosion mobilized Greens in the city and kept its officials under lengthy siege.

All of the furor and the fear might have been avoided. In 1974 an Occidental Petroleum executive had warned a highly placed Soviet official about the site chosen for the storage facility. "You could have a big problem with the environment down the road," he said.

"Environment?" responded Vladimir Alkhimov, then the deputy foreign trade minister, genuinely puzzled. "Environment? What does the word mean?"[78]

By 1991 no ordinary or official Soviet needed a foreigner to spell out the meaning of "environment." The nation had been taught, primarily if not perfectly, by its own ecological activists that a crisis threatened its natural resources, its public health, perhaps its survival. The ardent demonstrators, the student enthusiasts, the scientists who supported them and the officeholders who bowed to their pressure had awakened an environmental consciousness.

What they could not do as quickly or solidly was direct that aroused public understanding into coherent, cost-effective programs of cleanup and control. The investments required would be massive, and the Soviet Union was in deep financial distress. The policy guidance would have to be sophisticated, and reform-era Soviet politics, while vigorous and exciting, were both primitive and nearly paralyzed.

Prodded by Greens of various shades and ranks, the people of the USSR were demanding action. To get it, they would first have to settle on the kind of government they wanted and the price they were actually ready to pay to end the threat of ecocide. In the early autumn of 1991, those fundamental decisions still looked a long way off.

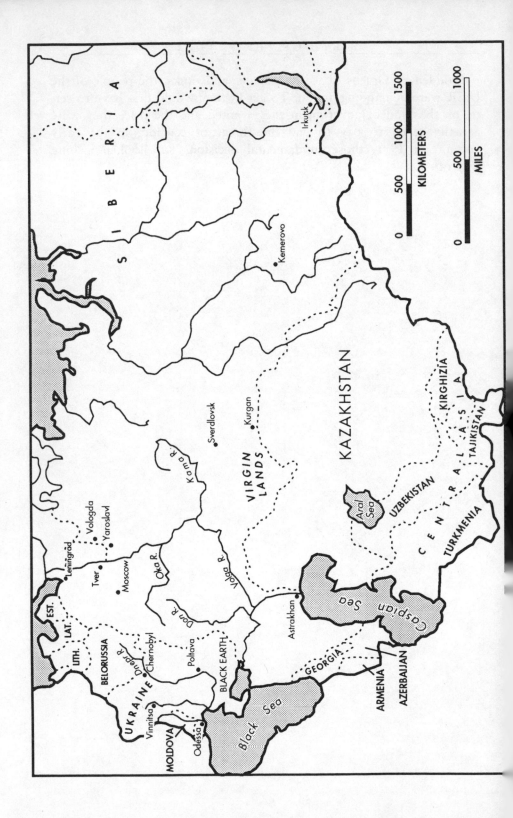

CHAPTER 3

Harvests of Neglect

ECOCIDE IS NOT just an urban phenomenon. In the Third World it is a burning rain forest or a spreading desert. In the United States its victims include the oystermen of the Chesapeake Bay. In the Soviet Union agriculture has been a major casualty. Reckless exploitation, skewed priorities and pernicious neglect have depopulated rural Russia. Throughout the USSR these forces have laid to waste productive fields and forests, poisoned food, water and people and denied the rural population adequate medical care.

City dwellers have also paid a high price for these losses. In the late 1980s domestic produce—whether healthful or toxic—became increasingly hard to find at reasonable cost. A kind of economic triage, moreover, reserved large amounts of hard currency for grain imports, denying enterprises and consumers alike the funds they needed to purchase modern technology, medicines, and consumer goods. The primary victims, however, were the Soviet peasants and the land they could not call their own.

"We treated the land without mercy," the chairman of the State Committee for the Protection of Nature (Goskompriroda) observed late in 1989. Like many Soviets he cited U.S. experience as a yardstick to measure Soviet failure and added: "Perhaps the point is that in the United States the land has masters, whereas in our country it belongs to the state—that is, to nobody."[1]

Ownerless by law and ideological imperative, cropland in the USSR was so ill tended that its 1984–86 average yield of grain was 35 percent that in the United States and only 55 percent Poland's average.[2] Nearly half of the arable land was under serious threat from wind and water erosion. Where it was irrigated or reclaimed, the job was so badly done that close to one-third of the acreage became unusable and another large portion was put in danger.

Under the stewardship of bureaucrats rather than farmers, the soil in the richest grain-growing areas was so abused that its organic content—a key index of fertility—fell by one-fourth. On Joseph Stalin's orders, revived by Nikita Khrushchev, the study of crop genetics that created high-yield and disease-resistant strains of cereals, vegetables and fruits for the rest of the world was kept a nonscience in the USSR until halfway through the 1960s. On the orders of chemical-production ministries, Soviet peasants were made to load the earth with both mineral fertilizers and toxic defenses against insects, pests and weeds. Uninstructed in the proper handling of these substances, the farmers used so many of them so ill-advisedly that their produce became dangerous both to harvesters and consumers.

Soviets can farm well. On their private plots—just 1 to 2 percent of all land—they produced "about two-thirds of the potatoes and eggs and about 40 percent of meat, milk and vegetables" consumed in the mid-1960s.[3] On those tiny patches of ground, they worked for themselves—hard and productively. On the huge holdings of the state and collective farms, their performance was miserable, even dangerous.

In the Ukraine's Donetsk *oblast,* where heavy industry and farming uneasily coexisted, the region's chief physician found in November 1990 that only 4 of 432 farms produced "healthy" produce or farmers. "A very alarming coincidence," he said, put human and animal illness in the region at similarly high levels. At the same time but far to the east in Kazakhstan, 300,000 head of cattle were found to be carrying tuberculosis, brucellosis and other diseases that made local milk "dangerous to human health." The cattle fell ill, it was reported, because—like many of the farmers who tended them—they were housed in dilapidated quarters and chronically underfed.[4]

AS YE SOW

"A coercive system of farming will never feed the people," thundered Yury Chernichenko early in the historic first session of the Congress of People's Deputies in 1989. A well-known television commentator on rural affairs who sought to mobilize Soviet peasants for their political self-defense, Chernichenko spoke with pungent sarcasm and a measure of inaccuracy. "There is no way," he said, "to explain to a sane person the kind of economy that turns out five times as many tractors per capita, ten times as many combines per capita as the United States, but produces [only] half as much grain."[5] Actually, average Soviet cereal grain production in the years 1986 to 1988 was three-fourths the U.S. crop, and the ratio of fifty-three Americans to every tractor is almost twice as high as the USSR's.[6]

Soviet agricultural failures were more the result of dreadful misman-agement than inadequate mechanization. The latter, though, played its part. Farm machinery was poorly maintained, often the wrong size and regularly out of service. Those factors helped explain why the average yield both of cereals and roots and of tubers per acre in the USSR was roughly two-fifths what it is in the United States.[7] But it was decades of error and indifference that brought Soviet agriculture to its low estate.

A day after the Chernichenko polemic, a farm official from Russia's breadbasket, a descendant of the Cossacks, gave the new parliament his explanation:

> For the Kuban, this [ecology] problem has two sides. One is irrigation on large areas, irrigation without drainage. . . . Over many decades, starting before the Revolution, more than 2,500 levees and dams have been built on the rivers of the steppes. As a result the rivers have silted up and are overgrown with reeds. Heavy equipment has compacted the black earth to a depth of about one meter, and the soil is no longer porous.[8]

The other bane of agriculture in his area, said V. V. Khmura, was industrialization. It took land out of production for factory sites and generated untreated industrial wastes, "poisoning valuable species of fish and polluting the waters." Then there were the pesticides and herbicides "which we have not yet learned to deal with—we apply them using homemade equipment, without laboratory analysis, by guesswork. You can imagine the situation today and what it will be tomorrow."[9]

An incident in point occurred in Belorussia in the 1980s when farmers sprayed a *double* dose of a herbicide made by DuPont onto flax fields that then needed two years to recover. "Such cases," recipes for disaster, said a plant protection specialist regretfully, "do happen, and not so very rarely. . . . [They] expose our economic irresponsibility and neglect [and] technical backwardness. And if you add to that our national custom of doing everything by eye, approximately, and adding on a little more 'just in case,' then the picture is certainly not a happy one."[10]

For writer Vassily Belov, a militant Russian nationalist, Soviet farm problems were not the fault of national customs but of misrule. Address-ing the Congress of Deputies, he flayed the central ministries for the "robbery" inflicted on the collective farms, denounced "destructive" plans to double the area of irrigated land by the year 2005 and then, to applause, threw down a challenge to the urban elite: "No country has so many academics as ours. There are academics all over Moscow—outer space specialists, all kinds of them! But why is it that in the countryside, the peasants cut grass with the same scythe they had in the twelfth century?"[11]

The short and over-simplified answer was that Soviet development policy from Stalin onward swung wildly between a conscious neglect of the country's rich resources and wasteful crash investment programs in them. The initial model, one that the USSR pioneered and that many Third World nations later followed to their regret, stressed growth of industrial production, of energy output, of cities. It left a crippling legacy of scorn for the land and the "dark masses" who lived on it.

Those peasants, freed from serfdom in 1861 only to return to it under the fierce coercion of collectivization seven decades later, were perhaps the Revolution's biggest losers. Lenin promised them ownership of the land. His successors not only denied them property and independence but confined them within a bureaucratic planning system that destroyed tradition, initiative and respect for nature. "Solitary, poor, nasty, brut-ish and short," for hundreds of years the life of most Russian peasants was a Hobbesian bog that began to change for the better only in the last quarter of the nineteenth century. As social and economic conditions improved, however, pressure on the land also rose. The increasing numbers of the rural population, 20 percent higher in 1914 than in 1900, diluted the impact of the modest pre–World War I reforms that allowed enterprising farmers to leave village communes and set up on their own. Post-1917 land reapportionment proved equally ephemeral, and by 1925 more than 90 percent of the peasants were once more tied to the rural communities some had tried to escape.

Technically, two years later 98 percent of the area sown in crops was still in the hands of private peasants, but on the eve of Stalin's forced agricultural collectivization, modern tools were as scarce as farm ani-mals. The wealthiest farmers, the 5 to 7 percent castigated and then eradicated as *kulaks*, rarely owned more than two horses, two cows and just enough land to produce food for market as well as their own table.[12] Their liquidation by expropriation and deportation and in the man-made famine of 1932–33 was the first, massive betrayal of the Bolshevik promise of land to the peasants.

It was far from the last. Collectivization served the political purpose of converting free farmers into a kind of agroindustrial proletariat, either as outright wage earners or as members of a collective, dependent on the state for employment, housing, tools, supplies and direction. The famine was partly a ruthless way to punish those who resisted seizure of their land, crops and labor and partly a result of Stalin's deliberate decision to maintain export sales of grain—3 million tons to Western Europe in 1932–33—while harvests shriveled in the turmoil of collectivization.[13]

The first casualties were the 6 million or more Soviets who died, many as they were being deported to such places as Kazakhstan. Millions of Kazakhs, for their part, fled to China, slaughtering the herds of cattle they could not take with them. The longer-term and nationwide loss was in experienced management and conscientious stewardship of the land. It passed from the control of those who lived on and from it into the hands of politicians and bureaucrats who held farmers in contempt.

Lenin had scorned farmers as "petty capitalists," but, judged Nikita Khrushchev, "Stalin deserves much of the blame" for the failures of Soviet agriculture. "He taught us to think of agriculture as a third-rate branch of our economy. For Stalin, peasants were scum" who would produce only under the pressure of forcible requisitioning for derisory compensation. "No wonder peasants weren't interested in working on collective farms [and] were plunged into the most pathetic conditions."[14]

Khrushchev's own seesaw performance as farmer-in-chief of the Soviet Union did little to improve those conditions. Initially a champion of private plots for collective farmers, he became their foe in 1958. Born a peasant, he seemed to understand the farmers' need for incentives and freedom but could provide neither on a steady basis. He lifted confiscatory taxes only to impose new, compulsory production quotas later. His almost manic reshuffling of the government and Communist Party agricultural bureaucracies disorganized both without, in the end, effectively restricting their power. Above all, he pursued a variety of what his successors called "hare-brained" schemes to rearrange and raise farm output. One shift was to plant corn for fodder on what proved to be unsuitable land in the European part of the USSR. The cereal grain which that region had produced was to come instead from opening up immense tracts of eastern steppe—the Virgin Lands of Kazakhstan and southern Siberia—equal in size to the total cultivated area of Canada.

Both campaigns were ambitious enterprises—and signal failures. Less grain was actually harvested in 1965 than in 1956, but to obtain it, farmers east of the Urals were forced to put large areas of fragile soil under intensive cultivation. As a result, erosion set in on almost half the

50 million acres (not 90 million as Khrushchev had planned) of steppe actually plowed and planted. Meanwhile, in European Russia and the Ukraine, crop rotation was replaced by heavy chemical fertilizer use, a switch that starved the soil of natural nutrients. Under Khrushchev, the seeds were planted for new harvests of neglect that plagued the economy of the USSR and the lives of its farmers for decades more.

A STINKING RUIN

For most of those on the land, life was cruel and primitive before and after Khrushchev's rule. Millions fled the harshness. In 1940 only one-third of all Soviets lived in cities; by 1961 half the population was urban and by 1990, two-thirds. Of the USSR's 273,000 hamlets and villages, only 29,300 have running water; only 7,000 have sewer systems. Only one such town in ten has a retail store, a health care facility or a movie theater, library or other cultural establishment.[15]

Of the 98-odd million people living in such deprivation, some 30 million worked directly in agriculture and forestry.[16] In thousands of joyless villages and on the USSR's 27,000 state (sovkhoz) and 26,000 collective (kolkhoz) farms, the proportion of women fifty-five and older was about 25 percent above that in the urban population. In the rural population of the Russian Republic, the Ukraine and Belorussia, elderly women constituted 44 percent of the total, one-third higher than in the cities to which their schooled and skilled younger kin had managed to move.*[17]

On one such kolkhoz outside the city of Yaroslavl, half of the villages incorporated in the collective were deserted by 1990, and only fifteen dairy maids were available for the three hundred cows still milked by hand. "The office workers were told to take turns milking the cows," said one woman farmer. "But if the cows don't know you, they give 30 percent less milk."[18]

Farther north, in the settlement of Spasskaya some 250 miles from Moscow, so many younger families left that there have been no births since 1965. With its population, once numbering in the hundreds, down to seventeen by the spring of 1990, Spasskaya was only one of some

---

*Until the mid-1970s, the denial of internal passports to most country people created an incentive for rural youngsters to move to cities before their sixteenth birthday, in order to qualify for the vital document that gave them mobility, within limits, in choosing where to get their schooling and subsequent employment. Even in 1991, however, authorities in crowded cities such as Moscow and Leningrad would only issue residence permits to new arrivals who could prove that their employers or families would provide them with housing.

seven thousand nearly derelict villages in the Vologda region where climate and soil are both unforgiving.

It was not always so bleak. Anatoly Zamokhov, a resident for more than seventy years, recalled that

> Before the Bolsheviks, my parents and their parents lived decently. They weren't rich—not by any means, God knows—but they had food and a cow and a table to call their own. Now everyone lives for himself. No one visits anyone on Easter. We were all supposed to be just one big family after collectivization. Just the opposite! Everyone was pitted against everyone else, everyone suspicious of everyone else. Now look at us, a big stinking ruin.[19]

Rural medical care was as primitive as most rural living conditions. Late in 1988, then-Minister of Health Chazov disclosed that there was no hot water in nearly two-thirds of all rural district hospitals—not just in the spartan facilities where midwives and paramedics attend childbirth. More than a quarter of all Soviet country hospitals, he said, also lacked sewage pipes, and 17 percent had no water at all.[20]

Rural medicine everywhere has always suffered from short supplies of doctors and facilities. The problem is not limited to the USSR. Many other advanced societies have found it hard to keep doctors down on the farm. But in the Soviet Union the uphill battle has clearly been a losing one. To put it in perspective, it helps to realize that in 1924,

> 80 percent of all physicians resided in large cities (more than one-third in Moscow and Leningrad alone), despite high levels of urban unemployment. Three years later [Health Minister] Semashko denounced a situation in which 1,500 unemployed physicians lived in Moscow while one-fifth of the rural physician posts went vacant.[21]

Sadly, six decades later the problem seemed only slightly less acute. A jubilee volume of Soviet statistics published in 1987 reported that only 7 percent of the 988,000 hospital beds put into operation from 1970 to 1985 were on cooperative farms, where 12 percent of the population still lived. "The problem of bringing medical assistance for the agricultural population closer to the level in cities," according to an editorial understatement, "is being resolved slowly."[22]

In fact, however, by a different Soviet measurement of health care facilities in the countryside, the problem was not being resolved at all. The 11,400 rural hospitals served only 34 percent of the total 1987 Soviet population living in rural settlements of 500 or more inhabitants. The

17,000 outpatient clinics reached 46.6 percent of that same population, and the 40,400 paramedic/midwifery stations—many of them horrifyingly primitive—70.7 percent.[23] Conditions in rural medical facilities are so bad that a large proportion of the rural population travels to urban centers for diagnosis and treatment.

In the Kurgan region of Western Siberia, the situation was grim enough to attract the attention of a Politburo member. According to his 1988 report to his colleagues, a special effort the year before to provide housing for doctors on the area's state and collective farms had produced 96 apartments instead of the promised 234. Physicians were needed because illness was sidelining 5,000 *sovkhoz* and *kolkhoz* farmers every day. Also in the course of the year, for every 100 workers, seventy-eight days were spent caring for sick children, who on thirty-seven of the region's farms had no free-standing school to attend when they were well.[24] Such backwardness in social services reflected the profound failure of Soviet agriculture to live up to its economic potential. The nation that exported an annual average of 11 million tons of grain in the years 1909 to 1913—30 percent of world grain exports at the time—never managed to sell more than 8 million tons abroad in any year since. A Soviet farmer in the 1990s was lucky to be able to feed himself and four others; his American counterpart produced food for fifty. By another measure, each of the 3.1 million U.S. farmers earned more than ten times the average yearly income of the 22.3 million Soviets engaged in agriculture full time.[25] Since 1972, the USSR has been a consistent net food importer, purchasing 35 to 45 million metric tons of foreign grain a year in the 1980s to feed its own people and livestock.[26] Hence the stinging joke Soviets told about the likely results of a Red Army conquest of the Sahara: "For fifty years nothing would happen. After that we would have to import sand."

Soviet agriculture as a whole was so poorly or wrongly supplied with labor, technology and basic infrastructure—silos, bins, roads and the like—that in 1989 some 30 million tons of grain, 14 percent of the total value of the crop, simply rotted in the fields or soon after harvesting. As in many other years, one-fifth of the loss occurred in the course of harvesting, primarily because of equipment failures, while two-thirds of the wastage was due to the lack of storage facilities either near the fields or at processing plants.[27]

Very similar problems generated similar losses of timber. In 1989, for instance, Soviet forests yielded only a little more than half the amount of wood designated for cutting. Just as in the fields, loggers left some of their crop—about 2 percent—behind to rot because of equipment and transportation failures or personnel shortages.[28] At the same time, they overcut coniferous forests that are easier to work in, neglected stands of deciduous trees and destroyed over 180,000 acres where saplings and valuable species of young trees were growing.[29] The Soviet Union did not practice "sustained-yield forest harvest in which the amount cut corresponds to the annual growth per year," a British scholar noted, and despite multiple reorganizations, including the 1989 dismissal of the minister of the timber industry, the "attempt to tie forest management more intimately to forest utilization" faced severe administrative and financial obstacles.[30]

With over 290 million acres of woodland theoretically available for timber cutting, the amount of wastage might have seemed insignificant, but nearly half of all forest land needed energetic husbandry. Seedlings were planted and tended on only 5 percent of that acreage each year, and "only 25 to 28 percent of the amount harvested [was treated to] aggressive forest restoration."[31] In the timber-rich Soviet Far East, the neglect seemed colossal. "As a result of many years of wide-scale, practically unlimited and uncontrolled continuous logging, accompanied by repeated forest and grass fires," timber experts reported, "many areas of the [Far East] . . . are turning into deserts hundreds of thousands of acres in size." This "ecological crisis," they added, is the result of "gross violations" of prescribed forestry practices in all parts of the region.[32] In the eastern Soviet Union, where "anything up to half of the world's conifers" are thought to grow, deforestation was already a real menace.[33] "A significant portion of the Soviet *taiga* [boreal forest] will be lost permanently," an American expert feared.[34] With it Moscow could lose much of the resource that earned 7 percent of the value of its exports in 1988,[35] $1.3 billion in hard currency in 1989.[36]

Given the resources available to them, Soviets could have made agriculture, including forestry, the base for a healthy economy. Conceivably, they still can, but decades of managerial incoherence and contemptuous neglect have left a pitiful legacy of wasted and abused resources, both physical and human. The erosion of the Soviet countryside is most vividly evident in the state of its most precious resource, the land itself.

ILL FARES THE LAND

Out of 1.5 billion acres of cultivated land in the Soviet Union, from the rich Black Earth Zone of the Ukraine and European Russia to the arid plains of Central Asia, by 1989 nearly half was seriously imperiled; an additional 13 percent was marginal—rocky, hilly, or overgrown. Of the endangered lands, some 388 million acres were saline; 279 million have been eroded; and 62 million were waterlogged or swampy.[37] Over the last fifteen to twenty years the levels of humus—decomposed organic matter—in the soil dropped between 8 and 30 percent, declining by an average of 20 percent in the Russian Federation and 9 percent in the Ukraine.[38]

Since the 1960s, the most fertile European sections of the country, lost "up to 25 percent of the soil humus," said Fyodor Morgun. Instead of traditional and effective techniques of farming—shallow tilling, contour plowing, crop rotation, letting land lie fallow, fertilizing with organic compost and animal manure—Soviets relied too heavily on mechanization and chemicals. Such policies, he declared, reflected "a unique fetish for scientific and technical progress. The belief that technology, fertilizers and pesticides can produce an infinite increase in crop yields has stalled agriculture and produced an endless consumption of soil resources."[39]

Morgun made his name as an agronomist in the area around Poltava, the site of Peter the Great's climactic 1709 victory over Sweden and the modern heart of the Ukraine's grain belt. There, however, he found that soil humus had dropped to half or less what it was at the turn of the twentieth century. He blamed such "degradation . . . mainly on tilling the land with plows" so deeply and so often that the richest upper layer loses the ability to renew itself and sustain plant life.[40] The loss of humus was matched by the loss of topsoil itself to the forces of wind and water. From 1975 to 1990 such erosion attacked some 135 million acres of farmland.[41] A major agricultural conference in late 1989 was advised that 376 million more acres of cultivated fields—one-quarter of the total—as well as 432 million acres of hay and pastureland stood in need of antierosion defenses.[42] During the years 1975 to 1985, water erosion damage rose by 12 percent, wind erosion losses by 20 percent and saline acreage by 95 percent.[43] The USSR risked losing productive land equal in area to all of Western Europe from Norway's North Cape to Spain's Costa Brava.

In the 1980s alone, experts reported, ravines and gullies over 600,000 miles in combined length ate up some 16 million acres of arable land. Expanding at the rate of more than 12,000 miles a year, they were taking between 245,000 and 370,000 acres out of service annually and adding nearly 2.5 million acres, twice the area of the state of Delaware, to the Soviet inventory of lightly, partly and severely eroded land.[44]

While U.S. conservation authorities classified some 40 percent of America's arable land as highly erodible, America—unlike the Soviet Union—took steps to reduce the danger. A 1982 study showed wind and water erosion claiming 3.1 billion tons of topsoil a year from U.S.

cropland, roughly twice the volume that is considered tolerable. When world demand was high, "for every pound of grain they harvested, [American] farmers squandered five pounds of topsoil."[45] Under a land reserve program begun in the mid-1980s, however, owners of 34 million of the 120 million most threatened acres contracted to take their land out of production for ten-year periods. Yearly excessive topsoil losses dropped by some 550 million tons.[46]

With vastly more cropland available than the 400 million U.S. acres, the Soviets could conceivably be excused for their prodigality.[47] In fact, however, of their total 575 million acres, nearly half lay in arid zones that, like the American Southwest, receive less than sixteen inches of rain and snow a year. In those areas, irrigation is essential. Throughout the USSR, the job has been immense and often badly botched.

Irrigation has brought water to nearly 51 million acres, about 9 percent of the total, a ratio similar to America's.[48] Irrigated acreage doubled between 1970 and 1986 and continued to expand at the rate of 1.1 to 1.3 million acres a year. In addition, land reclamation projects already covering 33.4 million acres by the mid-1980s incorporated an additional 850,000 to 960,000 acres each year.[49] The Ministry of Land Reclamation and Water Resources (Minvodkhoz)—"one of the prime Soviet leviathans," a British Sovietologist called it—employed "by its own account one and a half million people . . . something approaching 1 percent" of the Soviet labor force.[50]

A single, giant government agency until 1990, the renamed but un-reformed Ministry of Water Economy and its supposedly self-financing auxiliary, Vodstroi, continued to boast a political clout and a bureaucratic instinct for self-perpetuation that the powerful U.S. Bureaus of Reclamation and Land Management and the Army Corps of Engineers might envy. Having spent 130 billion rubles between 1966 and 1986—28 percent of all agricultural investments—on water management projects, Minvodkhoz managed to win a 50-billion-ruble budget for 1986 to 1990 capital construction projects.[51]

A major target of ecologists' scorn, the Soviet Gargantua has been notoriously inefficient. According to a 1988 survey, fully 14 percent of the land the ministry had irrigated throughout the USSR required restorative work; 4 percent of that portion was useless because of "flooding, salinization, failures of the irrigation system and other reasons."[52] Even more pessimistic findings came from a Soviet expert on hydraulic engineering. He claimed in 1990 that "nearly one-third" of the 50-odd million acres supposedly reclaimed since 1970 was unusable and that poor maintenance threatened further losses on large parts of the 86 million acres "with hydraulic land reclamation systems."[53] Crop yields on two out of every three acres of such land were consistently too low to justify actual outlays or meet projected potential.[54]

As V. V. Khmura angrily told his fellow deputies: "Money has been invested in the land on the principle of 'give it to the one who dug the hole and refuse it to the one who has to fill it in.' At present about 988,000 acres of Black Earth land in the Kuban needs to be saved from inundation. Hundreds of farms (stanitsas) are flooded."[55] The pattern was all too typical of the Soviet society and economy. In agriculture, as in industry, priority for gross output—the all-determining val—regularly justified huge investments in the wrong places and technologies.

One exception stood out. As the political boss of the fertile Poltava region before becoming the first head of Goskompriroda, Fyodor Morgun oversaw a strikingly successful return to a prerevolutionary system of shallow plowing. The experiment, his chief aide reported, pushed yields in 1981 to 1985 14 percent above the Ukraine-wide average and, with lower costs, raised per-acre income by nearly 100 rubles.[56]

Morgun, whose tenure at the Environmental Protection Committee was brief and frustrating, argued that his "soil-protection system" could and should be applied to 250 to 300 million acres of farmland in the European part of the USSR. Such a move, he claimed, would add the equivalent of 35 to 40 million tons of grain to each Soviet harvest, roughly equal to yearly grain imports.[57] Appealing for changed technologies in an address to the Communist Party's landmark Nineteenth Conference in July 1988, he said:

> The plow ruins and destroys, yet we make 200,000 of them every year. We find the metal and the money for this calamity [but not] for subsurface tillers, subsoilers, slotters and wide-span cultivators; there is no metal for equipment to handle manure properly, nor . . . for the production of modern drills and equipment for high-quality spreading of mineral fertilizers.
>
> So we are not applying the fertilizers properly, but are throwing . . . them away. But in nature nothing is lost. They are carried by streams into reservoirs and then show up as blue-green algae and all manner of impurities that destroy all living things in the Volga, Dniepr, Don and other rivers.[58]

CONTAMINATION FOR MASS CONSUMPTION

Chemicals from the fields also showed up in food. The Soviet minister who oversaw the world's largest production of mineral fertilizer—28 million tons in 1989—admitted that even though the USSR, on average, applied only 16 to 38 percent as much mineral fertilizer per acre as "developed capitalist countries," still "the presence of nitrates has been found only in our Soviet vegetables."[59] His statistic was somewhat misleading. Weighted to reflect different levels of national income, the USSR used "3.1 times more chemical fertilizers" than the United States.[60]

By one estimate, 30 percent of all Soviet produce contained nitrate levels above established limits.[61] According to the minister's deputy in charge of manufacturing, the problem was that fertilizers "are stored poorly and . . . applied without rhyme or reason, without taking into account the individual peculiarities of the soil or what is to be planted on it."[62]

One result was that Soviet health inspectors found unsafe levels of nitrates in close to one-third of all red beets and vegetable marrow tested in 1988 as well as in almost 15 percent of the carrots and cabbage sampled.[63] In produce from Kazakhstan and Uzbekistan, nitrates ran 12 and 19 percent, respectively, above the norms and even 100 percent above in carrot juice for infants produced in a plant in the Kazakh capital of Alma-Ata.[64] While vegetables from farms around Volgograd in July 1990 contained only "insignificant" above-norm nitrate levels,[65] Central Asian watermelons came to Moscow markets in 1989 with two to four times the legal limit.[66]

Soviet norms, while stricter in some cases than World Health Organization rules, were actually as far from being standardized as from being observed. All-Union, Russian Federation, Belorussian and Ukrainian authorities each set different ceilings for nitrate levels in potatoes.[67] Deciding that its limits were too strict, the Soviet Ministry of Health lowered them by 200 percent in May 1989, as casually as it had waived its ban on DDT use in Azerbaijan yearly from 1970 to 1988.[68]

Standards, in short, carried little weight. Farmers who routinely spread more than ten times the proper amount of fertilizer ran little risk of being severely penalized.[69] Only random checks were conducted on their produce, and even the honest sanitary inspectors usually had only outmoded, unreliable equipment to monitor the presence of chemicals or radiation in food or of pollution in the air and water that transmitted some of the poison.

On two farms on the receiving end of Moscow's industrial wastes, cadmium, a substance that can do irreversible kidney damage and may increase the risk of heart attack, was found at three to ten times permissible levels in beets and carrots tested in 1989. Zinc, also carried from the city's sewers to the rural water supply, showed up in the beets at twice and thrice the allowed norm.[70] It was no wonder that the Soviet publishers of a textbook on defining nitrate and pesticide levels printed only five hundred copies.[71] With paper supplies at a premium, it would have been hard to justify a larger press run for a guide so likely to be incomplete, outdated and ignored.

Nor was it surprising that an alarmed population, denied accurate information or reliable protection by official fecklessness, tried to fend for itself. Moving to answer the questions of worried consumers, a Moscow cooperative in 1989 began to market an easy home-testing kit that would indicate the presence—if not the precise level—of nitrates and nitrites. The price was high: two rubles and thirty kopeks for two hundred quick and cursory exams, a bit less than 1 percent of the average worker's monthly wage.[72] Still, demand was brisk. Ordinary citizens had become suspicious of the food put before them, both of the unhealthy substances added to it in the fields and of the dangerous way it was often processed and handled on the way to their plates. Increasing numbers became not just suspicious but sick, as the incidence of food poisoning cases hit 1.8 million in 1988, up 8 percent from the 1985 to 1987 average. While there were 64 cases per 10,000 population for the Soviet Union as a whole, the incidence in Tajikistan, the Russian Republic and Uzbekistan ranged from 71 to 113 cases for every 10,000 inhabitants.[73]

Publicity given to these perils seemed even to galvanize the Health Ministry's sanitary inspection service, previously a sinecure for bribe-takers. The functionaries whose job was to check hygiene in produce warehouses, markets, food-preparation factories, grocery stores and restaurant kitchens used to be notorious for their ability not to see filthy conditions if, as they checked the premises, their own shopping bags were filled. One senior female inspector in Yaroslavl was famous both for her capacity for alcohol and for carrying a box of live cockroaches that she would threaten to release unless she received a satisfactory payoff.[74]

In a display of glasnost-era zeal, the inspection service disclosed that in the course of examining some 850,000 food-handling establishments in 1987, its agents issued 511,000 fines, ordered 92,000 temporary closures, moved to fire 178,000 workers and initiated 6,000 administrative actions and 2,000 criminal suits. In 1988 the service also gave orders on 27,000 occasions to prevent the sale of one or another product, not just because of nitrate or pesticide contamination but also because of excess levels of antibiotics in 11 percent of the meat tested and 25 percent of the milk.[75]

One foray involved a low-level Moscow inspection service that briefly forced the two ten-day-old Pizza Hut restaurants in the capital to close in 1990 for violating various sanitary requirements having to do with the chemical makeup of the dishes used, the water system and the health of the employees. At a time when the Soviet government was supposedly encouraging joint ventures with Western firms, the episode suggested that some strategically placed functionaries were still marching to a different policy drummer. Actually, the stakes were lower: Once neighborhood officials got their share of tax and license earnings, Pizza Hut managers were allowed to reopen.[76]

Publicizing the campaign for food hygiene might have enhanced the reputation of the sanitary inspectors, but it did little for Soviet consumer confidence. It was shaped by reports that the dairy-inspection service, for example, checked milk and cheese for the presence of only eight out of nineteen known harmful and toxic substances. "The trouble is," affirmed a dairy industry technical expert, "it is impossible to consider [official] data on milk quality reliable. [Reported statistics] for 1988, for example, claimed that only 5 percent of the milk was of low quality. In fact, the real figure is six times higher *on average* for the country. In some regions it goes as high as 50 percent."[77]

Of all the Soviet consumers' worries, fear of radiation became the most acute after the Chernobyl disaster. Anxiety was kept well nourished by reports about trainloads of radioactive beef from contaminated pastureland being shuttled from one depot to another and occasionally turning up in sausages.[78] Here and there, citizens rebelled.

On one such occasion, a group of women on the outskirts of Tver, formerly Kalinin, set up a barricade after learning that a fertilizer factory "a stone's throw away" was processing phosphates imported from Syria that contained high levels of uranium, radium and thorium. Arguing with police who arrived to break up the picket line that they established to block the factory's trucks, the women said that they were "being showered" with chemicals in the polluted air. "That's bad enough," they added, "but yesterday they told us that they have some sort of radiation over there."[79]

Citizens fearful of irradiated raw materials had earlier blocked plans to build a fertilizer plant to process Syrian imports in Odessa. A public outcry also followed the use of such products on northern Russian fields and in 1990 forced a halt to construction work in Kursk and Bryansk on complexes to make phosphoric-based fertilizer from Syrian raw materials.

Arguing that such fertilizer was essential to modern farming, agrochemical industry officials accused the Soviet press of "tendentious, unsupported information . . . that disinformed public opinion." The result, they said, was a bill of "300 million rubles a year in hard currency" for imports of fertilizer that should be domestically produced. Environmentalists rebutted that the minerals imported from Syria contained "up to 30 harmful substances, almost all of which are first- or second-category hazards. Among them are uranium (up to 76 grams per ton), thorium (up to 90 grams per ton) [and] strontium (up to 3,000 grams per ton)."[80]

Radiation, however, was only a minor aspect of the pollution of farmland and produce traceable to man-made chemicals and their mismanagement. Nor was mishandling of chemical fertilizer the only wasteful and dangerous practice in Soviet farming. Throughout the USSR, as Fyodor Morgun told the Nineteenth Party Conference, "figures for organic fertilizer losses are astronomical." Just in the Non–Black Earth zone the volume of compost and manure "piling up around livestock sheds [and] poisoning ponds, lakes and rivers" more than doubled over two decades, from some 53 million tons in 1965 to 112 million tons in 1985. Soviet central planners set no targets for the use of organic fertilizers, indeed put no value on them. Farmers, thus, had no incentive either to apply them or to prevent their polluting surface water. "It is not so much the responsibility of the *kolkhozes* and *sovkhozes*," said Morgun, "as it is their calamity."[81]

PREFERENCE FOR POISON

The "calamity," however, went far beyond the dung heaps of rural Russia or their storage, transport and use. Arguably, if Soviet farmers could cut just those losses and, in the most promising areas, institute the kind of protective cultivation measures that Morgun tested, grain imports would become unnecessary. Under Mikhail Gorbachev, there was some movement toward more sensitive and sensible practices. Planners even pushed to introduce contour plowing on over 110 million acres of land by the end of the century.[82]

Long ago, however, Soviet agriculture's overlords chose a different course, the seemingly scientific "fetish" that Morgun named. The policy amounted to a quest for a chemical miracle to propel agricultural output high enough to compensate for the basic structural weaknesses Soviet leaders either would not or could not address. The state poured money into the land and, with the money, poison. A leading agricultural economist counted a fivefold increase in overall expenditures for agriculture from 1965 to 1989 and a 250 percent rise in the use of chemicals in farming. "The investments have been colossal," he said, "but the result is only a 20 percent increase in the production of crops and a 30 to 40 percent rise for livestock." Fertilizers, fungicides, pesticides and herbicides, he contended, contributed only marginally (4 to 5 percent) to increased output; land reclamation, just 14 percent.[83]

Whatever their impact on farm income, crop protection chemicals in Soviet hands proved unusually dangerous. Other countries have used them with little adverse effect on human health, although U.S. Environmental Protection Agency (EPA) officials have sought to ban some entirely as hazardous to farm workers and consumers alike. In 1991, for instance, the agency weighed a prohibition on parathion, a Danish-made insecticide said to be responsible for poisoning 650 California fruit-and-vegetable field workers—100 of them fatally—since 1966.[84]

In the USSR, where they were applied carelessly, to excess and by farmers untutored in handling them, the materials became a widespread hazard, in some areas even a threat to life. Out of four hundred pesticides whose use was permitted, only about sixty were controlled on "any significant scale," said a Soviet expert. "One hundred twenty are simply beyond the control capacity of the regulatory agencies."[85]

The most startling, even horrifying, case in point was DDT. Formally banned in the USSR in 1970, two years before the United States also outlawed it, DDT actually continued in secret use in the USSR into the late 1980s " 'by special permission' of the ministries of agriculture and forestry." Even twenty years after its supposed prohibition, standards defined "safe" levels of DDT in the soil, and scientists found its residues above the maximum permitted on 24.7 million acres of cultivated land. Average concentrations in Azerbaijan, Armenia, Moldova and Uzbekistan ranged from two to eight times above the limit.[86]

In the Kemerovo region of Siberia, aerial spraying of DDT went on for sixteen years, apparently starting in the late 1960s, as a way to control forest ticks that carried an encephalitis virus. Researchers in 1987 found that fish in the area's rivers still contained an average of 0.88 percent of DDT by weight, with concentrations ranging from 0.09 to 4.24 percent. They blandly concluded, however, that fish kills and higher concentrations of DDT discovered in 1971 and 1975 occurred either in "isolated reservoirs" or because of "violations of handling instructions" for the pesticide.[87] Until 1988, moreover, a pesticide identical to DDT but masquerading as a "polycyclical compound" was widely applied throughout the USSR. From 1978 to 1988, 6,000 tons of it were sprayed *every year* on fields in Uzbekistan.[88] In the Armenian village of Armash where the disguised DDT was used, Dr. Arsen Airiyan, a noted rural health researcher and practitioner, found significant increases since the 1960s in the incidence of cardiovascular disease, sugar diabetes, tumors and allergies.

In the 1980s congenital deformities, mostly retardation, appeared among children born to twenty-six of the town's five hundred families.[89] "We found a link," wrote Dr. Airiyan, who worked in the Ararat Valley since 1953, "between the extensive use of poisonous chemicals . . . and the rise in congenital diseases."[90]

The most widespread presumed damage to farming and farmers from toxic chemicals, however, was not done in secret but "according to plan." It resulted from the precise directives of central authorities who, for example, authorized the manufacture and use of the herbicide dioxin in 1965 but did not begin to acknowledge its lethal nature until late 1991. By 1989 one-third of all the soil and one-fourth of the vegetation that researchers sampled contained traces of pesticide. While the nationwide average of soil samples showing impermissibly high levels was only 4.6 percent, the incidence of contamination in Azerbaijan, 29.2 percent, was nearly seven times that rate. In both Belorussia and Georgia almost a quarter of the soil samples showed excess pesticide levels.[91]

The poisons were not only overused; they were also frequently ineffective. Only 15 percent of all Soviet state and collective farms had technical personnel on their payrolls even theoretically competent in the use of agricultural chemicals. As a result, one expert estimated that only 10 percent of all insecticides actually controlled the pests they were meant to attack. The remainder, which he conservatively put at some 200,000 tons a year,* went "to no purpose. The truth is, frequently we don't exterminate the bugs, we drown them."[95]

Aleksei Yablokov, who became the most vocal and respected ecologist in the Soviet parliament, once explained the practice in these words:

An "expenditure psychology" prevails in the USSR's agroindustrial complex; the basic growth measurements are not bigger harvests or lower production costs but the total volume of outlays (for pesticides, fertilizer, capital investments, etc.). The work indices for crop-protection units are tied directly to fulfilling the plan for chemical treatment of the crops regardless of the actual situation in a given month, season, economic zone or region. Thus in the race to put the highest figures in the ledger books, pesticides are sometimes simply carried out to the fields and dumped alongside them.[96]

* Other sources fixed Soviet pesticide supplies in 1988 at 308,000 tons, down by 15 percent from the year before.[92] And while disagreeing about the actual volume of land treated with pesticides in 1988, two experts concurred that it amounted to 87 to 88 percent of the total cultivated acreage.[93] In contrast, pesticides were used on only 61 percent of U.S. farmland and at per-acre levels slightly below Soviet ones.[94]

As other nations were reducing their agrochemical dependency, Soviets were getting more deeply hooked. While U.S. farmers cut back nearly 60 percent in the years 1976 to 1983—though still using insecticides heavily on tobacco, cotton, corn, soybean and vegetable fields and orchards—the tonnage of domestic and imported pesticides that Soviets applied rose some 70 percent in the same period.[97] By 1987, a year after usage peaked in the USSR, "about 30 percent of all foodstuffs contained a concentration of pesticides dangerous to human health," Yablokov reported, as did 42 percent of baby foods.[98]

Yablokov, a crusader on a multitude of environmental fronts in the USSR, made pesticide use a special target. He was impatient with arguments that the substances were not only essential for productive modern farming but, properly used, safe as well. To him "the magic wand of agricultural chemicals" was not only poison-tipped but unprofitable too. In rice-growing areas of the fertile Kuban, for instance, a 1.5-million-ruble increase in crop value attributable to pesticide treatments brought a 2-million-ruble loss in fishery income.[99]

What most alarmed Yablokov, however, was the human injury directly connected, he and many other Soviets believed, to the improper use of such chemical compounds. One example that bolstered, if not conclusively proved, their argument was the report of a senior doctor in vegetable-and-fruit-growing Moldova, where pesticide use was among the highest in the Soviet Union—nearly thirteen times the USSR average—and fertilizer applications per acre were six times the average in California. The doctor found that the Moldovan death rate from cirrhosis in 1985 was seven times the Soviet average and that children, many of them mentally handicapped, were 30 to 40 percent behind their healthier contemporaries in physical development.[100] Even the official, and thus suspect, statistics put Moldova's 1989 infant mortality rate—at 20.4 per thousand—almost exactly twice as high as in the neighboring, equally rural, Vinnitsa region of the southwestern Ukraine.[101]

Comparing disease rates on two collective farms in Azerbaijan, where the Soviet Health Ministry annually and officially authorized DDT spraying from 1970 to 1988 "as an exception," doctors found that skin diseases among children six and younger occurred 5.6 times more often on the farm "most polluted with chemicals" and nutritional and metabolic ailments, 4.2 times more frequently. "These are striking, scandalous facts," wrote Azerbaijan's minister of health. "Here is the high price we have paid—the price of our people's health, of our future generations—for our 'resounding' victories."[102]

BACK TO (HUMAN) NATURE

After studying the findings of an unprecedented, two-year Health Ministry inquiry into pesticide use and health, Yablokov concluded that "any increase in the pesticide load raises the frequency of a whole variety of pathologies . . . and illness among wide sectors of the population, especially children." As evidence, he cited the 68 percent increase in stillbirths between 1980 and 1984 in an Armenian area where pesticide use was "intensive." He also pointed to the eighteen- to twentyfold jump in pesticide poisoning deaths of Soviet farm workers in 1988 and 1989 over the levels from 1976 to 1985.[103]

The ministry's survey of tens of thousands of Soviets in hundreds of rural communities also produced data linking increases in anemia, tuberculosis, viral hepatitis and acute upper respiratory tract infections to the intensity of pesticide use. Infant mortality rates in one affected area of Moldova were 3.5 times higher than in a similar zone where pesticide application was minimal.[104] Among children six years old or younger in "high pesticide-use areas," illness rates ran 4.6 times above those in lower-use regions.[105]

Older children have also suffered. Parents of Ural University students, for instance, refused to let their offspring participate in the harvest around Sverdlovsk after fifty young temporary farm workers had to be hospitalized in August 1989 and twenty-six more onion pickers fell ill two months later. The concentration of chemicals on the land they were working was found to be 20 times—in one place 120 times—the maximum permitted, and "the most terrible thing," said one parent of an August victim after the story of improper pesticide handling became known, "is that when the same farm was checked in October, nothing had changed."[106]

A similar poisoning incident in the same region a year later was also caused by pesticide overload, specialists concluded.[107] The 1990 episode involved nine high school youngsters, all of whom succumbed while weeding carrot and turnip fields on a different Sverdlovsk area farm, and led the chief of the Russian Republic's sanitary control service to call for new laws to curtail the risk to farm workers.[108] On his own, he ordered all health inspectors to require farm managers throughout the Russian Republic to draw up charts showing the "chemical load" put on their fields over the preceding three to five years. The inspectors were to forbid manual labor in any fields untested for pesticide and "in no case" to permit fourteen- to eighteen-year-olds to work land where highly toxic insecticides had been recently used.[109]

That prohibition sounded very much like a case of postequine-escape barn-door closure. It also could prove as ineffective as the March 1989 ban issued by the head of the Soviet Union's sanitation service against the manufacture and use of a highly toxic defoliant called "butifos." Six months later the substance was found in wide use on Azerbaijani cotton fields, because the chief of the USSR's agrochemical enterprise had overruled the public health authorities.[110]

If the 1990 regulations saved some young Soviets from chemical poisoning, they could do little to alter the long-standing practice of recruiting city dwellers to work the land that full-time prerevolutionary farmers tended on their own. The incapacity of their successors to handle that job was demonstrated in September 1990 when Prime Minister Nikolai Ryzhkov went on television to call for a "total mobilization" of the population to salvage the potato crop rotting in the fields. He even ordered military units to join in the emergency harvesting. Party officials also put their functionaries into action around Moscow.[111]

That kind of improvised intervention may have rescued the potatoes, but it did not keep their prices from rising fivefold between 1990 and 1991.[112] With real prices put on their work and their product, Soviet farmers might eventually come closer to supplying the nation's food needs. In the meantime, the profound failure of centrally planned farm management showed up in rotting crops and poisoned fields.

Yury Chernichenko, whose indictment of "coercive" farming opened this chapter, has argued that the best hope of redeeming the agricultural promise of his nation is to revive family farming. Having founded a Peasants Party of Russia to pursue that cause, he hoped to see the number of family farms in the Russian Republic swell from 20,000 to 150,000 during 1991. New, still-limited rights for individuals to lease farmland could spur what Chernichenko calls a "comeback from . . . feudalism."

"The Kremlin's 'anti-crisis' fumblings are making life so unbearable in the cities that it is actually helping us," he claims. "It is horrible that a skilled person in the city feels compelled to go out to the land just to guarantee his family enough to eat."[113]

One such migrant was Misha Pavlov, a strapping, blond office worker in his twenties who was planning in October 1990 to double the size of his five-acre plot two hours by bad road from Yaroslavl and to hire himself and his tractor out to neighboring farmers. "I am just starting up," he told an American acquaintance, "and it is mainly a weekend project of trying to bring the land back to life. But I think I can make a real living from it in the future, an honest living."[114]

There was a measure of irony in his decision. The job he would be giving up, if his venture succeeded, was an office assistant's position in the Yaroslavl branch of the State Committee for the Protection of

Nature. For him, as for many Russians, the land exerted a more power-ful pull.

The same attraction was at work in Estonia. By the end of 1990, a 13,750-acre state farm near the border with Latvia was well along in a process of privatization. Thirty-four parcels of 110 acres each were already in operation as family farms, and sixty-six others were either just changing hands or listed for turnover.[115]

One 5,000-acre lot was to go to a group of three *sovkhoz* members, "who are taking the plunge into large-scale commercial farming," an American journalist reported. "Budding entrepreneurs are also taking over or have spoken for such businesses as the state farm's restaurant and supermarket, the motor pool, the equipment maintenance shop and sawmill."[116]

In the Russian Republic, Antonina Konopleva, a member of a large and thriving *kolkhoz* at Sokolniki some 150 miles south of Moscow, did not seem ready in 1988 to leave the shelter of the collective. She was nearly lyrical, however, in her attitude to nature. "The land is our bread," she said. "There's something intoxicating about working in the fields in the spring. You pick up the soil and it's almost like holding your mother's hand. The air makes you dizzy."[117]

"Dizzy with Success" was the *Pravda* headline over a March 1930 declaration by Joseph Stalin that the campaign to bring farmers into collectives had committed "excesses." It had been his brainchild, but in the face of stubborn peasant resistance, he treated it, for a time, as an unwanted stepchild. "Collective farms cannot be set up by force," he declared. "To do so would be stupid and reactionary."[118]

The judgment was accurate, but coming from Stalin, a lie. A year later he put the drive for collectivization back into force, sending mil-lions to their deaths and hundreds of millions more into lives of squalor and subservience. After decades of environmental abuse of the land and its people, it was something of a miracle that Yury Chernichenko could find any adherents for his efforts to revive an independent peasantry. Given the medical deprivation of the countryside and its acute shortage of so many modern amenities, it was also surprising that young city people, such as Misha, were considering a return to the land.

To Russians, whose tradition is rich with a mystical love of nature, however, Antonina Konopleva's image was still a compelling one. Hav-ing nearly crippled their "mother's hand," poisoned her milk and her offspring with chemicals, many Soviets now genuinely want to restore the earth's strength and bounty. There is a measure of hope, if not much more, in their survival and in their willingness to try to rise above the "stinking ruin" of their past.

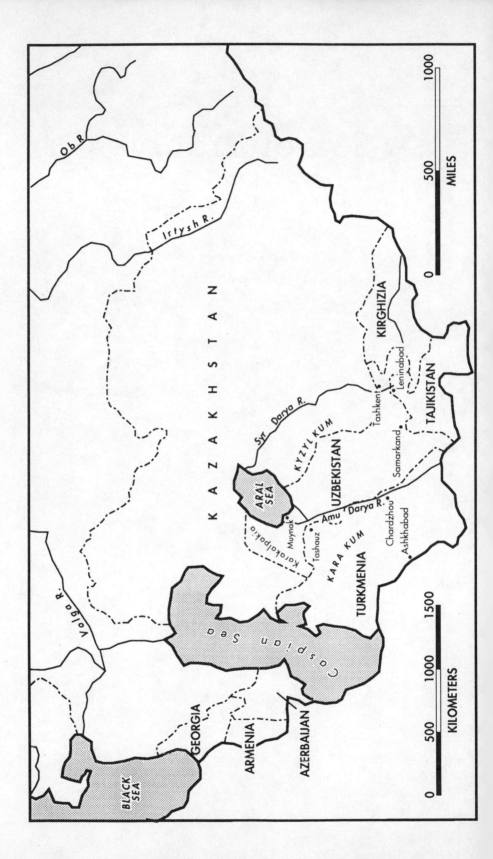

CHAPTER 4

A Sea of Troubles

"TELL ME," A writer-politician from Central Asia beseeched the Soviet Congress of People's Deputies in May 1989, "is there any other state in the world which permits its own population to be poisoned?"[1] His question echoed the agony of what he called a "doomed" people, the farmers and fishers of Karakalpakia who had elected him their spokesman to the historic parliamentary session.

His rhetorical question might seem extreme. In fact, it almost understated the worst single instance of agricultural ecocide in the Soviet Union: the murder of the Aral Sea and the contamination of the cotton fields that have swallowed the rivers that once fed it.

On the Aral's southern shores, just north of Turkmenistan, said Tulepbergen Kaipbergenov, "our earth no longer smells like soil but like chemicals." In the waters of the Amu Darya "the level of chemical residues washed back from irrigated lands is so high that the fish die," and "incomplete data" show that "two out of every three people examined in public health dispensaries are ill—mainly with typhoid, cancer of the esophagus and hepatitis. . . . Worst of all, most of the sick are children," and some "doctors recommend against breast-feeding because the mothers' milk is toxic."

Moscow was to blame, said the official of the Writers' Union of Karakalpakia, a nominally autonomous territory inside Uzbekistan. Faraway decision makers are the ones responsible for turning the Aral into "white, lifeless salt marshes," an "ecological disaster zone . . . soon to house only" people too ill to feed themselves. "We did not will these things on ourselves," Kaipbergenov insisted. "They came to us thanks to the tender mercies of the central planning bodies, essentially a consequence of an utterly criminal economic policy."

The goal of that policy was a monoculture of cotton, not just in Karakalpakia but throughout the Kirghiz, Tajik, Turkmen and Uzbek republics of Central Asia and in adjacent areas of both Azerbaijan and Kazakhstan. Propagandists and Party bosses had called the region's primary cash crop "white gold." They had exulted as their statistics showed the harvests swelling by 70 percent from 1965 to 1983 to make the Soviet Union the world's second-largest cotton exporter, after China.[2]

Cotton cultivation did make many people rich and powerful, if not as masters of what sometimes amounted to slave labor then as profiteers from falsified harvest reports. The latter were regularly inflated to earn both bonuses for exceeding the plan and profits from defrauding the state. While a corrupt Party elite waxed rich off mythical cotton, the real crop was ravaging the land—5.7 percent of the area of the USSR—and the 20.3 million rural people on it—60 percent of the four republics' population at the start of 1990.[3]

The region closest to the Aral and its 3 to 4 million inhabitants were damaged the most. During the last three decades of river diversion for massive irrigation and of saturation use of fertilizers, pesticides and herbicides for cotton farming, the inland sea's water level dropped forty-seven feet, more than a quarter; its volume shrank by two-thirds; its area, once larger than Lake Huron, by 44 percent.[4]

In 1989 only one-eighth as much water as in 1960 reached the Aral from its two main feeder rivers, the Syr Darya on the northeast and the Amu Darya on the south.[5] Diverted into a spreading network of poorly planned, usually unlined irrigation furrows that waste at least half—sometimes as much as 90 percent—of the water meant for the thirsty fields, the rivers also carried rising burdens of phosphates, ammonia, nitrites, nitrates and chlorinated hydrocarbons. Locked between the Kyzylkum and Karakum deserts, the Aral Sea was becoming a desert itself, three times more saline in 1989 than in 1961.[6] As it evaporated, the region's microclimate lost the moderating force the lake exercised. Unseasonal snowfalls damaged young cotton plants. Summer temperatures hit new highs.

Major storms of dust and salt "were first spotted by Soviet cosmonauts in 1975," a British analyst wrote, "and by 1981, 29 large storms had been identified. . . . [Their] frequency and magnitude is growing as the Aral shrinks."[7] Yearly in the 1980s the storms carried between 90 and 140 million tons of salt and sand from 11,000-plus square miles of exposed seabed to Belorussian farmlands 1,200 miles to the northwest and—more often—half as far southeast to the snowfields of Afghanistan where the Amu Darya rises.

In Karakalpakia and other areas near the Aral, as much as half a ton of mixed salt and sand from the seabed fell annually on each acre of irrigated land, depositing a toxic salt rain not just on the soil but in the lungs of those who worked it.[8] As a result, among Mr. Kaipbergenov's constituents, the infant mortality rate reached at least twice the Soviet average; maternal mortality rates tripled in the five years from 1984 to 1989 and eight out of every ten pregnant women were found to suffer from anemia.[9]

Karakalpakia's drinking water was foul. In every batch tested, its chemical content was above the prescribed hygienic standard, as was the bacteria count in two cases out of three. Waterborne infectious diseases such as hepatitis and typhoid were the leading regional causes of infant mortality, blamed for 27 percent of such deaths in Turkmenistan and 21 percent in Uzbekistan.[10]

"Utterly criminal" as such results were, the Aral disaster was only the most horrific and recent example of official Soviet policy toward the countryside and rural people, toward agriculture and toward Central Asia. The sea turning to desert was a symbol of a sixty-year pattern of ecocide by deliberate design.

It was also a measure of the second-class status of the southern Soviet republics. For the citizens of the region, their Turkic and Persian languages and cultures acted as internal dividers as well as barriers to assimilation with the Slavs of European Russia and with the ancient Catholic nations of Georgia and Armenia. Since at least the 1970s, the Muslims of Central Asia had been the fastest-growing ethnic minority in the USSR. They were also the poorest, the most rural and—even in the political turmoil of the Gorbachev years—the quietest.

That quiescence, however, showed some signs of fraying. Ecological disaster, including its frightful consequences for public health, had the potential to stimulate the first extensive political challenge to Moscow's rule since the Bolsheviks violently suppressed independence movements in Central Asia in the 1920s. Until the autumn of 1991 a new uprising seemed distant but not unforeseeable. The "Aral issue," judged an American scholar, "was made to order as a theme of nationalism. . . . As a symbol of environmental abuse, the Aral heightened public outrage over what outsiders had done to the Central Asian homeland."[11]

DEATHS AT AN EARLY AGE

Like sunlight concentrated by a lens into a burning ray, the full force of Soviet agricultural mismanagement seemed to come to an incendiary focus in the Aral region. Irrigation that began with the 215-mile-long Great Fergana Canal, dug primarily by hand between 1939 and 1941, proved a death-dealer, not a life-giver. As it threatened to turn the sea to desert, the practice also menaced the land it was meant to make bloom and carried poisons into the drinking water of the people it was meant to make prosperous.

After World War II, water projects in Central Asia spread far and fast. Between 1965 and 1986, acreage under irrigation expanded at an annual rate of 2.3 percent in Tajikistan, Turkmenistan and Uzbekistan. Construction, however, was so inefficient that rising water tables regularly inundated 985 settlements in the Aral basin. Despite a drainage network over 100,000 miles long and a system of 8,000 vertical drains, too much water used for irrigation stayed in the ground. Water tables that used to be twenty-two to thirty-three feet down in many areas rose to within a foot of the surface. Waterlogged soil on nearly 3 million acres of Uzbekistan became so saline that the land could not be farmed.[12]

Pumps and drains were supposed to draw off this excess. Where they worked, they put about 60 percent of the irrigation water directly back into the rivers or into fetid ponds and lakes along their course.[13] That water, often heavily polluted by chemicals and natural salts, supplied both the population's drinking needs in many places and, downstream, got recycled into other irrigation canals.

The drainage system, in any case, was a massive failure. By 1988 the Ministry of Land Reclamation and Water Resources (Minvodkhoz) was admitting that poor water management had taken an area bigger than Belgium, more than 8.6 million acres throughout the Aral Basin, out of production.[14] Irrigated fields had become swamps as groundwater rose.

Even in the once-arid Turkmen Republic capital of Ashkhabad, 150 pumping stations had to work around the clock to protect the city from flooding by underground waters.[15] One Soviet expert in hydraulic engineering was confident that wasteful "water consumption in Central Asia could be reduced by 40 to 50 percent which, incidentally, would largely resolve the problem of the Aral."[16]

Meanwhile, moreover, the water meant to slake the thirst of the cotton fields was actually fouling them with chemical salts from fertilizers, pesticides and defoliants. Turkmenistan's health minister described the Turkmen canal, a major source of drinking water, as an open sewer after finding impermissibly high bacteria counts in 60 to 98 percent of all water samples taken from it.[17] Pollution of the Amu Darya, whose mineral content runs as high as 1.5 grams per liter in Karakalpakia,[18] was responsible in some areas for illnesses, especially hepatitis, that afflicted seven out of every ten inhabitants.[19]

The poisoning of the river also made the land unhealthy. D. S. Yagdarov, Karakalpakia's top politician, warned that "soil conditions are deteriorating, the salt content of the earth is increasing . . . it is necessary to increase the amounts of water used both for rinsing and for irrigating plants. The end result is that the area of heavily salinated lands is rapidly expanding; such lands do not yield even half of their potential harvest."[20] In terms of actual cotton output, in fact, average Uzbek yields per acre in 1986 dropped 17 percent below their 1976 to 1980 level; the republic fell 1.5 million tons behind its plan commitment in 1987. Turkmenistan saw its crop decline from 23 million tons in 1985 to 17.5 million the next year.[21]

To make up for these deficits, Central Asian officials ordered peasants to give up the cherished private plots where they grew their own fruit and vegetables and to cut down the few trees that shaded the searing plains and held in fractional amounts of moisture. In protest, a popular slogan appeared as early as 1970: "Down with the cotton, long live the orchards."[22] Trees once grew on 15 percent of Uzbekistan; by 1987 they covered only 1 percent of its irrigated land.[23]

Along with the soil, the people began to hunger. As the cotton monoculture took over more and more land that had been used to produce fruit, vegetables and meat, rural diets worsened. By 1987 Uzbeks were getting only 26 percent of the meat and only 42 percent of the milk that Soviet authorities prescribed as a medical standard for good health.[24] Earnings from the "white gold" stayed in Moscow or with the political elite or were put back into new irrigation projects, more soil-destroying cotton plantations and increased loads of toxic chemicals. In the Tashauz *oblast* of Turkmenistan a medical researcher in 1988 found that for the preceding ten years, state stores had stocked no meat, poultry, butter, milk or milk products. Nor was such food readily available on the free market, since only 15 percent of local families along the banks of the Amu Darya raised livestock or poultry on private plots.[25]

The newspaper article that published his findings and its correspondents' broader conclusion that families in Turkmenistan were going hungry and their youngest children even dying of starvation shocked Soviet readers, not least because of the photograph of a skeletal boy at the edge of death used to illustrate the piece. Turkmen political figures denied that famine was claiming young lives in their republic, but the journalists documented repeated examples of children who "begin to starve even before they are born."

In the Ashkhabad *oblast*, medical records revealed maternal malnutrition so widespread that one of every three newborns in 1989 showed "symptoms of intrauterine starvation." In a town some fifty miles northwest, "literally, every second infant on the books of the local clinic is malnourished."[26] Separate inquiries by two local medical specialists revealed that 84 percent of a sample of 197 village children, aged three to twelve months, were underweight. Since the early 1960s, they reported, Turkmenistan had been providing free milk for youngsters and in recent years, free food, but the feedings "have not been observed to have the necessary effect in improving the health of younger children. There is no decline in the grave consequences of acute malnutrition among these children, especially in the rural areas of the republic."[27]

While the people of the region lacked food, the Aral Sea starved for water, and its dehydration, changing the face of nature, worsened the ecological crisis. The lake that once acted as a huge heat pump and cooling system lost its power to moderate the regional climate. Surrounding deserts gained the meteorological upper hand. "Winter has begun to come early and last a long time," recorded a Kazakh ecologist. "Summer now turns out to be rainless, dry and hot. Winter is snowless, severe and cold."[28]

"There is no water for the people," wrote Sagdulla Karamatov, an Uzbek novelist, as long ago as the early 1980s. "Where are we to find water for the trees?" A few years later Oktir Hashimov, editor of the literary magazine *Sharq Yulduzi*, posed the sharpest question of all: "Who can guarantee that a gigantic tragedy will not come to pass in Central Asia and that the land will not become uninhabitable?"[29]

Already, some places had reached that state. Muynak was once a thriving island fishing port in the Amu Darya delta, where most of the Aral catch—over 100 million pounds in the late 1950s—was brought for processing. By 1990, however, it was some forty-four miles inland from the still-receding south shore and nearly a ghost town. Hulks of abandoned ships and barges rusted on its sandbanks and salt flats along a dry canal dug in the 1980s in the vain hope of keeping the town connected to the sea. In 1990, however, the only fish to reach Muynak's canning factory had to "swim" two thousand miles in refrigerated railroad cars and the final sixty miles by truck, a surreal example of uneconomic improvisation.[30]

To the south, where the river had become a ditch, bacteria levels in the drinking water of the Tashauz *oblast* were more than ten times permitted levels; 70 percent of the population was sick, many with hepatitis; officially recorded infant mortality rates—66.1 per thousand live births in 1989—were the highest in the USSR. At a special session of the Turkmenistan parliament held in Tashauz in November 1990, more than one participant worried aloud that unless profound cleanup measures were instituted before the end of the century, "the people will have to move out of the *oblast*."[31]

In the nearby Bozataus subdistrict, 111 out of every 1,000 infants reportedly died before their first birthday, a frequency five times the *official* Soviet rate, more than twice the 1989 rate for Karakalpakia as a whole and higher even than the average for Africa.[32] In a farm settlement near the city of Tashauz, where 579 people—63 percent of them under the age of forty—were studied, a team of researchers found no sewers, no running water, no indoor toilets and almost no (4.2 percent) completely healthy residents. Just under half the population was seriously ill with respiratory, circulatory, digestive and nervous system complaints. Just over half of the most acutely ill were field hands cultivating cotton.[33]

That final statistic held no surprise. Wherever it is farmed, cotton consumes not just land and water, but people as well. Central Asian cotton is not only dosed with as much as fifty-four pounds per acre of pesticides against the boll weevil—some 180 times the average use of such substances in the Baltic Republics[34]—it is also treated with defoliants to make harvesting easier. Those who work unprotected in an environment so laden with toxic chemicals are bound to be poisoned. In the Soviet cotton belt such contamination seemed to be the rule, not the exception.

It was a rule of long standing. As early as 1974 Andrei Sakharov publicized complaints about Uzbek schoolchildren whose breathing had been affected by exposure to herbicides while they doubled as cotton field hands. To a group of writers in Tajikistan in late 1983, a similar case seemed shocking but not uncommon. It involved aerial spraying of defoliants on fields where sixth-grade youngsters, earning a miserable four rubles for picking 110 pounds of cotton, were actually harvesting. Their overseer, "a not unkindly man," refused to order the children out of harm's way before the crop-dusting aircraft made a second pass "because he had to fulfill his plan."[35]

In the land of King Cotton, the plan amounted to a royal decree, and the barons who supervised its execution could be executioners themselves. One such was Akhmadjan Adylov. Living like a feudal-style suzerain amid tigers and peacocks, he headed a huge *sovkhoz* that dominated the Fergana Valley town of Gurumsarai and 30,000-odd people in and around it. A bemedaled member of the Uzbek Communist Party's Central Committee and the Republic's Supreme Soviet, Adylov claimed descent from Tamerlane, the fourteenth-century conqueror of Turkistan, Persia and India. Until his arrest in 1984 and trial in 1991 on bribery and embezzlement charges, he exercised a cruel authority worthy of his putative ancestor. According to a Soviet journalist, Adylov imposed his rule by paying off higher authorities and keeping an iron hand over his subjects. If any of the latter offended him, he "cast them into an underground prison, tortured them with a red-hot iron and beat pregnant women with a whip before the eyes of their husbands."[36]

The money that such cotton lords commanded came from three sources: embezzlement of state funds meant for productive investments and social welfare, inflated harvest claims and protection payments from underground entrepreneurs, including some narcotics traffickers. Corruption permeated the society and its politics during what Gorbachev era Party boss R. N. Nishanov called "the triumphant march backward." He added:

> The Aral Sea represents our anguish . . . but not just the Aral Sea. Violations of crop rotation, overapplication of toxic chemicals, the mindless opening up of more and more new lands without a strictly scientific approach and without accurate calculations—all this led to a situation whereby our most fertile soil ceased to be so, and dozens of diseases proliferated.[37]

Medical care did not. With twice the population of Belorussia, Uzbekistan in 1986 had one-third as many hospitals. For the same number of people as Moldova, Kirghizia had only about 80 percent the number of outpatient clinics, women's consultation centers, pediatric polyclinics and independent paramedic-midwifery stations. Per capita, the people of the three Baltic Republics had nearly twice as many hospitals as Central Asians had[38] and, on average per ten thousand children, 43 percent more pediatricians.[39] Not only were those Baltic doctors almost certainly better trained and qualified to care for their young patients than their colleagues in Central Asia; they were also far better supplied with hospital equipment. The average value per child's hospital bed of medical equipment in major Soviet hospitals was just over 1,000 rubles in 1989. In the best-furnished children's hospital in Kirghizia the comparable figure was 700 rubles. It dropped to 200 rubles for *oblast*-level pediatric facilities.[40]

Comparisons with the more advanced regions of the USSR, in any case, barely began to measure the penury of medical services in the cotton belt. Half the birthing centers in Azerbaijan lacked hot water and sewage systems.[41] In 240 out of 325 hospitals in Tajikistan, there was no plumbing outside the operating rooms.[42] In the Osh *oblast* of Kirghizia 440 pediatricians were needed, but only 80 were at work; 152 midwife-gynecologists were required, but only 30 were on the job; in the *oblast* hospitals, beds were so crowded together that where Soviet norms specified seventy square feet of space, only twenty, at most, were available.[43]

The shortage of medical personnel in Tajikistan was particularly acute. Even in the second most populous *oblast,* around Leninabad, 80 percent of the children who died before their first birthday from acute gastroenteritis in 1989 received no "fully qualified medical care" before they were hospitalized, and 58 percent got none even in the wards.[44]

For a single *oblast* of Turkmenistan, where 30,000 of the 330,000 inhabitants were infants, there were only 330 pediatricians. Local physicians said they needed a total of 800, but the republic's medical training institute started graduating children's doctors only in 1978, and the 100 or so new pediatricians certified each year amounted to "just a drop in the sea." A spanking new child health care complex in the city of Chardzhou on the banks of the Amu Darya in eastern Turkmenistan had bed space for 400 patients and polyclinic facilities designed to treat another 500 a day. It stood half empty in 1989, however, for lack of funds—especially hard currency—to buy basic and advanced equipment.[45]

In the four republics together in 1987 there were, on average, fewer than 14 pediatricians for every 10,000 children, two-thirds the ratio for the Soviet Union as a whole. Even where they could be found, the child care specialists were often as poorly trained as many of their obstetrician colleagues, 70 percent of whom in Turkmenistan's Tashauz *oblast* lacked the skills to perform basic surgery.[46]

The chief epidemiologist of the Soviet Children's Fund, a private charity, stigmatized these doctors as "second and third rankers" sent as standard Health Ministry policy "to [rural] localities instead of principal specialists."[47] Once there, they frequently compounded their incapacity by trying to cover it up. In Turkmenistan, its chief obstetrician-gynecologist revealed in 1989 that "newborn babies and infants are not registered for a year and sometimes longer. In some cases, a physician reports in the registry book that a dead child is gaining weight."[48]

Alternatively, a live birth was sometimes recorded as a stillborn child. Such an incident happened in the Tashauz *oblast* in May 1988, when a *kolkhoz* mother gave birth at the central regional hospital to a child weighing less than four pounds who died within twenty-four hours. The infant was listed as stillborn. Another woman gave birth to twins later that year. Although one of them was stillborn, the hospital recorded only a single birth, that of the surviving child. Doctors also waited seven months after the death of a nine-month-old child before recording the fact, thus moving it out of the infant mortality statistics.[49]

Such deceptions seemed so routine and so widespread that it was safe, perhaps even overly conservative, to raise all infant mortality statistics from Central Asia by 50 percent. That adjustment—now made by Soviets themselves—would have a huge impact on Union-wide data, since half of the children who died in the late 1980s and early 1990s in the USSR before their first birthday were Central Asians. Instead of the official infant mortality rate of 22.3 per thousand, the real incidence—counting the underreporting in other regions as well—was at least 33 per thousand and perhaps higher. Using Western definitions of viable birth weight and prematurity, as leading public health officials in Moscow advocated, would adjust the Soviet figures even farther upward.

Beginning in 1987, emergency medical teams from other parts of the Soviet Union were flown to various cities of Central Asia for intensive campaigns to reduce infant mortality during the high-risk summer months. Even when this rescue effort, organized through the Soviet Children's Fund, was put on a year-round basis, however, it was hobbled by conditions such as those doctors found in a special rural health hospital in Samarkand, Tamerlane's ancient capital. In the intensive care ward where five incubators were needed, only one was working in 1990, and it frequently broke down. The unit had no sterilizing equipment at all; its only automatic respirator was made for adults. When American journalists visited, the device was hooked up by a makeshift adaptor to a one-year-old boy lying on a card table, since no crib was free.

While the journalists were present, the child died of gastrointestinal illness and dehydration that might have been curable had he been properly diagnosed a few days earlier. "We simply do not have any diagnostic equipment," said one of the Children's Fund physicians. "Even a bottle of oxygen is a problem here." Added an Uzbek pediatrician: "This is one of the best places. Still we have only our hands and our heads to work with."[50]

RESENTMENT RISING

The poverty of public health care in Central Asia, like the ecological damage done by the cotton monoculture, could be seen as a dramatic enlargement and intensification of the pillage and neglect inflicted on most of the Soviet countryside. Magnified in the Aral Sea region and the Amu Darya Basin, agricultural policy, however, looked to growing numbers of Central Asians like part of a historic conspiracy by Russians to exploit their Muslim subjects.

As old patterns of silence, collaboration and apathy slowly gave way to impatience and resentment, spokesmen such as Karakalpakia's Tulepbergen Kaipbergenov denounced Moscow's central planners as "utterly criminal." A passionate few spoke of genocide. Demanding redress, some (though not Kaipbergenov) sought to revive the vast design that the Kremlin shelved in 1986 for turning the flow of some Siberian rivers southward. Where Minvodkhoz planners had thought to put the Siberian resources into the Volga and Don rivers, Central Asians wanted the water to replenish the Aral Sea and its tributaries.

According to Russian ecologists who sympathized with the Central Asians' plight but not their proposal, the river diversion project was part of a long-standing bureaucratic scheme that actually hinged on drying up the Aral Sea. They claimed that the idea, dating at least to 1973, had envisioned using Siberian water resources to *expand* irrigation into land from which the Aral would retreat. A 1981 map presented the desiccation as an opportunity to turn exposed seabed into paddies that would produce 4,400 pounds or more of rice per acre.

As late as 1987 the chief backers of the idea were calling the Aral "nature's error" and voicing the hope that it would "die in a beautiful manner."[51] Scientists who studied the record angrily concluded that Minvodkhoz

has benefited from constantly digging canals and obtaining billions of rubles from the state budget for this purpose. To insure its operational territory for years to come, it set out to exhaust all the water resources of Central Asia and then to increase the area under irrigation. The resulting water shortage would be the pretext for promoting the "Project of the Century"—the diversion of Siberian rivers to expand irrigated acreage even further.[52]

After a fierce public and behind-the-scenes battle in which many prominent Russian writers enlisted to defend Siberia's resources, the ministry was compelled first to limit its design to a plan for replenishing the flow of the Volga and then barred by a Politburo decision from pursuing any part of the project. The Russian environmentalists' success, however, fed "us-against-them" conspiracy theorizing about Muscovite colonialism in Central Asia.

Some of the region's more ardent nationalists and even some members of the political establishment such as the reformist Party boss in Kazakhstan continued, therefore, to press the river diversion proposal. They saw Siberia's waters flowing relatively unexploited into the Arctic Sea while the desert encroached on their fields, oases and the Aral itself. The contrast allied them with the central water management bureaucracy behind a plan to dig a 1,470-mile-long canal that would take thirty to forty years to build and cost 90 to 100 billion rubles. The canal would eventually deliver 27,000 cubic meters a year of water from the River Ob to the Aral Basin to make up, in part, for the annual loss of 44,000 cubic meters in the flow of the Amu and Syr Darya.[53]

The Central Asians had a case, if not for the massive water redistribution, at least for a program of affirmative ecological action. Instead of shipping water from thousands of miles away, however, they should probably have been stressing ways to use their own resources less wastefully, to line leaky canals, adopt drip-irrigation technology and rotate crops as their forebears did, letting alfalfa, for instance, replenish the soil that cotton has depleted.

By 1991, in fact, local authorities along the Amu Darya's course were working to develop cooperative, basinwide water management projects to economize on their use of irrigation and to reduce contamination. "Unfortunately," reported a senior Uzbek scientist involved in the rescue effort, "decentralization of the land-reclamation program [once dictated from Moscow] . . . and the reduction of capital investments have effectively countermanded water conservation measures in our republic."[54]

As funds from Moscow were drying up, Central Asians could and did demand the right to retain more of their earnings for urgent social investments that they have been denied. One basic improvement would be in the supply of hot water and sewer connections to their rural homes. Nationally, only 10 percent of collective farm housing enjoys the amenity of piped-in hot water. In Belorussia, the average is 14 percent; in Kirghizia *kolkhoz* housing, it is just 4 percent. Where the national average for sewer systems on *kolkhozes* is 27 percent, it is just 9 percent in Uzbekistan, one-fourth Moldova's level.[55]

Drinking water, too, is precious but frequently poisonous in many parts of Central Asia. In Kirghizia, with 62 percent of its population rural, one-third has to slake their thirst directly from streams, rivers and primitive wells. As a result, reported a medical writer in 1989, annually "over 1,500 people die from digestive illnesses, and of these, more than half are children less than one year of age."[56] In the preceding three years, he added, water pollution was the main cause of the republic's

320,000 recorded cases of typhoid, viral hepatitis and other intestinal infections,[57] an average of one bout of disease for every fourth inhabitant every year.

One reason that the vast majority of Central Asians has to drink such dangerous water is that only 23 percent of the collective farms in Uzbekistan, 20 percent in Kirghizia, 14 percent in Tajikistan and just 2 percent in Turkmenistan had piped water for farmers' residences. In 1989 the national average for such utilities on *kolkhozes,* however, was only 39 percent, the same as for the Russian Republic.[58]

Being an urban Uzbek, it should be noted, is also no guarantee against pollution. Of the eleven textile fiber plants in the capital city of Tashkent and its environs, seven have no water purification facilities at all. Their wastes, 60 percent of them untreated, went directly into the Akhangaran River, a tributary of the Syr Darya. Applause and relief greeted the opening of a water purification plant in early 1991 to serve the republic capital of Ashkhabad. In the summer months, however, the facility was limited to nighttime operation. Soviet-made air conditioners needed to keep the imported machinery cool had not been delivered as promised.[59]

Despite their toxic environment and their terrible shortcomings in health care, Central Asians (including the non-Slavic residents of Kazakhstan) had the Soviet Union's highest population growth rate, 23 percent between 1979 and 1989, compared to 7.2 percent in the Russian Republic.[60] The region, however, also had the lowest proportions of skilled workers in its economy, a demographic combination that could be politically explosive on several fronts.

One volatile reality was a growing labor surplus where work opportunities were scarcest. In the 1970s the number of working-age Uzbeks grew two and a half times as fast as the number of nonagricultural jobs.[61] By 1989, an Uzbek educator told the USSR parliament, 760,000 people in the republic were unemployed. "Soon," he warned, "there will be millions."[62] Equally unsettling is the prospect that by the year 2000, when every tenth Soviet will be an Uzbek, more than one-third of the draft-age males in the Soviet Union will report for induction into whatever remains of a unified military from the southern republics—Central Asia, Kazakhstan, Azerbaijan, Armenia and Georgia.[63] Many will bring an Islamic heritage with them, relearned in mosques that in 1990 were "being reopened at the rate of one a day across Central Asia."[64] Few will share the Slavic outlook of the Red Army's officer corps. As their numbers grow, so, in all likelihood, will proposals to keep most of them out of the services by ending conscription and making the Soviet military fully professional—hence predominantly Russian.

Finally, there is the prospect that even before the turn of the century, the rising human pressure on arable land in Central Asia—in Uzbekistan the ratio is less than 6.5 acres per capita[65]—could bring a political explosion. The protest movement in that republic, headed by a popular front called Birlik, appeared for the first time in November 1988 as a student group trying to promote the Uzbek language and demote the use of Russian on television, in classrooms, on street signs and in courts. By the time Birlik staged an unauthorized mass rally in Tashkent's Lenin Square on October 1, 1989, its agenda had broadened to ecological and economic as well as linguistic resistance.

"We have come together to struggle for democracy, for a better future," Birlik's fringe-bearded leader, Abdur Rahim Pulatov, exhorted the crowd. "The Uzbek people must finally take control of its own land. We must feel that we are the true masters." Taking her turn with the bullhorn from the improvised podium at the foot of Lenin's towering statue, an intense young woman put a series of pointed questions:

> The Communist Party Central Committee has wasted all our treasures and keeps taking away the fruits of our land. A future generation is going to ask us: "What were you doing at that time? What were you thinking about? How did you get us into this situation? Where's our wealth?" And what will we answer them? How could we look them in the eye?[66]

To deflect such bitterness, Moscow made gestures and promises, but little progress on the burning social and environmental questions. The squads of doctors flown in by the Soviet Children's Fund did save lives, but their impact was localized and transitory. Indeed, some officials whom they came to help resented the intrusion, the publicity given to health problems and the local activism that outsiders nourished.

When Mukhamed Velsapar, a Turkmen writer and political dissident, managed to publish a short article in *Moscow News* in April 1990 asserting that "the majority of Turkmenistani children in our time are permanently undernourished," a Children's Fund official in Ashkhabad was furious. "It was a libel on all of us!" she protested. "No one goes hungry here. The Turkmenistani people love to eat! And poor? Oh, they have lots of money, cars—two sometimes. They could buy proper food if they wanted, but instead they buy carpets and expensive dresses."[67]

To save the Aral Sea, Soviet Party and government authorities mobilized a special study commission and then promulgated an October 1988 decree pledging to boost the flow in both the Amu Darya and Syr Darya and the efficiency of irrigation. The promise was specific: increases of 8.7 cubic kilometers of water by 1990, of 15 to 17 cubic kilometers by

2000 and of 20 to 21 cubic kilometers in the following fifteen years.[68] Performance, however, was slow to nonexistent. At the end of 1989, the USSR Supreme Soviet passed its own resolution calling for a competition to "develop concepts for restoring the Aral Sea." By March 1, 1991, none had been presented, and the Uzbek chairman of the parliament's environmental affairs committee asked for another six months to refine the "draft of a 'new' resolution." Ecologist Sergei Zalygin bitterly denounced the maneuver: "Strictly speaking, there is nothing in this 'new' document besides bureaucratic blather and wishes addressed to Lord knows who."[69]

As for executive action, experts meeting in Tashkent in September 1990 said that the 1988 Kremlin decree had proved a "mirage." Even with forty organizations involved and a startup budget of 5 million rubles allocated, the Aral was continuing to shrink, infant and maternal mortality to rise. A local Uzbek official could not say how much water had actually reached the Aral in 1990, and specialists estimated that 12 billion—not 5 million—rubles were actually needed to restore normal life in the region.[70]

Politically, life in Central Asia had not been normal since Party purges in 1986 removed the top layer of corruption in the ruling elite. Many of the successor politicians, however, still took a conciliatory line toward the Kremlin. But where popular fronts appeared, so did a kind of ethnic militancy, one reason that a reported 94,000 Russian-speakers fled Uzbekistan in 1989, with more than 200,000 expected to follow their example in 1990. These departures decimated the ranks of professionals, leaving vital installations such as the republic's largest thermal electric power station without skilled maintenance personnel for its turbines and halving Tashkent's ambulance service staff.[71]

That out-migration diminished hopes for rapid ecological recovery in Central Asia. Those hopes, in any case, had to be slim. The officials who decided in the 1960s to starve the Aral in order to feed the cotton fields knew at least some of the trade-offs involved. They opted to increase irrigation whatever the cost, spouting rosy forecasts of doubled rice and cotton harvests and quadrupled fruit and vegetable yields. Well after the fact, Minvodkhoz's chief compared projected Aral Basin cotton earnings of 11.2 billion rubles with what he calculated would be one-twelfth that amount in costs to "the [Aral] fishing trade, maritime transport and the coastal economy."[72]

His balance sheet took no account of the damage the cotton monoculture would do to human health, nor of the ecological consequences of the Aral's desiccation either for the regional climate or for the distant fields on which its salts fell as a poisoned rain. As early as 1968 the head of the Soviet Hydro-Technical Institute cautioned: "It is obvious to everyone that evaporation of the Aral Sea is inevitable."[73] His warning went unheeded. The greatest single, man-made ecological catastrophe in history advanced unhindered.

To some, it seemed that it was too late to be reversed. In the intemperate words of P. A. Polad-Zade, the USSR's top hydraulic engineer and, for many environmentalists, a favorite villain: "It is time for all the wailing to stop. The case is closed, and the people here will have to learn to live without the sea."[74] He recanted that December 1988 statement the next day, but his original verdict may have been all too honest. The truth was that the people of the Aral region might have to choose between migrating or dying along with their vanishing sea, their polluted rivers and their saline, waterlogged land.

They had a third option: rage. The merging of a demographic explosion with economic and ecological collapse made "Soviet experts . . . warn against 'revolutionary' migration of the 'countryside into the cities' " that could be "overrun by unemployed, uneducated, hostile youth, rocketing numbers of gangs and radical nationalist groups."[75] In the fall of 1991, as the Central Asian republics all declared themselves independent, their leaders initially sought to maintain working ties with Moscow and good relations with Russians. The region's low income and high population growth, however, made such accommodating policies look transitory, and ecocide—as a source of resentment—could easily become a pretext for revenge.

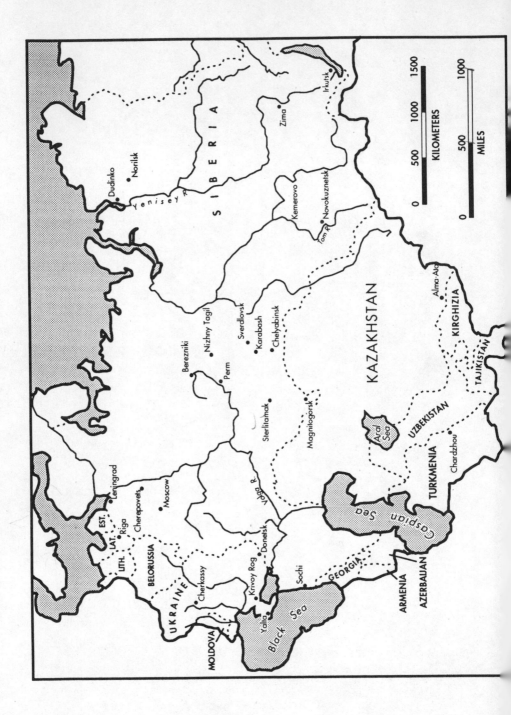

CHAPTER 5

Dark, Satanic Mills

UNTIL ENVIRONMENTAL CONSCIOUSNESS genuinely began to enter Soviet thinking in the late 1980s, factory smokestacks stood as symbols of the country's might, progress and, by extension, beauty. Along with towering concrete cliffs of dams, giant excavations of open-pit mines and the ordered march of high-voltage power lines, clouds of soot— black, orange, yellow—floated across the natural, political and psychic landscape as emblems of hope, rather than as portents of disability and death. Industrial development was high romance, socialist-realist style. The rule for it was the sooner, the bigger, the better.

In the modern world that attitude was no aberration. The dynamo, in Henry Adams' image, supplanted the Virgin as a source of inspiration from Kitty Hawk to Kamchatka. Nowhere was the transformation more warmly applauded or more energetically pursued than in the USSR, and nowhere has the corollary damage to nature and human health gone so long unattended. From the urgency of Stalin's first Five-Year Plan through the rot of the post-Khrushchev decades, the Soviet Union has been on a crash course that sacrificed vast human and natural resources to the goals of growth, prosperity and power.

During the Cold War, Moscow seemed to be achieving its aims. The appearance misled many outsiders and the Soviets themselves until, by the 1990s, a maelstrom of economic decline and political disarray exposed the deception. The means by which the USSR had pursued its goals had proved not just defective but destructive. And the cost of remedying past errors looked to be beyond reckoning.

Among the miles of largely uncatalogued celluloid decaying in a USSR State Film Archives depository at Krasnogorsk outside Moscow, there survives a pathetic, untitled tribute to the enthusiasm with which many Soviets embarked on the road to ruin. A partially restored, early "talkie" shows a well-dressed young woman arriving in a desolate *shtetl*, a tumbledown Jewish village probably in the Ukraine. She has come in a truck filled with consumer goods to hire laborers for a far-off construction site. The unemployed flock around her to sign up, and one urges his son, just returned from twenty-eight years as a brick mason in America, to enlist as well.

The ragged, illiterate father, played by Solomon Mikhoels, a famous Yiddish-theater actor murdered in one of Stalin's last outbursts of anti-Semitism, tries to impress the son with the magnificence of the opportunity. Stuttering with excitement but obviously ignorant of the actual location or the kind of factory to be built there, he blurts out, "It's Magnitogorsk. They're building there! Magnitogorsk!"[1]

The site, named for the Magnetic Mountain in the Urals, did become one of the giant industrial undertakings of the 1930s, turning the rich and easily mined iron-ore deposits into steel for factories, railways, tractors and—in World War II—for tanks and other weapons. Not all its workers came as volunteers. Some 40,000 were *kulaks* deported there in boxcars. Of them, "as many as 10 percent" died in the tents that were their only shelter through the first winter.[2]

Another presumed victim was Abram Kaminsky, a young Muscovite recruited directly from the prison camp to which he had been sentenced on political charges in the early 1930s. He told family members that as a trained economist he spent his four to five years of involuntary servitude in relatively comfortable living and working conditions. They believed, however, that he contracted his fatal leukemia at the site of what Party sloganeers hailed as an enterprise of "great socialist construction."[3] If so, his name should be added to the long list of casualties of the development of Magnitogorsk and the other huge industrial complexes that despoiled the Soviet landscape in the name of progress. Most of the dead, diseased and dying were known only to their relatives and friends. Their aggregate numbers told the story: Some 223,000 inhabitants of Magnitogorsk—34 percent of all the adults and 67 percent of all children fourteen and younger—suffered from respiratory illnesses; roughly 25,000 infants a year—forty-one out of every hundred in Magnitogorsk—were born with one or another pathology.[4] Birth defects in the city have doubled since 1980.[5]

To care for the sick there, Soviet medical standards specified a norm of 2,190 doctors. "The city had 1,205, including 68 of 109 surgeons, 99 of 137 gynecologists and 171 of 364 pediatricians. And the shortfall was growing. In 1988, 38 doctors left Magnitogorsk, primarily for lack of housing."[6]

In the city's filthiest section, a "prophylactic clinic" gave local children " 'oxygen cocktails,' a viscous soup of fruit juice, herbs, sugar—and a dose of pure oxygen. Older patients came in just to take a few breaths from an oxygen mask."[7] The local coroner estimated that more than nine out of every ten children born in the city—the center of a zone of atmospheric and soil devastation 120 miles long and 40 miles wide—came down with "pollution-related illnesses: chronic bronchitis, asthma, allergies, even cancers."[8]

Yet the city, site of the world's biggest steel complex, was not the most unhealthy place in the Soviet Union, even though the Magnitogorsk Works in 1990 still used open-hearth furnaces to produce 16 million tons of steel a year. The volume of the city's atmospheric pollutants—870,000 tons per year, 20 tons per capita—was unexceptional by Soviet industrial standards, as was the fact that only 50 percent of the emissions were filtered and then only to remove one-third of the toxic substances.[9]

At Krivoy Rog in the southeastern Ukrainian area called the Donbass, the air pollution, according to Goskompriroda's chairman, was "catastrophic." Plans to reduce the 1989 level of 1.3 million tons per year to 800,000 tons by 2000, he observed, would still leave the population in grave danger. "If we cannot perceptibly clean up the atmosphere of Krivoy Rog," worried Nikolai Vorontsov, "it might perhaps be more honest to tell the residents so. Will we really have to ship in migratory labor to the Ukraine?"[10]

Conceivably, temporary workers might come to what was once celebrated as the Iron Heart of the Land of the Soviets. They might, that is, if the pay and benefits met their demands and if the city spent some of the 2 billion rubles its officials estimated they needed to get gas and dust filters installed in factories and "to evacuate tens of thousands of people" from housing built too close to the polluting industries.[11]

In the last decade of the twentieth century, there are no major industrial cities in the Soviet Union where air pollution is not shortening the life expectancy of adults and undermining the health of their children. The growth that made the USSR a superpower has been so ill managed, so greedy in its exploitation of natural resources and so indifferent to the health of people that ecocide is inevitable. Its dimensions can be documented only imperfectly.

THE SHROUD OF POLLUTION

At best it is possible to sketch a rough portrait of the harm done to the Soviet environment in the course of industrialization. The picture has to be put together from statistics that no one quite trusts, drawn from samples taken by obsolescent monitoring equipment and inspectors who often gave factories advance warning of their arrival so that the dirtiest furnaces and assembly lines could be temporarily capped.

"On its days off the [pollution] control service takes no samples of air and water," *Pravda* correspondents reported from the smog-choked city of Cherepovets, two hundred miles due north of Moscow. "And on the night shift, to raise output the workshops at [the metallurgical combine] shut off their purification equipment" so that citizens wake up in the morning "as though from a drugged sleep."[12] The official figures for the factory's 1989 emissions were 584,000 tons of completely untreated carbon monoxide, nitrogen dioxide, ammonia and hydrogen sulfide, plus 42,000 tons of liquid wastes.[13] Those statistics, without doubt, understated the damage the combine was doing.

Similarly, much of the data assembled in these pages has to be construed as conservative estimates of actual pollution. Any depiction of the USSR's environment must begin with Soviet data and revise upward. The result should be understood as indicative, not definitive. What could be imperfectly documented were faltering steps toward controlling pollution and the damage it was doing to human health. What could not be discerned was a single instance of environmental turnaround such as the elimination of London's famous and deadly fogs or the cleanup of Cleveland's Cuyahoga River and Lake Erie.

Late in the 1980s Soviet scholars did begin to design comprehensive proposals for the kind of long-term economic and environmental revival that Pittsburgh undertook. Goskompriroda's chairman even cited the "two or three billion dollars" spent on overcoming pollution in the Pennsylvania steel center as an example for his country.[14] In mid-1991, however, such sweeping ecological projects—for the Armenian Republic, the Siberian city of Krasnoyarsk and the mining region of Kursk among others—existed more as drafts than as firm plans of action.[15]

Data made public in late 1990 did indicate some progress: Official measurements revealed a nearly 10 percent drop over nine years in the overall volume of stationary-source atmospheric pollution, with most of the decline occurring since 1986.[16] Since official 1985 to 1988 outlays for air pollution control averaged only about 1 billion rubles—far less than what was spent in those years *failing* to cap the growth of water pollution—the claimed reduction could be treated only with suspicion.[17] Certainly, the air in many major Soviet cities remained poisonous. Atmospheric pollution was counted a high risk in 103 Soviet urban areas.[18] In thirty, the index for dirty air has been *more than* fifteen times the allowable level yearly from 1985 through 1989, and forty-three more entered that crisis zone in 1989.[19]

Only in the cities of China, India, Iran and a few other rapidly developing Third World nations could such extremes of poisonous air be found so consistently.[20] In the United States, where the fight against air pollution began in earnest in 1970, it consumed at least $384 billion in constant 1982 dollars from 1972 through 1987.[21] As a result, by mid-1991, only in two places—around a Wisconsin engine factory and in the Steubenville, Ohio, area—did carbon monoxide from stationary sources still pose serious threats to what U.S. law defines as ambient air quality.[22]

The United States in 1991, however, was still far from meeting all of its clean-air goals. The atmosphere in forty-one U.S. cities contained excessive amounts of carbon monoxide, 90 percent of which, in a nationwide average, came from automotive exhausts rather than factory smokestacks. As far as the norms for particulate matter, seventy-two of America's urban areas were in violation of the standard; ninety-six exceeded the ceiling for ozone, a substance Soviets did not monitor.[23] Using air quality definitions and methodology quite different from Soviet ones, U.S. environmental controllers have concluded that "most areas meet the air quality standards for sulfur dioxide and lead."[24]

The Worldwatch Institute has attempted to make U.S.-Soviet comparisons according to a different yardstick. According to its calculation of comparative economic and air pollution indices, U.S. emissions of nitrogen oxides per unit of GNP were twice those in the Soviet Union. Soviet sulfur dioxide emissions per unit of GNP, on the other hand, were two and a half times higher than America's.[25] The most revealing difference between the two nations was in the presence of highly toxic air pollutants, the likeliest to damage human health. In these categories, the danger was very limited in the United States but widespread in the Soviet Union. In sixty-seven Soviet cities the 1989 level of benzopyrene, a carcinogenic coal-tar by-product, exceeded by five or more times the maximum allowable concentration (PDK, in the Russian abbreviation). Benzopyrene emissions were almost unknown in the United States.[26]

Levels of hydrogen chloride exceeded PDK by five times or more in thirty-eight Soviet cities; of hydrogen sulfide, in thirty; of nitrogen dioxide, in twenty-seven and of dust and ash, in twenty-six. Only Los Angeles, among American cities, recorded excessive nitrogen dioxide levels in the 1980s. In nine Soviet cities the 1989 levels of ammonia and hydrogen sulfide were ten or more times the PDK.[27]

America's fleet of privately owned cars was one of its worst sources of pollution. The USSR, with one-tenth the number of such vehicles and with truck freight one-half the U.S. volume, still managed to produce about two-thirds as much atmospheric poison from automotive exhausts.[28] Between 1988 and 1989, when Soviet industrial emissions, as measured, fell by 3 million tons to a yearly level of nearly 420 pounds per capita, reported automotive pollution in 538 Soviet cities and towns rose by 100,000 tons to a total of 35.5 million tons, or 250 pounds per capita.[29] Cars and trucks accounted for as much as 80 percent of the air pollution in the capitals of six republics from Alma-Ata in Kazakhstan to Riga in Latvia and in such Black Sea resort towns as Yalta and Sochi.[30] In Moscow, already ranked fifth in the nation in 1989 for the volume of pollutants emitted by stationary sources, an estimated 750,000 vehicles added as much as ten times more carbon dioxide to the atmosphere than health rules permitted.[31] In the first six months of 1990, the total tonnage of stationary-source emissions rose to almost 149,000 tons, a 5 percent increase over the first half of 1989.[32]

The situation in the Soviet capital, where fewer than 30 percent of the industrial polluters were said to have installed purifying equipment,[33] was aggravated by the shortage of trees and parks to act as urban lungs. Muscovites had 29 percent less greenery per capita than the Soviet norm; in the city center the deficit was nearly 80 percent.[34] Of the area's 9 million residents, only 720,000 were considered to live in "ecologically acceptable zones," and epidemiologists blamed pollution for one-fifth of all illness. Residents along the inner-belt road, inappropriately called the "Garden Ring," suffered from heart, vascular and nervous system ailments two and a half times as often as their neighbors in the Moscow region as a whole.[35]

Despite the scope of the automotive pollution problem, more than one-third of all Soviet auto inspection stations lacked the equipment to analyze the gaseous output of exhaust systems. Only about 10 percent could even measure the smoke in vehicle emissions.[36] Perhaps in recognition of this deficiency, Soviet authorities began 1988 by doubling the norm for the maximum rate of carbon monoxide emissions from 1.5 percent to 3 percent of exhaust gases. Arguing that their standard was still tougher than any other country's,* two officials rationalized that

---

*EPA regulations in 1991 permitted U.S. automotive emissions to average 8 milligrams of carbon monoxide (CO) per hour, apparently higher than Soviet tolerances, but states such as California have imposed tougher rules. The federal government has also targeted fuel emissions such as lead,

since the new limit would be easier to enforce, it would actually help retire "all defective cars."[38]

Officially, the 1989 level of air pollutants in the USSR as a whole was 94 million tons, with toxic industrial emissions down by one-fifth from 1976.[39] Soviet experts admit, however, that the real, overall figure should be "at a minimum" 20 to 30 percent higher. Underreporting was not just a result of factories that saved their worst pollution until monitoring devices shut down at night. It was also a function of an underequipped control effort.

The environmental inspection services of the State Committee on Hydrometeorology (Goskomgidromet), for instance, were not capable of monitoring pollution from rail, air, sea and river transport, home heating, trash burning or accidental fires. They also lacked the authorization to survey what went on in or came out of military facilities. And the underpaid inspectors were as prone to bribe-taking as other Soviet functionaries and under the same kind of political pressures to falsify inconvenient data as the doctors who concealed or misreported infant deaths. Under the circumstances, observers considered it justifiable to add 30 percent to the official count of harmful atmospheric emissions. The result was a total of over 122 million tons of air pollutants for 1989, or 854 pounds per capita.[40]

In the United States, according to data for 1986, the total was slightly higher than in the USSR: air pollution of 108 million tons, or 873 pounds per capita, almost equally divided between stationary sources and vehicle emissions.[41] U.S. emissions of sulfur dioxide were 20.4 million metric tons in 1987, compared to official (therefore understated by 20 to 30 percent) Soviet totals of 16.8 million tons in 1989. For suspended particulates, Soviet emissions as measured at 13.7 million tons were already almost twice the U.S. total of 7 million tons.[42] In other words, the Soviet Union, with industrial output valued at only about half that of the United States, had managed to make its atmosphere just as dirty and in many cities a clear and present danger to human health. And where Americans have been making a strenuous, if incomplete, effort to clean their air since 1970, Soviets, two decades later, had barely begun such work.

The American effort has been spurred by accounting methods that can, if imperfectly, measure the environmental costs of production and the market value of raw materials. Soviet economics put no real price on water, land, minerals or other goods held by the state. Until 1990,

---

which Soviets did not contemplate beginning to control before 1995. The EPA also required the petrochemical industry to hold average hourly CO output to 0.05 percent of total emissions.[37]

when an experimental range of fees for pollution began to be developed for projected nationwide implementation in mid-1991, minor fines were almost the only penalties for assaults on the environment.

The efficacy of the fee system was also in doubt. Only a fraction of the country's 46,000 industrial enterprises have begun to shift from dependence on plan targets of gross output to a measure of self-financing. Without such a changeover to market realities and an end to administered prices, it is impossible for managers to factor ecological costs—once they are established—into their calculations of profit and loss.

Started in 1989, that initial economic reform moved slowly. Self-financing did nothing, moreover, to strengthen the feeble system of pollution regulation or the ideology-driven presumption that natural resources, as common, social property, should be all but cost-free to the state and the ministries that served as buyers and suppliers. The plan that governed them and the Partocracy that in mid-1991 still formulated and oversaw the plan gave little weight to ecological concerns and less to environmental protection incentives.

SIBERIAN WASTES AND WASTELANDS

To Soviet planners, the imperatives that long mattered the most were the expansion of gross output, the prestige of the socialist state and its leaders and the Soviet Union's need to advance its security in isolation from Western rivals and markets. Such thinking dictated the crash course of industrial development. That model came from the 1930s, from Stalin's 1931 injunction: "The pace must not be slackened . . . those who lag behind are beaten . . . [and] old . . . Russia . . . was ceaselessly beaten for her backwardness."[43] Intensified by the wartime frenzy of production and postwar reconstruction needs, the commands of the center set the standard destructive pattern for investment and growth throughout the Soviet Union.

The disaster even spread through the vast expanses of Siberia. The Angara River, flowing out of the southern end of Lake Baikal, for example, has become an aqueduct for poisons. Yearly it carries 257,000 tons of chlorides, 140,000 tons of sulfates, over 30,000 tons of organic wastes and 10,000 tons of nitrates from factories built in the 1960s and 1970s along its banks.[44]

A 1989 study of that pollution in the Irkutsk *oblast,* including the city of Angarsk, found "increased illness and shortened life expectancy" due to "the intensive industrial exploitation of the region." Other ills included hyperacidity of over one-third of the region's arable land and "extremely irrational practices in timber procurement."[45] "The prevailing winds usually disperse the pollution from the Angarsk chemical plant over Baikal" some sixty miles south and east, an American journalist noted in 1990. "But sometimes, when the wind is in the wrong direction, it floats back over" the city, and "residents complain that breathing becomes more difficult and that the rain contains a corrosive acid."[46]

In comparison to the people of Zima, a Siberian settlement some 150 miles north and west, the inhabitants of Angarsk were almost well off. Until the late 1970s Zima was noted only as the place that poet Yevgeny Yevtushenko spent his wartime childhood. On geological maps, however, it stood out for a huge chlorine deposit, a literal Siberian salt mine that prompted the Chemical Industry Ministry to plan a major complex for the manufacture of polyvinylchloride and very pure alcohol.

To win the approval of Zima's townspeople, the ministry promised them employment, prosperity and rebuilt homes. Drawn by the bonuses given for hardship labor in the north, however, workers from other parts of the Soviet Union took the best-paid jobs. And as the plant was nearing completion about four miles from the village, its managers reneged on their original pledge to reconstruct Zima. Instead, they proposed to house its people in a new town at Soyansk on hills about eight miles beyond the plant.

Again they went back on their word. "They built a lovely city, but they only let about 10 percent of the population of Zima, the able-bodied workers, move into it," recounted Dr. Barenboim. " 'What do we need with the old people?' they decided. They even kept them out of the well-stocked stores in Soyansk.

"Now the prevailing winds carry the factory's smoke to Zima. Salt buildup has poisoned the subsoil. On some days the air carries ten times the PDK of an amalgam of alkali. On some days it's two hundred times the norm."[47] Benzopyrene in the air of Zima, in fact, *averaged* twenty-two times the tolerable level in 1989, the highest such reading in the Soviet Union.[48]

Zima and Soyansk were small dots on the vast expanse of Russia. The city of Norilsk, almost three hundred miles above the Arctic Circle, was the epicenter of a huge blot on the first authoritative, published map of USSR air pollution drawn in 1990 by the Soviet Academy of Sciences' Institute of Geography. A company town of 171,000 with another 96,000 living in the surrounding area, it housed huge deposits of copper and nickel, a giant ferrous metallurgy combine to process them and "the sickest children in the country."[49]

Youngsters in Norilsk were not just victims of an Arctic climate in which six months of darkness alternate with six months of daylight. When it shone, the sun was filtered through an omnipresent overcast of sulfur dioxide—1.2 million tons in 1989—pouring from smokestacks all around the city.[50] On windless days the "gas," as locals called it, regularly reached levels seventy-two times the maximum allowable daily concentration, five-tenths of a milligram per cubic meter.[51] Official measurements of Norilsk's atmosphere in 1989 recorded a sulfur dioxide high 26.4 times PDK, a carbon disulfide maximum of 49 PDK, and *average* levels of phenol and hydrogen fluoride of 3.5 and 1.7 PDK, respectively.[52] The men of the city were said to have the highest rate of lung cancer in the world.[53] Compared to the population of Dudinko, an industry-free town some sixty miles away, Norilsk's people were twice as likely, on average, to suffer from prolonged upper respiratory tract infections. The risk to children fourteen and younger was more than two and a half times as high as in Dudinko. The youth of Norilsk held fourth place in the USSR in the incidence of blood and kidney diseases and sixth place for skin diseases.[54]

At least in 1990 there were children. In 1935 when the Politburo resolved a turf fight over which ministry would exploit the minerals, Norilsk's few inhabitants were exiled *kulaks* like those rounded up to build Magnitogorsk. Their limited numbers were augmented over eighteen years by shipments of 250,000 political prisoners. There would have been more, but during the forty-five-day barge trip north on the Yenisei River, one-fourth of each shipment of 600 convicts usually died.[55]

The survivors were greeted in 1937 by the first camp director's exhortation: "Let us transform the entire contingent of prisoners into a vanguard of Socialist production!" Retired in 1938 after he and his involuntary shock-workers had brought the first furnaces on line, he was to return later to die in his own outpost of the Gulag, a prisoner like the geologist N. N. Urvantsev, who first discovered the fabulous ore deposits in the 1920s. "Nikolai Nikolaievich," his barrackmates used to tease, "couldn't you somehow or other cover up Norilsk and rediscover another, just a bit farther south?"[56]

DEATH TRAPS IN THE RUST BELT

Indeed, farther south in the Urals and in Siberia were more rich veins of minerals and more industrial infernos where the ore, coal and other raw materials were mined, smelted and turned into heavy machinery, such as the giant strip-mining steamshovels produced in Sverdlovsk, to pull more metals from the scarred earth. Through the Urals from Perm to Nizhny Tagil to Sverdlovsk to Chelyabinsk to Magnitogorsk and then east to Kemerovo and Novokuznetsk, a vast, toxic rust belt of mines and metallurgical combines stretched across the Soviet Union. Some dated to Stalin's first Five-Year Plan; some to the heroic evacuation of Russian industry east, away from Hitler's advancing armies in 1941–42. Few were modernized; all were fearsome sources of pollution, killing grounds for those who had to work in them and for their children.

In Berezniki, a small city near Perm, for instance, children under the age of fifteen were over eight times more likely to suffer from blood diseases in 1987 and 1988 than the average of their contemporaries in 121 other badly polluted Soviet urban areas. In Sterlitamak, at the southern end of the Urals, and in the Ukrainian city of Cherkassy on the banks of the Dniepr River, the incidence of eye and lung ailments among youngsters was not only 1.5 to 2 times as high as the 122-city average, but also—for lung diseases—100 to 200 times the rate in the impoverished Turkmenistani town of Chardzhou.[57]

Kemerovo was not necessarily the dirtiest of these cities, just one of those most closely studied. The figures were staggering. Discharges of such pollutants as sulfur dioxide, hydrogen sulfide, sulfuric acid and nitrous oxides ran to over five tons *per hour*. Dust and ash entered the atmosphere at the rate of more than 7,000 pounds an hour; carbon monoxide emissions were half as high. To bring nitrous oxides down to a safe level would have required adding over a million cubic meters of fresh air daily to the city's atmosphere. To do the same for the sulfur dioxide concentrations would have taken about half that volume of clean air.

Cleaning the Tom River that flowed through the city, carrying 100 tons of untreated industrial wastes from upstream polluters a year, was another mission impossible. In addition to enormous volumes of oil products and formaldehyde, the Tom contained forty times the permissible concentration of arsenic, five times the PDK of nitrates and 2.4 times the PDK of phenol, a poison derived from coal and wood tar.[58]

The consequences of such contamination for public health were as sad as they were predictable. Adults in Kemerovo were more than three times as likely to suffer from endocrine system ailments as others in the USSR and 2.7 times as often victimized by chronic bronchitis. Their children, in turn, came down with infections of the kidneys and the urinary tract almost three times as frequently as the average of their Soviet contemporaries. The incidence of respiratory illness among Kemerovo youngsters up to fourteen years of age was 145 percent of the

Soviet average; of endocrine disorders, 129 percent. In one heavily polluted neighborhood of the city, 7 percent of the newborns in 1989 were retarded—a rate roughly three times the national average.[59]

In the northern Urals metallurgical center of Nizhny Tagil, citizens finally took to the streets in April 1988 to protest pollution that had raised the rate of children needing hospital treatment for heart and lung ailments by one-third.[60] After a rally by over 10,000 people and a petition with some 8,500 signatures, two coking batteries were closed. The impact, however, was minimal on the "city-factory" where all but 13 percent of the territory was occupied by industrial plants.[61] In September 1988 the local paper, under a regular heading—"Ecology [is the] Mirror of *Glasnost*"—reported that ammonia in Nizhny Tagil's air was twice the allowed limit and formaldehyde, three times PDK. In one city district levels of both nitrogen dioxide and ammonia were quadruple the maximum allowed.[62] Young people tried to organize a follow-up demonstration but were made to defer it until a week after the public holiday on which they wanted to capitalize. Meanwhile, officials flew in from Moscow to draw up plans for pollution abatement.

They should have come sooner and studied the problem at more length. But as in Magnitogorsk, where factory managers had tried and failed as long ago as the 1960s to get funds for a switch from open-hearth steelmaking to a closed, converter process, Nizhny Tagil metallurgists could look forward only to marginal pollution abatement measures.

"If we changed from the open-hearth to the converter method, many of the ecological questions would disappear," argued the city Party's first secretary. "We are always rushing things under deadline pressures. Often what we gain is minimal and the losses are a lot larger. We built the Number 9 coke boiler in a hurry and fired it up still unfinished. Now it puts out as much smoke as two normal batteries."[63]

The result was that in 1990 the city's 400,000 residents were still breathing in harmful industrial pollutants at the rate of 1.5 tons per capita a year, to which vehicle emissions added another quarter ton. A Soviet journalist concluded,

it is not surprising that the most widespread children's illnesses in Nizhny Tagil are respiratory: bronchitis, bronchial asthma and acute pneumonia and that nervous system disorders are on the rise. The children are twice as likely to suffer from skin allergies and eye disease as those in nearby towns. Infants arrive in the world in a weakened condition, with lowered immunity and birth defects. After all, the ecology of childhood starts with the ecology of motherhood.[64]

Walking around the city, the reporter came to a school for mentally handicapped children. Across the street the metallurgical complex's coke batteries fumed. Around the corner a cement factory pushed clouds of gritty dust into an atmosphere judged to be 16 percent more polluted than the air of Nizhny Tagil in general.

"You go to school sometimes in a thick haze of smoke with your teeth gritting from the cement dust," teachers told the visitor. "And you must never open the classroom windows. The sills turn gray in an instant."[65]

NO PLACE TO HIDE

Why would anyone live and work in such hellish conditions? Why did more than half a million people stay in Kemerovo's lethal surroundings? Why did the workers at Norilsk's hearths, obliged to wear gas masks throughout their six-hour shifts, run high risks of impotence and sterility so that they could spend their free time in a barren moonscape where, for a twenty-mile radius, berries and mushrooms were toxic? Why would anyone choose to remain in a place about which an appalled Muscovite wrote "there could be no more perfect setting" for a film of George Orwell's novel 1984?[66]

The questions could be answered in more than one way. Of all the answers, one was not just accurate but appalling: There were few if any other Soviet cities where industrial workers could find markedly better conditions, truly clean air and, overall, safer living conditions.

Even if there were such havens, Soviet industrial employees—though free in principle to roam after their initial job assignment—generally seemed unready and unlikely to move to them. In surveys in the 1980s Soviet sociologists found that more than half of those who put a high value on their health nevertheless would not give up even harmful employment to preserve it.[67] While one worker in six—about 25 million people—did find a new job every year, the shift was usually a short-distance one, rarely from one city, or even one skill, to another.[68] One reason for this relative lack of mobility was the "company store" nature of labor relations. Enterprises and trade unions often doubled as the sole providers of housing, cafeteria meals, take-home food supplies and fully paid vacation trips for blue- and white-collar workers alike. At the richer factories, higher-quality medical and child care and recreation facilities constituted added inducements to keep labor turnover low.

Welfare agencies within a welfare state, the industrial enterprises were also conduits for hard-to-get consumer goods, including automobiles. But they usually did not teach new hands to master new skills; job training was reserved primarily for workers already on their payroll. The government, additionally, provided only a skimpy network of employment exchange offices and next to no help in the hardest part of any change of job and address: finding new housing.

With 14.3 million urban families and single persons (100,000 of them in Magnitogorsk alone[69]) seeking better quarters at the start of 1990—nearly one household in four[70]—any Soviet had to think hard before giving up a job to which an apartment was attached. Although Stalin era internal passports were no longer needed for moves from one city to another and farmers, who were denied such documents until late in the 1970s, could obtain them, Soviets had to register their addresses with municipal authorities if they stayed in one place for any length of time. In especially crowded cities such as Moscow and Leningrad, residence permits were issued only to new arrivals who could prove that they were essential employees or close kin of a registered city dweller.

Finally, where working conditions were bad, pay and perks could also be good. In Norilsk, bonuses were paid for working so far north. In Siberia as well, hardship premiums and lengthy vacations at sought-after resorts were used to attract labor. In the Chelyabinsk region of the Urals, just north of Magnitogorsk, a 400-ruble-a-month salary (including premium payments for exceeding output quotas) was a major consideration for Vasily Karlenko, a crane operator at an open-hearth furnace since 1959.

"He doesn't deny that the smelter is hell on earth," a Soviet journalist reported, "that the steelmakers suffocate from smoke, that there are days, depending on the wind, when they can't see each other and have to work by groping around." The job, however, has brought Karlenko an apartment and a car for which he had to save ten years. His grown son returned alive but wounded from the war in Afghanistan. "For that I thank fate," he said. "I don't know what else I need. I'm just like everyone else."[71]

He and his co-workers were grateful and resigned. At least, they pointed out, a roof was finally built over the factory many years after it started wartime production. The smelter was one of the hundreds of installations constructed hurriedly in the Urals or brought there from the European part of the Soviet Union to escape advancing German armies. Built for emergency conditions, few have been modernized or reequipped. During and right after "the terrible years of the war," Fyodor Morgun observed, such industries were moved or begun "with good intentions to 'fix it later.' But 'later' . . . we are still tearing nature to pieces and trying to plug up the gaps from the mismanagement.

... We whipped it like a beaten horse. And what we have now is what we have."[72]

Industrial infrastructure has been as much abused as nature. The smelter's furnace had hardly been modernized since it was installed in 1942, and Karlenko's co-workers did not expect to see it or their working conditions improved. Alexander Uglichin voiced their general sense of futility. "How can it be any different?" he asked. "Okay, we gulp down dust and ash—a kilogram [2.2 pounds] per shift. All right, we dig our health into the ground, but what's the sense in trying to save it? There's nothing but emptiness out ahead.

"What are you going to achieve? An apartment—say you get it—is going to be the last one you get. There won't be anything better. There are 150 guys signed up and waiting now in our shop, and 'they' hand out two a year. If you're at the tail end of the line, you'll get your moving permit 75 years from now."[73]

In Karabash, also in the Chelyabinsk *oblast,* a foundry dominated a township of 18,000 people, blackening their air, their homes, their clothes, their lungs with soot. Annually the factory put 162,000 tons of sulfur, lead, arsenic, tellurium and other metals and gases into the atmosphere. The total worked out to nine tons of pollutants a year for everyone, including the three thousand children. Yury Babkin, a smelter, has two.

"Are they sick?" he was asked.

"Of course."

"Why of course?"

"Because there are no healthy kids here."

"Then why don't you quit, get out of here?"

"Where to? It's the same everywhere. Besides, who's waiting for me to show up? Where?"[74]

The incidence of first-time diagnoses of cancer in the Soviet Union—57 percent higher than the U.S. rate in 1987[75]—was 268 cases per 100,000 inhabitants in 1989. In the Chelyabinsk *oblast* it was 291, according to the region's chief public health official. In Karabash, he said, the rate was 338. Vladimir Makarevich, the doctor in charge of sanitation for the town, acknowledged that its intense pollution meant only one thing for the residents: death.

"But it's a slow death," he added. "That's why many aren't afraid of a tumor. They think it will go away. Go away? Already, the army turns down half our kids who are up for the draft as total invalids. The other half only get assigned to auxiliary units. They're invalids, too, but still good for a bit of work.

"I could order the furnaces shut down, but it wouldn't happen. The manager would just go to the *oblast* Party committee and the regional executive authorities, and they would take the seal off. I tried once. An official told me, 'The workers themselves will beat you down. They'll spend a week breathing fresh air, then they'll get hungry and run back to work at the factory.'

"I agree with him. People here have no choice. The foundry is the only place that hires workers."[76]

The Karabash metallurgical complex had been so dangerous for so long that in November 1985 Moscow took notice. The USSR Council of Ministers promised remedial action for it and similar industrial polluters in the cities of Chelyabinsk and Magnitogorsk. The decree spoke of closing factories, reconstructing some and taking others out of operation entirely.

As of early 1990, however, nothing had changed. A joint circular from central planners and the Metallurgical Ministry, in fact, deferred all action. It called on the inhabitants of these infernos in the Urals to understand "the difficult situation" in the country and "to demonstrate responsibility and provide help to the nation's economy."[77]

POLITICS, ECONOMICS
AND POLLUTION

"Responsibility" in that sense means accepting the prolongation of ecocide, neither an economically nor politically responsible course. Environmental damage comes at a high price to future growth and, where it generates popular protest, a cost in political stability as well. Both bills were coming due when the country's purse was empty and its old-guard rulers were on the run.

Despite all the commissions from Moscow flown to trouble spots around the country, despite the promises made and the investments allocated for pollution abatement, industrial contamination went largely unchecked even as environmental awareness rose. For almost every indication of improving atmospheric conditions, for instance, there was counterbalancing evidence of deterioration in water supplies and of mounting problems of solid and toxic waste. The more reliable Soviet environmental monitoring became—and it had far to go—the more overwhelming seemed the decay.

A major contributing factor was the inertia of the giant government agencies, the industrial conglomerates of the USSR. Proprietor polluters such as the Ministries of Energy and of Metallurgy together accounted for just over half the measured stationary-source air pollution in 1989,

29.8 million tons of emissions out of 58.5 million.[78] They and others like them had a history of unaccountability and a legal status as "All-Union" entities that shielded them against most pressures from local or even republic-level authorities.

The issue of controlling these ministries and their subsidiaries—their finances and, secondarily, their impact on the environment—was a key part of the disputes between the Kremlin and the fractious Soviet republics as pressures for decentralization escalated in the Gorbachev era. In mid-1991 the issue of sovereignty—of whose laws represented final writ—stood at the center of Soviet political debate. The consequence for ecological action was near stalemate. Although the Russian Republic's parliament ordered a stop to construction on the Katun Dam, a giant hydroelectric project environmentalists had long opposed in Siberia, the minions of Minvodkhoz and the Ministry of Energy went right on digging.

Earlier efforts brought some reported diminution in air pollution traceable to industry. As stationary sources stabilized or even shrank their output, however, contamination from vehicle exhausts was on the rise. In 190 Soviet cities cars, trucks and buses accounted for half of the recorded 1989 air pollution.[79] Unleaded gas and catalytic converters, measures long ago adopted in the United States and later in Europe, are not likely to be widely available in the USSR before 1995 at the earliest. In the meantime, the 16 million passenger cars, 300,000 buses and uncounted trucks on Soviet roads continue to foul the air.[80]

A fundamental set of obstacles to effective constraint on the emissions of manufacturers and processors was economic. Closing large installations either for good or for retrofitting with expensive purification equipment entailed high costs, not only for equipment but in lost jobs and output. Soviet production of antipollution devices was limited in any case, and central planning created another hurdle: production monopolies. Measured by value, at least one-third of all products made in the USSR came from a single factory.[81]

When a sole supplier of a key component—needles or elastic, for instance—could not make or deliver its wares, a Moscow establishment that turned out socks and stockings had to idle its production lines.[82] The resulting hosiery shortage, one of many in the consumer sector, was a symptom of the Soviet Union's general economic breakdown. In other instances environmental concerns were blamed—not always fairly—for the disappearance of basic goods.

One such case was an aspirin famine. After an installation near Sverdlovsk was shut in January 1990 at the insistence of environmental, health and safety agencies, a variety of nonprescription pain-killers began to vanish from Soviet pharmacy shelves. The factory had been making chlorosulfonic acid, a component of many analgesics. Drug makers who said they could not find it elsewhere railed at meddling ecologists. In fact, twelve days after the chlorosulfonic acid line was closed, the roof of the empty factory fell in and crushed the machinery beneath it.[83] The pain-killer scarcity would have occurred anyway.

The incident suggests that Soviet environmental laws have muscle. That is not the case. Ecological regulations as well as the agencies meant to administer them more usually lacked both the power to punish and, at least until 1991, the incentives to stimulate cleanup. Three years after its 1988 creation, Goskompriroda, the State Committee on Environmental Protection, was upgraded to ministry rank but with dual responsibility to defend nature and to oversee the use of natural resources.

Sensing a crippling internal contradiction, Aleksei Yablokov moved in the Supreme Soviet to delete the second half of the new agency's title. His amendment got 242 votes, 30 short of the majority needed. At midyear, though Nikolai Vorontsov had been designated its minister, the agency had no authorizing directive to establish its duties and powers. "In real life," Yablokov forecast, "it will have no power at all, because even on the issues of ecology, the republics do not want to follow the central government. They want to go their own way."[84]

Under vocal pressure from worried constituents, the republic, *oblast* and municipal environmental protection agencies did seem positioned to be more energetic pollution fighters than any Moscow-based body. In practice, they were not up to the job. One of their critics was the ubiquitous Valentin Rasputin, respected as a literary talent but loathed in some quarters for his ties to extreme Russian nationalist groups and their anti-Semitic views. Many local environmental protection committees, Rasputin charged, "have become cozy and peaceful spots for people who no longer have any influence, are just waiting for retirement and are ready, pen in hand, to sign any document whatsoever."[85]

Even if the lower-level committees had had better staffs, they were hardly better financed than the impecunious Goskompriroda. As Yablokov pointed out, the 11 billion rubles supposedly spent in 1990 on environmental control by Soviet governments at all levels equaled the cost of a single Soviet aircraft carrier. "And we are building three of them," he noted gloomily.[86]

For a mere 8 million rubles, the children living in the vicinity of the Tajik Aluminum Plant at Tursun Zade could have gotten a variety of social services built—two dispensaries, twelve schools of various levels, surgical and obstetrical facilities and twenty-six wells for drinking water—to enrich their impoverished environment. Those investments, however necessary for basic welfare, would not have reduced the plant's toxic emissions that not only caused teeth to rot but also increased the rate of "congenital development defects" to eight times that in a nearby, pollution-free zone. The funds needed for pollution abatement should probably have come from the Soviet Ministry of Metallurgy, but the factory straddled the border between Uzbekistan and Tajikistan, and neither republic accepted full responsibility for cleaning up the operations and pressing Moscow for the funding.[87]

The Tursun Zade case was an unusual example of an overriding feature of Soviet bureaucratic life. Repeatedly, lower-level health and nature protection bodies ran up against the reality that enterprises controlled by Union-wide ministries recognized only the commands of central authority. Those decision makers, reluctant to sacrifice their own interests in normal times, appeared nearly impotent, if not totally paralyzed, as the USSR groped toward a new decentralization of power and a market economy.

Late in 1990, to give another example, the city council of Magnitogorsk was given the responsibility to mount a cleanup effort and the authority to use 7 percent of the earnings from the city's enterprises and 10 percent of their foreign exchange reserves to pay for the work. In theory, that should have been a very large sum, for Magnitogorsk produced 10 percent of all Soviet metal and one-fourth of all the goods containing metal. In reality, however, the grant of authority amounted to a permit, not an order. The enterprises could choose whether or not to follow it. And since the *laissez aller* was issued by the Russian Republic's Council of Ministers, not its all-Union counterpart, it was not binding on the giant metallurgical ministries or, in the case of foreign currency reserves, on Soviet central banking authorities.[88]

Political chaos at least opened new possibilities. Among the 50,000 coal miners who struck the twenty-one mines in the Donbass city of Donetsk in the spring of 1991, their own Dickensian working conditions—poorly ventilated, ill-lit shafts, some of them hardly changed since they opened during World War I—were the prime concern. But the miners were also parents aware that childhood leukemia cases in Donetsk had risen 20 percent between 1985 and 1990. Their hope, a naive one, was that their protest action would speed progress toward privatization and that the play of market forces would bring them social as well as capital investments.[89]

The political impasse that stalled even efforts to write new, effective environmental laws offered little encouragement to such aspirations. "We are entering the market," lamented Goskompriroda's chairman in November 1990, "without possessing in fact any systems at all (either economic, or legal) for environmental regulation."[90] He might have added that the USSR also did not possess anywhere near the necessary modern equipment to monitor accurately the use of such basic resources as water or such dangers as radiation.

The persistence, even the spread, of industrial pollution on Mikhail Gorbachev's watch was thus a function of established practices hard to overcome in any setting. In the midst of internal political stalemate and economic collapse, wholesale environmental rehabilitation could be only a distant dream. Piecemeal efforts on disparate fronts, plant closings that inflicted unanticipated damage on the tightly woven chain of production, were the most that Soviet ecologists achieved. Such victories were too small and too short-lived to make a difference to the national crisis. But in one of the longest environmental struggles on record—the fight to save the largest body of fresh water in the world—shutting two factories could reverse decades of environmental degradation. Like Stalin's commitment "to build socialism in one country," the salvation of one lake could prove a turning point in Soviet history. As late as 1991, that turning point for Lake Baikal still lay in the uncertain future.

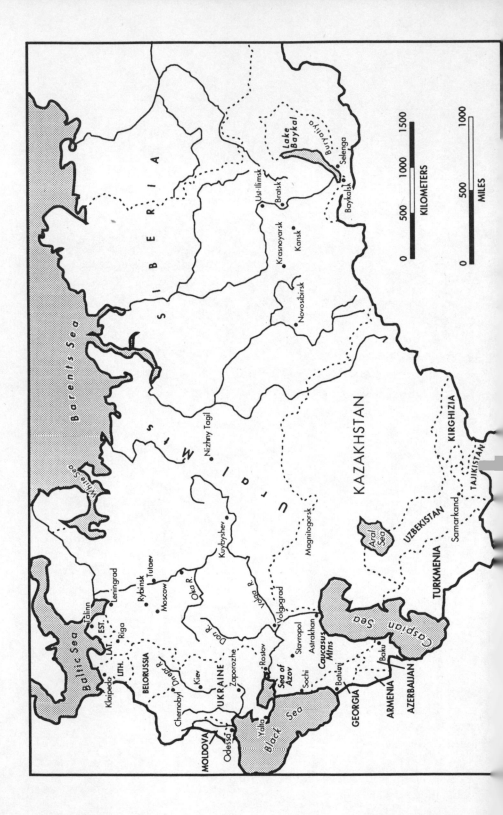

Barents Sea

White Sea

S I B E R I A

Lake Baykal

Buryatia

Selenga

Baykalsk

Ust-Ilimsk · Bratsk

Krasnoyarsk · Kansk

Novosibirsk

U r a l   M t s.

Nizhny Tagil

KAZAKHSTAN

KIRGHIZIA

TAJIKISTAN

Aral Sea

Samarkand

UZBEKISTAN

TURKMENIA

Baltic Sea

Kuybyshev

Magnitogorsk

Leningrad

Rybinsk · Tulaev

Moscow

Oka R.

Volga R.

Volgograd

Talinn

EST.

Riga

LAT.

Klaipeda

LITH.

BELORUSSIA

Chernobyl

Dnepr R.

Kiev

UKRAINE

Zaporozhe

Don R.

Rostov

Stavropol

Astrakhan

Caucasus Mtns

Caspian Sea

Baku

AZERBAIJAN

ARMENIA

GEORGIA

Batumi

Sochi

Sea of Azov

Black Sea

Yalta

MOLDOVA

Odessa

CHAPTER 6

Water Torture

THE POLLUTION OF Lake Baikal was to Siberia what the destruction of the Aral Sea was to Central Asia: ecocide engineered with malice aforethought. But while the Aral's doom seemed almost certain, in the early 1990s salvation is possible for Lake Baikal. A crusade to preserve its purity, under way since 1963, has won both Moscow's attention and, over the years, some incomplete, ameliorative action.

The unfinished victories achieved in the name of Baikal attested to its uniqueness and to its stubborn defense by a remarkable coalition of grass-roots nature lovers, prominent scientists and literati. Its symbolism as the vessel for roughly 20 percent of the world's entire supply of fresh water and 80 percent of the Soviet Union's also drew stronger champions to it than to many, even more endangered Soviet water resources. Conceivably, the fight for Baikal could serve as a model for other Soviet environmental campaigns. More immediately, the lake mirrored the recklessness of much Soviet development.

Imprudence, if not extremes of folly, in the pursuit of growth did even greater damage to the great Soviet seas, lakes and rivers than to the "pearl of Siberia." Lying far from the biggest urban centers, Baikal was peripheral to the nation's economy. The Baltic, Black and Caspian seas as well as Lake Ladoga and the Volga, Dniepr, Don and other major rivers were the nation's lifelines. In the 1990s some were dying. All had been poisoned.

Water in the USSR, unsurprisingly, is every bit as compromised as the air. Of the total volume of surface water, measured in 1989 as 44 billion cubic meters, 32.7 billion—nearly three-fourths—were classified as polluted.[1] Fully one-third of the unclean water was *totally untreated*. The Russian Republic did manage to treat, though not fully, an average of all but 31 percent of its polluted water in 1989. Armenia, by contrast, purified almost none of its wastes, and the untreated portions of polluted water in Azerbaijan, Uzbekistan and Georgia were 76, 78 and 83 percent, respectively.[2]

From 1986, a notably dry year, to 1987, when runoff from rain and melting snow overloaded already inadequate storm drains and sewage treatment facilities, the volume of unclean water drawn from Soviet reservoirs for urban use rose by more than one-third. The polluted portion of the stock of drinking water went from 9 percent of the total to 12 percent.[3] Of water samples taken from two hundred major rivers, only 21 percent did *not* show dangerous levels of bacterial and viral agents.[4] In the city of Novosibirsk on Siberia's Ob River, bacteria content went four thousand times over the established health limit in 1988.[5]

In comparison, a 1989 survey by the U.S. Environmental Protection Agency found only 10 percent of America's "rivers, streams and bays to be significantly polluted."[6] Of 17,365 segments of U.S. surface waters contaminated by one or more of 126 toxic chemicals, just 595 bodies of water averaging six to ten miles long were considered severely affected.[7] To achieve that degree of cleanliness, however, Americans had to spend an average of $24.3 billion (in constant 1982 dollars) yearly from 1972 through 1987, just a bit above U.S. outlays for air pollution control in the same period.[8]

Even the ambitious program that official Soviet environmental scientists proposed in 1990 for a fifteen-year cleanup effort envisioned maximum average annual outlays of only 32.3 billion rubles for *all* air, water, land and other nature protection and for improved efficiency in the use of natural resources.[9] At the unrealistic commercial exchange rate of $1.37 to the ruble, that total would come close to average U.S. spending for clean water alone. At the mid-1991 tourist rate of twenty-seven rubles to the dollar, the Soviet plan projected an all-threat ecological defense costing just $1.2 billion a year.

The danger that Soviet water pollution poses to human and economic health is severe enough to require far higher remedial investments. Given the fact that 84 percent of all surface water in the USSR is in Siberia, Kazakhstan and Central Asia, where only 29 percent of the people live,[10] measurements of average, nationwide contamination understate the degree to which most Soviet citizens have to rely on unsafe water supplies. West of the Urals and in the Caucasus, where population density is high, so is water pollution.

In the 1990s the danger was on the rise, but remedial action was far behind schedule. "The huge sums that the state allocates for construction of water purification systems are not being used," Aleksei Yablokov complained in 1990. Less than half the planned 1989 outlays were actually expended, he said, and the Ministry of the Chemical Industry, a major polluter, met only 13 percent of its target for installing new water treatment facilities.[11] Along with chemical production, the chief menaces to clean water came from metallurgy, forestry, agriculture and energy producers. In the inventory of Soviet water pollutants they and others discharged in 1989, pride of place went to 21 million metric tons of sulfates, 19 million tons of chlorides and 4 million more tons of mercury, zinc, chrome, nickel, iron, copper and petroleum products.[12]

Sometimes, as well, there was gold in them thar rills. One example was the river that flows through Nizhny Tagil, the city whose name spelled pollution to every sentient Soviet. When municipal authorities used the fees they imposed on the smoky metallurgical combine to finance a cleanup of the Tagil River in 1991, the workers who drained and dredged the riverbed recovered 422 ounces of gold. Assuming it was pure, the cache was worth a minimum of $350 an ounce, at least $148,000 in all or, at the mid-1991 official tourist rate, about 4 million rubles.[13]

That seemed a handsome sum. In fact, it was just a bit more than twice the six-month fine that environmental authorities in the small Siberian city of Kansk tried in 1991 to levy against the municipal sewer system managers who had been pouring 100,000 cubic meters of waste water through a treatment facility designed to handle only two-thirds that volume. The overflow of detergents, phenol, sulfates, oil products and heavy metals had made Kan River water unfit either to drink or to use for irrigation. Work on expanding the treatment facility moved at a snail's pace. "It's the old tradition of throwing everything you have into building housing, industry and social-cultural facilities," said the chairman of the district nature protection committee, "and leaving environmental considerations till later. That has been and still is the policy of the city executive."[14]

One reason such practices continued was that the financial penalties imposed on polluters usually were negligible. In the Krasnoyarsk region, bordering Kansk, seventy factory directors were personally assessed during 1990 for discharging polluted water. The fee in each case was a mere fifty rubles, enough to buy two packs of imported cigarettes.[15]

The entrenched policy of leaving nature until last also left six hundred Soviet cities with inadequate water treatment systems and impure water.[16] It put many Soviet lives in danger. As the volume of discharges of Soviet waste water rose nearly five times in the twenty years after 1970,[17] so did the incidence of parasitic diseases, many of them carried in the water.

Infestations of worms (helminths) in Siberian and Volga Basin reservoirs, some of them polluted by the wastes from cattle feed lots, were just one of the phenomena that led to a reported 4.5 million cases of parasitic infection in 1987.* In the 1980s new cases of pinworms more than doubled, to the point that one out of every hundred Soviets suffered from them in 1987.[19]

Cholera, one of the mass killers during the famine period of the Civil War, also reappeared. An August 1990 outbreak in Samarkand, the ancient city in Uzbekistan where Tamerlane is buried, was blamed on the use of open water cisterns.[20] Another episode followed quickly at a camping ground in Stavropol, the city in the northern Caucasus where Mikhail Gorbachev had been Party boss, and then a third, farther north, in Rostov at the mouth of the Don River. The victims in Rostov had drunk river water without boiling it first.[21]

Some Soviet waterways, in short, were dangerous to human health. Some were so polluted—the Volga River, the Caspian Sea, the Baltic— that fish were dying and commercial fisheries with them. In most cases the fault lay with officials who invested too much in promoting industry, too little in protecting people and nature. In only one place, Lake Baikal, have people fought back long and effectively enough to begin to save an irreplaceable asset from the threat of ecocide.

"CONSERVE THIS GLORIOUS SEA"

The fight for Lake Baikal, the best-documented tragedy of official hubris and of scientific and popular protest, is also the longest-running ecological drama in the Soviet Union. The lake, the deepest and eighth largest in the world, is a natural wonder 25 to 30 million years old, an ecosystem as distinctive as the Amazon rain forest, a scenic marvel on the order of the Grand Canyon, but seven times as deep, and a laboratory for the study of what may be the oldest freshwater organisms on the planet.

---

*The director of the Soviet Health Ministry's Institute of Medical Parasitology and Tropical Medicine told an *Izvestiya* reporter late in 1990 that official statistics which he used in writing for medical journals probably understated the incidence of parasitic disease by ten times on average. Among 290 million Soviets, the actual number of cases of illness traceable to contaminated water and similar causes should therefore be some 45 million a year. Medical schools, he also noted, "have virtually no courses in parasitology" and because laboratories are poorly equipped to identify such diseases, "a great many cases go unreported in our country."[18]

Until one hundred years ago, the lake was undisturbed by man. Running along a geologic rift between towering hills 420 miles north to south across southeastern Siberia, it reaches depths of 1.2 miles and holds water so translucent that the mint date on a tiny coin "can be read through 1,000 feet of water."[22] In a space roughly equal to the territory of Denmark, there have developed 1,200 forms of aquatic life found nowhere else, including a fish-eating flatworm that can grow over a foot in length and the only freshwater seal on the planet.[23] Not until the Trans-Siberian railway cut around the lake's southern end in 1896 did the modern world begin to intrude on this aquatic Eden. Only since 1957 has the invasion really posed a threat.

In 1991 it was still a limited hazard. Sedimentary pollution from the wastes of an outsize cellulose-processing combine affected a bit less than eight square miles of the lake bottom at its southern end, less than 0.07 percent of the total area. But a second pulp-and-paper mill on the east side and other industries brought to the north end by the construction of a second railroad, the Baikal-Amur Mainline, have added new dangers. In 1988, for instance, the 191,000 metric tons of inadequately treated waste water poured into the lake was nearly triple the 1986 volume of 66,000 tons.[24]

Considered "the cleanest large lake in the world," Baikal may be able to absorb heavy human punishment in the 1990s, but only at the risk that its "ancient ecology could unravel" rapidly and irreparably.[25] A report produced in the mid-1970s by a special USSR Academy of Sciences commission concluded that, given its size, "Baikal is not easy to pollute, but it will be impossible to clean up."[26]

The plan to exploit it and the fight to save it began at the same time but remained a behind-the-scenes struggle until April 1963. Then an article in a mass circulation magazine disclosed that the cellulose-cord processing facility under construction at Baikalsk and the smaller, cardboard-making factory at Selenga had both been opposed by authoritative national institutes of botanists, zoologists, geographers, hydrobiologists and microbiologists and by the Siberian division of the Academy of Sciences.[27] What the publication did not reveal was the reason that the forestry-product manufacturers succeeded in overriding their opponents. Later, an insider uncovered the truth:

At that time the Ministry of Defense needed new durable cord for heavy bomber tires. Such things are referred to tersely as "strategic interests of the country" and are not subject to discussion even within the Council of Ministers. The immunity of the Baikal projects to any criticism is explained by these "strategic interests." They had sealed Baikal's fate by 1959.[28]

The decision, based on the need for exceptionally clean water and the availability of timber in the Baikal area, had a number of positive appeals to Soviet planners. Governed by an autarchic outlook inherited from Stalin's fear of "capitalist encirclement," they instinctively wanted to produce heavy-duty tire cord domestically, so as not to rely on Western imports. Siting the production in the nominally autonomous Buryat Republic was an added plus. It meant development for one of Siberia's most primitive areas, a leap from the near nomadism of the indigenous Mongol people to the presumed blessings of twentieth-century socialist progress.

The Buryat equivalent for the United States would be to put a major defense plant on an Indian reservation near Glacier National Park in Montana. American environmentalists would fight the proposal tooth and nail, and Indian leaders would almost certainly join them. In Buryatia in 1963, however, the Party first secretary denounced the head of the Baikal Limnological Institute as "an enemy of the Buryat people" for voicing his objections to the mills in a little-read scientific journal as early as 1961.[29] "Enemy of the people" was a familiar Soviet charge. In Stalin's time, it usually heralded a death sentence.

Further anathematized as an "accomplice of imperialism," the scientist, Grigory Galazy, not only continued the dispute but drew colleagues and eminent writers into it on the side of nature conservation. Not even three successive secrecy orders from 1963 to 1975—the last a press gag on publishing *any* ecological information, not just arguments about Lake Baikal—stilled the controversy. At the Communist Party's Twenty-third Congress in 1966, novelist Mikhail Sholokhov, usually a reliable mouthpiece for political orthodoxy, urged that only nonpolluting development be allowed in the area. "Later generations," he said, "will not forgive us if we do not conserve this glorious sea, our blessed Baikal."[30]

Under such pressure, Soviet authorities vowed to install state-of-the-art waste treatment facilities at the Baikalsk combine where, initially, none had been planned. A special Academy of Sciences report in late 1966 pledged that all would be well, but its authors went through three hotly argued drafts before dropping their blanket opposition to the cellulose plants. In return they won commitments that a special pipeline would carry the factories' wastes twenty-five miles across a high ridge away from the lake and that pulp processing would be banned in large zones along its shores.[31]

The promises were not kept. Only two decades later, in 1986, did the government establish a nature preserve and two national parks, totaling just over 5,000 square miles. In that year the Baikalsk combine was still pouring 58,000 tons of inadequately treated wastes into the lake, 88 percent of the total of polluted water entering it.[32] As recently as 1988–89, atmospheric pollution from the Baikalsk and Selenginsk plants together came close to 100,000 tons a year. The second combine, supposedly equipped to recirculate its liquid refuse, put "over 15 million tons of mineral, suspended and organic wastes directly into the lake," one-fourth the volume emanating from Baikalsk.[33]

Those effluents, in fact, made it difficult if not impossible for the original mill to do the job for which it was built. Without intakes of pure water, it could not manufacture durable cord from cellulose. And the water it used every twenty-five hours, Grigory Galazy has computed, was worth more than the combine's annual earnings, even using the low, official price of two kopecks for a cubic meter of water. "The damage," he calculated, "is 150 to 200 percent the benefit."[34]

Worst of all, since 1964, even before Baikalsk went on stream, *the USSR has had no need for its main product*. Petroleum-based cord for tires, even for those on heavy bombers, had become the standard, and the USSR, at that time, had no shortage of oil. By 1977 the controversial mill was reduced to turning out 160,000 tons of ordinary cord—50 percent below its planned output—3,000 tons of coarse brown wrapping paper and 100,000 tons of nutrient yeast, mostly for pig fodder.[35] In 1987 Moscow ordered the combine closed or converted to furniture making by 1993, but a visitor in late 1990 found "no sign of this happening."[36]

Lake Baikal, thus, has been held hostage to easily replaced goods, to the jobs connected with them and, presumably, to the bureaucratic *amour propre* of the Ministry of the Timber Industry. Meanwhile, sewage dumped in 1989 by the growing settlements around the lake brought a 25 percent rise in pollution by organic wastes over 1988.[37] Other major oxygen-eaters in the lake came from the decomposition of the 2 million cubic meters of logs that were rafted over it to the pulp mills. They left 70,000 tons of wood and bark a year to rot in Baikal's waters, consuming two and one-half times their weight in oxygen.[38]

Any degradation endangered the entire aquatic structure. The unique environment of Lake Baikal was built on the presence of a zooplankton called *epishura*, so dependent on the full functioning of the ecosystem that it cannot survive even in a test tube containing only Baikal water. This tiny, indispensable crustacean is not only food for the other life in the lake but a biological filtering agent for all of Baikal's waters. In the late 1980s, it was rapidly disappearing around the Baikalsk combine. No one knows for sure at what point the decline in *epishura* could begin to spiral out of control. By 1977 algae were already flourishing in what had been crystalline depths. Worms were so prevalent "that sometimes nine out of ten *omul* salmon caught by ichthyologists [were] teeming" with them.[39] Mass deaths of both fish and nerpa, the unique freshwater seal, occurred in 1987, with incomplete data showing a 10 percent drop in the seal population that winter.[40]

"Nature is taking its revenge," said Grigory Galazy, Baikal's earliest defender, in 1990. "By destroying Baikal, we are destroying the basis of our own life . . . pure water, not water that has first gone through a pulp plant."[41] The only solution, he argued, was "to exclude entirely" all pollution of the lake's air and water, not just out of "concern for Baikal's unique ecosystem" but also for the basic economic reason that the cellulose combines cause "far more" harm than they do economic good.[42]

WASTING AWAY

Such unprofitable polluters dot the whole map of the Soviet Union. Hurriedly built in many cases, they are, as a rule, also poorly maintained and badly equipped with both productive and protective technology. Often hazardous to the health of their neighbors and employees, they drain natural resources and the state's competitive ability. The wastes they and the cities around them discharge have turned great Soviet waterways into infected sewers.

The Volga River, ancient symbol of Russia, is a prime victim of pollution from such sources. The waters of the Volga Basin, source of one-fourth of Russia's agricultural output and one-fifth of its catch of river fish, were so filthy in 1989 that teeming masses of worms infected 70 percent of the fish in the reservoirs behind the dams at Rybinsk, Samara (formerly Kuibyshev) and Volgograd and between 80 and 100 percent of those upstream from Gorky, the once and once-again Nizhny-Novgorod.[43] The more than three hundred reservoirs formed by these dams[44] have turned "Mother Volga" into a turgid stream; water from Rybinsk that used to reach Volgograd in fifty days now takes five hundred.[45] When it does arrive, that city's outdated water system annually adds 200,000 tons of untreated sewage to a river already carrying the effluents of two hundred major industrial complexes.[46]

Even though one measure of the Volga's load of unpurified wastes put it at less than half a percent of the total flow, the pollution was enough to produce eighty-two massive fish kills in 1988 alone.[47] In the water storage area for Ivanovsk, one of the cities upstream from Volgograd, the average 1989 level of copper compounds was thirty-six times the PDK, with a one-time high of 294 PDK. That February, concentrations of petroleum by-products were 1,320 times the allowed limits near Tutaev, close to Nizhny-Novgorod.[48]

The Volga, in turn, was the main tributary of the Caspian Sea, the repository for 40 million tons of polluted waste water, more than a fourth of the 153 million tons produced in the entire USSR in 1989.[49] Spills from the many oil fields under the Caspian's waters and on its coasts raised the level of petroleum by-products from ten- to a hundred-fold the sanitary limit in its southern reaches and three to four times too high at its center and northern end.[50] Among the result were outbreaks of skin infections among bathers so widespread that authorities closed several popular beaches near Baku in 1990. Calling the situation "preca-tastrophic," Azerbaijan's environmental protection chief blamed it on the "irrational use of natural resources" by producers each one of which processes "only 'its own' components and throws away the rest."[51]

Pesticides and industrial wastes carried south by the Volga were more to blame than oil leaks for cutting the sturgeon catch from 56,000 tons in 1974 to 27,000 tons in 1987. The haul of pike perch dropped by a factor of twenty-four over thirty years. "The grave ecological situation of recent years," analysts concluded, "constitutes a real threat of losing the entire stock of sturgeon" in the Caspian, where 90 percent of the world supply of those caviar-bearing fish live and breed.[52]

Sturgeon were not the only endangered species around the world's largest landlocked sea, and dirty water was not the only threat to life in the region. An aluminum plant in Sumgait, just north of Baku on the Caspian's west coast, emitted some 70,000 tons of toxic discharges into the city's air every year. Petrochemical industries in the town poured another 67,000 tons of waste products into the sea.[53] Four months before one of them was shut down in 1989 for emitting more than 150 times its allowed quota of soot and dust, a leading Soviet scientist observed that 90 percent of the Sumgait chemical industry's purification equipment was "worn out."[54]

Oleg Nefodov, a vice president of the USSR Academy of Sciences, applied that same description to one-third of all the Soviet chemical industry's waste control machinery and added that one-fourth was "in a dangerous state."[55] When an international conference on the problems of the Caspian Sea met in Baku in June 1991, experts testified that "the irrational use of natural resources" constituted one of the chief environ-mental plagues of the Soviet Union in general and the Caspian in particular. "Specialists gave tens of examples" of industrial practices that used, on average, "20 tons of raw materials to produce one ton of finished product."[56]

The figure was surely exaggerated, but the inefficiency and wastefulness of Soviet industry were unquestionable. From their forests, for example, Soviets got 67 to 75 percent less value in final output than other industrialized nations. Those losses start with the wood left to rot—12 to 20 cubic meters per acre—on harvested timberland. In addition, every twenty-fifth or thirtieth log floated downriver to Soviet sawmills sank or disappeared, so many in fact that "for many years Norwegian ships in the Barents Sea made a nice profit out of retrieving them."[57]

The sunken logs gave off toxic substances, phenol in particular, that poisoned the rivers and reservoirs where they rotted. Considering the vast stretches of Siberian forests that were not harvested before dams near Bratsk, Krasnoyarsk and Ust-Ilimsk flooded the woodlands, Yablokov may have been right to call the forestry industry "one of the chief destroyers of living nature in our rivers."[58]

Yet Soviet loggers were hardly alone in the race for that dubious distinction. Many Soviets would have awarded the title, hands down, to chemical manufacturers and cited Lake Ladoga as their evidence. Lying just east of Leningrad, the largest freshwater lake anywhere in Europe was once pure enough to be considered as a site for the cellulose-cord factory built at Lake Baikal. No longer. Not since industries in the region raised their output of untreated effluents from 271 million cubic meters in 1985 to 392 million in 1988, a 45 percent increase.[59]

One-seventh of that total comes from a single chemical combine, Azot. Like most of its neighbors, it fell well behind its target for installing purification devices. At the Pikalevsky alumina plant, for example, only one-third of the ample funds budgeted for a water recycling system had actually been spent by the end of 1989.[60]

Another exhibit in the case against Soviet industry, the 1,420-mile-long Dniepr River received an annual load of one billion cubic meters of polluted water, including radionuclides from Chernobyl. The contaminated water was blamed for a 40 percent rise in cancer cases in the city of Kerch over fifteen years and for an illness rate among that town's children of two or more diseases per youngster.[61]

The water treatment facilities in the Ukrainian capital of Kiev receive 6 percent more effluent from the Dniepr than they were designed to handle. Dioxin was reported in the city's water supply in the spring of 1991, and scientists conferring there advised Kievans that they would not have clean drinking water until the brewery switched over to bottling it from artesian wells.[62]

The fees to be levied on polluting industries in the city—a projected 20.3 million rubles in 1991—might be enough to finance the conversion. But they could not begin to rectify the ongoing destruction of the Dniepr. These "pathetic crumbs," said an infuriated ecologist/independence advocate, mean that "we have little choice: either we meekly stand in line to buy pure water in bottles or we work to achieve life in a truly sovereign Ukraine with a healthy economy and effective legislation. The hard truth is this: only a free people will survive in the land which experienced the disaster of Chernobyl."[63]

If fees were to be assessed in Moscow to equal the water pollution damage caused by the nine hundred or more enterprises in the Soviet capital that galvanize iron and steel products, ecological analysts said the annual amount would approximate 70 million rubles. Every day the factories, almost none of which recycle their liquid wastes, put about three tons of heavy metals into the Moscow sewer system in their incompletely purified discharges. A sophisticated cleansing process could turn these toxic wastes from slurry into ceramic tile and save on water intake at the galvanizing plants as well, one environmental scientist has argued. Until that happens, however, Muscovites will be getting cadmium and other poisons in their water and, from it, in their food.[64]

Before user fees can be levied anywhere in the Soviet Union, water meters that work will have to be installed almost everywhere. "If you could find one water meter in a thousand that was actually functioning," said a Kharkov engineer who had spent thirteen years in her city's water supply agencies, "it would be almost a miracle."[65]

Theoretically, Soviet municipalities in the 1980s charged residential users an insignificant 2.5 kopecks per cubic meter for sewer use and 4 kopecks for each cubic meter of drinking water. Water charges to commercial enterprises started at a still-negligible rate of 10 kopecks per cubic meter up to varying limits, but, because of faulty measuring devices, almost all surcharges had to be based on guesswork and bargaining. On one occasion, the Kharkov engineer recalled, "we levied a huge charge for excess water use against officials at a railroad car repair factory, but after my boss got them to agree to fix his car, he tore up the fine."[66]

CURRENTS OF CONTAMINATION

As Soviets wasted their water, they also loaded it with waste products. Where those substances were as toxic as dioxin, cadmium and phenol and whether they came from rotting logs, untreated household sewage or industrial discharges, moreover, few barriers stood between them and the nation's water supply. From dirty water, of course, it was only a short step to diseased humans.

In the course of extensive testing of drinking and surface water for chemical and bacteriological contamination in 1989, Soviet scientists found chemical pollutants in 19 percent of all their samples of the nation's drinking water and excessive bacteria levels in 12 percent. In the samples of surface water, both kinds of pollution occurred 27 percent of the time.[67]

In all categories, the most dangerous water was to be found in Central Asia, where poverty and pollution nourish each other. The rate of new cases of typhoid, a waterborne disease, ran from over three times the Soviet average in Uzbekistan to thirteen times the average in Tajikistan.[68]

The very highest level of bacteria-infested surface water—71 percent of the samples—was recorded in Georgia. Its inhabitants and the tourists who flocked to Georgia's Black Sea beaches also suffered the highest rate of digestive system ailments in the Soviet Union, almost double the 1989 national average.[69] Only 18 percent of the waste water in Georgia's main port at Batumi received any purifying treatment.[70]

Alarmingly elevated percentages of bacteria in samples of surface water were also found in Latvia (49 percent), Lithuania (38 percent) and Moldova (39 percent). The latter also had the highest count of chemical contaminants (44 percent) in its rivers, streams, reservoirs, ponds and lakes.[71] Above and beyond its problems with pesticide-related diseases discussed earlier (chapter 3), Moldova registered roughly twice the rate of new cases of viral hepatitis in 1987 and 1988 as the Russian Republic and a significantly higher rate of bacterial dysentery than its immediate neighbor, the Ukraine.[72]

Polluted water and the illnesses it spreads do not stop at political borders. Runoff from Moldovan and Ukrainian farms was the major source of the agricultural chemicals that contaminated the Dniestr River in the 1980s with pesticide loads six times the prescribed limits.[73] The Dniestr, which carried 13,000 metric tons of completely untreated waste water in 1986, held 21,000 tons in 1989.[74] Cleaner or dirtier, the river was the chief source of drinking water for the 2.6 million people in the city of Odessa and the region surrounding it. The Dniestr may be their nemesis as well.

The Odessa *oblast,* where the incidence of cancer rose by 27 percent in the fourteen years after 1975, had the highest 1988 infant mortality rate in the Ukraine. While that key measure of overall health conditions improved 28 percent for the Ukraine as a whole and most of its urban regions between 1975 and 1988, progress in the Odessa region was a much slower 10 percent.[75]

Water was a life-and-death issue in Odessa. A cholera epidemic that hit in August 1970 and forced a quarantine that delayed the opening of school by two and a half months gave "an early sign of the mounting crisis."[76] Two decades later water quality was one of the major ecological dangers that doctors blamed both for the majority of the birth defects killing 300 to 320 Odessan infants a year and for a mortality rate of 30 per thousand among children up to their fifth birthday.[77] That toll was 60 percent greater than the 1989 average for the entire Ukraine.[78]

Drinking water—in which the chlorine dose had to be doubled or tripled during summer months[79]—also became a cutting political issue in Odessa in the 1980s. Fed by the rising frequency with which municipal beaches had to be closed, popular anxiety helped ecological activists mount powerful campaigns in local elections. (See chapter 11.) Their successes in early 1990 prompted Odessa authorities first of all to consider supplying bottled drinking water to the population, then to spend a reported $250,000 in hard currency for Western technical advice on a new water treatment system.

"It has become a scandal," recounted one of the Green leaders. "We got no return on the money. The [bosses] are digging new artesian wells, and that's it." Living in the center of the lovely but rundown city, once a great health resort as well as a busy port, she said, "I have to make my own water by boiling it for 20 minutes with manganese and soda."[80]

Odessa's water problems flow onward into the Black Sea. Its gravest peril may be eutrophication—the disappearance of dissolved oxygen without which fish die, algae blossom and harmful bacteria multiply rapidly—which was first registered in the Bay of Odessa in the summer of 1990.[81] More widespread was pollution from hydrogen sulfide. Considered the substance most damaging to water quality, its level in the Black Sea rose by two-thirds from 1935 to 1985.[82]

Off the Bulgarian/Rumanian coast in the Danube River delta, moreover, levels of oil and petroleum by-products tripled in a single year to three times the permissible limit (PDK) in 1989; off Odessa they jumped from five PDK to six.[83] The Danube turned quickly from blue to muddy brown as it ran from the Black Forest to the Black Sea, where it dumped some 241,000 metric tons of untreated waste water each year to join almost 35,000 more tons of equally filthy Soviet river water.[84] In addition to the pollutants carried by the Danube and the Dniestr, the sea received heavy loads of ammoniates and nitrites from the Dniepr River and the South Bug, which experienced episodes of eutrophication itself.[85] In the Sea of Azov, connected to the Black Sea by a narrow channel north and east of the Crimean peninsula, similar deficits of dissolved oxygen have also been observed along with residues of DDT and other pesticides and high levels of oil pollution.[86]

Not all the Black Sea oil slicks were of civilian origin. A remarkably candid passage in the Goskompriroda environmental survey for 1989 even fingered the military as a major culprit:

> Among the significant sources of maritime pollution are the ships and support services of the USSR Navy. Over many years in the areas of the Bay of Sevastopol where the Black Sea Fleet is moored and fueled, the level of pollution from oil and petroleum products has been high, sometimes up to 100 times the PDK. Work on preventing oil leaks . . . is being carried out extremely slowly. There is no effective system in place to catch the overflows from heavy rains that carry higher loads of oil products into the bay. Still, the Defense Ministry plans to finish work on water catchment installations only in 1992.[87]

LAST RESORTS

Wherever the greatest fault lay, thoughtful Odessans believe that the Black Sea is dying. The tourist industry along its shores has been imperiled by pollution and breakdowns such as the leak from an inland oil pipeline in Georgia in August 1991 that closed the beaches at Sochi, some of the USSR's most popular.[88] To give summer visitors a chance at clean water, entrepreneurs at the resort of Yalta opened a water-shuttle service to a huge, floating pool they anchored several miles offshore.

The pebble beaches below the dramatic Crimean cliffs where Czarist aristocrats once came to vacation and the seventy-six major health resorts[89] dotted along the sixty miles of coast around Odessa still overflowed in 1991 with visitors from all over the Soviet Union. They sunned themselves, ate, dozed and promenaded, but fewer and fewer spent much time swimming. The water seemed dangerous, not health-giving. Off Yalta's beaches, for example, water samples infected with harmful bacteria were found in 43 percent of all the tests made in 1988. In 1989 the percentage was 60. Onshore, the town supplied drinking water for only three hours in the morning and another three in the evening.[90]

A first-time visitor to the Soviet Union in 1974 was bemused by an immense sign erected on the hills behind the complex of hotels outside Yalta. "Citizens of the USSR," the slogan boasted, "are guaranteed the right to rest."[91] But while the Soviet Constitution, even as amended in 1977, proclaims that inalienable social privilege, pollution makes it harder and harder to enjoy, either on the Black Sea or at the beaches along the sandy, pine-lined southern shores of the Baltic.

Bordered by 70 million people living in six full-fledged nations and three Soviet republics that regained their sovereignty in 1991, the Baltic, too, came under heavy pressure from the land on all sides and from the 15 percent of the world's industrial output produced around it.[92] While Poland was thought to contribute the highest volume of pollution to the almost tideless sea, the USSR was a major force in cutting the stock of spawning fish in the Baltic from 777,000 tons in the 1983 harvest to 311,000 tons in 1989.[93]

That year the Soviet Union was the source of 3.6 million metric tons of polluted surface waters that annually carried 352,000 tons of organic matter, 58,300 tons of nitrogen, 375 tons of zinc, 167 tons of copper salts and 42 tons of lead into the Baltic. Much of that poison passed through the overloaded and antiquated sewage treatment systems of Leningrad, Riga, Klaipeda and Tallinn, but one-fifth of the organic matter was traced to the fourteen Soviet pulp-and-paper plants in the region.[94]

One such plant, on the Lielupe River in the popular Latvian beach resort of Jurmala, was the target of strong environmental protests in 1988 and 1989. Its shutdown was even ordered at the start of 1990 after many candidates in Latvia's first free elections chose it as an example of Moscow's "colonialist" exploitation of their country. The closure, though made politically easier by the fact that most of the Sloka mill workers were Russians rather than Latvians, had to be rescinded within a few months. The fledgling politicians ran low on the newsprint needed for their propaganda battles.

On January 23, 1990, no local papers were printed in Latvia.[95] Within weeks, the Sloka mill was operating again with minor technological adjustments. "Nationalist sentiment triumphed over ecological feelings," commented Juris Ekstcins, a young but worldly-wise Latvian Green. "You can't run a revolution without newspapers."[96]

The greater irony was in the belated discovery that the Sloka combine was not really guilty as charged. Its liquid wastes were fouling the Lielupe as it entered the Daugava River on its way to the nearby Baltic. They were relatively minor factors, however, in the pollution that was killing the lovely pine trees along the Jurmala beach. The real culprits, as a study team directed by Dr. Grigory Barenboim discovered, were the city of Riga, upstream on the Daugava, where the sewer system had not been overhauled since 1938; the 14.2 million annual man-days of auto-borne vacationers crowding into the fifty-eight-square-mile beach area; and the 219 coal-fired hot-water heaters in the town of Jurmala itself, where tourists washed off the salt and the sand of the Baltic.

"The pulp mill was responsible for only 12 percent of the air pollution and between 17 and 20 percent of the harmful effluents in the Lielupe River," concluded Dr. Barenboim. "Its wastes accounted for just 3 to 5 percent of the problems on the Baltic beaches" that had to be closed to swimming ten days in 1989 and twenty-five the next year.[97]

Swimming had been forbidden in the Lielupe River itself since 1982 thanks to coliform index counts that rose to half a million bacteria per liter of water in the summertime. In the Daugava River, much of that filth came from Riga—104,000 tons of pollutants in 1987. One expert claimed that a 20-million-ruble investment in sewage treatment for the Latvian capital would significantly cut the Daugava's load of muck.[98]

On November 3, 1990, a polymer factory across the republic border in Belorussia added its contribution: Tons of an organic cyanide compound were accidentally discharged into the Daugava over a fifteen-hour period. The factory did not report the accident or admit responsibility until after a massive fish kill alerted people downstream two days later and Riga shut off its intake of drinking water from the river. Even then the Belorussian managers "refused to disclose details of the spill . . . because they are under contract with the Soviet military," perhaps to help make chemical weapons.[99]

Pollution abatement in Riga, where work on a wastewater treatment plant began in 1971 and was still unfinished in August 1991,[100] would not end toxic accidents, but it might pay for itself. Cleaner water could help bring the commercial catch of herring, sprat and eels in the Gulf of Riga—one-fourth the size of the original Aral Sea—back up to 90,000 tons—twice the peak Aral catch—after a two-thirds drop over twenty years.

In terms of the lost 50 million rubles in fishery income, "we are losing two Aral Seas in the Gulf of Riga," declared a construction engineer whose passion for ecology sparked much of the Jurmala protest. In addition, while cancer rates among the town's population doubled between 1975 and 1985, "not a single session of the Jurmala city council," he said, addressed ecological problems "for many years."[101]

In the midst of larger political contests and economic chaos, Soviet politicians found it increasingly difficult to deal coherently with environmental issues. Dr. Barenboim's findings, supplemented by proposals from a group of French water system engineers, went to Latvian authorities who had commissioned the Jurmala study. Preoccupied by the struggle for sovereignty and short of funds, officials deferred action.

One problem, Dr. Barenboim surmised, was that "lots of National Front deputies were elected on the promise to close the mill. They have a hard time adjusting politics to scientific reality. The truth is that scientists can't run the world; they can only advise on ways to make it better. Their tragedy is that they know what needs to be done, but no one listens to them."[102]

No one in authority was listening carefully when, to exploit a seemingly cheap source of energy, engineers in the 1960s began to drain Armenia's Lake Sevan through a new hydroelectric power plant. The lake's volume dropped so rapidly over the next decade that climatic changes brought on by the loss of water evaporation began to cut into the republic's agricultural output. Just to stabilize Sevan at a much-reduced level, Armenia has had to pump in faraway water through a mountain tunnel that cost more to cut than the energy from the power plant has been worth.[103]

Nor were Minvodkhoz planners sensitive to public or expert opinion when they set out in 1980 to construct a billion-ruble flood-control system across the Gulf of Finland at the mouth of the Neva River, the artery on which Peter the Great built his capital. The design had been repeatedly criticized over the preceding decade as both too big and too dangerous a bottleneck in the flow of Leningrad's waste water to the sea.[104]

As construction proceeded, the warnings came true with a vengeance. Not only did dissolved oxygen dwindle while algae bloomed in the Neva Bay, but water backed up to undermine the foundations of the graceful palaces that gave the city, as St. Petersburg, the soubriquet of the "Venice of the North." Elected on a wave of ecological and other protest, Leningrad's new mayor declared in 1990 that the system of dikes threatened "a real catastrophe."[105]

The city council voted in October 1990 to permit no further work on the dikes.[106] Whether or not the prohibition is honored, it did not address the main danger to water quality in the Neva and its delta: the untreated industrial and human wastes that made the river a "giant sewer pipe" and its now-constricted outlet to the Gulf of Finland "a cesspool." City treatment facilities under construction in 1990 were due to be up to handling all the household sewage in 1992, but connecting pipes will take another six years or longer to install.[107]

In the meantime, a Soviet journalist complained:

> What is frightening is not even this chronic "unrestrained filth." What is frightening is that we have gotten used to it. . . .
>   The habit of living in filth is no less contagious than other harmful habits. And we have grown accustomed to the crush on busses, wearisome waiting lines, leaking roofs, boorishness, empty store shelves, defaced facades and bad roads.

In the midst of all this we have children growing up. They look at us with amazement. And then they, too, get used to it.[108]

Habituation to sloppy lives also produced sloppy work. It did so in the 1970s at Atommash, an important machine-building installation some five miles from the giant Tsimliansky reservoir on the southern reaches of the Don River, created as part of Stalin's megalomaniacal plans to transform the face of Soviet nature. The enterprise was turning out enormously heavy equipment that had to be calibrated in microns, the kind of precision required for a new generation of a vital and risky technology. But because the factory was built on soil that no one knew to be severely waterlogged, the floor of the factory settled a few millimeters. State purchasers repeatedly found the equipment defective and sent it back for repairs that cost millions of rubles and months of delay. As a result, the installation got a poor reputation for on-time delivery, and the technology it was pioneering became suspect. Designers who needed its product had to make do with a cruder, earlier version.

One place where the old technology went was a sleepy Ukrainian town close to the Dniepr River. Instead of being able to build a power facility around the new pressurized water reactors (VVER) from the discredited Atommash assembly line, the experts in charge at the site of the Chernobyl nuclear energy plant fell back on the less-advanced channel-type uranium graphite reactors (RBMK).[109]

Under pressure to bring one of their reactors on stream, they actually did so ahead of schedule—almost an unheard-of feat—on December 20, 1983.[110] Although they did not, it was later revealed, conduct all the safety tests they should have before commissioning the facility,[111] it developed no severe or unusual problems for a number of years.

On April 26, 1986, however, in the course of tests that were both improperly run and greatly delayed, the reactor at Unit Number 4 in Chernobyl exploded. It is only somewhat exaggerated to trace the disaster back to the builders of the Tsimliansky reservoir on the Don and to the engineers who left behind no topographical charts that might have helped designers prevent the settling of the Atommash foundation which slowed the introduction of VVER reactors into the Soviet power grid.

For want of a nail . . . a kingdom can be lost. The chain reaction of ecocidal negligence that marked so much Soviet history took decades to generate an explosion that rocked the world. The chain reaction has since been slowed but it is far, far from stopped.

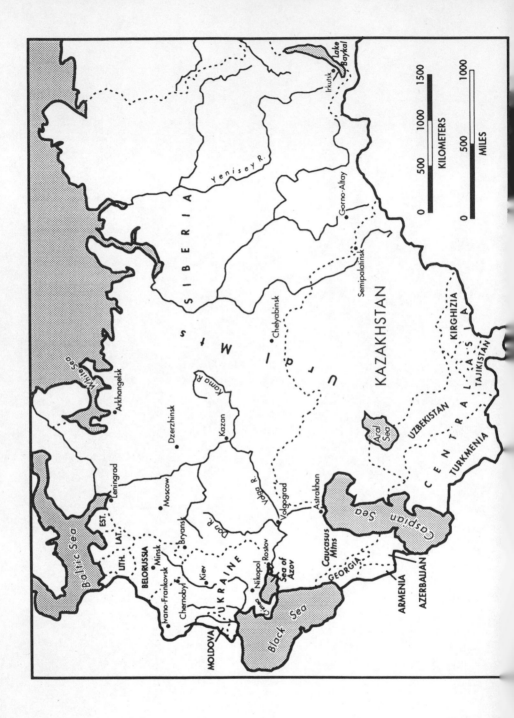

CHAPTER 7

". . . Plus Electrification"

In developing and over time draining their energy resources, Kremlin planners long behaved as if there were no tomorrow. Late in the 1980s, more than a decade after energy crises hit Western industrial nations, tomorrow finally dawned in the USSR. Accustomed to thinking themselves rich in oil, gas, coal, water power and nuclear energy, Soviets awoke, as though from an alcoholic binge, to the reality that they could no longer count on easily available and environmentally clean fuels to drive a future as prodigal as their past.

They faced a crisis on every energy front. Stagnant in the 1980s, oil output was expected to drop steeply in the 1990s.[1] Much of the remaining oil lay deep in fields that were hard to reach, tough to drill and costly to pump. Similarly, the high-grade, low-sulfur coal in the Urals and the Don River Basin—the fuel that powered decades of Soviet industrial growth—was all but used up. Untapped coal reserves were huge, but far away in Siberia, and their fuel content was as low as their capacity to pollute was high. To be turned into energy without further poisoning Soviet air, this low-grade coal would have to be burned or converted to gas through processes that looked technologically and financially beyond Moscow's short-term reach.

Expanding natural gas production could conceivably make up a large part of the domestic energy deficit, but for two considerations: its importance as an export commodity and the expense of either switching coal and oil burners to gas or replacing them with new ones.

Sales of natural gas abroad—almost half of them for hard currency—more than doubled in the 1980s, to 13 percent of total output.[2] Significantly cleaner as a fuel than most alternatives, every cubic foot of gas, like every barrel of oil, that goes to domestic use is lost to export. Holding about two-fifths of proven global reserves of natural gas[3] and seeing oil export earnings drop, the USSR faced painful trade-offs between its appetite for energy at home—especially nonpolluting power—and its need for the industrial technology, consumer goods, medical supplies and pollution control equipment available only abroad.

In Soviet energy planning before the April 26, 1986, Chernobyl disaster, controlled nuclear fission was supposed to cover a good part of the gap between rising energy demand and the stock of fossil fuels and hydroelectric power. That option died in the radioactive and political fallout from the blast. Strenuous efforts to resuscitate the peaceful atom were largely undone by continuing revelations of deception and secrecy engineered to conceal the extent of human and environmental damage stemming from Chernobyl. The lies that were told and the truths left untold have created an antinuclear public mood that seems unlikely to soften in this century.

With dam builders also under heavy attack from ecological activists, it is almost easier to imagine old hydroelectric installations being dismantled than new ones being built. The giant, costly dams on the Volga, the Dniepr and other rivers were the pride of an era inspired by Lenin's proclamation: "Communism is Soviet power plus electrification of the whole country." In those early years, some enthusiastic Soviets actually named their daughters Elektrifikatsiya (and their sons Traktor). By mid-1990, instead, Moscow crowds protesting the policies of the Communist Party of the Soviet Union were chanting "Hey, hey CPSU! Chernobyl is the place for you."[4]

The anger, when it focused on energy production, was evident on picket lines outside a new gas-condensate refinery in Astrakhan, around the construction site for a thermal power station in the green belt north of Moscow and in front of bulldozers trying to move earth for a giant dam on the Katun River in the Gorno Altai region that borders Mongolia. Intensified by fear, the bitterness breached barricades at atomic energy stations from the Ukraine to Lithuania and on to Arkhangelsk on the White Sea, to Kazan on the Volga and to Rostov, where the Don River enters the Sea of Azov.

As part of a broader political upheaval, such alarm and loathing proved a potent force. It made nuclear energy almost a pariah in a nation where the atom was once the bright, clean hope of the future. In the first five years after Chernobyl, no new reactors opened; two operating atomic energy stations closed and construction halted on thirty-nine targeted by demonstrators.[5] On eleven of them, work was cancelled.[6]

Early in 1991 the Ukrainian legislature even demanded that the three undamaged reactors at Chernobyl shut down for good by 1995, though they provided 8 percent of the republic's energy.[7] Nuclear power stations throughout the USSR should have had a generating capacity of 77 million kilowatts by the end of 1990.[8] In 1989, however, capacity reached only 37.4 million kilowatts, less than half the planned level.[9] It has declined since.

Defective steam generators in the nuclear power plants were a major source of trouble. Accidents put twenty-six out of the fifty-six supplied to just one reactor station out of commission in 1990. At another plant, generators that were supposed to have lasted thirty years worked for only five. As a result, many Soviet nuclear power plants were able to function at only half capacity.[10]

A senior energy bureaucrat may have been right, from an economic standpoint, in insisting in 1991 that in the industrial regions of the USSR where "there is a rising deficit of fossil fuels," there is "no alternative to atomic energy."[11] From a political perspective, however, he was whistling in a graveyard. The ministries of energy and of nuclear power seemed to recognize that reality when they released their joint draft twenty-year program for energy development. It offered three variants: 30 million kilowatts of new nuclear energy output, 13 million kilowatts or—if "the negative attitude of the public and local authorities cannot be reversed"—an end to building atomic power stations.[12]

Soviet power engineers faced a profound dilemma. Somehow, they had to adjust the economy's need for stable and expanding supplies of energy to the political and technical reality that Soviet conventional power resources were increasingly high-priced and increasingly under attack from environmentally conscious citizens' groups. As the appetite for energy grew, production options shrank. But the USSR had not yet made a serious start on improving efficiency in fuel use or developing alternate sources of clean power such as wind, tidal power and sunlight.

Environmental protests did not just stymie growth in nuclear power. Armed with the knowledge that the Ministry of Energy alone produced a quarter of all harmful atmospheric pollutants, ecological activists aimed their anger at the aging electricity-and-steam-generating plants, many of which were straining to keep up output at the expense of long overdue maintenance. Such leading cultural figures as the Siberian writer Valentin Rasputin, a seasoned veteran of the Baikal campaign and a controversial spokesman for militant Russian nationalism, also made hydroelectric projects a target of public scorn.

"If the energy that writers have expended in the battle with Minvodk-hoz [the Ministry of Water Resources and Land Management] could have generated kilowatt hours," Rasputin claimed in 1989 with a large measure of literary license, "we would not need any nuclear plants."[13] Many Soviets—the victims of Chernobyl, the Volga Basin farmers whose land now lies beneath the reservoirs of giant power dams and the Siberian tribes displaced by oil wells and pipelines—undoubtedly wished that writers generated electricity instead of polemics.

But eloquence turned no turbines. Without more efficient, more ecologically sound and more acceptable sources of energy, Soviet lamps could start to dim from the Baltic to the Pacific. To paraphrase the prophecy of a British diplomat on the eve of World War I, the lights may not come on again at full strength for a very long time.

ROCKS AND HARD PLACES

The paradox was one of poverty in the midst of plenty. The USSR, in fact, was richer in energy reserves and alternatives to nuclear power than any industrial nation. According to published Central Intelligence Agency estimates in 1990, the Soviet Union held 38 percent of the world's reserves of natural gas, produced more oil and gas than any other country and was third in coal output after the United States and China.[14]

Oil and gas, however, were important not just as domestic fuel sources but as generators of hard currency. Together, by the CIA's count, exports of the two fuels brought the USSR the equivalent of $30.2 billion in 1985—57.5 percent of total commodity revenues from the West that year—and, with falling world energy prices, $28.7 billion, or 42.5 percent of earnings, in 1986.[15]

The flow of both black gold and hard currency started to shrink in the mid-1980s. Crude oil production fell 9 percent in 1989 from 1987–88 levels, with another 7 percent drop predicted for 1991.[16] The CIA estimated that by 1988 Soviet hard-currency sales of oil had dropped to $9.8 billion and of gas, to $2.6 billion, just slightly more than one-third the total receipts three years earlier.[17] Partially cushioning that fall was the soaring rate of gas production, up more than 80 percent in the nine years after 1980 to the point that it supplied 53 percent of domestic energy needs in 1989.[18] If West European demand remained strong, something like that rate of expansion could be sustained into the twenty-first century. But before the turn of the century, domestic consumption could also rise, depending on the rate at which Soviet utilities and enterprises switch from polluting fuels to natural gas.

In 1991 the USSR had no shortage of oil in the ground. A single unexploited field near the Caspian Sea was thought to have reserves 250 percent larger than those of Alaska's North Slope.[19] Pumping the crude oil out of this Tengiz field and then moving it to market, however, posed major technical problems and considerable environmental risks. The former were supposed to be overcome through a twenty-five-year joint venture with the Chevron Corporation, but even after the August 1991 coup attempt against Mikhail Gorbachev, the deal remained stalled by political feuding and an expressed fear of capitalist exploitation.[20]

In the huge Tyumen fields of Western Siberia, opened in 1964 and severely depleted within fifteen years, drillers could not inject conveniently located gas to lift the oil to the surface because the USSR did not manufacture and could not afford to import the necessary compressing equipment. "We have been asking for [the compressors] for 15 years, and they are still not making them," an angry geologist protested. "So we inject water instead,"[21] a technique that had huge drawbacks. It made the oil fields so waterlogged that by 1989, two-thirds of the liquid brought to the surface was water, not oil—compared to 38 percent in 1982.[22] The mixture corroded the poorly built and maintained pipes that carried it.

Major breaks in Tyumen region oil pipelines, numbering 698 in 1988 alone,[23] contributed to an estimated loss of more than 1 million tons of spilled oil that year, about 9 percent of all Soviet output.[24] In the first six months of 1990, the number of breaks rose 15 percent over the first half of 1989, to a total of 1,132 and a loss of 300,000 tons of Tyumen oil. A single leak and fire in July at the Belozerneft field cost another 400,000 tons.[25]

Additionally, oil and gas exploration activities were blamed for putting a yearly load of some 27,000 tons of petroleum and chemical pollutants directly into Soviet waterways.[26] That volume of waste accounted for 36 percent of the petroleum and oil by-products that official monitors said they detected in Soviet water supplies in 1989. The substances were so toxic that ten grams could make one cubic meter of water (267 gallons) unfit to drink or to use in many industrial processes.[27]

Without even calculating such environmental costs, Siberian oil was becoming too energy-consuming to extract. Specialists believed that the relatively small fields located farther north of the Tyumen deposits, and others in Central Asia, could produce only half the daily output of oil needed to cover the expenses of exploration, drilling and transport.[28]

If those fields were developed with existing Soviet technology, it would be just one more example of the besetting sin of the Soviet energy sector: outrageous wastefulness. The maintenance program for the Siberian oil pipelines was typical. They broke down because even in such harsh climate and terrain, only 1 to 2 percent of total system outlays went to keep them functioning properly. U.S. and Middle Eastern producers spent five to ten times as much on pipeline maintenance as a proportion of their costs.[29]

One result was the oil spillage noted earlier. Gas pipelines also posed a growing hazard. Too often manufactured from materials that did not stand up to Siberia's frigid winters, they were guaranteed reliable for only ten years, when they should last for thirty. Every third section of pipe tested on the West Siberia-Urals-Volga line was found to be corroded.[30]

On June 3, 1989, one such pipeline had been steadily leaking gas into a huge natural bowl of Urals woodland through which ran railroad tracks and, late that evening, two heavily loaded passenger trains. A spark ignited the fumes and set off an explosion equal to 10,000 tons of TNT, or half the force of the Hiroshima atomic bomb. Of the estimated 1,200 passengers, 300 died outright. Another 700 were hospitalized.[31]

Less catastrophic but still a serious problem, the gas pipelines damaged the settled land they crossed. The builders were supposed to compensate for such destruction with financial help to housing, health care, educational and pollution-control budgets in the affected areas. The payments, if made at all, were rarely adequate.

In the Sverdlovsk *oblast* alone, complained a whistle-blowing public health doctor, the construction of 3,750 miles of natural gas pipelines and pumping stations cost over 30 billion rubles, none of it spent to "recultivate land damaged" by the pipe-laying nor to "create decent living conditions for the local population."[32]

Energy-related pollution, moreover, only started at ground level. It was a major threat to clean air throughout the USSR as well. The Ministry of Energy and its aging utilities produced 14.5 million tons of stationary-source emissions in 1989. Only the metallurgical industry had a higher pollutant output. Harmful emissions from direct production of energy, including 10 million tons of soot from gas flares in West Siberia alone, were not far above the 12 million tons further attributable to gas and oil processing and refining.[33]

These statistics understate the actual volume of pollution caused by the energy sector. (See chapter 5.) Until the late 1980s, the USSR made little systematic effort to define the social costs of such pollution in a way that would let citizens and their leaders weigh the value of industrial production against the damage done to human and economic well-being. The calculations were not easy to make, and the results achieved by two senior Soviet economists were at best approximations. Their conclusions, reached by assigning air pollution a 43 to 45 percent weight in "worsening public health," were nonetheless noteworthy.[34]

Counting the cost of a day lost to illness at ten to thirty rubles, they fixed the total financial harm caused by nonnuclear power generating, oil, gas and coal extraction and refining and energy transport in 1989 at 4.6 billion rubles.[35] A significant fraction of GNP, that sum equaled the 1983 capital costs of bringing 8,000 megawatts on stream.[36] The Soviet economists concluded that 61 percent of the ecological harm, in ruble terms, fell on the Russian Republic and 83 percent derived from thermal and other conventional-fuel power stations—the venerable, even decrepit, installations that produced four-fifths of the nation's electricity.[37]

Another, though more disputed instance of cost-*un*consciousness was the flooding behind hydroelectric dams. A senior energy official put those losses at 15 million acres of Soviet territory since the 1920s, including 6 million acres of cropland. In his telling, the inundation of 3 percent of the nation's arable land was a fair trade-off: Hydroelectric power produced the same amount of energy as 70 tons of fossil fuel that, if burned, would emit 1.2 million tons of ash and 2.2 million tons of sulfur and nitric oxides.[38]

Soviet ecologists countered that such a calculus was too primitive. In their ledgers it failed to take into account the effect of slowing down the naturally self-cleansing flow of rivers and the consequent rise in species-destroying bacteria and other pollutants in waters that should have been rich in fish. The official equation of clean hydroelectric energy against flooded farm fields also, they said, left out the seepage that turned fertile riverside soil into swamps. Finally, they disputed the arithmetic itself. Valentin Rasputin argued that dam builders on the Volga and Kama rivers alone had flooded 6 million "highly fertile" acres in the heart of Russia in order to add an equal amount to the total of irrigated land along the Volga. But their work was so badly done that one-fifth of the supposedly improved acreage was severely waterlogged, either completely useless or in urgent need of reclamation.[39]

In the Saratov region, between Volgograd and the Caspian Sea, a plan to double the amount of irrigated land by the year 2000, Rasputin warned, would also presumably require doubling the existing network of 3,000 miles of canals, 5,500 miles of water pipes and 3,800 pumping stations. To power those added stations would require half again as much electricity as the 1 million kilowatts that the existing Saratov hydroelectric station provided to all consumers in the region.[40]

Rasputin professed to see a conspiracy by the "monstrous edifice" of the water and power bureaucracy to ignore technical reality and public opinion everywhere in order to take "long-range precautions against possible abundance."[41] Infuriated that the Katun dam in the mountains of Gorno Altai was being built despite assurances it would not be, in the absence of any approved plan or environmental impact assessment and in opposition to the "seething emotions" of nature lovers, he stormed:

> Will the hydroelectric stations on the lower Volga be enough? Will the Ural and Don lands [where other water projects are planned] be enough? And what about the water of the Volga? . . .
>
> For whose benefit? Who can explain why this is being done? We usually say it is a result of narrow [ministry or agency] interests. Why do we call them "narrow" if they are broader than the national interest?[42]

"WE SIMPLY SQUANDER ENERGY"

Overriding all interests, "narrow" and "broad," was a seeming instinct for profligacy. The trait was pervasive in a land where resources always appeared to be limitless and in a culture long noted for its expansiveness and nonchalance about material concerns. In energy use, these grasshopper attitudes produced astonishing waste.

"The idea that we are extravagant is undoubtedly true. We simply squander energy," conceded a highly placed Soviet power industry official in the fall of 1990.

> Our wastefulness at times reaches fantastic proportions. But statements that we can solve all our problems just by energy savings alone . . . put me on guard. This is an illusion, an extremely dangerous one.
>
> Yes, ideally we could save a third of the power generated . . . an estimated 900 million tons of standard fuel equivalent by 1995. But . . . a more realistic figure is 150–160 million tons a year. At present, we save about 80 million.[43]

Forecasting the need for huge new outlays in machinery and machine-building capacity to effect such economies, he defended nuclear power as the cheapest course and an urgent one to pursue. Soviet reserve energy capacity, the industry spokesman revealed, stood at only "4 to 6 percent, versus a standard of 13 to 15." Overloaded by demand, he added, traditional power stations were having to work their machinery "in simply barbarous fashion" to the point that equipment with "a total capacity of 40 million kilowatts [12 percent of all generating capacity] has completely exhausted its service life but continues to operate."[44]

The deputy minister of power told a Soviet radio interviewer a few months later that the energy "situation is very alarming, even critical." While thirty years earlier the country was bringing 10 million kilowatts a year on stream, it is now "commissioning between three to four million." The old generators, he added, are "becoming obsolete" faster than their output can be made up, and instead of "preventive maintenance, I would say . . . they should simply be written off and put out of service."[45]

Something would have to replace them, and until the end of the century or a somersault in public attitudes toward atomic power, it is hard to see what that something would be. Yet without steady power output *and* huge strides in energy efficiency, the Soviet economy will be crippled, and standards of living, already depressed, will plummet further.

Presumably, industrial activity would be first and hardest hit. Industry accounted for two-thirds of the energy used in the USSR in 1985— compared to its 37 percent share in the United States—and severe power cutbacks would be likely to slow or shut many large assembly lines from the Urals westward into the European regions of the USSR.[46] Soviet drivers would probably not face as many of the long waits at the fuel pump that infuriated Americans in 1973 and 1979; transport in 1985 took only 12 percent of USSR energy consumption. Residential and commercial demand amounted to 23 percent.[47] But producers and householders alike would have to drive farther and wait longer to find supplies of all sorts. The intensity of the shortages would depend on where managers of the Soviet Union's unified power system decided to cut back first, but a drop in energy availability would soon show up in reduced production of steel and chemicals, then of machinery, appliances and fertilizer and, rippling through the economy, of food, clothing and new housing.

Conceivably, such an energy crunch could drive manufacturers to raise their energy efficiency and cut the volume of power they waste. Such therapy is long overdue, and the twenty-year energy-sector development plan assumed that conservation would result in "reducing the rate of increase in electric power output by 35 to 40 percent."[48]

Goskompriroda's chief said in 1990 that it should be "possible to save 40 percent of our energy, one-half by better insulating apartment houses, the other by changing economic policy. We have too many tractors, which, in addition, are too heavy. We use too much steel [and too much energy in its manufacture]."[49]

Such savings require not just changed economic policies but heavy initial investments as well from limited Soviet capital. "How hard it is to live within our means!" lamented Moscow's deputy mayor. "Especially if we have none."[50]

A long-term cure could work. Clearly, it is needed. Power projects consume 15 percent of all capital investments in Soviet industry. But the capital is so inefficiently utilized that it takes Soviets ten times as much energy to produce a ton of ammonia as Americans or Japanese and 24 percent more power to manufacture a ton of steel from electric furnaces.[51]

Over time it should be possible to cut losses in the transmission of electricity from 9 percent to about half that level, the standard in many Western countries.[52] Over time and with effective pricing, it should be possible to put ferrous metallurgy producers on a diet so that *just the energy they waste* would no longer "exceed the output of all nuclear power plants."[53] Over time it should be possible for Soviets to apply the advanced technology in underground coal gasification and in gas turbines that they pioneered decades ago only to hand off to American and Japanese firms for practical development.[54] Over time and with a radically revised approach to energy and to economic management, the USSR could reach 1991 U.S. efficiency levels—far from the highest in the world. That progress alone would enable Soviets to get by on 72 percent less power than they generated in 1987.[55]

But in the early 1990s time was running out, and popular indignation was running high. It threatened to generate more heat and light than the overtaxed political power grid could handle without an explosion.

Early in June 1990 nearly three hundred residents of the city of Nikopol rowed across a reservoir on the Dniepr River below the Zaporozhe hydroelectric station, a hallowed, functioning relic of the first Five-Year Plan, to confront engineers building a sixth nuclear reactor. In nearby Nikopol, the protesters claimed, pollution from radioactivity was already dangerous.[56] Six weeks later and some four hundred miles west, a different group of Ukrainian Greens camped out in tents around the construction site of three new reactors at the Khelmnitsky atomic power station, where "thirty-five shutdowns and several fires" at the original unit in a three-year period had given "grounds for people to be alarmed."[57]

Anxiety overwhelmed all official reassurances that nuclear energy was safe, that the number of accidents and unplanned power outages were few and on the decline. "We understand and approve of these Greens' activities," the Nikopol plant's chief engineer told a Soviet reporter. Claiming to be as concerned for the environment as the band of protesters, he added, "The difference consists of the fact that we have information and do not hide it, and the people we are talking to do not want to hear anything."[58]

The dialogue of the deaf left the journalist despondent:

> People already do not believe anyone: neither reports, nor dosimeters, nor opinions of foreign experts. . . . It is impossible to blame Nikopol residents for this. They and really all of us have been deceived too many times.
>
> But it is also irrational to close the plant just on the wave of emotion. [The] picketing . . . is an act of despair.[59]

Irrational or not, the Ukrainian parliament on August 2, 1990, echoed the cry of *vox populi*. Legislators pronounced the entire republic an "ecological disaster area" and ordered an immediate, five-year halt to all construction work on nuclear plants.[60] Only a few years earlier that decree would have been as hollow as the environmental regulations the Ukraine had adopted in the 1970s to mandate closed-cycle water-cooling systems at atomic energy installations. Central authorities overruled that requirement in 1977 to let a reactor near Nikolaev be built without the eighteen-month delay and without the 10 to 12 percent cost increase that compliance would have entailed.[61]

In 1990 as well, the Ukrainian deputies' sweeping decision might have been dismissed as another skirmish over turf in the fierce "war of laws, war of sovereignties" being fought between Moscow and its restive subjects. Even five years after Mikhail Gorbachev launched *perestroika,* the Soviet nuclear industry—like the ministries of energy, of metallurgy, of machine building, of water resources and land management, of the timber industry—might still have brushed off the attempt by local authorities to have a say in the workings of the command economy and its massive, centralized bureaucracies.

"WE NEED A PROPAGANDIST"

But by 1991 the aftershocks of the April 1986 Chernobyl disaster had irrevocably changed the political landscape and the internal balance of forces. One sign of the new times was the July 1990 order from nuclear safety monitors to limit all RBMK reactors—the Chernobyl model—to operating at no more than 70 percent of capacity. Admitting what had long been suspected, the agency disclosed that the aging units, installed between 1965 and 1975, had been started up "when there were no national standards and safety rules for atomic power stations."[62] By year's end the cutbacks had gone beyond curtailing the load on Chernobyl-type reactors. On December 9, 1990, an independent Soviet news agency reported a Kremlin decision to suspend construction on most nuclear power plants.[63]

The retreat from the promise of the "peaceful atom," a tactical withdrawal in political terms, amounted to a near rout for Soviet energy planners.

- They had seen coal production drop almost one-fourth, to 552 million tons in 1990 from 718 million tons in 1985, partly because of miners' strikes that also cut 1991 deliveries.[64]
- They had watched oil and gas condensate output begin to slip from its peak of 624 million tons in 1987 and 1988 to 607 million tons in 1989 and 570 million tons in 1990.[65] At midyear Soviet statisticians projected 1991 oil production at just 528 million tons, a precipitous 15 percent drop in a short three years.[66]
- Soviet power managers even saw Valentin Rasputin, the ardent foe of their plans to build ninety-three new hydroelectric stations, installed in 1990 as a member of Gorbachev's short-lived but imposingly titled Presidential Council.

Facing a shortfall in the 1990s of 109 million kilowatts[67]—almost one-third of 1989 capacity[68]—and an onslaught of criticism, the Soviet power industry tried to clean up both its act and its image. As protests against nuclear reactors swelled in mid-1990, safety monitors released data to show that although unscheduled shutdowns rose by 15 percent in the first half of the year, "no nuclear violations or serious technical violations were recorded" at any of the forty-six Soviet power reactors, eleven research reactors or twelve reactors on nuclear-powered civilian ships. They claimed as well that it was "extremely rare" to move radioactive wastes away from reactor sites, but admitted there were "breakdowns in discipline" even in that area of nuclear safety.[69]

To fortify the statistics, the Party and government orchestrated a public relations effort that mixed threats with reassurances. *Pravda*'s deputy science editor reminded readers, "You cannot help wondering: In freezing nuclear power engineering, will we not freeze ourselves next winter?"[70] In an appeal to President Gorbachev in the fall of 1990, workers as well as managers from the nuclear energy industry termed "radiophobia . . . fear of the unknown." They asked for "legal protection . . . from the acts of extremists," expanded international monitoring of reactor safety and wide publication "of the full truth about the state of power engineering, the place of nuclear power in the ecology and the economy and the consequences of the energy crisis for our country."[71]

The same official journal that printed their plea gave a senior spokesman for nuclear power considerable space to argue that "not only ordinary people but even those in power do not recognize the danger" of the approaching Soviet energy crisis.[72] While he conceded that energy efficiency was needed, he weighed the fact that "about 60 percent of the [conventional] thermal stations are half-way worn out . . . becoming decrepit and entering a period of increased risk" against an immediate capacity shortage of 6 million kilowatts and concluded that the risk associated with nuclear power could be made "acceptable." With a bitter edge to his words, he observed: "Note that none of those who call for closing down nuclear power stations dare to tell the people that they will live even worse than now. Moreover, when various councils of people's deputies approve moratoria on atomic-energy-station construction, is there not one deputy who will think about who will provide the region with electricity?"[73]

The nuclear industry's efforts to regain public confidence were impressive but unavailing. "Fear of the unknown" was fed by a torrent of information, not all of it accurate, about the aftermath of Chernobyl. Against such a flood of anxiety, the official public relations campaign was an exercise in futility.

In a way it seemed to echo the cry for help that Anelia Romanovna Perkovska heard not long after the explosion. She was then a secretary of the Komsomol committee in the town of Pripyat, home to the workers at the Chernobyl atomic station and their dependents, 50,000 people in all. Not until more than eighteen hours after the blast did experts flown in from Moscow finally acknowledge that the reactor had been destroyed, that its burning core was still pouring out radiation and that helicopters had to be used to dump thousands of tons of sand onto the nuclear conflagration. Crews were put to shoveling the sand from a town stockpile, but the work was hard, the weather was hot and the pace began to slacken.

Anelia Perkovska then witnessed a scene that could have been drawn from the most hackneyed films about ardent Party agitators exhorting weaker colleagues to greater effort at crucial moments. As she recalled it, "The sand was loaded into sacks. There were many people [from other cities] who had been posted to the town. Lads ran up from Ivano-Frankovsk. And they said: 'We need a propagandist.' That sounded really military. 'We need a propagandist, the guys there are already exhausted.' "[74]

145

CHERNOBYL: COSTS OF CATACLYSM

In May 1986 the last bag of sand, tied with strips of red bunting that the Pripyat Komsomol had been saving for May Day festivities, plunged into the glowing crater of Chernobyl reactor Number 4. That month Pripyat itself became a ghost town. Its residents were the first of 100,000 people required to evacuate land and homes inside a twenty-mile radius from the reactor. Over the next four years 90,000 others, from farther away, were forced to move; in April 1990 orders were issued to relocate 14,000 more.[75]

In November 1986 a concrete tomb fifty-nine feet thick in some places closed—at least for a while*—over the remaining 180 tons of radioactive fuel, most of it uranium, but including more than half a ton of plutonium.[78] And in 1987 Soviet authorities decided to blame the explosion on the human errors of the plant's on-site operators—and on no one higher up.

Few ordinary citizens accepted any of the verdicts as a full disclosure. Fewer still accepted as final the official count of 145 cases of blast-induced radiation sickness, including 31 deaths. The Chernobyl Union, a citizens' lobby, claimed in 1990 that roughly 300 people had died because of the accident.[79] In 1989 the group put the total of fatalities among civilians and soldiers pressed into cleanup duty and known as liquidators at 256.

Yury Shcherbak, a Ukrainian cardiologist who became a Chernobyl chronicler, a Green leader and, in 1991, the republic's highest appointed environmental official, contended that the figure should be 5,000.[80] One researcher who had worked in the zone ever since the blast said that Shcherbak's estimate "is not unrealistic. More than 500,000 people were irradiated, so it is a probable percentage."[81] The top scientist in charge of the evacuation zone put the toll of fatalities in the first five years at 7,000 to 10,000.[82] Weighing his assumptions against actuarial data for the age groups concerned, others thought it more likely that 4,000 of the liquidators brought in to help remove and bury the lethal debris had died prematurely by the spring of 1991.[83]

Even the estimated costs of the disaster—9 billion rubles, 4.8 million

---

*Designers of the sarcophagus gave its useful life as twenty to thirty years, but scientists soon began working on ways either to replace the containment structure or to disassemble and move the parts of the shattered reactor so that no new chain reaction could begin in the rubble.[76] A Soviet legislator investigating the accident and its aftermath has charged that an explosive dust buildup inside the tomb was still possible and that underground water contamination from leaking radiation could ruin the Dniepr River as a water source for 38 million people in the southern Ukraine.[77]

people harmed and 200,000 resettled, 50,566 square miles (a bit more than the area of Alabama) contaminated with cesium-137[84]—are widely acknowledged to be understatements. A senior energy industry analyst put long-term economic charges at 160 to 205 billion rubles over and above cleanup costs.[85]

Crop losses from the contaminated land, by his calculations, will amount to 57.5 to 94.5 billion rubles by the year 2000, and the cost of power not generated by the destroyed reactor over those years will run to almost 67 billion rubles. Another 35 to 45 billion, he estimated, will go to resettlement costs, extra payments to radiation victims and decontamination work. He assigned 10 billion rubles more as losses on nuclear reactors that have to be closed and on improving safety controls for those that stay open.[86]

The question of radiation-induced illness became the most disputed of all the unresolved issues. A top Ukrainian health official told fellow parliamentarians in February 1990, for instance, that 1 million of their 52 million constituents—250,000 of them children— were still living in places where background radiation was too high. Additionally, some 120,000 liquidators resident in the republic needed more and better medical attention.[87] In the eight months after the Chernobyl blast, he added, 5,800 children and 7,000 adults were exposed to doses of radiation affecting their thyroid glands in ways expected to impair and shorten their lives.[88] Statistics for 1990 showed twenty-two cases of thyroid cancer among Ukrainian children, an affliction he said had been "isolated" before 1986.[89]

An American journalist who reported from the USSR in 1986 returned five years later to find that of Ukrainian and Belorussian peasants and townspeople in the fallout zone, as many as 75,000, by her count, were still farming abnormally radioactive soil and eating the produce from it.[90] In summary, she wrote: "Far more land was poisoned than can ever be cleaned—or evacuated. Far more people are eligible for resettlement than will be moved. Far more illness is evident than Soviet officials ever predicted. Far more clean food, far more medical care, far more money is needed than a country staggered by other troubles can give."[91]

Far more truth remained to be told, as well, both about the origins of the accident and about its long-lasting effects on human health. Some of the latter would not be known for decades. One American biologist expected only 1,000 to 7,500 Chernobyl-related cases of cancer in the USSR over fifty years. A U.S. biophysicist, by contrast, predicted that Soviet *fatalities* will total 50,000 and perhaps reach five times that number. Both forecast that eventual radiation-caused deaths outside the USSR will equal those within it.[92]

MIND OVER MATTER

For their part, many Soviet experts stuck to the official line that radiation sickness was basically a mental problem. They claimed that fear and accompanying stress were the primary causes of the many complaints of illness among Chernobyl's liquidators and people who live or lived in the fallout zones.

While largely accepted by several prestigious international bodies, among them the International Atomic Energy Agency (IAEA), the World Health Organization and the International Red Cross,[93] the contention was also widely disputed. The official Soviet view gained support from a study released in 1991 by Columbia University and Audubon Society researchers who focused on "a small wave of excess cancers" among people who lived near the Three Mile Island power plant when an accident imperiled its reactor in 1979. The "modest post-accident increase in cancer," the report said, "is unlikely to be explained by radiation emissions . . . [and] might reflect the impact of accident stress."[94]

Confusing, though not necessarily contradicting, that finding were the results of a long-term study of American laboratory workers exposed to "very low levels of nuclear radiation for many years." The group examined—8,318 white males who worked at the Oak Ridge National Laboratory in Tennessee from 1943 to 1972—included 1,524 who had died, 28 of them from leukemia. That proportion put the sample's leukemia death rate 63 percent above the level that would be normal for such a population group. The "association between cancer mortality and radiation doses at a very low level . . . is disturbing," said the epidemiologist who oversaw the research.[95]

His guarded conclusion would tend to back up the arguments many Soviets have made against the official guidelines on what constituted a maximum permissible lifetime level of exposure to radiation. A senior radiobiologist, for instance, said the allowable dosage (35 rem) used to judge the degree of danger in contaminated areas was too high and too broad. It had to be lowered, she argued, for children and adjusted to reflect radiation's demonstrated effect on the immune system and possible effect in mutating human genes.[96]

The initial IAEA study on the Chernobyl aftermath released in May 1991, after a year's work, held that "reported adverse health effects attributed to radiation have not been substantiated."[97] The authors checked 22,000 people living on 10,000 square miles of Ukrainian, Belorussian and Russian territory in the path of the Chernobyl plume, but did not monitor the health of those evacuated from homes within twenty miles of the reactor. A spokesman for Greenpeace, a militant environmental group, promptly denounced the report as a "white-wash," and even the USSR's representative at the IAEA said the study had not looked hard enough at long-term health issues.[98]

Early indications were that illness rates were on the rise—and apparently not due to stress alone. Two Belorussian immunologists, for instance, found tuberculosis occurring by mid-1989 twice as often among young children and adolescents in the Gomel *oblast* where fallout was heavy as in the republic as a whole.[99] Widely dispersed by the first evacuation, the children of Pripyat and the smaller town of Chernobyl itself were not traced by the outside researchers. Nor were Soviets willing to divulge the results of any studies they might have done on the youngsters.[100]

One early analysis showed relatively little change in the Gomel region's cancer rates or thyroid illness, but "an increase in the number of children born with congenital developmental defects, including mental retardation."[101] Whatever reassurance that data provided was dissipated by the disclosure in mid-1991—coming from the *oblast* Party committee—that thyroid cancer cases among the region's children were running nine times above their April 1986 level and that the overall incidence of cancer was up to 246 cases per 100,000 people, compared to 202 per 100,000 five years earlier.[102]

The Belorussian minister of health at the time of Chernobyl also acknowledged increasing incidence of relatively minor ailments—anemia and chronic ear, nose and throat complaints—among children in the most affected areas. Among adults there, along with stress-related hypertension and peptic ulcers, he saw "a trend toward a rise in the incidence of leukemia."[103] He noted, with considerable justification, that comparative statistics were probably skewed by the more intensive levels of post-Chernobyl medical attention the population was getting, including better and earlier diagnoses of disease. More to the point was the history of illness in Hiroshima after the 1945 bombing, which released one-tenth the radioactivity of the Chernobyl blast.

The risk of fatal leukemia, higher for youngsters than for adults, appeared to rise noticeably in the first three years after the atomic explosions in Japan and to peak after six or seven years. Nearly 42,000 survivors of Hiroshima and Nagasaki were studied between 1950 and 1985. Because the youngest of them only entered their most cancer-prone years in 1985, researchers who did find a "remarkable excess risk" of cancer among those who were less than ten years old at the time of the blasts had not been able to determine conclusively by then the effect of early radiation exposure on their lives and lifespans.[104]

Not until nine years after the March 1954 fallout from a U.S. bomb test in the Pacific exposed 290 Marshall Islanders to radiation levels similar to those generated by Chernobyl did the victims grow precancerous thyroid nodules. "And the cancers themselves didn't show up for several years after that," an American science journalist has noted.[105] If illnesses among Chernobyl victims follow the Japanese and Marshall Island patterns, the full health effects of the accident will not be known for several decades.

COVERUP AND CONTROVERSY

Vladimir Lupandin, a Soviet psychiatrist with forty-five years of clinical experience, however, found what he called persuasive evidence that even exposure to very low doses of radiation was responsible for a distinct rise in ailments of the nervous system among the young and not-so-young. Rebutting the contention that "radiophobia" (or "accident-stress," as it was called by Americans), and not radiation itself, was to blame, he reported that careful pediatric surveys in the Bryansk *oblast*, the Russian Republic region most subjected to Chernobyl fallout, found "70 to 80 percent of the children up to the age of fourteen suffering from severe headaches, unusual fatigue and depression."[106]

The Bryansk youngsters' symptoms, he contended, matched similar data from the areas around the Semipalatinsk nuclear testing ground in Kazakhstan and the Chelyabinsk region of the Urals, where a nuclear accident in 1957 remained a state secret until the late 1980s. (See chapter 8.) He also asserted that in a group of eight hundred liquidators whose health had been scrupulously monitored, the "same curve" of nervous-system complaints was evident.[107]

Another well-informed Soviet who asked not to be identified said that a 1990–91 study of 10,000 soldiers brought in to clean up the off-limits zone established around the Chernobyl reactor in 1986 found similar indications of rising illness rates, especially nerve diseases, among those whose exposure had supposedly been low. The study, prepared for the USSR Supreme Soviet under the direction of the chief of the Obninsk Institute of Medical Radiology, still bore a top-secret stamp in mid-1991. In the face of evidence that many Soviet scientists took as proof that even low-level radiation damaged health, the unpublished report endorsed the theory that "radiophobia" was the major cause of post-Chernobyl distress.[108]

Given the battle of wills between pro- and antinuclear forces inside the USSR, full and frank disclosure of the health consequences of Chernobyl will inevitably be long in coming. A good deal of the data will be publicized as much to argue a point of view as to advance scientific inquiry. The first detailed but very incomplete admissions just of the scope and intensity of the fallout did not emerge until nearly three years after the blast. Even then, Yury Izrael, head of the State Committee on Hydrometeorology, sought to reassure *Pravda*'s readers: "Radioactive contamination will always be a cause for concern, but if the norms and instructions of the USSR Ministry of Public Health and the State Agro-Industrial Committee are observed, it poses no danger to the health of the population."[109]

He also tried to keep public opinion on the side of nuclear power, "when properly operated . . . the cleanest source of energy."[110] Very much on the defensive in 1990 for not having made public the State Committee's maps and findings showing radiation contamination in Bryansk *oblast* and other Russian Republic areas, he pleaded to a special Supreme Soviet session on Chernobyl's fourth anniversary that in 1986, "the procedure was such that in the event of serious accidents, this information was privileged and was being offered to all the organisations dealing with eliminating this accident."[111]

By then residents of the Russian Republic and their elected representatives were infuriated that the "privileged" nature of the data had been used to hide contamination, especially fallout in the rural Bryansk *oblast*. Not until September 1989 were the people there told that their area had been widely and severely hit, and only in February 1990 were middle-level officials in Bryansk and neighboring regions allowed to see a formerly top-secret map of radiation dangers on their territory.[112]

Higher authorities had already quietly ruled that forty-four settlements in the region had to be evacuated. They had also decided to provide the grand total of one refrigerator and one washing machine per 1,000 people to residents who, to protect their health, would have to avoid food grown on their own soil and wash radioactive dust from their clothes almost daily.[113]

With contamination in one Bryansk subdistrict running at 15 to 40 curies per square kilometer in early 1990, children were developing enlarged thyroid glands and chronic fatigue. Their parents, moreover, were forbidden to gather the local berries and mushrooms that had long served as vitamin supplements in an area where imported fruit and vegetables cost more than most peasant families could afford.[114]

In April 1991 Soviets found out even more about how much had been kept secret from them and by whom. A Ukrainian journalist, a member of the Soviet Congress of People's Deputies, exposed a pattern of secrecy inside the Ministry of Public Health. Its Third Main Directorate, a special and little-known unit formed in 1947 to monitor health and treat illness among those who worked on atomic energy, had issued a June 27, 1986, gag order to its 100,000 staffers in 153 medical units and 12 research installations.[115]

Items in the directive, "On Intensifying the Regime of Secrecy" about Chernobyl's consequences, read: "4. Information about the accident is to be kept classified. . . . 8. Information about the results of medical treatment is to be kept classified. 9. Information about the extent of radioactive injuries suffered by personnel who took part in the elimination of the consequences of the accident . . . is to be kept classified."[116]

THE WAGES OF FEAR

Despite those strictures, more and more, mostly fragmentary and perhaps misleading, reports of health problems leaked out and fed public anxiety. The coverup backfired to the point that out of four hundred patients at a Kiev radiation study center, all but one told opinion surveyors that they did not believe their doctors.[117] Fear of radiation even kept some young doctors from reporting for duty in the Gomel *oblast* three years after the explosion.

"Of 329 medical school graduates who were assigned to us," said the region's chief public health administrative officer, "86 did not show up. Many experienced doctors are leaving the *oblast;* 45 went abroad. It used to be a good place to work and live. It's bad now, and people are running away."[118]

The doctors, at least, were probably fleeing public anger. A Soviet journalist in the Belorussian capital of Minsk reported in September 1990 that authorities there had dropped criminal charges against a group of Gomel region doctors accused of a kind of collective malpractice in the wake of the explosion. Not only had they reportedly failed properly to examine 50,000 local residents, 5,000 of them children, but they had also, it was said, falsified data to conceal health "anomalies" in every one of their patients under three, in 62 percent of those three to seven years old, and in 13 percent of those up to fifteen years old. Administratively disciplined, in a few cases fired, all the physicians went unprosecuted, and the statistics they produced went into the records as more evidence that Chernobyl fallout had caused only limited harm to human health.[119]

Those statistics were human beings. They had grievances and no longer feared to air them, to demand recompense and to insist on truth telling. A young Donbas coal miner from Dzerzhinsk, pressed into cleanup duty at Chernobyl in August 1986, apologetically but determinedly wrote to the editors of *Komsomolskaya Pravda* a simply worded, harrowing account of "the real truth" about Chernobyl.

The paper, in the 1990s a particularly bold source of investigative reporting on Chernobyl, put Vladimir Shilov's *cri de coeur* on its front page:

> We wore no means of protection except for a gauze mask. They called us the "green robots" . . . and we worked hauling bricks, washing the walls of unit number 4, up on the roof tossing down shards of graphite, down in the cellar bailing out radioactive water in buckets. . . .
>
> It went on that way for about a month in the zone. The whole time we were there no doctor looked at us. The food was so-so, but you could drink as much mineral water as you wanted. . . .
>
> Every trip to unit number 4 was recorded as an exposure of either .5 roentgen or 1.5 roentgen even though we worked in special places where you could only stay 10 to 15 minutes. . . . Once six of us were carrying water out of the basement—we were there an hour, I counted. . . . As the senior member of the group, I measured the radiation: up to 70 roentgens coming from the dirt and up to 45 from the water. But the supervisor who had put us on that detail would only record an exposure of 1.5 roentgens for us for the hour.
>
> I put it to him straight: "How can you write down such a low dose when we were in the cellar for a full hour? You ought to write the truth, the way it really was." But he told us: "I don't have the right to record any dose that high. I can see it, but I can't do anything about it. The bosses would chew me out."[120]

Shilov, complaining of aching legs and bouts of dizziness and amnesia, worried that he and his co-workers dared not have offspring because "our children would be cripples." He and other "liquidators," he said, "have been cheated" of privileges and protection, financial compensation or the right to go to the head of the line for an apartment or even a kitchen appliance. "We carried out our duty, and now, slowly and in silence, we are dying."[121]

That epitaph was not quite accurate. If anything, the noise level of post-Chernobyl alarm and protest rose with each anniversary of the disaster. The anger fed independence movements in the Ukraine and even in long-suffering, politically long-dormant Belorussia. Fear sparked strikes in the Gomel *oblast* and even a July 1990 march from there to Moscow, ending in an audience with the Soviet prime minister.[122] And the anxiety won a steady trickle of compensatory payments to Chernobyl victims who pressed their demands as voters.

The trickle might have been larger and faster, the Soviet press charged, if Party officials had not misused Chernobyl relief funds. Out of 500 million rubles that were authorized in 1990 to help children uprooted by the evacuation or exposed to fallout, a Moscow paper reported in 1991 that almost all had gone to regional Party committees and almost none to the victims.[123] An angry Party member in Belorussia wrote that while Chernobyl survivors' needs were going untended, *apparatchiks* had "spent 7.9 million rubles alone for the upkeep of official automobiles!"[124]

In response to such anger, Belorussia's government agreed in August 1990 to send an extra 15 rubles a month to more than 1,250,000 of its citizens living with background radiation of 1 to 5 curies per square kilometer.[125] A month earlier the Ukrainian parliament voted to let evacuees take ownership of state property free of charge as well as be reimbursed for the expense of building themselves new rural homes. Adding to earlier bonuses for the refugees—25 percent salary boosts, thirty-ruble-a-month food supplements, early retirement rights—the legislators also granted free prescription medicines to radiation victims.[126]

The republic's Council of Ministers quickly sweetened the pot with a decision that raised wages by 20 percent for farmers in settlements where the land remained too radioactive to produce safe food.[127] And the Ukrainian minister of health saw even higher bills to come: 2.5 billion rubles just to supply his ministry with needed equipment and expertise and, perhaps, 7 billion rubles more to inhabitants of Kiev, if they and the city are designated as Chernobyl victims.[128]

"LETTING THE CHIPS FLY"

Most such responses to the Chernobyl tragedy, even more than five years after the event, had an air of improvisation to them. So, of course, did Soviet political life in the crucial battle for power at the center and for a new ordering of individual and state rights and responsibilities. And so, inevitably, did Soviet energy policy across the board.

In the face of mounting crisis, officials could contrive only temporary expedients, half-measures, splints on an increasingly crippled structure in need of radical surgery. Fortunately for them, Soviets were adept at making do.

Workmen have learned to patch, to tinker and to keep obsolete machinery functioning in the energy and other sectors. The Soviet engineers who would have to mine and move Siberia's coal, oil and gas reserves have learned to live with and often to master the distances and the climatic and terrain difficulties involved. But the decades of profligacy in the pursuit of megawattage left barriers that are more than technical impediments to new power resources. The obstacles were political, economic, even psychological.

Against such a background, Soviet energy problems will not yield to quick or cheap remedies. As shortages grow more acute, at least in the short term, environmental costs already incurred and those that lie ahead are likely to narrow options for change and are certain to raise the price of new growth.

Yet by 2010, according to one researcher, the Soviet Union must *add* 20,000 megawatts of electricity to its current capacity to meet projected demand for industrial and residential power consumption.[129] Solutions are not impossible to conceive. Soviet engineers have been working since the 1970s on a steam-and-gas internal cycling technique that its advocates claim has been successful in German and American applications and that could raise fuel efficiency in thermal power stations 43 to 45 percent while cutting sulfur dioxide and soot emissions by one-tenth to one-fifth. In the USSR, the technology had not been tried on a commercial basis, but its supporters hoped that raising the ridiculously low fees that individual and industrial users paid for power would be the incentive to turn the experiment into reality.[130]

In the much longer term, alternative sources—wind and solar power—could also provide increments of new energy, at least from the mountains of the Urals and the Caucasus and from the warm plains of the Crimea and Central Asia. Even in the West, such technology has received only limited support. In the Soviet Union, it is barely at the trial stage.

While waiting, perhaps in cold and discomfort, for such advances, Soviets need to learn an entirely new attitude toward energy and all natural resources. They are heirs to a spendthrift psychology that is partly a product of the vastness of their land and partly a function of a Communist pricing system that put no realistic value on assets that everyone owned and no one husbanded.

Along with higher prices for heat and light, they must also assimilate the waste-not-want-not ethic of Benjamin Franklin. For it, however, they will find few historic models. The rare exceptions were some prerevolutionary woodsmen, Ivan Appleseeds or Genrikh Thoreaus of the time, who set examples of respect for nature and of economy in its exploitation. Among the contemporary, spiritual descendants of those largely forgotten foresters are the leather-coated members of Lyubei, a rock-music band. In the fall of 1990 they could be seen on Soviet television and heard on tapes played in Moscow taxis, pounding out a catchy admonition to save not just Russia's forests but its soul as well from home-grown plunderers. "Beyond the village, by the river," went their lyric, "the good old boys are out chopping down the woods, making any mess they want, letting the chips fly every which way."[131]

It is possible to read in that last phrase a sarcastic reference to Joseph Stalin, who used the same image to proclaim his indifference to the victims of his purges. The songwriters, in any case, moved on to a verse on preserving natural beauty and the idealism of an earlier Russia. Then came their chorus:

> *Don't destroy, guys, don't destroy.*
> *Don't cut the trees, don't chop them down.*
> *For the nesting rook, guys,*
> *Stay your hand. Keep your cool.*
> *Don't bring ruin, don't destroy.*[132]

In the tradition of Alexander Solzhenitsyn—"A great writer is, so to speak, a second government in his own country"[133]—Soviet poets, novelists, essayists and other respected intellectuals began in the Gorbachev years to preach a message very much in tune with the musicians'. Valentin Rasputin, for one, put ecological issues in terms of ultimate morality.

"Although we have admitted many of our errors in recent years in keeping with the moral renewal of our society," he told fellow members of the USSR Writers' Union at the start of 1989, "we have been contented with half-truths in discussions of the state of our ecology. . . . We let things go to the point of lifelessness and then leap to their aid. This is what happened on the Aral and this is what is happening on the Volga, to Baikal and Ladoga."[134]

It was also, to a degree, what threatened to happen to the energy sector, the source of life for the entire Soviet economy. By 1990 it was probably too late for rock lyrics. It was also too early for funeral marches. But somewhere on the musical spectrum, Soviets had to orchestrate a new anthem that could harmonize energy with ecology and move a great nation away from self-destruction.

CHAPTER 8

Crippled Giant

MAY 9, 1990, was a sunny spring day in Moscow, a midweek holiday, given over to a stirring parade of men and weapons. Missile launchers, museum-piece T-34 tanks from the 1940s and T-80s, their huge modern successors, rolled through Red Square. The parade ground echoed to the rumble of heavy machinery, the firm, lighter rhythm of booted ranks of uniformed marchers and the applause of enthusiastic crowds. Afterward, around the city, Soviet veterans of World War II staged a huge, informal, emotional reunion to celebrate in their own way the forty-fifth anniversary of their victory over Nazi Germany, to remember the triumph and the fallen.[1]

It was a day to recall past glories, legendary valor and terrible sacrifice, to summon from memory the finest hours of the Red Army. It was also, but unacknowledged, a last hurrah.

Despite the proud display, the enormous Soviet defense machine—nearly 5 million uniformed troops backed by an estimated 12 million civilians employed in defense industries and controlling 20 to 30 percent of Soviet GNP[2]—was an institution of diminished status and declining strength.

The military's slide from grace and power had begun some years earlier. After the great victory commemoration of 1990, the downhill drift only picked up speed as the most revered single institution in the Soviet state apparatus emerged in a double role of villain and victim, a moving force in creating the country's economic and ecological woes and a casualty of their acceleration.

In a classic case of power corrupting, of strength concealing and contributing to weakness, the Soviet armed forces represented the polluter contaminated by its own negligence. As guardian of the USSR's security, it had helped undermine both the health of the nation and of the young men it needed in its own ranks. By direct assaults on the nation's ecological balance and by tolerating a destructive physical and psychological environment in its own ranks, the USSR military shot itself in the foot. Like the Soviet Union more generally, as an American statesman wrote in 1984, it became a "crippled giant."[3]

As the August 1991 coup attempt against Mikhail Gorbachev revealed, political divisions in the once-monolithic uniformed ranks followed the fault lines of the civic earthquake set in motion by Gorbachev's off-and-on drive for domestic reform and military retrenchment. Open opposition to military budgets and to the ferocity of military discipline—both formerly as unquestioned as the teachings of Marx and Lenin—became as vigorous in the Gorbachev years as ecological protest against Soviet nuclear weapons testing. Many Soviet troops returned from assignments in Eastern Europe to find themselves not only unwelcome presences in independence-minded republics but caught as well in a situation remarkably analogous to the one-third of Depression-era Americans whom Franklin Roosevelt described as "ill-housed, ill-clad and ill-nourished."

Some Soviet soldiers were also ill served by military doctors as hampered by poor training and poor equipment as their civilian colleagues. Many of the newest recruits were so ill treated by their superiors that not only did many desert, but—*in extremis*—they killed themselves or suffered mental breakdowns with a frequency far greater than in the past. And high numbers of soldiers—like the civilian population from which they came—turned out to be just plain sick both with diseases they had when they put on their first uniforms and with other ailments acquired on duty.

A few episodes—far from a comprehensive account—can sketch in the story of the army's precipitous decline in fitness, strength and prestige during the Gorbachev years. Only vignettes, they nevertheless record a humiliating descent from glory to infirmity, a fall that mirrored that of the USSR itself.

May 28, 1987: Red Square, Moscow. A special day (though not a holiday) to honor the KGB units called Border Guards that patrol the Soviet Union's closely watched frontiers. Three times a tiny plane buzzes the great open space outside the Kremlin walls before landing on the cobblestones in front of St. Basil's Cathedral. The pilot steps out. He is nineteen, Mathias Rust, a West German. In a rented, single-engine Cessna, he has just pierced what are supposed to be the toughest air defenses in the world.

Within hours the Soviet minister of defense and the commander of the Air Defense Forces are both fired. A "major dereliction of duty," the Politburo charges.[4] A humiliation. More are to come.

May 15, 1988: Soviet troops begin to pull out of Afghanistan after more than eight years of bloody, inconclusive fighting and, according to a senior officer, over 49,000 casualties, including 13,310 dead.[5] Nine months later the last combat unit is gone.

September 25, 1989: Presenting the draft 1990 state budget to the Soviet legislature, USSR Minister of Finance Valentin Pavlov forecasts a 6 percent reduction in outlays for "maintaining the Army and the Navy" and a 15 percent cut in military construction spending. Expenditures on housing for troops will be kept at current levels, but as officers are made to retire, pension payments will rise.[6]

February 28, 1990: The 1,000-man Chinstakhov tank regiment, one of the units used to crush the Prague Spring Communist reformers in August 1968, begins its part of a withdrawal that will take all 80,000 Soviet soldiers out of Czechoslovakia.* By October the regiment is based in Dzerzhinsk, a "petrochemical sewer" of a city 225 miles east of Moscow, where one-third of its troops spend "much of the fall on neighboring farms harvesting potatoes and building greenhouses. . . . Others were deployed to bakeries to combat a bread shortage."[7]

Together with their dependents, the 250 Chinstakhov officers are badly housed—"14 families in one-room hostels; nine families in a dormitory in town; 25 in a five-story dorm on post." They are also anxious about pollution. "One officer worried openly about the environmental effect on his sexual potency. Mothers fretted for their children."[8]

July 3, 1990: Foreign Minister Eduard Shevardnadze, at a session of the Twenty-eighth Party Congress in Moscow, counterattacks Communist diehards who charge him and other Gorbachev aides with weakening the USSR by surrendering control over onetime Soviet satellites in

---

*When Mikhail Gorbachev visited Prague in 1987, journalists asked his spokesman to explain the difference between the Soviet leader's *perestroika* aims and those of Alexander Dubcek, the Czech Communist leader ousted after the Soviet invasion. Replied Gennady Gerasimov: "Nineteen years."

Europe. Shevardnadze claims that the military, monopolizing one-fourth of the national budget, had wasted 700 billion rubles in Cold War spending excesses.[9] In the first quarter of 1991, a Soviet economist reckoned, defense expenditures were running 50 percent higher than the total revenues of the Soviet government.[10]

December 22, 1990: Two days after announcing his resignation as foreign minister in protest against a trend toward "dictatorship," Shevardnadze concedes that the attempt to reduce armaments and to convert defense industries to civilian production "is a huge task. You want to help us?" he asks Westerners. "Buy some of it!"[11] A few weeks later the Soviet press agency, Novosti, reports that military-civilian conversion is underway at the Northern Mechanical Engineering Plant, which "has manufactured the first Soviet tourist submarine."[12]

Earlier in the year U.S. intelligence officials testified that at least one out of every five young Soviets was ducking the summons to military duty. In response "thousands of crack troops" were deployed to enforce conscription.[13] In the Ukraine and in the breakaway Baltic and Transcaucasian republics, some draft boards have been described as "combat theaters of operation" because local politicians and protest groups have called for guarantees that draftees will not have to serve outside their homelands. Reporting on 1989 draft evaders, *Pravda* revealed that their numbers were twenty-three and twenty-four times higher in the Ukraine and the Baltics, respectively, than in 1988.[14]

March 6, 1991: Marshal Dmitri Yazov, the Soviet minister of defense, admits that draft-dodging is on the rise. He discloses that 100,000 fewer eighteen- to twenty-year-olds than expected reported for induction in the fall of 1990. "Armenians, Georgians and inhabitants of the Baltic Republics" stayed away in droves.[15]

April 18, 1991: In response to a Russian Republic parliamentarian's accusation that defense spending is rising by 30 billion rubles in 1991, a top General Staff officer claims outlays have been cut in real terms by 6 billion rubles and that the apparent rise from 68 billion to 95 billion rubles is due to inflation, "the slump in the ruble exchange rate." The army, he adds, is "seriously understaffed," at 3.4 million men, almost 10 percent below its authorized manning level.[16]

May 13, 1991: On top of political unrest, the physical debility of Soviet youth, says the head of the Defense Ministry's medical commission, is aggravating military manpower shortages. Because of ill health, draft boards had to excuse 3 percent more youngsters from service in 1990 than the year before. During the decade of the 1980s the incidence of disease among conscripts on duty rose by 30 percent. At the same time, military hospitals became so overburdened that soldiers sent to them for treatment had to wait several days for admission.[17]

June 19, 1991: The military recruitment problem worsens when the spring 1991 callup is 353,000 men short. More than fifty times as many young men were missing as in all of 1989. Marshal Yazov warns a closed session of the USSR parliament that draft-dodging encouraged by leaders of secessionist republics means "Soon we will have no armed forces." They can exist "only under a unified command," he insists. "There are no armed forces when everyone is in command."[18]

June 24, 1991: General Mikhail Moiseyev, chief of the USSR Armed Forces General Staff, receives a representative of McDonald's, the fast-food chain, and announces that "we are ready for the broadest cooperation" in improving Soviet mess halls.[19] A month later Moiseyev's American opposite number, General Colin Powell, arrives in Moscow for a seven-day tour "that will include talks on Soviet efforts to convert military factories to civilian commercial use."[20] In a speech at a military training center near Moscow, Powell criticizes the slow pace of defense industry conversion and "the oversized Soviet force" as "unjustified [and] potentially wasteful."[21]

July 23, 1991: The deputy defense minister and the general who led the Soviet army's exit from Afghanistan join ten other opponents of reform and conservative Russian nationalists, including writer Valentin Rasputin, in an ominous public warning that the "Motherland . . . is dying, falling apart and sinking into darkness and nothingness." Appealing for a "patriotic movement . . . to lead the country to a sovereign future without humiliation," they name the military as a shield against "fratricidal war . . . and a safe guarantee of security."[22]

August 19, 1991: Army tanks roll through Red Square and surround the Kremlin as a State Committee for the State of Emergency, a front for military, police, old-guard Party and military-industrial leaders, attempts to seize power and roll back the changes of the Gorbachev years. Civilians pour out to block the putsch, to argue with the soldiers, to hurl eggs and, the next day, Molotov cocktails at the military vehicles and to inveigh against Defense Minister Yazov. The commander of Soviet airborne forces is said to be under arrest for refusing to join the plot, and

Marshal Yazov, on the second day of the attempt, reportedly quits his post as well.

"Why tanks?" an American reporter in Moscow hears a gray-haired woman scream on August 19 at a passing column of armored cars. "Tanks against whom? Boys! Boys! You are our children. What are you doing? What do you want?"[23]

If they wanted to regain the people's once-unquestioning respect and the military's political preeminence in setting Soviet industrial and foreign policy priorities, the armed forces had moved too late. Though they had sophisticated weapons and more men at arms than any other nation, the Soviet armed forces were not in true fighting trim. They had too long neglected the human factor in military preparedness—the health of soldiers themselves—and too long ignored the underlying economic and ecological well-being of the land they were meant to defend.

The fault for this state of affairs could not be laid exclusively at the door of the top military command. Nor were the remedies for it entirely in the power of the defense establishment to find and apply. On the eve of the coup, however, the General Staff of the Armed Forces of the USSR was barely starting to move to be part of the solution—even to problems of its own making. Insisting on entrenched privileges and siding against most proposed reforms—such as proposals to establish a smaller, professional army—the one combat for which top military figures showed themselves ready was domestic and political.

The final issue of that fierce contest for the body and soul of the Soviet Union is not likely to be decided before these pages are printed and bound. From afar, though, the Soviet Army, so heroic in other fights, so feared for so long in the West, seemed to have chosen the wrong side in a historic battle at home. Rigid at the top, disintegrating from below, it was prey to the same ills that shook the foundations of every Soviet institution. In its case, many of the wounds seem self-inflicted.

SICK CALL

A measure of the Soviet military's internal strength also measured the general state of Soviet health. Both were alarming. By 1991 army recruiters were finding fifty-two out of every one hundred potential draftees physically, mentally or otherwise unfit to serve.[24] The statistic was not surprising. It tallied with the 1988 report of the USSR minister of education that 53 percent of all Soviet schoolchildren suffered from poor health.[25]

According to two top Soviet medical corps generals, the trend lines pointed only to a progressively weakening society. During the five years after 1985, Health Ministry data showed chronic illness among youths (presumably the fifteen- to seventeen-year-olds who make up the pre-draft cohort) up by 34 percent and the incidence of psychiatric disturbances higher by 50 percent.[26] Major General E. A. Nechayev, head of the Armed Forces health services, focused more narrowly on actual recruits among whom "year by year, the percent of individuals in good physical condition is declining (in 1988—74.5 percent; in 1989—70.3 percent)."[27]

Who or what was to blame? In Tajikistan—where, as in Uzbekistan, infant deaths attributable to infectious and parasitic diseases were thirty or more times as frequent as in Estonia and Lithuania—the top military commander accused Central Asian mothers of being ignorant and uncivilized.[28] General Nechayev's two colleagues offered a broader and more convincing explanation. "Disregard of sanitary and hygienic requirements," they wrote, "the unsettled state of everyday life, environmental pollution, inadequate diet, poor bathing and plumbing facilities, violations of safety rules—all of these contribute to the incidence and spread of illness and trauma."[29]

Demographic shifts inside the Soviet Union heightened the military health crisis. The fastest population growth was occurring in the poorest regions. With 37 percent of its 1988 intake coming from the four Central Asian and three Transcaucasian republics, compared to 28 percent in 1980,[30] the military was more and more dependent on the least able-bodied Soviet citizens.

Karim Bakhiryev, an Uzbek politician who kept track of the deaths of 430 young recruits from his republic in 1989 and of 190 more in the first seven months of 1990, worried that the "mass meetings and funerals" organized by nationalist groups when the coffins of alleged suicides are brought home from army service "have almost led to riots and [anti-Russian] pogroms." The suspicion fanning such emotion was that the racist taunts and brutality of their Slavic fellow conscripts drove the Uzbek youngsters to kill themselves.[31]

While confirming that such mistreatment was common, Bakhiryev also contended that many young Uzbeks were simply unfit to serve. Debilitated by toxic chemicals "applied to the soil of Uzbekistan 3.5 times more intensely" than in the USSR overall, they were still accepted for military duty, he wrote,

by officials in white coats [who], for a specific sum, classify perfectly healthy people unfit ... or, on the contrary, send obviously ill people into the army in their place. . . . The result: puny boys with congenital diseases to whom a soldier's garb is offered when they attain their majority.

How can we draft a young man from a remote rural area into the rocket troops, when we have around 2,000 schools in an emergency state in the republic and many children attend school in two or even three shifts?[32]

Also least fluent in Russian among the USSR's major ethnic groups,* the Central Asian draftees were more likely to have been malnourished as infants and young children. In adolescence, their health was often further undermined by contaminated water and, as Bakhiryev noted, excessive exposure to agricultural chemicals. (See chapters 3 and 4.) Although those problems stemmed from civilian policy errors, the failure to reverse them and to deliver compensatory social investments, especially in Central Asia, reflected the huge, ongoing diversion of resources to the Soviet defense sector, which accounted for 35 percent of the government's 1991 budget,[36] compared to 3 percent allocated for health care.

In the late 1980s the Soviet military was paying the price for its high-spending ways. In 1988 it had to classify 10 percent of the young men it inducted in Kirghizia as "fit only for noncombatant duty."[37] In the same year it actually had to dismiss twice as many ailing Kazakhs from active service as in 1987.[38] Draft boards in the industrialized Karaganda *oblast* of Kazakhstan issued 40 percent more deferments for ill health in 1987 than in 1985.[39]

Until tougher health standards were introduced for the fall callup of 1989, many eighteen-year-olds were put into uniform regardless of their disabilities. Inevitably, the poor quality of medical care in civilian life then affected military readiness. To fulfill draft quotas, recruiters accepted the lame and the halt and even some who were classifiable as legally blind. Unhealthy civilians made unhealthy soldiers.

As long ago as 1984, a former Soviet Army doctor who had served in three different military districts estimated that at any given moment, 10 to 15 percent of soldiers were on sick leave and others, though on duty, should have been excused.[40] As recently as 1989, another Soviet physician reported that only one inductee out of fourteen could qualify physically for duty on a flight crew.[41]

Once in service, Soviet troops fell prey to illnesses that afflicted

---

*The major nationalities range from the 145 million Russians, 44 million Ukrainians and 17 million Uzbeks, to smaller groups such as the 2 million Germans, 1.4 million Bashkiris, 1.1 million Poles and 1 million Estonians.[33] The four Central Asian republics in 1989 had the USSR's lowest rates of high school graduates as a percentage of adolescents and adults,[34] and in 1987 their rural settlements were producing draftees 90 percent of whom spoke virtually no Russian.[35]

civilians as well. When Moscow was hit by a diphtheria epidemic in 1990, for instance, 171 soldiers in the capital's military district caught the disease and 5 died. With Soviet parents increasingly fearful of impure vaccines and unsterile needles, many of their teenage children skipped being revaccinated, even against diphtheria. Alert to the danger, the army and navy started in 1987 to inoculate recruits who could not prove they had already received revaccinations. Seventy percent of the soldiers posted to the Moscow district over the next two years were in that category.[42]

Most of these vulnerable young men probably came from Central Asia and the Transcaucasus, where uninoculated recruits numbered from 63 to 68 percent of all draftees between 1985 and 1988, compared to 35 and 42 percent in the central and western regions of the Soviet Union, respectively.[43] Revaccination apparently did not go far enough, since it only brought "collective immunity" in three military units in the Far East and two in Central Asia to 88 percent, when the level needed to insure against disease outbreaks was a minimum of 95 percent.[44]

MAYHEM IN UNIFORM

Diphtheria, however, was not the main cause of noncombat deaths and disabilities among Soviet soldiers, sailors, and airmen. Alcohol abuse was and long had been a significant factor. Before he defected by flying his MiG-25 fighter to Japan in 1976, Lieutenant Viktor Belenko had observed enlisted men and officers on drunken binges at every base where he was posted.

Because it used large quantities of highly distilled alcohol as aircraft coolant that could be and was siphoned off for consumption on base or black-market sale outside, the jet he piloted had a pet name in the air force: the *Flying Restaurant*. Training flights often were cancelled because the vital lubricant was so extensively diverted. A few months before Belenko flew his MiG to Japan, a visiting political officer scolded the unit for being "too drunk to defend our Motherland."[45] Similar problems affect readiness in the fleet. Alcoholic sailors surveyed in 1986 were found to be five times more prone to disease than the population at large.[46]

In 1990 authorities disclosed the existence of drug abuse in the military as well. A sampling of army men found 69 percent who said hashish was available on post. Among those who had served in Afghanistan, 11 percent spoke of having access to LSD and twice as many, to heroin.[47]

A 1987 survey of young Muscovites, moreover, found almost 27 percent who said they first used drugs while doing their military service.[48]

If drugs and drunkenness were abiding threats to health in the Soviet armed forces, discipline and indiscipline were the most publicized causes of lowered morale, death and even desertion. The Defense Ministry cited "accidents at construction sites" as the most frequent cause of death, but admitted that of twenty-three Uzbek recruits who died between August 1 and September 3, 1989, four were murdered and five were suicides. Eleven others met their death breaking "safety rules in the performance of various construction and other jobs."[49]

The nine homicide or suicide victims were almost certainly casualties of *dedovshchina*. The word put a name to the brutality regularly inflicted on the newest recruits, especially those from the Baltics and Central Asia, by senior conscripts—the *dedy* (grandfathers), serving the last quarter of their twenty-four-month enlistments. A military justice official, granting an ethnic "tinge" to the practice, claimed that it had peaked in 1985 with about 4,000 convictions that year of soldiers who tormented their barracksmates.[50]

Hazing was still a sufficiently severe problem in the navy in 1987 that commanders, political officers and Komsomol activists in the fleet were issued a red-paper-covered "official use only" brochure of "Recommendations" on how to deal with its various forms. The headings for different abuses range from "oral insults . . . threats . . . blackmail . . . thievery" to the practice of forcing juniors to perform menial and hard physical labor and, the final category, "homosexuality and perverted sexual behavior."[51] In the elite navy, fights even broke out over shortages of sinks, toilets, clean linen, hot water and food.[52]

At the ignoble bottom of the armed forces, *dedovshchina* was especially prevalent in the construction battalions where about 330,000 unskilled troops served as hod-carriers, ditch-diggers, plasterers and even nannies for officers' children. Often put to work on such nonmilitary projects as facilities for the 1980 Moscow Olympics, one out of every seven enlisted men in these units had a criminal record.[53] The same statistic, coincidentally, appeared in Interior Ministry data identifying every seventh Soviet criminal as a minor.[54]

In one celebrated case in 1988, a Lithuanian recruit turned on the *dedy* who had not only beaten him and forced him to stand guard duty for three days without sleep but also made him submit to a gang rape. He killed eight of his attackers, an action for which he was committed to a psychiatric institution.[55]

It was not known how many such cases occur or even the precise number of peacetime fatalities in the Soviet military. The total averaged either 6,000 a year, according to the State Planning Committee, or 8,000 annually over a fifteen-year period, by the reckoning of a special commission of the Russian Republic's parliament formed to investigate *dedovshschina*.[56]

The commission's existence and the mail that flooded it were both proofs of how serious the previously hidden problem of military discipline had become and how angry the brutality had made many Soviets, especially the parents of recruits. A group of three hundred women formed a Committee of Soldiers' Mothers in 1989 to get their victimized sons released from army duty. That battle won, they continued to publicize the issue, even picketing outside the Kremlin walls with signs that said: "It's time to make the military aristocracy answer for hazing . . . for the deaths of our sons, for their mothers' pain and tears."[57]

The mothers' group was bold enough to demand that commanders be punished if their soldiers die as suicides or murder victims. The women were also insistent enough to start their own inspections of military hospitals, discovering them "filled to capacity," some beds holding "recruits [who] were maimed for their reluctance to be humiliated" and, in Central Asia, "lice . . . found not by army physicians but by soldiers' mothers."[58]

MILITARY MEDICINE: AN OXYMORON?

That revelation tended to support the unnamed source who told an American reporter in Moscow that 21 percent of military deaths were due to illness contracted while on active duty.[59] If correct, the figure was appallingly high, five or more times above what North Atlantic Treaty Organization (NATO) medical authorities in 1987 regarded as normal for their troops.[60] Given the state of Soviet military (and civilian) hygiene and medical care—the low qualifications of the uniformed personnel and the decrepitude of their equipment—the figure was also all too believable.

The fact that lice, the targets of Lenin's early exhortation on hygiene, were still a threat seventy years later probably came as no surprise to senior military doctors. In 1984 some of them persuaded the Defense Ministry to form an Extraordinary Anti-Epidemic Commission.[61] Its backers warned that commanders concerned about the battle-readiness of their troops needed to give urgent attention to preventing "mass epidemic diseases, such as typhoid fever and typhus, paratyphoid, viral hepatitis, dysentery and other diarrheal diseases."[62]

Civilian and presumably military hygiene efforts made some progress against typhoid and viral hepatitis in the next years, but not against contagions such as dysentery and influenza. Their incidence per 100,000 population rose 86 percent and 40 percent, respectively, from 1980 to 1988.[63] One contributing factor, openly identified by military doctors in 1988, was the army's own laxness in installing water purification systems at garrisons in the Far East, Transbaikal, Baltic, Turkmen and Leningrad Military Districts and in insuring the level of disinfection needed to prevent the spread and improve the treatment of viral hepatitis and digestive illnesses.[64] As those and other health problems increased, the power of military medicine to deal with them declined. The problems range from incompetence to overcrowding to obsolete equipment, the same weaknesses that afflict civilian health care. (See chapter 9.) Doctors in uniform were products of the same educational system that produced doctors in mufti whose "ignorance, criminal negligence and indifference" caused the head of the Military Medical Service in 1988 to advocate a professionwide purge.[65]

He had good reason to be indignant. Among the various military districts, the error rates in diagnoses reported in Soviet military medical journals in 1983 and 1984 ran from a low of 17 percent of measles cases to 95 percent of angina cases and between 68 and 100 percent of thyroid cancers.[66] Delayed or mistaken diagnoses of ulcers occurred 38 to 62 percent of the time; of typhoid, 42 to 67 percent; of intestinal infections, 60 percent and of diphtheria, in 68 to 95 percent of the cases.[67]

Considering that thousands of soldiers who had done duty as Chernobyl liquidators in 1986 had been exposed to radiation, the inability of their doctors to spot thyroid cancer—one of the likeliest early effects of radiation overexposure—could prove fatal. The same analytical failure might have been responsible for the five 1990 Moscow Military District deaths from diphtheria, a disease that can prove mortal if identified too late. In that year, according to the official status report on the work of the military health services, troops in the field often suffered from incorrect or tardy diagnoses of skin diseases, acute infections and respiratory illnesses. One out of every four abdominal surgeries was performed on the basis of erroneous diagnoses.[68]

Senior army physicians argued for some years that the medical school graduates entering the ranks were not up to the job and needed either to be assigned to military hospitals before being attached to field units or further trained while on duty. A program that began in 1986 made it theoretically possible for uniformed physicians to upgrade their skills and specialized knowledge. In reality, over the next two years only 15 percent of the eligible doctors took advantage of the opportunity.[69]

A top military medical personnel administrator also proposed expanding the armed forces' training institutes for physicians so that they could give postgraduate training to doctors already in service and put newly fledged civilian doctors into special two-year courses to ready them for military-grade medical work.[70] The success of the proposal hinged, in part, on the army and navy's ability to keep and to keep on attracting medical staff when even a 50 percent salary increase in September 1990 left uniformed health workers at lower pay levels than most of their civilian counterparts whose wages also rose.[71]

One reason that doctors quit the service was that unit commanders could overrule them on the issue of a soldier's or sailor's fitness for duty. The 1990 Defense Ministry status report, moreover, indicated that doctors who pushed for improvements in the living conditions and hygiene for the troops saw their ideas implemented only 30 to 50 percent of the time.[72]

Meanwhile, the physicians' own working conditions—and those of the patients who need hospitalization or sophisticated care—were often dreadful. Medical personnel on active duty in Afghanistan were instructed to wash bandages for reuse.[73] The chief of the Leningrad Naval Base's medical service described the equipment in his facilities in 1989 as "antediluvian" and asked colleagues to "imagine how much worse things are" at remote posts.[74] A 1991 training exercise to simulate emergency conditions was conducted by a special medical detachment in the Kiev Military District that could muster only fifteen of its assigned fifty officers, had no transportation of its own, used outdated operating room equipment and tents "from out of the past."[75]

In 1988 a Health Ministry official had characterized 61 percent of all military hospitals as dilapidated and reported that 33 percent lacked hot water and 13 percent had no sewer systems.[76] In 1990 things got better—and worse. The military medical service acquired 27 CAT scanning machines, 347 ultrasound apparati, 1,317 imported endoscopic devices for examining lungs and intestinal tracts and other "modern equipment."[77] By selling some old ships for scrap metal, the navy was also able to acquire hard currency, some of which it allowed its medical service to commit for the purchase of imported medical equipment and medicines.[78]

To Deputy Defense Minister General Vladimir Mikhailovich Arkhipov, however, the situation looked bleak. Asked to itemize perestroika-related problems in the armed forces, he cited as his first concern the refusal of Soviet enterprises, even defense contractors, during 1990 to accept more than ten out of sixty state orders for essential drugs and equipment. Fifteen orders for uniforms and footwear worth 250 million rubles in all were among those that enterprises declined to accept, either because they were unable to fulfill them or because they chose to pursue more profitable activities.[79]

Only a few years earlier, state orders, *goszakazy,* amounted to edicts. In 1991, with 48 percent of all military medical buildings so deteriorated that they were beyond repair and 25 percent of the total severely over-crowded, the Ministry of Defense could not even count on the factories it sustained for many years to provide help.[80] In some cases, the basic facilities at military posts, as well as the medical ones, were so rundown that hygiene suffered and soldiers fell ill. In the 1970s an overcrowded air force base in the Far East had no soap or hot water in which enlisted men could wash their dirty dishes. "Usually they elected to simply brush the plate off with their hands."[81]

Lack of hot water, still a serious problem fifteen years later, led to skin disease. Lack of clean drinking water brought on intestinal ail-ments, but in 1987 only 59 percent of the funds allocated for garrisons to use in buying and installing water purification systems were actually spent. The following year, of five such installations that were to have started working, not one actually functioned.[82] Poor food storage—one-third too few refrigerators, one-half too little cold storage for vegeta-bles—and mess halls without plumbing also bred dysentery and diar-rhea.[83] The sanitary situation that appalled Lieutenant Belenko in the 1970s remained desperate in the 1990s, and desperate men, not prepared to defect as he had, took desperate actions of their own.

The wackiest may have been the decision some Soviet Navy doctors made to study on their own with the well-publicized and publicity-conscious Moscow faith healer, Djuna Davitashvili. An aging exotic famous in the past for having used her psychic powers to treat Politburo members, including Leonid Brezhnev, she claimed to incarnate an an-cient Syrian deity.[84] The head of the fleet's medical services, who also spoke with pride of officially sanctioned instruction given to his subordi-nates in acupuncture and massage therapy, told readers of the Soviet military's daily paper, "Djuna is prepared to offer the fleet some of her techniques, and we are considering her proposal." One obstacle to wider pursuit of "non-traditional medicine," he added, is financial. "A month-and-a-half-long study period these days costs about 1,500 rubles. No one will let us have the money for that kind of training."[85]

HOIST BY ITS OWN PETARD

If funds had been available to deal effectively with the core problems of Soviet military health, they would have been far better invested in pollution control than in faith healing. Much of what ailed troops in the USSR stemmed from their own disregard for nature on the 183 million acres—4 percent of the land in the USSR—that the military owned or administered.[86] Another component of the combined assault on Soviet health and ecology was the pollution generated by industries that, at least until they stopped automatically accepting *goszakazy,* were "just carrying out orders."

The orders, as often as not, came from defense planners. They and complacent civilian officials defined the "strategic interests of the state" in terms of swords, not plowshares; tanks, not sewers or sewage treat-ment; SCUD missiles, not smokestack-emission scrubbing devices. Since 1988, 60 percent of the output of enterprises in the military-industrial complex has qualified as consumer goods.[87] But whatever their output, producers gave little attention to accompanying environmental damage. Also unheeding the pollution their priorities generated, military chief-tains long sanctioned or, at least, ignored the abuse inflicted on the environment by uniformed troops in the ordinary course of business.

There was profound irony, then, in the worries of the Chinstakhov regiment about the polluted state of its new garrison town, Dzerzhinsk. If the unit's conduct while stationed in Czechoslovakia had been any-thing like that of other Soviet tankers, the army at home was only getting as good as it gave abroad. An American environmental analyst reported on part of the legacy Moscow's military left behind in Eastern Europe:

> The groundwater is so contaminated where Soviet troops ran a tank maintenance depot in Frenstat, Czechoslovakia, that "you could practi-cally drill for diesel there," says Deputy Environment Minister Jaroslav Vlcek. As much as 3,000 square miles—6 percent of Czechoslovakia's territory—has been polluted or despoiled by the Red Army. . . .
>
> In Swinoujscie, site of the largest Soviet naval base in Poland, [environ-mental inspectors] found groundwater supplies contaminated by fuel . . . [and] discovered sewage from Chojno airfield flowing untreated into the Rurzyca River. . . .
>
> In the former East Germany, at least 90 Soviet installations are severely polluted. At Laerz Air Base in Mecklenburg, for example, 50,000 tons of fuel leaked into the soil. All told, an estimated 10 percent of East German territory has been fouled.[88]

In the United States, the General Accounting Office called the Ameri-can military "the single largest generator of hazardous wastes."[89] In 1991, to start remedying its past abuses at thousands of military and defense installations at home and abroad, the Pentagon announced that it would spend $6.9 billion on efforts to clean up the poisons it had allowed to endanger drinking water sources, to remove radioactive contamination and to moderize pollution control equipment. Analysts estimated that the effort would require three decades and cost $400 billion.[90]

In the USSR, where the military-industrial complex by conservative estimate "accounts for over a third and perhaps as much as half of the Soviet Union's total industrial output," the armed forces' role as polluter was almost as secret as most of their weapons development programs.[91] Only a few officers were even assigned to monitor the army's treatment of nature. In 1988 one of them cautiously revealed in an obscure military journal that the conduct had been less than sensitive.

"There are so many deficiencies in our [military] environmental protection practices," he wrote, "that we simply cannot remain silent about them." Citing forest fires that "we cause," uncontrolled garbage dumping and petroleum wastes leaked into the water supplies of garrison towns, he added that the installation of emission-control devices on military cars, trucks and armor "is catching on slowly." Even though inspectors traveled widely to prod commanders to clean up their bases and educate their troops, it is, the officer admitted, "too early to speak" of improvements.

The main problem is that people persist in their ingrained view of environmental protection as an unimportant, secondary business and remain convinced that shortcomings . . . will [only] be punished by a mild reprimand.

Despite the Minister of Defense's insistence, many units and agencies have not yet appointed outside environmental protection inspectors [and] despite the enormous volume of work they must accomplish, the ranks of [military district staff inspectorates created for the first time in 1987] have been cut in half, and the remaining personnel is assigned to other tasks.[92]

The role of the Soviet military in contaminating land, air and water with ordinary as well as toxic wastes, while also undoubtedly immense, showed up only in separate incidents, not comprehensive studies available to the public. If the armed forces knew the extent of the pollution they caused, they kept most of the knowledge to themselves.

One exception was the disclosure that while the navy had a fleet of sixty ships for processing trash and oil wastes, only a single ship was properly equipped for effective purification work. "We need at least 30 such ships," the Defense Ministry's environmental inspection chief complained in 1989. "Only one-half of all [the navy's] effluent is treated, and only 24 percent is biologically clean."[93]

The armed forces also kept civilian monitors out of military facilities. Except for the passage on Black Sea pollution from the Sevastopol navy base cited in chapter 6, Goskompriroda's comprehensive report on the state of the Soviet environment made no reference to the military role in ecological decay. Completed in December 1990, its 350 single-spaced typed pages did not discuss reports of leaks of radioactivity from underground nuclear testing at Semipalatinsk in Kazakhstan, of nuclear waste exploding in 1967 near Chelyabinsk in the Urals or of mysterious mass deaths of White Sea marine life that some ecologists blamed on the navy and its nuclear-powered missile submarines.

All those episodes have been traced, though not always irrefutably, to military activities. All were widely publicized in the Soviet press. The Semipalatinsk test site became the target of a substantial and largely successful protest movement that pushed Kazakh parliamentarians in 1990 to order an end to nuclear testing in their republic. (See chapter 11.) But until 1989 the subject of radioactive and other pollution emanating from the defense sector remained a nearly forbidden topic for uniformed Soviet officials to discuss in detail.

Secrecy bred distrust. When navy officials admitted that a 1985 nuclear submarine accident in the Pacific not far from Vladivostok had resulted in the onshore burial of 2,500 cubic meters of radioactive waste, they also insisted that it would be more dangerous to move the deposit—as local residents demanded—than to leave it. "One gets the impression that military people have their own outlook on the environment and the measure of [their] responsibility for its condition," snapped a Soviet journalist. "Ship graveyards in once thriving bays and the sea's pollution with oil products are routine facts of the Navy's activity."[94]

A different kind of fallout angered Soviets living near the Baikonur rocket launching and test site in Kazakhstan, the center of Soviet space activities. Local environmental authorities brought rocketeers down to earth with a suit filed to recover 1.7 million rubles for the value of a single year's lost harvest on land used as "a veritable scrap-metal heap." The space agency had promised in 1989 to clear up its litter, leaking fuel tanks from more than "890 whole and unexploded stages of multi-ton rockets," but had failed to act.[95]

"The military started to demand a deferment 'until the first snow,' " the head of the Dzhezkazgan *oblast* environmental protection committee recalled. "We gave it to them. What then? Winter arrived long ago, but about one-fifth of the territory . . . has still not been cleared. . . . The only course left to us was to resort to fines."[96]

The deaths of millions of starfish in May 1990 and, a month later, of a large number of whales and seals on the White Sea coast, north of the Severodvinsk nuclear submarine base, set off a tidal wave of rumors. An extensive and seemingly dispassionate scientific investigation could find no convincing evidence of natural causation. A Murmansk politician, however, revealed in September 1991 that the Navy had dumped 11,000 large containers of nuclear waste in waters nearby between 1964 and 1986.[97]

Aleksei Yablokov had little doubt that the defense establishment was covering up its responsibility. "We do not know at all the amounts and composition of the pollution which comes from the naval bases," he commented on a journalist's thorough report of the scientific postmortem on the starfish. The reporter's own editors agreed that the "military themselves have caused" their troubles with "public opinion. For [as long as] it is practically impossible to get into their archives . . . society will be hyper-suspicious and biased against the armed forces and the military-industrial complex."[98]

To an American audience, Yablokov added that a 1985 to 1990 doubling in the incidence of two types of cancer among adults and a reported sixfold rise in birth defects among infants in the Arkhangelsk *oblast,* which includes Severodvinsk, strongly suggested radioactive pollution from the military sources in the region.[99] Submarine builders at the Severodvinsk works, said to be the world's largest, clearly shared his alarm. Threatening a strike—unheard of at defense industry installations—in October 1990, they demanded that funds from the USSR budget be allocated both to convert their plant to civilian output and to clean up "radioactive pollution from the adjacent territory."[100]

No informed Soviet citizen doubted the defense industry's role in two terrifying and long-concealed nuclear accidents in the Urals. The first, in September 1957, occurred when a cooling mechanism failed in an 80,000-gallon storage tank for nuclear wastes at Kyshtym, a secret site near Chelyabinsk. When an emigré Soviet scientist revealed what he knew of the episode twenty years later, Soviet officials flatly denied his account.[101] In fact, 70 to 80 tons of radioactive material had been blasted into the open, sending contamination over what came to be known to officials and, finally in 1989, to the public, as the "East Ural Radioactive Trace." In the year following the accident, nearly 11,000 people had to be evacuated from the zone. Farming was banned on 410 square miles surrounding the site for anywhere from four to twelve years.[102]

Soviet investigators claimed that "[no] deviations in the incidence of

diseases of the blood and . . . of malignant tumors have been registered."[103] Survivors told a different story, one of "numerous instances of
cancer and leukemia among the victims of the Kyshtym accident," and
Yablokov and two parliamentary colleagues leading an investigation of
the disaster insisted that "it is too early to reach an optimistic verdict
and file the tragedy away in the archives."[104]

Soviet authorities also failed to quiet the anxieties of people living
near Lake Karachay, a Chelyabinsk region nuclear waste storage area
called a "slow-motion Chernobyl." Starting in 1951 and continuing for
at least ten years, the Mayak bomb-making enterprise based in a town
so secret that it appeared only on military maps pumped 1.2 billion
curies worth of cesium- and strontium-laced nuclear waste into the
bottom of the 100-acre lake. The result was a reservoir holding (and
leaking into adjacent groundwater) *nearly twenty-four times* the radioactive content of the debris released by the Chernobyl reactor failure.[105]

The summer of 1967 was hot and dry. Lake Karachay evaporated in
part, and winds blew the radioactive dust from its exposed bed onto
nearby land, buildings and an estimated 41,000 people, some as far as
fifty miles away.[106] Visitors in 1990 found radiation levels on the lake-
shore along the path the wind had followed still high enough at about
600 roentgens per hour "to provide a lethal dose" in sixty minutes of
exposure.[107]

UP IN ARMS

A famous visitor went to the Chelyabinsk area in June 1991. He was
Boris Yeltsin, nearing the end of his successful campaign to win election
as president of the Russian Republic and complete his revenge on the
Communist Party hard-liners who drove him from the Politburo in
1987. Although he hedged on making a flat promise to give the region
the same costly "ecological disaster" status and benefits as Chernobyl
received, Yeltsin did commit himself to "try to find ways to help."[108]

Warming to the opportunity to criticize the Soviet establishment's
past sins, he spoke of the expanding threat of radioactive pollution in
groundwater and added: "You or I are not to blame. There is a guilty
party somewhere, however, is there not? They have been concealing the
truth about this radiation pollution from the people for thirty years.
There has been silence. How many people have suffered? I hope that we
know better now."[109]

Part of what Yeltsin knows he learned from the elected head of the
Chelyabinsk *oblast* legislature. In an emotional December 1990 address

to colleagues in the Russian Republic parliament, Pyotr Somin called the radiation poisoning of his region "one of the greatest human tragedies of our age."[110] Denouncing the "criminal negligence" of officials who had tried to conceal the accidents, he said that 437,000 people had been exposed to radioactivity. "Chronic radiation sickness," Somin added, "was diagnosed in 935 people. More than 18,000 rural inhabitants were resettled. Compensation for the damage is taking a long time and is not commensurate, which causes justified indignation from the population. . . . There is no other such radiation-soiled and explosive situation on our globe."[111]

That judgment was not one that military authorities, including their civilian employees at the Mayak complex, were ready to share openly. Their attitude was better measured by an article that appeared in the armed forces' daily paper, *Krasnaya Zvezda*, two months before Somin's passionate speech. Conceding that "times are changing," the reporter, a colonel, described a visit by French journalists to Mayak headquarters in the area formerly off-limits even to Soviets without special authorization.[112]

The account, praising the Mayak reactor engineers as "aces, like test pilots," claimed that the plutonium-making enterprise was shutting down most of its facilities and discontinuing any output for weapons. Questioned by the visitors from France, the Mayak head did admit that there had been radiation accidents, "especially at the beginning, when we lacked experience." Without going into detail and apparently without admitting the fallout from the 1967 evaporation of Lake Karachay, he added, "We are paying for past sins."[113]

The bill kept mounting. "At present," USSR Supreme Soviet investigators said in late 1990, "the USSR has 500 million cubic meters of radioactive open water which could, in theory, cause irreparable harm to 7.5 million people who live near the Iset, Irtysh and Ob Rivers," the first of which rises in the Urals near Chelyabinsk and joins the flow of the other two northward through Siberia.[114]

At Krasnoyarsk in southern Siberia, nuclear waste had not yet gotten into the water of the Yenisei River when 60,000 petition-signing citizens of the city launched a preemptive attack against the potential danger. Their 1989 protest won postponement of a project to reprocess spent nuclear reactor fuel and to carry liquid wastes from that work through a tunnel dug under the river. The design might have been sound, but city residents "were angered by the revelation that the scientific study justifying the selection of the site was actually produced nine years after construction started."[115]

The 300,000 citizens of Ust-Kamenogorsk in Kazakhstan, by contrast, began their protests against the danger around them too late. Only after a September 12, 1990, explosion in one section of the Ulba Metallurgical Combine released beryllium compounds into neighborhoods with 120,000 residents, including twenty-three schools and forty-two kindergartens and nurseries, did they take to the streets to demand that the installation close.[116] They were hardly placated by medical teams that tested 2,700 people and found 236 of them, including 86 children, with beryllium levels 50 to 400 percent above the allowable limit. "Less than 3 percent of all residents exposed to the beryllium attack were examined," an *Izvestiya* correspondent who, with his family, was among the 120,000 exposed, noted with unconcealed anger. He added,

> the maximum allowable concentration was worked out in 1959 when many [such definitions] were established in our country less out of concern for people's safety than [to reflect] the capability of existing technology. Studies made public in 1984 . . . confirmed that the maximum allowable concentrations of beryllium now in effect do not protect people from contracting cancer.[117]

Beyond closing the nuclear fuel branch of the Ulba metallurgical works, the protesters demanded the removal and safe storage of about 100,000 tons of radioactive wastes created since 1949 and dumped, mostly in nylon-wrapped canisters at an unguarded, open-air site. One resident of the city, situated south of the Soviet nuclear testing grounds at Semipalatinsk and north of China's parallel site in Sinkiang province, had mounted a vain one-man crusade against the dump for about a year before the accident galvanized his fellow citizens.

Gennady Medvedev was an electrical engineer whose story is bound to remind Americans of the late Karen Silkwood's crusade against carelessness in uranium processing.[118] He attempted to interest politicians, scientists and journalists in Moscow and Kazakhstan as well as the impoverished people living in shacks near the waste-disposal site. At every turn, he found military secrecy stifling the alarm he tried to sound.

When his account of his campaign was finally published, he was a cancer patient, hospitalized in Alma-Ata for treatment. As such he was also one of his own statistics, one of the cases of oncological disease "the incidence [of which] is 11 times higher in East Kazakhstan *oblast* than in Alma-Ata *oblast* and two times higher than in Semipalatinsk *oblast*."[119]

Medvedev found that officials and ordinary people alike ignored his alarm in part because authorities constantly and accurately reported that *gamma radiation* levels in the city were safe. A sign at the Ust-

Kamenogorsk sports stadium even posted the day's radiation count along with the time and temperature. What was not measured, except secretly, was *alpha radiation* from uranium-238 and thorium-232, radiation that "radiology textbooks say . . . is dangerous when its source ends up in the lungs and the stomach together with dust."[120]

That was the real hazard from the dump, a place where gates that should have been guarded were always open, where fences had gaping holes, where cows roamed, children played and scavengers collected containers to use at home as water cisterns for themselves and their vegetable gardens. Getting no response to his appeals, Medvedev went as public as he could.

> June 28, 1990. Thursday. I went to a city ecological rally. I could not resist it and took the floor. The "conductor" of the rally gave me a limit of five minutes; it is a pity I did not say everything. Perhaps, we can solve our problems only with women. Only women were in many of the front rows, and only in their eyes did I see involvement and interest. . . .
>
> July 2, 1990, Monday. [With a TV director and cameraman to photograph the dump and the nearby] slums and their residents. Once again I found out how active women were. Only women came up to us, and they talked sharply, with pain and resentment. They said there was not a single healthy person on their street, that women gave birth to either deformed babies or babies like themselves, that is, sick, and that their living conditions were horrible. In some cases, six people [shared] 11 square meters of floor space. There was no school nearby, no shop, no water, and so on.
>
> In the evening I flew to Alma-Ata for treatment.[121]

In the Kazakh capital, Medvedev discovered that the management of the Ulba combine had talked the local television station into dropping its planned broadcast about the dump. He also learned that activists in the Nevada-Semipalatinsk ecological movement had persuaded a special USSR Academy of Sciences committee to visit Ust-Kamenogorsk on September 14 with precision instruments to verify his charges.[122]

Two days before the Moscow specialists were to arrive, the explosion spread beryllium dust from the Ulba plant over the city. By November 21 Vitali Fyodorovich Konovalov, Soviet minister of atomic energy and industry, was in the city to promise those who greeted him "with more than a few insulting words" that his agency "would take an active role in speeding up the provision of medical facilities, housing and harvesting machinery and in resolving other acute problems."[123]

Soviet citizens in hot spots far from Moscow were used to hearing such promises from high-level visitors sent to pacify them. Soviet citizens everywhere were also used to having the promises forgotten once the emergency passed.

In terms of health care, however, the emergency was nationwide and of indefinite duration. It affected military readiness and morale and civilian fitness for the hard work of converting a rusted, self-contaminated command economy—including its defense contractors—to market-stimulated consumer-oriented production.

None of those concerns, however, was on the announced agenda of the State Committee for the State of Emergency that moved to take power by force in the Soviet Union on August 19, 1991. Its leaders spoke that day of fighting "economic disintegration, crime and corruption," of making "food and housing our top priority," of "patriotic feelings" and a political "situation that has gone out of control."[124]

They proposed to put "our house in order" by force, if necessary, by central command, as before. They did not mention environmental or public health concerns. They were the leaders of the old political establishment, of the military and police and of the industrial sector so long dominated by defense planners. As such, they were simply being true to form.

CHAPTER 9

Gathering Ills

THE AUDIENCE OF about five hundred drawn through the sleet of a late autumn night in 1990 to the circus building on Freedom Street in Yaroslavl brought with it a palpable aura of pathetic hope. Almost as strong a presence as the reek of horse manure in the air of the cavernous auditorium, the credulous longings of the people who had paid three or five rubles for their straight-backed wooden seats focused on a self-proclaimed "Russian Orthodox miracle-worker." Among the spectators, a few young men had come to scoff at the performance. Most of the sparse crowd of solid, drab and expressionless middle-aged men and women had come to pray.

Many had placed tokens of their faith along the raised wooden barrier that enclosed the single ring: jars of water, woolen caps, scarves, sweaters, photographs, set out to be blessed by Anatoly Kondratiev, the tall, lank-haired faith healer. Wearing a rusty black caftan with cuffs, hem and front decorated by shoddy, silvery embroidery, he seemed, to an American spectator, like a defrocked priest turned medicine man. His "miracles," explained as manifestations of a God-given psychic power that redeemed sinners could also tap, included putting a pregnant young woman in long-distance telepathic touch with her mother and curing two boys of stuttering, an affliction demonstrated only out of the audience's sight and hearing.

The "healing" was accompanied by a rapid patter, a great deal of arm-waving and, at most, muted applause. The event lacked the fervor that U.S. televangelists generate in dispensing their cures or the disturb-

181

ing power of Anatoly Kashpirovsky's weekly seances on Soviet television. A hypnotist and self-styled "psychotherapist," Kashpirovsky began broadcasting in the fall of 1989 and managed, in some cases literally, to entrance his viewers.

At the height of his popularity, when public opinion polls recorded 61 percent of Soviets as "unreserved" believers, Kashpirovsky boasted, "Today, I know how to direct the masses, how to get results from them. . . . I have brought millions of people into the movement. Naturally, [what I do] is to distract people from their painful, everyday problems, and, perhaps, that's not so bad."[1] After getting an enormous ovation in the sports stadium of Minsk, the Belorussian capital, in mid-October 1990, he confided to the press that he was working on cures for three pressing problems: radiation sickness, AIDS and cellulite scars.[2]

The Minsk appearance was among his last in the Soviet Union. Facing what proved to be false charges of sexual misconduct and under fire from both physicians and professional circus and variety-theater hypnotists, Kashpirovsky shifted his base of operations to Poland in the fall of 1990 and went on to perform for Russian-speaking audiences in Israel and America.[3] He left behind several hundred would-be imitators staging seances all over the USSR, except Latvia, where the Ministry of Health banned them on the grounds that "people's health often seems to worsen" after such ministrations.[4]

What the sad little show in the Yaroslavl circus put on display were not the gifts of an extraordinary psychic—Kondratiev emphasized the healing power of Christ and of herbal concoctions he offered for sale— so much as a desperate hunger for miracles among simple people who had lost their trust in Soviet medicine and, by extension, in the scientific rationalism of Soviet Communism. Assessing the success of Kashpirovsky and others like him, a Moscow journalist noted that with only 2,500 professional psychologists—compared to some 200,000 in the United States—the USSR was "a wide open space for charlatans."[5]

The void in health services extended far beyond the field of psychology. Into the breach poured legitimate herbalists and presumed frauds— the makers of a medicinal, "magnetized" vodka that allegedly destroyed cancer cells and even a private Volgograd spa advertising its mineral compounds as a treatment for radiation sickness.[6]

The nostrums and the swindles revealed alike the same basic truth: After nearly seven self-congratulatory decades, Soviet medicine was deep in crisis, in public disfavor and internal disarray. Poorly staffed, furnished with obsolete technology, chronically short of drugs and shockingly neglectful of basic hygiene, the Soviet health care system was a victim—along with many other social programs—of the same misplaced priorities that had let environmental damage go long unchecked and unacknowledged.

Tasked by the early Bolsheviks with the job of disease prevention and control, Soviet medical personnel, even during the horrors of World War II, made genuinely impressive progress toward their goals. Julian Huxley had accurately gauged the health conditions he saw in 1931 as "near the general level of other European nations." Nor did he seem overly optimistic in forecasting for the 1950s "not only a very good medical service, but—what does not always follow—a very healthy population."[7] Time proved his hopes misplaced.

ENVIRONMENT AND HEALTH

A huge gap opened in the 1970s between promise and performance in Soviet medicine. Infant mortality rates rose, life expectancy at birth declined and by the middle of the decade, Soviet health officials, unable or unwilling to combat the trend and the forces behind it, conspired to conceal the truth. (See chapter 2.) Unconfronted, health care problems inevitably grew more acute.

Environmental pollution not only added to their severity; by introducing or aggravating a host of infirmities, it also complicated the task of already overworked and underqualified doctors in underfinanced and badly equipped clinics and hospitals. The tie between ecological degradation and the advance of disease was rarely clear beyond doubt or expert rebuttal. In the Soviet Union, however, the circumstantial evidence was overwhelming.

As data-gathering improved, a running survey of cities and regions with high levels of contamination began to uncover a striking correlation between poisoned air and sick people. Measuring illness rates in 122 Soviet cities with severely and less acutely polluted atmospheres, Ministry of Health statisticians found in 1988, for example, that children under the age of fifteen in Perm—the fourteenth-ranked Soviet city by volume of harmful atmospheric emissions in 1989—were 3.4 times more often diagnosed with blood diseases than their contemporaries in the 122-city average.[8]

In the neighboring Urals industrial town of Berezniki, as noted earlier (see chapter 5), the rate of reported juvenile blood-disease cases was 8.4 times the 1988 average. Adults fifteen years and older in Perm suffered from similar illnesses 4.3 times as frequently in 1988 as did those in other cities.

In Sterlitamak, where airborne mercury levels regularly reached ten times the maximum permissible concentration, as in Kremenchug, roughly one thousand miles to the west, the rate of adult hypertension cases in both 1987 and 1988 ranged from 1.8 times the 122-city average to 2.6 times. North of Kremenchug along the Dniepr River, children in the Ukrainian manufacturing city of Cherkassy fell ill with upper respiratory tract infections 1.5 times more often and with other breathing problems twice as frequently in 1988 as the average.[9]

It is in studying infants and children, epidemiologists believe, that environmental effects on health can be shown most convincingly, if not conclusively determined. Adults move around more than youngsters and may fall ill because of their work conditions or their exposure to alcohol, tobacco and other harmful substances. Although not a perfect set of indicators to establish definitive connections between pollution and disease, correlations between levels of air pollution and levels of infant and childhood diseases can at least set alarm bells ringing. In various Soviet cities, the noise should be deafening.

- Bronchial asthma among children rose sevenfold in Moscow from 1949 to 1981, and in the most polluted neighborhoods of the capital physical retardation among the young was 1.5 times higher than in areas with cleaner air. Even in a Moscow maternity clinic reserved for the elite, eight out of every ten children born between late 1990 and mid-1991 arrived either prematurely or with birth defects or both.[10]
- In Podolsk, a city near Moscow with 64,000 tons of smog a year and a storage-battery plant that refined 23,500 more tons of lead a year than its purification system could process, childhood diseases were 80 percent more prevalent than in Russian Republic cities on average. Among the entire Podolsk population lung diseases occurred 70 percent more often than they did on average in the RSFSR.[11]
- In Magnitogorsk, not only was infant mortality high—an average of 17 per 1,000 live births in 1986 to 1990—but one-fourth of all the infants who died were born with congenital development defects.[12] The national average for such infant deaths in 1989 was one-third of 1 percent of all live births.[13]
- Pneumonia rates among children in Novokuznetsk, one of the metallurgical centers of the Urals, were 4.3 times higher than those in Arkhangelsk, a northern port city with much lower levels of atmospheric pollution.[14]
- From 1988 to 1990 in Yaroslavl, also the site of a major lead-processing factory, an oil refinery and a number of other large polluting enterprises, rates of congenital abnormalities among children quadrupled and of malignant tumors almost doubled, while the incidence

of digestive tract infections and kidney diseases rose 79 and 74 percent, respectively.[15]

LOSING GROUND

Such statistics were not the kind that a prosecutor could take to a jury, but put before the jury of Soviet public opinion in the Gorbachev era, they brought a resounding verdict of condemnation. Yet, as one Soviet biologist pointed out, it was hard to go from general disapproval to specific remedies. "It's absolutely essential to have information about the substances enterprises emit," he said. "In the West, before you can put something into production, it has to be tested for its toxicity. . . . Here, we include an ingredient in the production plan, and then—if there are signs of danger—we start to do research on it."[16]

Even without the hazards of industrial pollution, Soviet health problems were genuinely severe. In a formal report issued in the spring of 1991, USSR Minister of Health Igor Denisov revealed how far his nation was from having the "very healthy population" Huxley had anticipated and Soviet propaganda had boasted.

Over the last 15 years, there has been a steady tendency for infectious diseases to increase—from 60.9 million cases annually in 1974–78 to 80.2 million in the last five-year period. The resulting direct economic losses run . . . by conservative estimates to 20 billion rubles a year.

More than 90 percent of all infections are in the category of influenza or acute respiratory viral illnesses. . . . [Their] undeviating rise . . . has gone from 6.7 percent of all cases in 1974 to 62.8 percent . . . with overall economic losses to the state calculated in the range of 3.5 billion rubles . . . .

In the last 10 years not only did the decline in the incidence of [infectious diseases] slow, but the rates for whooping cough, diphtheria and polio actually rose. Since 1985, cases of whooping cough have almost doubled, . . . [and] since 1980, cases of diphtheria have risen more than two-fold. . . . [In the USSR] there are 312 recorded cases of polio, four times more than in 1989. . . .

Every year the country's treatment facilities handle 70 million patients, most of them elderly or very aged. Five million fall ill from infections acquired while they are hospitalized, half the time during post-operative care. As a result the length of hospital stays has increased by 23 million bed-days at a cost of over 800 million rubles in lost production.[17]

Denisov blamed what he called an "epidemic situation" primarily on the failure of immunization efforts, especially the poor quality and inadequate supply of vaccines. The single Soviet enterprise manufacturing measles vaccine, for instance, closed for five months in December 1988, and in 1991 it was still not matching previous levels of output.[18]

Only twenty-seven Soviet-made vaccines out of forty-nine, he said, met World Health Organization standards of purity and effectiveness. Because many of the preparations had a short shelf life as well and because so few were multipurpose dosages, an average Soviet youngster received nineteen shots—not always from single-use syringes—before the age of fourteen.[19] The recommended number for American infants and children is twelve.[20]

In the Central Asian and Transcaucasian republics immunization efforts have lagged so badly that in 1989—when 79 percent of all Soviet infants received diphtheria shots—only 57.5 percent of Uzbek babies and 67.7 percent of Georgian ones got such inoculations before their first birthdays. To control the spread of infection, 95 percent of the vulnerable population must be immunized, but only 60.3 percent of Russian Republic infants, 54.6 percent of Uzbeks and 60.2 percent of Kirghiz were vaccinated against whooping cough in 1989, Denisov reported. In 1990, he added, the incidence of polio throughout the Soviet Union quadrupled over the 1989 rate as more than 25 percent of the nation's children failed to get vaccinations against the disease during their most vulnerable years.[21]

What Denisov did not examine was the growing tendency of Soviet parents—especially the urban and well educated—to keep their children at more than arm's length from the medical system. Too many reports of contaminated vaccine, of single-use needles resharpened and attached to imperfectly sterilized syringes and of AIDS infections spread by such unhygienic practices had weakened public trust in Soviet medicine.

Vladimir Umnov, the muckraking health care writer for *Komsomolskaya Pravda,* for instance, wrote in 1988 that Soviet drug manufacturers had consistently been using a dangerous germicide in preparing batches of the basic vaccine against diphtheria, tetanus and whooping cough that was supposed to be administered in three separate doses to Soviet infants before they are six months old. The antiseptic was specifically labeled by its Western makers as unfit for medicinal use, but that warning—and even the severe and occasionally fatal allergic reactions that followed inoculations—went unheeded, Umnov reported, "for the simple reason that the enterprises where vaccine is made are too dirty."[22]

Not completely unheeded, it turned out. By 1988 many pediatricians were already advising parents against the full series of immunizations. Two years later, however, Health Ministry officials took to blaming the

Soviet media for scaring parents away from their duty to their children and to the prevention of epidemics. "But no one said shots weren't necessary," Umnov rebutted. "The real problem is how to do them properly. . . . It seems that we've reached the point where [the authorities] are trying to shift the guilt for childrens' deaths onto journalists."[23]

Whether infected by their doctors, their newspapers or the grapevine, Soviet parents had indeed become injection-gun shy. A vice president of the Academy of Sciences, according to a Moscow acquaintance, warned his two adult sons not to get shots in Soviet clinics before taking business trips abroad in 1989. Both ignored his advice. Both came down with hepatitis after their injections.[24]

A Moscow cabdriver and his wife explained to an American friend why they had delayed giving their two-year-old daughter a variety of inoculations. "Except for skin rashes which go away when we take her out of the city for a few weeks, she is healthy now. But if she has to have shots for nursery school, we don't know what bugs she could pick up. The polyclinic may be fine, but how do we know that the equipment is really clean and that the vaccines are all right?"[25]

As the outbreak of diphtheria in Moscow in 1990 dramatized, the proudest accomplishment of Communist health care—disease prevention—was being undermined from within. Soviet citizens had not just stopped trusting their professional political leaders, they had also lost faith in the professionals trained to heal them.

DRINKING AND DYING

That apostasy, moreover, became virulent just as Soviet industrial growth and the pollution that shadowed it were lengthening and altering the list of death-dealing dangers. The near epidemic of infectious diseases was a mortal threat to the youngest and oldest. It was only an added threat to an already endangered species—*homo Sovieticus*.

The age-old scourge of alcoholism and the more recent rise in circulatory and cardiovascular diseases, cancer and respiratory illnesses were killing people prematurely at a rate that lowered life expectancy for Soviet men from sixty-five years in 1986–87 to 64.6 years in 1989—and to around forty-two years in some mining areas of the Donbass and Siberia. The sixty-five-year life expectancy level for males recorded in 1986–87 was actually an increase from a 1980–81 low of 62.3, an improvement widely credited to the antialcoholism campaign mounted—but then relaxed—during Mikhail Gorbachev's first years in power.

Alcoholism was all too familiar a menace to longevity in the USSR.

Not a modern affliction, it was a steadily worsening one. In 1989, 5 million Soviets were officially registered as chronic drunks by public health authorities.[26] The real number of alcohol abusers in the USSR was assumed to be four to six times higher, but the official count was alarming enough: about 20,000 alcohol-related deaths a year, including 11,000 from drinking poisonous surrogates such as perfume and moonshine in 1987; 250,000 cases of on-the-job intoxication reported in 1987, compared with 117,000 the year before; 133,000 juveniles disciplined as drunks in the first eight months of 1989.[27]

At the height of the three-year campaign against Demon Vodka, Mikhail Gorbachev claimed that restrictions on its manufacture and sale were "saving 300,000 lives a year." The gains from the effort—a reported 37 percent drop in alcohol-related deaths among the working-age population—were offset, however, by heavy losses of state revenue from alcohol sales. The liquor trade "in the early 1980s . . . provided about 13 percent of the state budget," and many economists dated the onset of the USSR's disastrous inflation to the rubles printed to make up for the missing income. Estimates of those losses vary—from 37 to 49 billion rubles—depending on different estimates of what sales of vodka, beer, wine and brandy from 1985 to 1988 would have been had prices risen and supplies not been cut.[28]

The human casualties of Soviet intemperance are at least as devastating to the nation's long-term health as the economic toll. A senior sociologist, for instance, tied the 22 percent increase in children born mentally retarded between 1984 and 1988 directly to their boozy parents.[29] And despite reformers' strenuous efforts to cut consumption—echoing campaigns Stalin launched in the late 1920s, that Khrushchev attempted in 1958 and those Brezhnev toyed with in 1972 and 1979—alcoholism, a Soviet journalist concluded in 1989, took "a powerful and steep upward jump."[30]*

The evidence of drunkenness is everywhere, from the prostrate human forms in Moscow subways and doorways, to the men lined up during working hours outside liquor stores or before working hours outside perfume stores. It is as much a plague in the countryside as in cities. Visiting the town of Sogra, population about three thousand, near Arkhangelsk in November 1990, an experienced Western correspondent

*Official data cast some doubt on that judgment. Where there were 601,000 new cases of alcoholism and alcoholic psychosis registered in 1985, the 1988 total was 439,000, dropping to 426,000 in 1989. The more alarming increase, actually, has been in drug addiction: up from 9,600 registered as addicts in 1985 to 17,100 new cases in 1988 and 15,400 more in 1989.[31] Even 1991 data was probably an undercount since the cumulative total of registered addicts at the end of 1990 was 131,000, and Soviets who have studied the problem estimate that habitual drug users in the USSR numbered from 500,000 to 900,000 in the years 1989 to 1990.[32]

from Moscow found "alcohol . . . the main entertainment, the main currency and the main scourge" for the settlement's farmers and loggers.[33]

Urged by a middle-aged village woman to discover how much vodka her neighbors consumed, the journalist put the question to the chairman of the village council, Valentin Popov. In reply, he learned that "the provisions barge shipped in 120,000 bottles of vodka and spirit last May. That works out to something like 60 bottles a year for every adult, perhaps the most telling statistic of all about life in Gorbachev's crumbling Soviet Union. It's nowhere near enough, Popov says."[34]

NEW ILLS, OLD STRATEGIES

Among the officially defined working-age population and, informally, those of drinking age—Soviet men sixteen to fifty-nine and women sixteen to fifty-four years old, inclusive—the death rate rose 20 percent between 1970 and 1989, from 399 to 480 per 100,000. Heart attacks and related complaints were responsible for 22 percent of all deaths in that age group in 1970, but for 31 percent in 1986. Cancer was the killer in 19 percent of the 1970 cases and in 23 percent of the 1989 cases.[35] These afflictions came as the lethal by-products of civilization's advance. Cancer and circulatory diseases together accounted for almost 72 percent of all deaths in the USSR in 1988, a statistic very similar to that in the United States and Western Europe.[36] Measured in terms of cause of death per 100,000 population in 1989, circulatory ailments were the fatal agents 51 percent of the time for Soviet men and 62 percent of the time for Soviet women. Cancer was the second most frequent killer, accounting for 18 percent of male mortality in the USSR as a whole (19 percent in the Baltics and 20 percent in severely polluted Kazakhstan) and 15 percent of female deaths.[37]

Cancer's unbridled growth in the Soviet Union seemed extraordinary. In less than two decades and with population growing by just 19 percent, the incidence of lung cancer more than doubled from 50,000 cases in 1970 to 120,000 in 1988—growing roughly three times as fast as in the United States in those years. Where an annual average of 500,000 Soviets contracted cancer in one form or another during the 1980s, oncologists diagnosed 677,000 new cases in 1988 and 676,500 in 1989. They expected 700,000 more in 1990.[38]

The Ukraine, which recorded 74,800 cancer deaths in 1980, registered 99,300 in 1989, an increase of one-third. The increase ran to 40 and 50 percent even in regions untouched by Chernobyl fallout.[39] The 1989 cancer death rates in the republic—identical to those in the USSR as a whole—were not the result of better diagnoses and more honest record keeping.

The truth, if not the whole truth, was that Soviet doctors were caught sadly unprepared to mount effective resistance against such modern killers. Too many medical professionals lacked training in advanced techniques. Additionally, they often lacked both equipment and know-how to perform advanced surgical procedures and were chronically short of medications to prescribe. Still conducting the prophylactic campaigns of the past, they were fighting a rearguard action at best against polluted air, impure water, the stress of urban, industrial life and nitrate-laden food.

Many Soviet health analysts, in fact, believed they were witnessing the progressive decay of an entire population's immune defenses just as new threats appeared and as old diseases, once thought under control, resurfaced. These health risks put the Soviet Union's labor force in evident jeopardy and menaced the productive assets the nation needed for economic recovery.

In the Russian Republic, approximately one-fourth of all those who died in the 1980s were men and women of working age. Despite a leveling-off in such deaths in the middle of the decade, demographers calculated that the *1990 mortality rate for this contingent of the population was 20 percent higher than it had been three years earlier.* Although the jump was due primarily to increases in fatal accidents, poisonings and injuries—including a doubling in the murder rate from 1987 to 1990—high levels of fatal tuberculosis, heart attacks and respiratory diseases among men also played significant roles.[40]

The figures on invalidism in the entire USSR were almost as frightening as those on mortality in the Russian Republic. Half of the approximately 17,000 Soviets *disabled* by tuberculosis every year, for instance, were under forty-five, and 7,000 of the 100,000 *diagnosed* as new tuberculosis victims every year were children under fifteen.[41] Similarly one-third of the 552,000 men and women first certified as invalids in 1988 were in what should have been the prime of life. Nearly two-thirds of all working-age Soviets forced by illness to give up work that year were victims of cancer, circulatory diseases or accidents and poisonings.[42]

Such data reinforced the view of three Soviet demographic specialists who saw their country in the midst of a transition from the "old pathology," where malnutrition and infectious and parasitic diseases were the main forces determining rates of illness and death, to a later stage in the "epidemiological revolution." The new or imminent phase, they said, required a "new strategy" as well to combat the effects of pollution and of stress induced by modern life, production methods and machinery.[43] Given the altered nature of the public health challenge, in their words,

> the need has now arisen to carry out broad-scale social measures, sometimes political actions, that can seriously affect an entire way of life. To implement [the new strategy], the role of political, economic and lawmaking institutions is much more important than that of the health services. The latter have to be reoriented . . . not so much against infectious diseases, many of which [but not including AIDS] have almost lost their previous vigor, . . . as to combat the dangers of technogenic origin: environmental pollution from [industrial] production and unhealthy technologies. . . .
>
> We have an incongruously higher percentage of deaths among children and the working-age population due to outside [nongenetic] factors than other developed countries. For instance, of every thousand newborn boys 20–30 times more die of infectious and parasitic diseases than in other large developed countries. . . .
>
> Of the total number of men dying of [respiratory diseases], 30 percent are under 60 in the USSR, only 7 percent in France and less than 4 percent in Japan. . . .
>
> In the mid-1920s, when the foundations of [the Soviet] health protection strategy were laid down, only 118 per thousand newborns were likely to die of [circulatory diseases and cancer]. . . . But in 1988, 712 per thousand newborn males and 829 per thousand newborn females [faced the risk of eventual death] from those causes.[44]

The appearance of AIDS in the USSR was one sign of the new times. Spread first in hospitals through the use of unsterilized hospital needles and infected blood, the disease terrified many Soviets and gave rise to doomsday predictions of an epidemic. Health Ministry officials forecast more than 30,000 AIDS patients by the year 2000 and as many as 1.5 million people who are HIV positive.[45] Those levels would roughly equal the incidence of the disease in the United States in 1988, when, with about 40,000 reported AIDS cases, epidemiologists were estimating the presence of 1 million HIV carriers.[46] But the USSR had far to go before AIDS reached epidemic proportions. The registered number of Soviet HIV cases as of March 1, 1991, totaled 1,176. AIDS patients numbered 54, of whom 33 had died. Among the HIV carriers, 49 percent were non-Soviets—most of them, presumably, students, workers and visitors from Third World countries.[47]

These statistics could have been skewed—up or down—by poor lab work. The USSR Ministry of Health allowed ten to fifteen blood samples to be analyzed using diagnostic tests designed to examine one sample each. Such disregard for standards could well have resulted in missing a number of HIV infections. In Estonia, however, testing worked the other way. A sample from 1987 to 1990 of some 400,000 blood donors produced 44 whose first tests showed the presence of the human immunovirus, 38 of whom proved, after further testing, to be false positives. Only 5 men and 1 woman were actually confirmed as HIV carriers.[48]

The spread of AIDS infection through unsanitary hospital practices and the error-ridden AIDS testing practices exemplified some of the weaknesses in the Soviet health care system. The three demographers provided a broader picture of the ways in which Soviet medicine succeeded and the ways in which it failed. The incidence of measles, whooping cough and polio that so worried Minister Denisov, for instance, actually fell by factors of 34, 18 and 2,160, respectively, between 1940 and 1989, although the polio level of 312 cases remained enormously higher than the U.S. rate of 0 to 3 cases a year.

In contrast, respiratory diseases killed Soviet men 70 percent more frequently in 1988 than American males in 1987, and circulatory ailments proved fatal to Soviet men and women 59 percent and 53 percent, respectively, more often in 1988 than to Americans of both sexes in 1987.[49]

Comparing 1988 Soviet mortality rates with those in France in 1987, the researchers also found shocking contrasts: an incidence of infant deaths from infectious and parasitic diseases twenty-seven times higher in the USSR and from respiratory ailments fifty-five times higher. The mean age of death for Soviets who succumbed to contagion or parasites was 37.3 years for males and 26.9 for females compared to 73.2 and 75.9 years, respectively, for French men and women.[50]

The "new strategy" the analysts believed was needed to bring Soviet mortality rates closer to those in the West clearly required a massive effort to improve the chances for survival just among newborns and infants in Central Asia, where deaths in the youngest age groups soared along with birth rates. (See chapter 4.) The statistics that showed such phenomenal differences between Soviet and Western youngsters' vulnerability to infections and parasites reflected, in part, the enormous discrepancies within the USSR itself between the depressed standards of living of Kirghiz, Uzbeks, Tajiks and Turkmen on one hand and the better-off inhabitants of the European parts of the nation.

The comparison of death rates and ages at death due to circulatory and respiratory diseases showed most clearly of all how far the entire USSR lagged behind other industrialized states in protecting people against the ills of modern times. Soviet men between the ages of thirty and fifty-nine were 2.5 times as likely to die in 1988 from heart attacks and other cardiovascular illnesses as their French contemporaries. For Soviet women in the same age group, the risk was 3.5 times as high as among *les Françaises*.[51]

SHORT-CHANGED

One reason for such disparity was the technological frailty of the entire medical support system. In 1987, then USSR Minister of Health Yevgeny Chazov, himself a cardiologist, reported that "we can't even manage to perform 900 [coronary bypass] operations a year."[52] In the United States, 131,000 such procedures were performed on men in 1987.[53] In 1988 physicians estimated that 200,000 Soviets stood in need of one or another form of heart surgery, but that the system could provide a maximum of 22,000 operations.[54]

As for kidney transplants in the USSR, Chazov said that in 1986, "we performed fewer than 400. In other developed countries, they do ten times that number."[55]

Another measure of Soviet medical failings was the death rate for cancer among youngsters under the age of fifteen: 6,000 fatalities a year among 11,000 cases.[56] The cure rate for the approximately 3,000 Soviet children diagnosed annually as leukemia victims was 10 percent in the USSR, compared to 70 percent in the United States and somewhat higher in Germany.[57] Although some 500 young leukemia victims in the USSR—and an unknown number of the 4,300 adults who contract the disease annually—were reported to need bone-marrow transplants in late 1990, only two such operations had been performed successfully in the Soviet Union by then.[58]

With leukemia rates expected to rise in the wake of the Chernobyl disaster, the Ministry of Health pledged to start providing 90,000 rubles per child in 1991 for each marrow transplant. Considering that the procedure can cost as much as $200,000 in the West, hematologists hoping to open ten specialized leukemia treatment centers in the USSR appealed for charity—Soviet and foreign—to support their plans.[59]

"Nowhere near enough"—the verdict on vodka shipments to Sogra—was all too fitting a description for almost every vital ingredient of health care in the Soviet Union. The shortages only began with measles vaccine. They ran from syringes to scalpels to surgical gloves, from the simplest analgesics to insulin to cancer drugs, from catheters to CAT scan machines, from hot water in hospitals to kidney dialysis equipment. After the December 1988 earthquake in Armenia left a reported 55,000 dead and thousands more homeless, rescue workers retrieving corpses from the rubble were seen washing their hands in *samogon,* home-brewed alcohol. No ordinary disinfectants were available.[60]

Western governments and charities rushed large shipments of emergency medical supplies by air to the Soviet Union after the Armenian disaster. Among the goods provided were a number of kidney dialysis units. Clinics in Moscow alone had only 147 such machines and needed 500.[61] Within a few months after the airlift, however, Western diplomats spotted several tanks from the imported dialysis machines for sale on Moscow's pedestrian shopping street, the Arbat, as home aquariums.[62]

Such corruption was an everyday part of Soviet life and a longstanding feature of medical practice. Many doctors supplemented their pitifully low salaries by writing work- and draft-deferment medical excuses for patients who paid in cash. Hospital attendants often demanded under-the-bed rubles just to change sheets, clean floors or provide food and bedpans. Pharmacists dispensed scarce medicines to favored (and appropriately grateful) customers, one of whom, a female writer, told an American acquaintance about the moral burden such practices create.

"My father has glaucoma, and I have a friend who is in charge of medical supplies for our region of Moscow," the woman recounted in October 1990. "Last month she got her quarterly shipment and let me buy enough eyedrops to last my father through the year. That was fine for me, but it meant that I bought half of her whole stock, and there are one hundred others among whom the rest will have to be shared. Should I have let my father go blind? I couldn't do that, but now I am guilty of the suffering that strangers will undergo because I had a friend in the right place at the right time."[63]

There was, of course, another danger in the back-door trade in medical supplies—the risk of getting caught. In the Brezhnev years it was a marginal hazard, but Yury Andropov launched a law-and-order campaign in 1983 and Gorbachev era reformers continued it, partly as a weapon against the entrenched and often illegal privileges of the old Partocracy. Soviet prosecutors, appropriately encouraged from above, brought criminal charges in 1988–89 against 33,000 health care personnel and 2,000 more medical industry employees, mostly for bribe-taking, extortion and black-market diversion of goods. "Criminal gangs," the law enforcers reported in 1990, "are systematically stealing medical preparations and selling them to profiteers." Agencies that imported vital medicines and supplies, meanwhile, were warehousing many such goods supposedly to await translations of the accompanying foreign-language instructions, but just as probably storing them for under-the-counter resale.[64]

The shortages that fed the underground economy bedeviled every Soviet citizen and every productive activity. In health care, they were in part the legacy of decades of financial neglect. The "residual principle," often criticized by Health Minister Yevgeny Chazov (1987–90), assured that only budgetary crumbs went to the Soviet social sphere—health, housing, education and culture. As a result, Aleksandra Biryukova, then a candidate member of the Politburo charged with social welfare issues, reported in 1990, "We have really had to engage in a salvage operation [since 1986] to resuscitate our entire health care system."[65]

Money was meant to be the kiss of life. A 10 percent increase in the USSR health budget from 1989 to 1990, for instance, raised planned outlays to 27.3 billion rubles. The higher amount, though, left government spending for health at about 3 percent of Soviet GNP as officially calculated. In Europe, public health got twice or more that share of public outlays.[66]

Besides, the increase was illusory. Although state financing for health care in the Russian Republic rose from 9.1 billion rubles in 1986 to 14.3 billion rubles in 1990, the growth, as A. I. Potapov, then the republic's minister of health, explained, "went primarily to cover inflation and not for development. The health budget today is based only on caring for *healthy* people."[67] Minister Potapov, who lost his job in late 1990, estimated that a proper level of expenditures— part from the state budget and part from employer-financed insurance funds that were just a glimmer in legislators' eyes in 1991—should provide health care based on costs of 250 to 300 rubles per person per year by 1995. The 1990 expenditure level for the Russian Republic, by contrast, was 89.8 rubles per capita.[68]

Even with such increases, 1995 Soviet expenditures on health would come to a maximum of 90 billion rubles or, at the 1991 tourist-exchange rate, about $3.6 billion. America's health care spending in 1989, public and private, was estimated at about $600 billion, or 167 times the projected Soviet rate.[69]

The U.S. health bill is the world's highest. It is regularly and convincingly denounced as grossly inflated by medical profiteering, unnecessary procedures, unrealistic cost-accounting and wasteful overhead. Still, to reach just one-fourth the American rate of spending in 1989 and to improve its own health care standards radically, the USSR would have to plan on outlays forty-two times higher than those now being contemplated.

OPIATES FOR THE MASSES

One area where new investments have long been crucially needed is the medical supply industry. As early as 1976, thermometers were so hard to get—with 22 million produced and 28 million needed—that pharmacies would sell them only on prescription and then, in many cases, only to customers who would buy other, slow-moving wares as well.[70] That same year domestic producers fell 30 percent short of filling the Health Ministry's orders for medical equipment.[71] In 1982 and 1984 shortages of diagram paper idled electrocardiogram machines all over the USSR, while blood pressures went unmeasured for lack of cheap rubber padding needed in sphygmometers.[72]

The upheavals of *perestroika* aggravated a deep-seated problem in medicines as well as medical furnishings. The central planning system that gave a single Moscow enterprise a monopoly on measles vaccine was the same one that allocated to Moscow's once-compliant Eastern European partners a huge share of the Soviet drug market. Purchases by the USSR even financed the "fraternal socialists' " pharmaceutical industries, with Moscow investing from 1977 through 1989 three times as much—an estimated 15 billion rubles—in the then-satellite nations' drug-making capacity as in its own.[73]

When Germans, Hungarians, Poles and Czechs began demanding payment for their medical and other goods in hard currency, the terms of the old trade came undone. Wholesale and retail medical customers in the USSR found themselves forced to cut back and even to do without goods for which there was no domestic producer. The availability of drugs and medical supplies in 1988 fell 14 percent short of overall demand, and 70 percent of Soviets polled at the end of the year said they were having trouble finding medicine.[74]

In 1989 Soviet hospitals spent 600 million rubles more to buy drugs than the year before, but their outlays robbed Pyotr to pay Pavel. The stock that the hospitals laid in almost equaled the value of the medicines that disappeared from the pharmacies.[75] But even hospitals ran short. A despairing Tajik physician wrote that in many cases his hospital received "less than 20 percent of the drugs" it needed. "How bitter it is to admit, but in the years of *perestroika,* our work in medicine has become much harder. In my opinion, in the field of health we have taken two steps backward. . . . What is most painful for us as doctors is to see children die before our eyes because we have no means to cure them."[76]

As public, press and Party anger rose in the spring of 1989, experts prepared a report on the state of the pharmaceutical industry for a joint session of the top policy planners in Soviet health care and drug supply. The study revealed that "more than one-third of [Soviet] medicinal preparations have lower shelf lives than analogous foreign" drugs. Noting that domestic manufacturing capacity was severely underutilized, the report also said that "72 percent of the machinery and equipment in chemical-pharmaceutical factories is worn out."[77]

Even with those problems identified, remedies were slow to come. By 1990 the overall drug and medical supplies deficit was running at about 28 percent, twice the rate in 1988. The shortage of blood and plasma substitutes was estimated at 72 percent of Soviet needs. Anticipated output and import of antiseptics, antituberculosis medicines, anesthetics and vitamins could meet as little as three-fifths and only as much as three-quarters of requirements. Domestic production of vitamin B-1 in 1990 dropped by one-tenth, of vitamin B-2, by half.[78] Even with imported medicines, the system was short 35 percent of the antibiotics that patients needed, 62 percent of the heart and circulatory system drugs and 90 percent of the insulin. In the first two months of 1991, production of "nitroglycerine, analgesics and other life-saving medicines" dropped 45 percent below the January and February 1990 output.[79]

The deficits were the sharp edges on a pyramid of failures in the Soviet economy and planning system. The heavy reliance on the availability and affordability of Eastern European products was an unadmitted consequence of letting domestic pharmaceutical and medical equipment manufacturing and standards slip to disgraceful lows. A few examples:

- Shipments from a Tomsk chemical and pharmaceutical plant labeled aspirin that were actually powerful antibiotics.[80]
- Shards of glass in an ampoule of heart medication to be taken by mouth; bits of insects in tablets of drugs made in Baku.[81]
- A Tashkent vaccine maker forced to close down its tuberculosis line in 1989 because of unsterile conditions had its output of antityphoid vaccine shut off as well a year later and for the same reasons; in 1990, however, it opened a measles-vaccine production line.[82]
- The Ministry of Medical and Microbiological Industry, given responsibility in 1987 for overseeing the modernization of Soviet vaccine production, instead put its primary focus and investments into manufacturing an economically profitable and ecologically disastrous protein-vitamin concentrate for animal fodder.[83] (Before becoming minister in charge of drug making, Valery Bykov had headed the concentrate factory at Kirishi near Leningrad. Its atmospheric pollution was held responsible for a spate of asthma attacks, some fatal,

and other respiratory illnesses suffered by local children, and their complaint came to be known as "Bykov disease."[84])

- In 1989, two years after Bykov's ministry announced that it would build, expand or reconstruct thirty-nine pharmaceutical plants, work was underway on fewer than half. By May 1990 the ministry was supposed to have signed contracts with Western firms to build four turnkey drug-making factories in the space of three years; in November 1990, however, the English firm that beat out twenty-nine other bidders still lacked the final go-ahead to start construction.[85]

By 1991 Soviet health authorities had to admit that their own industry would be able to satisfy only 19 percent of the year's demand for medicines. Shortages of raw materials, moreover, meant that in 1990 USSR drug manufacturers could operate their plants at only 60 percent of capacity.[86] In August 1991 *Pravda* called the situation "catastrophic" and warned that, without added supplies of medicine, "inevitably, many thousands of patients will die."[87]

"How can the sick be cured in such conditions?" asked an angry medical writer near the end of 1990. "According to official reports, deliveries of 77 out of 473 important drugs will cover less than a third of the demand."[88]

At the same time, pharmaceutical enterprises in the USSR were making or buying as many as 3,000 medicinal preparations, many of them duplicating one another. While about 5,000 different drugs were available in the United States at any one time, the American listings were renewed by dropping and replacing approximately one-fifth of the medications every year. Brazil, a contemptuous Soviet journalist noted, cut its pharmacopoeia to 700 products, and, she added, experts in Moscow "recently . . . suggested that 200 obsolete drugs be taken out of production. Who kept that work from being started and finished years ago?"[89]

The officials responsible for those errors of omission were presumably the same ones who let Soviet physicians so often prescribe the wrong drugs for their patients. According to a pharmaceutical researcher, who had checked "tens of thousands" of treatment charts, in some years more than 1,500 tons of drugs to reduce fever and fight bacterial infection were improperly administered. The economic harm from all adverse reactions to drugs ran to 35 billion rubles a year.[90]

The researcher's bill of indictment went on:

More than 63 percent of patients diagnosed with non-specific lung ailments receive potentially dangerous, irrational and pharmaceutically inappropriate [drug] compounds. Almost 92 percent of those suffering

from bronchitis are given prescriptions for antibiotics and sulfa drugs
. . . which in most cases do more harm than good. . . .

By our calculations, about 20 percent of the nation's hospital beds are
occupied by patients with complications due to the medications [used in
treating them]. More than 84,000 are treated for infections following
surgery, and between 1.5 and 6.5 percent of them die. At a minimum,
according to the data of Academician V. I. Pokrovskiy, 25 percent—and
perhaps 55 percent—of all injections given to patients are improper.[91]

FAILING ACCORDING TO PLAN

Such data reveal the ignorance and poor training that characterized all
too many members of the Soviet medical profession. But their lack of
qualifications was compounded, at least in the acute shortage of drugs,
by the built-in indifference to efficiency, especially as measured in profits, that ruled in the Soviet medical industry as decisively as in steelmaking or land reclamation. Raw materials rolled in; finished products
rolled out—often wastefully and improperly made—and if physicians
and patients did not get what they needed, at least the central planners
who set production quotas more or less did. Perhaps the saddest by-
product of this innately flawed system was the way it stifled innovation
by genuinely talented and dedicated scientists. In the Soviet Union, it
was an oft-told tale of opportunities missed and ideas suppressed in one
branch of knowledge after another, from genetics to electronics to art,
music and literature.

One of the grimmest stories was in the field of medicine. It happened
in secret and it took years to emerge. But emerge it did in the pages of
the newspaper *Izvestiya,* first in January 1991 and then in a follow-up
article in May of the same year.[92] The first clue of a newsworthy event
was a speech by a high Communist functionary given at the Twenty-
seventh Party Congress in 1986 attacking an experimental biochemical
research laboratory for "wasting" 50 million rubles without producing
a single new drug.

The criticism was a typical tactic of the new, insecure Gorbachev
regime seeking to discredit its predecessors as inattentive spendthrifts.
The true story proved more complex. The research institute had, in fact,
not only produced promising drugs to treat nervous system disorders
and epilepsy—from which 2 million Soviets suffered—but also invented
the nation's first and reportedly highly sophisticated method of screening new chemical compounds to find the most promising ones for future
pharmaceutical use.[93]

All three of these breakthroughs ended up gathering cobwebs. The medical and microbiological industry ministry vetoed the epilepsy drug on grounds that it was too hard to synthesize, although its discoverers, turning to colleagues in a military think tank, demonstrated otherwise. The neurological medicine was handed over to Soviet medical export firms to market abroad but not put into production at home. And the screening method was given a state patent but never funded for use.[94]

Worse—but very much part of the reigning culture in Soviet science in the Brezhnev years—the inventors and some of their associates were purged from the research institute or demoted inside it in a campaign of "persecution on grounds of ethnic origin." Their names—Avidon, Moshkovskiy, Raikhman, Attaulakhanov, Piruzyan, even Kuznetsov and Zhdanov—spoke of Jewish, Muslim and Armenian ancestries that made the bearers suspect as *inorodtsy,* aliens.[95] Higher-ups feared that their first loyalty might not be to the Soviet Union or to the Russian-run scientific and political establishment. They posed a danger. They might seek to emigrate. Indeed, once they were ousted or humiliated, some did. Their bosses, bureaucrats looking out for their own reputations, judged it safer to persecute them than to advance them and their work.

In theory, such self-destructive practices should vanish with the discrediting of Stalinism undertaken in the Gorbachev era. History may not prove easy to overcome, however. Anton Chekhov, a pre-Revolutionary physician who became one of Russia's great writers, described the agonizing, lifelong process by which he "squeezed the slave out of myself drop by drop."

That process remained arduous in the 1990s. One Soviet commentator, for example, reserved judgment on a mid-1991 governmental decision to liquidate the Ministry of Medical and Microbiological Industry and rearrange most of its parts inside a profit-oriented public enterprise called *Pharmindustriya.* "Does this mean that the difficult drug-supply situation is to be looked after at the highest level and, most importantly, that the newborn corporation can count not just on well-intentioned concern but also on genuine government support?" the doubting journalist asked. "Let's remember that all too recently the highest authorities did not exactly pamper the domestic pharmaceutical industry with their attention. That is why it has fallen so low."[96] So low, in fact, that researchers had neither "pure strains of laboratory animals" nor decent facilities to house them, and Soviets had to spend about 100 million rubles' worth of hard currency to cover their laboratories' inability to manufacture "pure, monoclonal and human insulin" every year.[97]

High-level indifference—bred of ignorance, complacency and a willingness to accept slogans as reality—inevitably fostered a pernicious neglect that harmed far more than the Soviet drug industry. The gathering ills of industrialized society that attacked the USSR and its people did not spring, like Venus, from the ocean foam. They were nurtured and, in effect, speeded on their way by conscious governmental policies that put more value on pesticides than on people, more emphasis on energy production than on conservation or pollution control, more money into armaments than medicines, more investments into the symbols of international power than the reality of domestic well-being.

THERE OUGHT TO BE A LAW

By the time Mikhail Gorbachev (and many reformers whose sensitivity to health and environmental dangers far surpassed his) called for a drastic change of direction, ecocide had so damaged the nation's health that the prospects for near-term recovery looked bleak. In the spring of 1991 the deputy chief sanitary inspector of the Soviet Ministry of Health itemized some of the effects of environmental neglect and came to his own gloomy conclusion:

> In 125 cities a tenfold excess of the maximum permissible concentration of harmful substances in the air . . . means that 40 to 50 million people are subject to constant threat.
>
> Drinking water [infects] approximately half a million people with viral hepatitis. . . . Every fourth sample of water is dangerous to health because of its chemical content; every fifth sample, for its bacteriological content.*
>
> Soil contaminated with pesticides and the salts of heavy metals also makes the situation worse. . . . There exist 14 natural, permanent breeding grounds for plague . . . and the potential for infecting a total area of 512 million acres.
>
> One more significant factor is the occupational disease that arises from harmful working conditions. . . . In 1989 more than 6,000 workers were declared victims of vibration, and every year there are 12,000 new cases of poisoning and disease due to job-related problems. . . . Each represents a cost to the economy of about 20,000 rubles.
>
> If we use military terms, today this "army," though morally prepared for any battle, is stripped, barefoot and poorly armed. We lack the main weapon—a law to bar the way against this calamity.[100]

*From 1988 to 1990, the incidence of hepatitis B, the most dangerous form of the disease, doubled in the Soviet Union, with more than two-thirds of the cases being transmitted in medical facilities by infected blood or unsterilized needles, according to a USSR Health Ministry specialist. The spread of hepatitis and other viral infections, however, is also thought to be linked to the worsening quality of big-city water supplies in which bacteria levels rose from two to five times in the 1988–90 period.[98] Epidemiologists in the 1980s blamed polluted water for one-fourth of all Soviet intestinal infections.[99]

The law the inspector had in mind was an innovative environmental consumers' rights act. It would entitle citizens to know what dangers lurked in their air, water, soil and food; to find out who put the hazards there; to sue government agencies and officials and private persons for damaging public health and to impose on polluters both stiff fines and, perhaps, prison terms. Adopted by the Russian Republic parliament, the legislation awaited action by the USSR Supreme Soviet in June 1991.

Startup costs for the legislation amounted to 2.5 billion rubles. But its backers estimated that the absence of legally enforceable "sanitary-epidemiological well-being" was costing the state "much greater losses—about 33 billion rubles a year. . . ." As one Health Ministry official put it, "Economizing on health has always turned out to be very expensive."[101]

The concept behind the law postulated a direct link between pollution and disease. Origin and causation are hard to question in the case of poisoning by lead, mercury, cadmium, beryllium, dioxin, untreated human wastes in sewage, phenol, formaldehyde and some other chemicals. But neither Soviet nor Western scientists knew for a certainty—the kind that could pass a court test—just how much sulfur dioxide combined with how much nitrous oxide over how long a period of exposure would be a disabling or even fatal dose for an otherwise healthy adult.

It was rare for Soviet urban air or water to hold just one hazardous substance or for an isolated poison—uranium-238 in Ust-Kamenogorsk or DDT on the fields of Azerbaijan and Moldova—to act alone as a lethal agent. Medical research has established the harm that individual atmospheric, aquatic or foodborne toxics can do, but the combinations of such substances in the daily diet of millions in the Soviet Union have not been studied enough to allow forensic specialists to point to one compound or one source as the pollutant and polluter to be brought to justice.

The presumption that environmental damage produces human illness was easy to demonstrate in the declining health of large numbers of people but very hard to prove for a single individual. It was one thing to joke, as a Soviet wit has done, that because of ecological damage to the resort area where they are located, the sanatoria of Crimea should be renamed "crimatoria."[102] It was another to trace back to the shoddy refuse disposal practices of the Black Sea Fleet based in Sevastopol a case of viral hepatitis contracted by a vacationer in Yalta.

The danger in the assumptions underlying the proposed USSR law was that the pursuit of the guilty—a time-honored Soviet sport carried over into environmental affairs with a very literal sense of vengeance—could distract from the urgent effort to reduce pollution and rebuild human health. The law may prove most useful in providing reliable epidemiological data and in forcing its disclosure so that experts can compare rates of pollution with rates of illness and mortality to help focus cleanup efforts sensibly. The law could help dedicated researchers such as Yaroslavl's Aydin Guseinov, a professor who has been using the health records of factory workers to draw a map of environmental illness in his city. Describing the extensive data-gathering work he and his colleagues have done in the region, he told an American guest, "We are like the dogs who sniffed the rubble after the earthquake in Armenia. We tell the rescuers where to dig."[103]

Those who would salvage the Soviet environment and, to repeat Biryukova's image, "resuscitate our nation's health care system," must have such guidance. But they must also have pollution-control equipment to install and the funds to pay the environmental control bill. They must have the financing to build modern, sterile pharmaceutical plants, to further their own promising drug research and, above all, to treat and cure the sick.

Those resources, however, were precisely the ones on which the state scrimped in the past. Short of a miraculous economic turnaround, the necessary funds looked impossible to create or divert in the sixth year of Mikhail Gorbachev's tempestuous rule. Too many other urgent problems—from the impending energy crisis to the challenge of converting military production facilities to civilian output—demanded attention and investment.

The "residual principle" that put human welfare last was a hard habit to break. Those who would suffer because of it through the 1990s were those who had suffered in the past: Soviet hospital and clinic personnel—administrators, nurses and doctors—and the patients in their care—mothers and newborn children first and most of all.

CHAPTER 10

Cradle to Grave

"EVERY FOURTH DOCTOR in the world is Soviet." So proclaimed a propaganda poster printed in Moscow in 1973, typical of that smug era's sloganeering about the state of social well-being in the USSR.[1] The boast, though statistically accurate, revealed little about the quality either of Soviet health care or of Soviet life. Then and in the Gorbachev years, Soviet infant mortality rates gave a truer picture of a medical system calamitously failing to protect the nation and its most vulnerable people.

In 1989, 1,115,000 doctors were on duty, still more than four for every 1,000 inhabitants of the country. The ratio in the United States was only half as high. But in 1989 as well, according to *official* Soviet data, of the 5,062,200 children born in the USSR, 116,300—22.7 per thousand—did not live 365 days.[2] In all probability, as noted earlier (see chapters 1 and 4), the *actual* number of Soviet births that ended in death before the babies reached their first birthday was closer to 170,000 in 1990. According to leading maternal and child care authorities in the Soviet Ministry of Health, "about 200,000 babies died" in 1989, more than one in four a victim of improper medical care.[3]

With so many physicians on hand, an infant mortality rate higher than that of China—one of the world's poorest countries—and closer to Botswana's and Bulgaria's than to South Korea's was hard to explain and harder to excuse. The overall health crisis and its effect on children brought cries of rage from a once-passive population, directed not at the medical profession but at the nation's political leadership. An extreme example was a vitriol-laden call for Mikhail Gorbachev to leave the

Kremlin "before our children suffocate under the emissions of our chemical, metallurgical and atomic 'giants.' "[4]

Printed as a signed open letter to the Soviet president in the crudely produced independent paper of one of the most radical democratic factions to spring up in the *glasnost* era, the vicious attack targeted both Gorbachev's wife's alleged extravagance and the penury of Soviet health care. "Unlike Raisa Maximovna," wrote the polemicist, "our wives don't have money in Swiss bank accounts that we could use to have our kids treated abroad. And our 'free' Soviet medicine, as you very well know, gets only the leftovers from the budget. It is no help. It hasn't the power to cure children, only to infect them with AIDS."[5]

SIEGE CONDITIONS

Hysterical as the tone of the letter seemed, much of its substance was sound. "Free" Soviet medicine inflicted terrible human costs. For years the health budget had been too low and too often misspent on producing impressive statistics such as high numbers of doctors and hospital beds. Elementary hygiene, a less glamorous concern, had been neglected to the point that hospitals were severely overcrowded or dilapidated or both and that the instruments doctors used were too often unsterilized and obsolete.

None of those conditions could fairly be blamed on Gorbachev himself. He inherited a health care system on the edge of collapse and one that, until his arrival, had tried to hide its shortcomings behind meaningless statistical flourishes and conscious statistical deception. From 1975 until 1986, Soviet health officials knowingly concealed and even fudged the *official* tally of infant mortality. Only in the Gorbachev era did they begin to disclose the incomplete truth in an effort to mobilize political support for higher funding and deep reform. As part of that campaign, some leading figures pressed for both public candor and the use of standard World Health Organization criteria of viability at birth.

Deputy Minister of Health Alexander Baranov, for example, insisted: "We can no longer write off as a miscarriage, as was done before, the death of an infant weighing 980 to 1,000 grams (34–35 ounces) within the first few hours of birth." Such self-deception, he said, had blinded Soviet leaders to the real crisis. The "blissful ignorance" was so widespread even in ruling circles that "when some of us started talking about a catastrophic situation in this particular field, we met with incomprehension."[6]

The catastrophe ran the full gamut of Soviet medicine. It extended from prenatal care to postoperative attention. It began with the poor qualifications of many new-fledged physicians and went on to the meager salaries they and other medical personnel received even after long service. It ranged from the quantity and quality of drugs, to the quantity and quality of baby food, of essential medical supplies, of hospital equipment and hospital plumbing.

There were exceptions, some of them striking. A Moscow eye clinic, the creation of an extraordinary medical entrepreneur, has been the site of pioneering work in assembly-line-style cataract surgery. In basic and sometimes even applied research, as on juvenile diabetes, specialized scientists in the USSR could claim a place of honor. And even in the disorder, often the dirt, of Soviet sickrooms, doctors and nurses sometimes managed to show a human and humane touch missing in too many highly efficient, highly mechanized and gleamingly sterile American treatment facilities.

In the last decade of the twentieth century, signs of hope and change began to appear in the Soviet Union. The complaints of a newly informed public spurred the self-scrutiny of a medical profession under fire. Legislators began to consider health insurance plans as an alternative to the system of free treatment. Administrators acted to raise the pay of skilled physicians. Private philanthropy, some of it Western, responded to emergency appeals for financial and technical help.

But the emergency was everywhere and overwhelming. It was not like the plagues and famine of the early 1920s that the American Relief Administration came to fight. Those had struck mainly in Central Russia. Seven decades later Soviets everywhere were under siege on almost every health front.

To stay well and to administer medication to the sick, they needed single-use needles and disposable syringes by the billion. To improve treatment, they needed hundreds of millions of dollars worth of primary and advanced diagnostic and therapeutic equipment and years of training in its use. To survive surgery, they needed reliable supplies of antiseptics, scalpels, disposable surgical gloves, medications, bandages, bedsheets, running water, hot water and skillful nursing care.

In fact, they needed something far beyond the healing arts: a healthy standard of living. In the midst of the accelerating economic failures of the 1990s, the basic indices of Soviet daily life—income, food and housing—all pointed down, not up. Poor nutrition alone eroded overall public health and jeopardized the survival chances of many newborn children. Cramped dwellings and empty wallets were the main factors that Soviet women consistently cited to explain their decisions to spare unborn children lives without proper clothing, housing or food.[7]

DESPERATE REMEDIES

Even though only five or six out of every one hundred women in the world in 1989 lived in the USSR, every fourth recorded abortion in the world was performed on a Soviet woman.[8] The frequency of Soviet abortions was a social scandal and a major health hazard. With contraceptive devices, even condoms, hard or impossible to obtain and without "a single, practical, popular brochure" on how to avoid unwanted pregnancies available in the USSR as late as 1988,[9] abortion, with all its potential for physical and psychological complications, was the only reliable birth control option open to most Soviet women.

"When will those idiots in Moscow realize that the damage done to our women by abortion is quite equal to the harm done by narcotic addiction, alcoholism?" raged a well-known Georgian gynecologist to an American writer in May 1988. "Do you really want to know why so many of our doctors oppose birth control?" he continued. "In many areas of the Soviet Union—Georgia is one of them—much shame is still attached to abortion, and our doctors oppose birth control because they make so much money out of *criminal* abortions performed at home."[10]

In the USSR in 1989, according to official statistics, 6,974,000 legal abortions were performed, almost ten for every one hundred women between the ages of fifteen and forty-nine.[11] The official data, however, were not to be trusted. Statistics on abortion were printed in 1987 for the first time in more than fifty years. Even then the figures went back only to 1975. For most of its history, the Soviet Union has not officially reported on the abortions that it legalized in 1920, banned in 1936 and made lawful again in 1955.

The real ratio of abortions to live births was not seven to five, as the published figures indicate. In all likelihood it was two to one, since Soviet women averaged at least four abortions during their lives, an aggregate figure that ran much higher in non-Muslim regions and cultures. Many Soviet experts calculated that the number of self-induced and illegal abortions—carried out by fee-charging doctors after their regular duty hours, or performed after the first trimester or in order, as in Georgia, to avoid family and community disapproval—is close to 50 percent of the total carried on the record books.[12]

No medical remedies, Soviet or other, could cure the host of socioeconomic ills that degraded the quality of life and health in the USSR. But Soviet physicians could do much to heal themselves. They could improve their professional education and skills and weed incompetents from their ranks. In their daily duties, as a single example, they could take better care of the women whom circumstances and the lack of other contraceptive methods compel to seek abortions.

A decent level of care could make anesthesia a standard practice instead of a rarity often costing 200 rubles in bribe money.[13] It could also reduce the appalling rate of sterility in the 90 percent of Soviet women reported as using abortions to end their first pregnancies.[14] In the 1980s as many as one out of every six such women suffered a punctured uterus or other complication that made them barren for life.[15]

For Soviet women in the 1980s only childbirth represented a more harrowing, though less frequent, encounter with medical reality than abortion. On average over the decade, approximately 2,500 pregnancies each year ended in the mother's death. The average *official* rate of roughly 49 fatalities for every 100,000 Soviet women giving birth— again, an undercount—was more than five times higher than America's between 1980 and 1987 and only slightly lower than Chile's or Uruguay's during the same years.[16]* The number of acknowledged maternal deaths in the USSR climbed above 2,900 in 1989. The number of anemic mothers reached 698,000, and 360,000 women "suffered from toxemia during the second half of pregnancy," the senior Soviet official overseeing maternal and child care revealed. That blood infection increased "the chances of a pathological childbirth by one and a half or two times."[17]

The official figure of 49 maternal deaths per 100,000 live births in 1989 represented an admitted increase of six such deaths per 100,000 over the previous year, but the 1988 statistic was yet another misleading number. The "true indicator," Deputy Health Minister Baranov disclosed in 1990, was almost 52 such fatalities—not 43—per 100,000 births in 1988. And, mirroring the region's high infant mortality rates, mothers in Central Asia died far more often in childbirth than their counterparts in the rest of the USSR. The 1988 maternal death rate in Tajikistan was 1.6 times above the Soviet average; in Uzbekistan, 1.7 times higher and in Turkmenistan, 2.6 times higher, or nearly 135 maternal deaths per 100,000 births.[18]

A WOMAN'S STORY

But the threats of death during or after labor or of giving birth to a defective child were statistical flyspecks compared to the all-but-univer-

---

*Soviet statistics did show a drop in maternal mortality rates from 56 per 100,000 in 1980 to 43 per 100,000 in 1988.

sal horror of maternity ward conditions. Sonya Shmatova, barely eighteen when her first son was born in Moscow in April 1988, thought she would be among the privileged few to get special treatment. Her Rh-negative blood entitled her to admission to one of the capital's three clinics specially equipped to look after pregnant women with similar, threatening conditions. Her father's friendships helped secure her the entitlement in practice.

"I arrived at seven in the morning, and I couldn't believe how dirty the place was," she recalled eighteen months later. "It looked as if the floors were never cleaned. There were flies stuck to all the light fixtures. Everything was slimy." The specialists on hand, however, seemed superior to their surroundings, and one supervising physician took a personal, reassuring interest in her.

After changing to a hospital gown and slippers, Sonya gave her own clothes to her parents. They had accompanied her to the reception area but could go no farther nor stay in the clinic to await the outcome of her labor. Their daughter then walked up three flights of stairs—there was no elevator—to a curt nurse who gave her a quilt and a pillow and pointed to a chair in the corridor where she was to wait.

Sonya began to cry. The nurse asked her if she had any infection. "A little head cold," Sonya replied. On those grounds, she was sent down a flight of stairs to the ward for contagious patients. It too was full, but in the corridor Sonya found and took possession of a bed the back of which was permanently stuck in an upright position.

There she waited for six hours until, with birth imminent, a nurse directed her to the delivery room. She walked to it and joined a dozen other women in "pandemonium, all of them screaming in pain and using the most ferocious Russian curse words." The actual delivery was uncomplicated, but for two days afterward Sonya's only accommodation was the broken bed in the corridor.

No visitors were permitted. Finally admitted to a "super," a private room with its own refrigerator, she had four more days of convalescence to undergo. To wash herself, she had to share the ward's single bathroom with the other new mothers. The one available spigot dispensed only cold water.

Home at last, Sonya began to suspect that her son was not as perfect as he had first seemed. At the age of three months, he was found to have a dislocated right hip, something she suspected came from the rough handling he received on entering the world. He spent his next six months immobilized in a plaster cast.

At eleven months, Sonya took him to a Moscow children's hospital for minor surgery, the removal of a subcutaneous cyst over his right eye.

The hospital required him to stay for three days after the procedure and put him in a crib in a room with a dozen other youngsters. Sonya stayed with him, common though not universal practice for Soviet parents of sick children. Adults often seek to stand guard over their young to shelter them from clinicians' indifference. The first night, she made her bed out of two chairs and slept as best she could.

"Then my mother came and saw how things were," Sonya recollected. "She knows how to talk to people the right way, and she got us into a private room. I had walked past it along the corridor many times, but never realized it was even there."

At home again with the convalescent boy, she managed both to buy her own supply of a vitamin solution for injections to speed the healing and to acquire, through a medical student friend, a sterilizer and a needle and syringe with which to administer the shots. Such exploitation of a social connection was a modest example of the universal practice of *blat,* an untranslatable word for the ad hoc arrangements that Soviets have to use to gain access to goods and services without going through clogged channels.

Sonya's exercise of *blat* saved her the standard 100-ruble price of a packet of ten disposable needles, home-delivered by underground medical entrepreneurs. Equipped with her own supply, she was also able to decline the services of the district nurse who, though a provider of home treatment that Americans might envy, was also part of the medical system Sonya had come to fear.

"My boy ran a very high fever after his first polio vaccination, so I never gave him the second or third shot, nor the series against diphtheria, whooping cough and tetanus. There were a lot of articles in the newspapers about vaccines contaminated with mercury, and then there was a sudden silence in the press. Along with the AIDS business, it was just too scary."[19]

The "AIDS business" was the outbreak of the disease in a Volgograd children's ward in January 1989. Ten children in the hospital were diagnosed as HIV-infected. The disease was traced back—at least to the satisfaction of most authorities—to blood drawn in the nearby Kalmyk city of Elista from a child whose mother's husband, a translator, had been stationed in Africa. Unsterilized, the contaminated needle and syringe passed the sickness on to a number of youngsters in the Elista hospital.[20] When some of those same children were moved to Volgograd for better medical care, their condition was not correctly diagnosed. Their diseases, again carried by unsterilized needles, entered Volgograd's pediatric wards. By early May 1990, four of that city's youngsters had died of AIDS.[21]

Sonya Shmatova's anxiety about Soviet needle hygiene predated those tragedies. Many other parents, as noted in the previous chapter, shared her fears, but not all experienced the particular epiphany that Sonya had when she took her son to have the stitches removed from the incision above his eye.

"The cut was badly swollen with blood, and when they pulled the stitches out, he cried from the pain, and blood gushed all over his face," Sonya recalled. The doctor did not apologize, only explained. The original stitches had been sewn with silk thread, because no other material was available. If she had wanted a higher-quality of suture used, Sonya should have supplied it herself.

"I thought, 'This is what *free* medicine is.' And for the first time in my life, I totally lost my temper with the system. I went and raised hell with the hospital authorities. Nothing changed, but at least I stopped submitting in silence."[22]

She might not have emerged unscathed had she thrown her tantrum in the polluted Urals town of Berezniki where blood infections (see chapter 9) afflict a disproportionate number of children. In Ward 43 of Unit 2 of the First City Hospital of Berezniki in 1990, a list headed "Mothers' Duties" hung on the wall. It specified the following code of conduct:

a. Keep the bed and night table of each child neat.
b. Nothing is allowed on the night table except a drinking glass and juice.
c. Nothing is to be placed on the windowsill.
d. Hang the towel at the back of the bed.
e. The number on the bedpan must match the number of the bed.
f. Maintain the security of the furniture.

Do not argue with the medical personnel. Mothers who disobey will be ordered off the premises. Address the nurses by their first name and patronymic.[23]

MOTHERHOOD AND ITS DISCONTENTS

Far from Berezniki, the women of Muslim Central Asia, the most fertile and the most often bereaved mothers in the Soviet Union, have suffered in silence, subservience and sorrow. With 12 percent of the country's population, the Kirghiz, Tajik, Turkmen and Uzbek republics accounted for 22 percent of the births in the USSR in 1989 and no less than 39 percent of the infant deaths.[24] The average Central Asian infant mortality rate of 40 per thousand live births—even as calculated from the suspect official data—was nearly twice the Soviet average, and among rural people, more than twice. In Turkmenistan, infant death rates in 1989 were actually higher than in 1985.[25]

The lethal forces at work on Central Asian children and their mothers include malnutrition, environmental poisons, incompetent health care and inadequate medical facilities. The fact that respiratory and intestinal tract diseases, respectively, killed infants three and five times more often in Central Asia in 1987 than in the USSR on average suggests how unavailing the mothers' defenses were against their toxic diet and surroundings.[26]

The stunted health care structure was clearly unequal to the battle against such debilitation. Because the number of doctors could not keep pace with population growth in the region, some parts of Central Asia in 1987 had only half as many pediatricians per capita as the USSR overall.[27] Uzbek women were twice as likely as other Soviets to go through nine months of pregnancy without a single medical examination.[28] When Kirghiz and Turkmen women went to give birth, they found as late as 1991 that only 24 and 15 percent of the maternity clinics in the respective republics had piped-in water.[29]

The absence of family planning and government support for programs of birth control made the situation worse. The young woman whose appointment as minister of health of Turkmenistan in early 1991 seemed to signal a more vigorous official response to the infant mortality crisis worried aloud about the powerful traditions in Islamic culture and belief that encouraged women to produce as many children as possible. At the same time that she praised the legislature for appropriating an extra 50 million rubles to combat the highest infant mortality rates in the USSR, she regretted the lawmakers' refusal to finance family planning measures. Conceding the difficulty of quickly changing entrenched customs, she spoke of the harm many of the republic's mothers did to their own health and to their children's by "giving birth every year and sometimes twice a year. . . . It's a very delicate question," she added,

> and it is impossible for authorities on high to order families below to observe a set interval between births. Still, education is a different matter. It is essential. . . .
>
> Mothers who have a child every year double the risk that their baby will die or that they will suffer serious complications. But it is hard for doctors to get this message across when, especially in the countryside, women only come to the hospitals in order to give birth.[30]

Women in the cities of Central Asia had almost as hard a time as their rural sisters getting guidance and prenatal care. At a special clinic and counseling center attached to Maternity Hospital Number 5 in the Uzbek capital of Tashkent, 200 to 300 women waited daily for attention in 1989–90. They crowded into facilities where doctors who needed 100,000 single-use needles a year got only 5,000 to 6,000, where ordinary rubber gloves were a rarity and where the director observed, "our clinic is not the worst off, . . . [but] our gynecologists have only one diagnostic apparatus they can use—their own two hands."[31]

The one ultrasound device on the premises, made in Lithuania, cost 18,000 rubles and broke down within a few days of its installation. At the only clinic in Tashkent where such equipment actually functioned, "the waiting lines are enormous."[32]

Soviet women, so long suffering, finally began to speak out in the kind of fury that seized Sonya Shmatova. Strangers to her but not to her anguish or to the travail of Central Asian mothers, many took their protests to the press.

"I was seven months pregnant and in hellish pain," began a letter to the editors of the *Magnitogorsk Worker* in 1989, "and had to go to an 'alien' clinic because it was 'my' specialist's day off. Without even looking up at me, a pregnant woman standing there in agony, the registrar refused to give me an appointment because I lived in a different district of the city.

"Tell me, please, is there really such a rule? . . . If there is, let's open clinics where you have to pay but where anybody can go no matter where she works or lives. . . .

"I stayed in bed at home for three more days in unbearable torment until I got to see 'my' doctor. The diagnosis was furunculosis [infected swellings in the uterus]. They treated me with antibiotics. My child was born dead."[33]

A mother in Kiev wrote to her newspaper about giving birth in 1987 in a hospital where "senior, middle level and junior medical personnel see you as a potential source of bribe money. . . . My ten-day stay in the gynecology department cost me 300 rubles." For those payments she got no special attention or help during the pain of delivery, and, along with most new mothers, "no training on how to pump breast milk . . . and no [predischarge] gynecological examination."[34]

Another letter came to the Magnitogorsk newspaper from a grieving and embittered father. "For her first year and four months our daughter never had a sick day," he wrote. "Then suddenly on a Wednesday her temperature shot up to around 101 degrees.

"On Thursday we called the district nurse to come look at her. She got an injection, but it didn't help. We called the ambulance service. They took her to the hospital with a diagnosis of 'acute laryngitis.' My wife asked to stay with her, but the hospital wouldn't permit it.

"On Monday they told us our daughter was dead. Her heart had stopped.

"The doctor came out. 'Your daughter died. They brought her in too late. Well, am I needed for anything else?' He turned around and walked off. Am I right in thinking that if her mother had been allowed to stay with her, maybe this wouldn't have happened?"[35]

The question is imponderable. In the late 1980s only 20 to 25 percent of Magnitogorsk infants were born completely healthy. The rest suffered from a range of illnesses, many of them congenital.

"Why," a Magnitogorsk journalist asked local health authorities, "do we have such a high infant mortality rate?"

"Because the index of maternal health is so low."

"And why is it so low?"

"The city's environment is very unhealthy. That's the first reason. Second, many women are production workers. They don't get away from the harmful surroundings of the assembly line until late, if ever. Third, the level of medical help is low."[36]

EQUAL RIGHTS, UNEQUAL BURDENS

Magnitogorsk (see chapter 5) is among the most poisoned and poisonous of Soviet industrial cities. In its sanatoria, among a special category of children classified as "frequently ill," 60 percent of the young pneumonia patients in 1988 and 37 percent of those with gastroenterological disorders were the offspring of metallurgical workers.[37] Some thousand miles to the west, in the residential neighborhoods around the metallurgical combine in the city of Novolipetsk, miscarriages tripled and infant deaths rose 78 percent between 1985 and 1990.[38]

Not all female industrial workers in the USSR were exposed to quite the hazards of those whose jobs put them next to raging, smoky furnaces. But Soviet statisticians counted 44 percent of all women laborers in industry and 17 percent of those in the building trades as working in what were defined as "particularly difficult or harmful conditions."[39] Among those conditions, Turkmenistan's new minister of health found one particularly horrifying: "It's way past time for us to reexamine the standards that were set God knows when for heavy lifting. In Japan, for example, the law prohibits women from hauling more than 440 pounds per shift. Our permitted norm is seven [metric] tons [15,400 pounds]."[40]

In 1990, more than 3 million of the 59.3 million Soviet women employed in industry and services toiled in conditions that did not meet minimum occupational safety standards.[41] One-fifth—500,000—of all those engaged in heavy manual labor in industry were women and one-fourth of all construction workers.[42] So were 38 percent—4 million—of night-shift workers, 34 percent of the personnel on Soviet road-building crews, 20 percent of those who laid and repaired railroad tracks, 13 percent of the ditch-diggers, 12 percent of the bricklayers (who may haul 40 tons per shift) and 6 percent of the cement pourers.[43]

One more occupational statistic is relevant. In 1989 approximately two-thirds of all Soviet doctors were women, 838,100 in all.[44] They were, with few exceptions, the worst-paid and the least skilled members of a medical profession that in 1990 provided doctors of both sexes an average wage of only 175 rubles a month, 80 percent of the then-standard industrial worker's salary.[45]

In 1969, when women held 85 percent of all medical jobs in the USSR—midwives, nurses, paramedics and physicians—a Soviet economist noted that men occupied 50 percent of the best-paid and most prestigious health care posts.[46] Twenty years and more later the ratio had probably not changed much.

The 6 million Soviet women working in medicine at all levels in 1989 were not just eyewitnesses to the declining state of the country's health care system. They were also, with many commendable exceptions, contributing to the downward slide. They were like the millions of other Soviets who said, in effect, "We pretend to work and they pretend to pay us." The women who predominated on the staffs of hospitals, clinics and neighborhood examination and treatment facilities across the USSR had little financial incentive to do more than go through the motions of medical care.

Starting salaries for nonspecialists assigned to work as polyclinic physicians were 110 rubles a month in 1989, in theory enough to buy the least expensive Soviet-made automobile—if they saved every kopeck of their wages—after nine years. New nurses got 80 rubles, not enough to pay for a child's winter coat or a decent pair of shoes. While medical workers' wages rose 20 percent in the four years after 1985, the average salary in the USSR increased by 24 percent.[47] For 15 percent of Soviet doctors' families in 1991, combined income was reportedly below subsistence level.[48]

Not surprisingly, health workers could and did supplement their official earnings with money from the people they were supposed to treat for free. In 1987, when three Soviet patients in four were making payments to their doctors as a matter of course,[49] 25 rubles in cash or a relative's donated unit of blood could get a patient hospitalized ahead of others waiting their turn, and 300 rubles could cover the costs of making a twenty-day hospital stay possible and minimally comfortable.[50] In some specialties and some regions, such as the Transcaucasus, these supplementary payments could act as potent lures for doctors-to-be. The bribe a student had to pay for admission in 1991 to the Dagestan medical institute at Makhachkala, for example, was reported to range between 40,000 and 50,000 rubles.[51]

In a special 1989 survey for official use focused only on health care and on public support for putting it on a paid basis, pollsters found that 30 percent of their sample were willing to admit reimbursing medical personnel either in cash or with presents, in most cases to get quicker and better attention and to thank those who provided it. In almost half the cases where payment was made, the patients said they were buying access to hard-to-find diagnostic equipment.[52]

Female physicians were probably not major beneficiaries of such illicit but widespread largesse. They had little time to invest in their clients beyond their overcrowded duty hours and next to no time to spend on training in new medical skills or learning to operate sought-after machinery. The Russian proverb, "Women can do everything; men can do the rest," accurately described the division of labor between the sexes.

Soviet women have long been the nation's sturdy, victimized work-horses. Double-yoked to jobs and family needs, to cleaning, shopping, cooking and child care before and after their paying jobs, they had only the illusion of equal status with men. The reality was overwork and undercompensation.

HANDICAPPED HEALERS

Given the prevalence of women in primary care medicine and the low level of qualifications most of them attained, it was little wonder when a 1990 public opinion survey of 36,000 people in the Russian Republic found that 38 percent mentioned poor medical service as one of the six problems that disturbed them most. Although shortages of decent food and consumer goods and the high prices of both generated complaints from 74 to 84 percent of the sample, health care was the third most frequent noneconomic gripe. City dwellers cited it after environmental pollution (52 percent) and housing conditions (42 percent).[53]

Nor was it surprising that 70 percent of Soviet doctors, male and female, who emigrated to Israel and took qualifying exams to practice there failed the 1990 test. Two-thirds of Argentinean physician-emigrés and three-fourths of those arriving from Western Europe passed it without any preparatory studies. Of the Soviets who succeeded, only 15 percent managed to do so without a cram course.[54]

They came, after all, from the ranks of a profession where the standing joke had doctors examining a patient asking one another: "Well, shall we treat him or let him live?" Not so funny was the discovery made by a motor-pool dispatcher in the Belorussian capital of Minsk, who had not visited her polyclinic doctor for nine years.

"Recently," she told a Soviet journalist in 1990, "I felt very poorly and went to the doctor. Just imagine. She found in my chart the results of analyses made in the last three years [the period since the Chernobyl disaster and subsequent official instructions to monitor closely the health of the entire population in areas, like Belorussia, where fallout had been heavy]. Naturally, all the findings were normal. We can't endure such blatant deceit any longer!"[55]

The lying was more than a manifestation of a health care structure corrupted by years of pressure to conceal alarming truths in clouds of false statistics. Diagnostic errors were products of the inadequate training, equipment and time available to the doctors in polyclinics—Soviet patients' first contact with the medical system. A veteran physician in one such Moscow establishment explained to a reporter in 1990 just what constraints he worked under:

> I've understood for a long time that the only thing that sustains us is enthusiasm. The building was put up 20 years ago to handle a case-load of 1,600, but the population in the district we serve went above 2,000 some time ago, and our facilities haven't changed. . . .
>
> The rules of the system are set in concrete. A district polyclinic internist is allowed 12 minutes with each patient. Specialists get even less time. All by themselves, those norms are simply absurd. Doctors should be able to plan the use of their own time. . . .
>
> Doctors get sick themselves fairly often,* but our defenselessness against germs is nothing compared to our social vulnerability. After all, we are not to blame for the fact that there aren't enough medicines or hospital beds.[57]

The diagnostic errors that originated in such dismal, overtaxed facilities spread through the entire course of treatment, often in hospitals not much better staffed or furnished than the neighborhood centers. As an experiment in 1987, a surgical institute sent blood samples from a single patient to three different laboratories for analysis. "The results," re-

---

*In a kind of pep talk to a 1989 physicians' congress, then Minister of Health Yevgeny Chazov noted: "Today, more than 350,000 medical workers do not have their own housing. . . . The rates of illness and death among health-care workers are among the highest in the country, but we have almost no sanatoria or preventive clinics for ourselves and no health-improving centers, not to mention how bad the working conditions are in most medical institutions."[56]

ported the institute's chief engineer, "came back scandalously different, and none of them was correct."[58]

Mistaken and misleading analyses would remain commonplace, he added, until Soviet diagnosticians had standardized equipment and proper training in its use. That day is far off. Even where considerable numbers of computers made their way into large hospitals, as in Moldova, "physicians and mid-level medical personnel were essentially unprepared to use them." As of the spring of 1990, only Moldovan medical students, not practicing physicians, were getting a twelve-hour introductory computer course.[59]

For more sophisticated apparatus, the gap between medicine in the USSR and the West was a chasm. In 1990, for example, when the United States had 4,800 CAT scanners and Japan, 4,000, the Soviet Union had only 62 such machines, of which only 25—all imported—"were capable of reading the whole body." Soviet-made fetal monitoring devices were "good, on average, for only 500 uses, compared to 30,000 for U.S. devices."[60]

Under such conditions, Soviet healers were bound to err. Examining analyses made in 2,531 cases culled from records in various cities, three Soviet researchers concluded in 1990 that diagnostic errors occurred 59 percent of the time. Their study did not indicate how many mistakes proved fatal, but it did find an 88 percent error rate in cases of heart failure, a 60 percent rate for acute pneumonia and a 79 percent rate for all cases of severe illness.[61] Another group of researchers reviewing patients' records in 1,232 cases of chronic lung disease in Uzbekistan in 1985–86 discovered a narrower but still disquieting pattern of errors. Ten percent of the time the initial diagnoses were "gross blunders." In 26 percent of the cases, chronic bronchitis proved to be either *acute* bronchitis or an unrelated ailment. Fifty-nine percent of the diagnoses of chronic pneumonia were wrong.[62]

The problem is not limited to Central Asia. An eleven-year-old boy in Kuibyshev, renamed Samara in 1991, underwent unnecessary and harmful lung surgery in 1990 for what was later discovered to be a congenital defect in his immune system. In his case, and in many others where diagnoses were mistaken, sometimes fatally so, the fault lay not with his doctors but with the lack of technical support. No laboratory in the region where over 3 million people live possessed the equipment to analyze the youngster's health problem correctly.[63]

Even when diagnoses were correct, quick attention was not guaranteed. A 1990 study of patients in the Russian Republic showed that more than one-fourth of those with intestinal blockages and one-fifth of those with acute appendicitis were admitted for treatment only twenty-four hours or more after the onset of their illness.[64] Problems even plagued emergency ambulance services, "most of which," an analyst concluded, "have too little space and are housed in buildings unsuited for the purpose. Practically all [the emergency squads] are handicapped by the low quality of their diagnostic, laboratory and treatment equipment."[65]

An American who visited Moscow's central emergency medical service in August 1990 found that its 2,000 doctors and paramedics were handling cardiac problems on 60 to 70 percent of their calls, but had only 126 defibrillators, each of them a bulky fifty-five pounds, to use to stabilize failing heartbeats. Like all other Soviets in the health care field, the first aid teams suffered from a terrible shortage of disposable needles and syringes. They could count on annual governmental supplies of approximately 150,000, normally enough to last two weeks.[66]

If the paramedics successfully delivered a patient to Moscow Hospital No. 63, whose 104 doctors and 740 beds served the 120,000 people of the Dzerzhinsky district in two forty-five-year-old buildings attached to a main wing built in 1987, the hospital would have been able to provide the following services:

- Two Hungarian-made X-ray machines in the radiology department, both "of an outmoded design," and X-ray films developed at the rate of 1,000 a month "exclusively by hand" so that "the image quality . . . is quite poor."
- A twenty-three-year-old electrocardiograph, the only one in the sixty-bed cardiology department, as well as a single, eighteen-year-old apparatus for reading brain-wave activity that uses "monitors which were built by hospital technicians themselves."
- A laboratory without "any modern testing equipment" where "all glassware was washed by hand . . . [and since] the distillery for sterile water was out of commission, the hospital" used "a home-made still."[67]

Whether an emergency case or a regular admission, a Soviet patient before and during the Gorbachev years was also likely to be put in the hands of a doctor who, as one member of the profession in Leningrad put it, had been "deprived of professional rights."

[Such a doctor] does not have the right to issue a medical excuse to a worker when and for the period that the doctor considers justified. Often, he [more often, she] cannot prescribe the appropriate drugs because the choice of medicines in our pharmacies is so severely limited. . . .

The new Health Ministry order that all physicians must raise their professional qualifications every five years cannot be fully implemented. One reason is that there is often no one to take the doctor's place, above all in the polyclinics. Besides, there are not enough training spaces [at postgraduate medical institutions] in any case.[68]

UNARMED, MAYBE DANGEROUS

In a variety of ways in 1990 and 1991, many Soviet doctors were saying what Winston Churchill had said fifty years earlier: "Give us the tools and we will finish the job." But the tools of modern medicine can be astronomically expensive, and the Soviet Union had only severely limited funds to spend on them—or on any other medical supplies. Unable to rely on government support, many physicians took up figurative arms to fight their way toward professional competence, independence, higher status and better patient care.

Two senior female doctors in Novosibirsk led the way with a short and partly successful hunger strike in January 1989. Camped out on a city sidewalk in harsh winter weather and sneered at by passersby who asked, "When do hunger strikers take their lunch break?" they demanded that authorities move their rundown polyclinic from its overcrowded, hot-waterless quarters into a new, five-story building. It had been promised to them five years earlier but was occupied instead by the construction enterprise that had put it up.

Protesting that the two physicians were behaving in very un-Soviet fashion, flustered officials nonetheless agreed on the spot to let the polyclinic take over the first floor of the building as a start. "We agree that our methods were 'out of bounds,'" said the polyclinic's Party organizer, "but what are we to do if those are the only kind of tactics that work? At least, we got the first floor."[69]

Two years later the "out-of-bounds" tactics had become almost routine, and doctors, nurses, pharmacists and other health workers were following the examples of hundreds of thousands of coal miners, striking for better wages and working conditions.* In February 1991, for instance, personnel in Moscow's hospitals and clinics—except for emergency services—declared a two-and-a-half-hour daytime strike to protest the lack of financial and technical support for their work.

---

*On occasion, strikers targeted environmental hazards as well as economic grievances. Ten thousand Donbass miners did so in May 1990 after fifty of their co-workers were overcome in the shafts by what were suspected to be toxic wastes seeping into the earth from a nearby explosives' plant's evaporation ponds. The Donbass protest followed by only a month the formation of a twenty-five-mile-long human chain of protesters in the city of Ufa, where a chemical plant accident that released phenol into the city water supply deprived more than 500,000 residents of drinking water for two weeks.[70]

At a prewalkout press conference, strike-committee members described the problems of patients for whom drug supplies covered only one-third of the need, of doctors for whom wages averaged only 60 percent those of industrial workers, of a city burn unit with no anesthetics and of hospitals that could provide neither decent food nor sharp scalpels.[71] Ranging beyond Moscow, they could have mentioned the surgeon in a distant part of the Russian Republic who told his colleague, the head doctor of a Moscow hospital, about regularly performing appendectomies with a straight-edge razor, as no scalpels were available.[72]

The Moscow strikers could also have called attention to the situation in one of the capital's best-equipped and most advanced organ-transplant establishments, where "delicate suturing" often had to be done with ordinary thread of the kind used on Sonya Shmatova's child. Or they might have cited the shortages of "scalpels, clamps, sutures, cauterizers, etc." in the main pediatric teaching hospital of Moscow. After a brief tour of its surgery department in 1990, an American visitor observed, "I have kitchen knives in my home that are sharper than the scalpels they use, [and] they are forced to re-use suturing needles, sharpening them as best they can."[73]

In Petropavlovsk on the Pacific Ocean, an American physician visiting what was "probably the largest children's clinic in the [Soviet] Far East" in April 1991

> found doctors' equipment [that] looked like leftovers from a 1950s yard sale: a Frankenstein X-ray machine and, in the maternity hospital, a creaking sterilizer the size of a Volkswagen.
>
> [Dr. Matison] White [a family practitioner from Anchorage, Alaska] saw technicians resharpening disposable needles and cleaning disposable syringes and cringed. "I haven't seen a single computer," he said, dumbfounded; his private office in Anchorage had far more advanced hardware than did this giant clinic. . . . All they had to offer, it seemed, was a human touch.[74]

The "human touch," however, was hard-pressed to compensate for a system in collapse. It could certainly not make up for the near disappearance from pharmacies and hospital supply rooms in 1989–90 of something as basic as cotton wool. Although Soviet cotton-wool production increased by 13,600 tons, or 38 percent, from 1980 to 1989, the shortage remained acute. At least one-fourth of the deficit could have been overcome just by packing the cotton wool instead of leaving it in long, loose bolts. Manufacturing such finished goods as tampons—an article not mass-produced in the USSR until 1989—would have economized on 30,000 tons of raw material a year, nearly two-fifths of all 1989 output.[75]

Nor could the "human touch" make up for the absence of sterilizing equipment and the indifference to basic hygiene inside so many Soviet medical institutions. Together, the two factors were responsible for 1.5 million cases of postoperative, suppurating infections *among outpatients alone* in the Russian Republic in 1990. In RSFSR hospitals, such infections occupied 35 to 40 percent of surgeons' efforts.[76] In Moscow maternity wards, the Soviet minister of health said in 1988, staphylococcal infections were rampant.[77]

A 1988 study of 150 departments in twenty-one hospitals in three separate regions of the USSR found in-hospital maladies affecting from nearly 3 to 28 percent of all patients. Primarily, they struck as uterine infections among women who had just given birth (almost 21 percent), and as a range of contagions among newborn children (166 to 233 cases per 100,000) and among those over sixty-five (114 to 118 per 100,000). Death rates for such patients fluctuated from a low of 3.5 percent to an appalling high of 60 percent.[78]

PROGNOSIS GUARDED

Given such fundamental problems, enormous investments targeted to implement sweeping reforms seem the only expedient that might put the Soviet medical system in shape to meet the nation's critical health problems. In mid-1991, with funds pinched, though increasing, and change coming more from below than by central directive, the odds against speedy recovery for the full system were enormous. Still, medicine in the USSR displayed some encouraging symptoms of new life and hope in its scattered parts.

Medical professionals, for instance, began to organize an independent association in 1990, launching it with coordinated rallies in numerous cities on August 18. Organizers in Leningrad pointed to a "crisis of confidence" in the entire Soviet health system and insisted that until their own "material conditions" were bettered there could be no improvement in medical performance overall.[79] Threatening that strikes could follow if the initial display of medical solidarity reaped no prompt dividends, a Russian Republic activist pointedly reminded doctors who usually worked a shift and a half that they were not legally bound to stay on duty for more than a single shift.[80]

When the rallies actually occurred on August 18, demands varied.

A pharmacy student in Khabarovsk, near the Chinese border, proposed turning the local Communist Party training school building over to pharmacological studies. At Komsomolsk-on-Amur, a few hundred miles north, some two thousand protesters staged a two-hour demonstration for higher salaries, better housing and upgraded hospital facilities. In Leningrad, on the opposite side of the USSR, marchers brandished the slogan: "Let's have some material support for the Hippocratic Oath."[81]

"Material support" would presumably have to deal with the renovation or replacement of the 45 percent of Soviet hospitals and 41 percent of polyclinics built before 1960 and with the fact that in mid-1989 "almost one-third" of all Soviet health care facilities needed a complete overhaul while one hospital out of eleven and one polyclinic in twenty were in "disastrous condition."[82] One almost universal disaster was overcrowding. Where Soviet medical standards prescribed a norm of 7 square meters per bed, the actual allotted space on average in 1988 was only 4.2 or 4.3 square meters.[83]

Although the pace of construction did accelerate and 13 percent more hospital beds were built in the Russian Republic between 1986 and 1990 than in the previous five years, the total still fell more than 30,000—16 percent—short of plan.[84] In the Moscow area in 1989, less than half of planned hospital construction was actually carried out and only 58 percent of the polyclinic-building program.[85]

In Belorussia officials estimated in 1987 that they needed to install 71,400 new hospital beds and build polyclinics to handle 169,800 visits per working day.[86] In Kazakhstan at the start of 1988, the minister of health calculated that his sprawling republic needed not only to create 6,200 extra beds just for maternity and gynecological patients, but to move 13,600 of those then in service to quarters that were not "dangerous and unfit."[87]

In the face of such overwhelming nationwide problems and an underwhelming response to them from Moscow, individual medical institutions and doctors improved where they could, improvised when they had to and tried to get on with the business of healing. Kazakhstan claimed impressive progress, for instance, in bettering sterilization work, setting up 563 central units in major hospitals and polyclinics and 104 more in facilities with fewer than one hundred beds to disinfect all medical instruments between uses. Even though 66 existing units did not meet sanitary standards "and some had to be shut," researchers said that the incidence of in-hospital hepatitis B infections in the republic stabilized in 1987. In Ust-Kamenogorsk, the rate actually dropped 37 percent from 1986 to 1989.[88]

Such success stories were few and far between. More typical was the history of doctors in one of Magnitogorsk's three maternity clinics. They "managed to turn a small operating room into an intensive-care unit, but they couldn't find any space for a biochemistry laboratory, even though they had the equipment for it."[89] Pediatricians in a Yaroslavl hospital got the funds to buy a long-sought, imported bronchoscope to examine their young patients' lungs by agreeing to cooperate in publicizing their benefactor, a factory manager campaigning for election to the USSR Supreme Soviet in 1989. He lost, but they won.[90]

New equipment was also coming off Soviet production lines from a variety of small firms set up by energetic medical technician–entrepreneurs trying to fill part of the huge demand and bolster the finances of their research and treatment centers at the same time. At a hospital in Penza, for instance, computer programmers perfected a diagnostic apparatus capable, they said, of monitoring sixty vital functions in a patient.[91] From a cooperative—that is, private—firm in Mogilev, an ultrasound device just to measure fetal pulse rates and temperature went on the market in 1989.[92]

Similarly, a Saratov medical institute created an association to combine diagnostic, clinical and technical work on blood diseases under a single roof and to offer itself as an example and guide to other hematologists in cities where, like theirs, factory workers in polluted surroundings frequently came down with such ailments.[93] Some medical entrepreneurs, not bound by stringent ethical rules, went directly to the public, especially to advertise diagnostic facilities. In Moscow a joint venture with Swiss technicians promised that Western stress tests combined with Soviet-developed techniques of physical therapy would help patients lose weight, reduce the risk of heart attacks and "improve general condition and mood."[94] A medical cooperative in the city of Kurgan, advertising a diagnostic and treatment method it said had been introduced in the regional hospital and in the RSFSR gastroenterological center, urged ulcer and gastritis sufferers as well as those afflicted with varicose veins to enroll for cures.[95]

Such signs of energy and activism were part of the life throes of Soviet medicine in the early 1990s, as it tried to shed its reliance on negligent central authorities and find a base for survival and growth in self-reliance. In just two years, 1988 and 1989, the number of medical cooperatives went from near zero to 3,289, with 61,000 people employed and an annual income of 286 million rubles.[96] Their growth and especially their profit-making offended many Soviets still wedded to the promise of free medical care provided by the state. But the old guard in medicine, as in Soviet politics more broadly, was being forced to retreat.

Characteristically, the self-assured father of Soviet medical entrepreneurialism, eye surgeon Sviatoslav Fyodorov, had no doubts about the therapy needed for his country's health and health care: reorganization and privatization. Creator in the 1970s of the Moscow assembly-line clinic that performed roughly eight thousand cataract operations a year and investor—through the clinic—in a 17-million-ruble-a-year company producing optical instruments,[97] in car rental services, in a Moscow luxury hotel and in agricultural training, Fyodorov spelled out his prescription to *Pravda* in 1990:

> I am convinced that medicine today should divide itself into three levels or categories. Let the family physician be the discoverer of diseases that show themselves early. We need about half a million such practitioners.
>
> Then there should be diagnosticians grouped according to their specialties and working in separate institutes, cardiovascular, gastrointestinal and so forth. Of those, we need about 150,000.
>
> Once an ailment has been diagnosed as requiring surgery, there should be fully equipped surgical clinics [to handle it] . . . and 50 to 60,000 surgeons to staff them.
>
> It is completely obvious that doctors' earnings should correspond directly to the results of their work.
>
> Today more than 1.2 million doctors work in our health care system. In quantitative terms, we have swamped the world, but as far as quality goes, we have slipped tragically to the bottom.[98]

The fact that Fyodorov was elected to the USSR Supreme Soviet, where, a Moscow physician said, doctors were the best-represented profession,[99] probably had less impact on the Soviet medical establishment than the cries of outrage from below and the energetic push for reform initiated by Health Minister Chazov and continued by his successor, Igor Denisov. In an interview in May 1991 Denisov bluntly dismissed the once-sacrosanct but rarely implemented concept of administering annual clinical examinations to every Soviet citizen. "Tell me, how was it realistically possible to examine each of 285 million people once a year and diagnose the sick and have readily available results of blood and urine sample analyses and blood-pressure tests?" he asked. "This was a parody of preventive medicine."[100]

Sounding very much as though he had studied at Fyodorov's knee, the minister went on to endorse the concept of family doctors as the first stop for care and treatment, of 40 and 60 percent wage increases for physicians—already enacted, respectively, by Russian Republic and Ukrainian parliaments—and of payment according to skill levels. "The present [May 1991] guaranteed minimum for a surgeon is 460 rubles a month. When supplementary pay and pay based on workload are taken into account, the total is over 1,000 rubles per month [only 40 dollars at the free-market exchange rate]. I believe that with that level of protection, we can now move into a market economy."[101]

Along with movement toward legislating employer-financed health insurance plans and the spread after the rallies in August 1990 of independent, professional medical associations, Soviet medicine was, as Denisov indicated, trying to shift gears. Dr. Pyotr Prodeus, the energetic administrator of a Moscow children's hospital and an active figure in the capital's new medical association, was a good example of reform in practice. Full of plans in the fall of 1990 to run competitions to attract the best staff, he was also busy rearranging his strapped finances so that he could pay doctors and nurses what they were worth. Walking the grounds of his mini-empire with an American physician on temporary assignment to help install modern burn-treatment equipment donated through Project Hope, Dr. Prodeus said of the Soviet health ministry officials with whom he had once clashed, "A year ago, they saw us as enemies. Now they realize we are allies."

He pointed to a little playground in the complex—a sandbox, some swings, a slide. "I proposed that we build that just so there would be a bit of esthetics here. And I got a lot of rough talk from my staff. 'We need so much, and you want to put in a sandbox.' But I went ahead. I want kids to go home from the hospital and remember that some of it was pretty and even fun.

"We need a holistic approach, a wide understanding that everything is connected, that the environment—even in such little ways—has a lot to do with health."[102]

CHAPTER 11

The People Speak

IF HISTORY-MINDED Odessans were ever to place a marker on the low-rise apartment building known as the "Aristocrats' Nest on Proletarian Boulevard," the plaque might read: "Here lived Georgy Korneyevich Kryuchkov, First Secretary, Communist Party, Odessa *oblast*, 1988–90. Defeated in local elections, March 17, 1990, by a female environmentalist. Casualty of the times."

They were hard times for many Communist Party officials in the Soviet Union. Even those, like Kryuchkov, who represented the generation and, reputedly, the modernizing outlook of Mikhail Gorbachev found themselves on the defensive. From top officeholders in the Kremlin to minor chieftains throughout the USSR, the old guard was being challenged for abusing its power and special privileges and for neglecting the needs of ordinary people.

Arriving in Odessa in the fall of 1988 from a Party ideology post in Moscow, Kryuchkov was said to be a Gorbachevite, one of a new breed of *apparatchiks* trying to shake up the Party and shake off its tainted reputation. In his early sixties, he was courteous, businesslike and astute enough as a politician to try to keep both his personal profile and his visible perquisites initially low.

Having no children to house, he and his wife sought modest living quarters, rather than one of the handsome villas they could have taken in the elegant neighborhood overlooking the city's Black Sea beaches. In prerevolutionary times that area of the 200-year-old port had been a resort for Czarist nobles and magnates. Under Communist rule, it became the preserve of the local Party elite.

Despite Kryuchkov's efforts to stay out of the spotlight, his housing arrangements quickly became a subject of Odessan gossip. The three-room apartment to which he moved in the "Aristocrats' Nest" had, it seemed, been occupied by a retired military officer who was hustled off to a four-room apartment more commodious than his rank and prior service merited but not as prestigiously located as the Proletarian Boule-vard address.

The shuffle did not stay a secret. Odessa, though home to 1.7 million people, had the intimate social climate of a Mediterranean city. Every-one knew everyone else's business, and the grapevine—if not always the most accurate means of communication—was rarely still. The new Party secretary might have wanted to make a discreet entrance. Instead, he was greeted scornfully as yet another exemplar of the highly placed Soviet for whom all doors opened and all privilege was routine.

But real-estate manipulations were not the cause of his downfall. A hardy band of ecologists turned political activists was. Their victories in the city and suburban precincts of Odessa in March 1990, though not unique, were remarkable. By winning seventeen of the thirty-seven races that their candidates entered—a record bettered only by sixteen Ecology Club members, all of whom won their contests in Volgograd—and by humiliating an *oblast* Party boss, the Odessans scored a major triumph.

They doomed Georgy Kryuchkov to the role of King Canute. The tide that carried him away from Proletarian Boulevard after less than a year and a half swept on to restore the tree-lined street's prerevolutionary name: *Frantsuzky Bulvar,* Boulevard of the French. But, as tides do, the wave of ecological politics soon crested. Environmentalists and leaders of other opposition movements took legislative offices in 1990 only to confront both well-ensconced Party functionaries in executive posts and the deep-rooted ills of decades of misrule. Short of funds and longer on promises than on real power, the scattered victors—even in Moscow, Leningrad and Sverdlovsk, where reform slates won handsome majori-ties—faced the perennial challenge summarized in *The Candidate*. In that movie, Robert Redford, as a just-elected insurgent, turned to his manager and asked: "What do we do now?" As Ilya Zaslavsky, one of the radical Moscow democrats, put it in the summer of 1990, "It's a terrible thing to have a democracy that talks but doesn't work. After so many years of silence, people expect great change."[1]

Some of the Soviet ecological activists tried to meet those expecta-tions by turning to coalition-building. In the process, they often had to subordinate their priorities to the agenda of nationalists, as in the Baltics, Armenia and the Ukraine. Others clung to a purely Green identity and formed political parties of their own, most of them destined to achieve marginal influence in the struggle for power. And a third segment—sometimes with members drawn from the other two—concentrated on keeping public awareness high, on spreading the ecological alarm and, where possible, on organizing civic indignation and scientific expertise to promote change. Through the three overlapping and shifting categories there ran a persistent Luddite animus against modern technology. The syndrome was not surprising among Soviets who had been taught as schoolchildren to honor England's nineteenth-century counter–Industrial Revolutionaries as primitive, if unaware Communists. NIMBYism—the not-in-my-backyard attitude familiar in many Western societies—also characterized much Soviet environmental protest.

It proved easy to mobilize *against* nuclear power almost everywhere, *against* phosphorite mining in Estonia, *against* a dam on Siberia's Katun River and, as in Odessa, *against* an ammonia-storage facility. It was much harder to galvanize support *for* specific environmental cleanup and pollution control measures. Remedial action was expensive, complex and long range.

All the same, the pressure from below did bring responses from above: plans made in Moscow, in individual republics and even in city councils for conservation, cleanup and for new user fees and polluter penalties to help pay the bills. But like the Soviet environmental movement, the efforts lacked coordination. In mid-1991 they and parallel plans for reforming and rebuilding the health care structure occupied more space on drawing boards than in practice.

Nevertheless, the various initiatives were a start toward recovery. An enormous change from past neglect and abuse, they were also the first signs that civic activism on behalf of nature and the nation's health might generate real progress, not just halt what had passed for progress in earlier times. No easy victories lay ahead, but a campaign born of frustration and sometimes of tragedy had begun to move down the long, potholed road from protest to *perestroika*.

GREENING AROUND THE EDGES

The earliest marchers appeared on the volatile fringes of the Soviet Union. In the Baltics and in Armenia, pollution and related health concerns served as both camouflage and catalyst for nationalism and other subversive sentiments that in 1986 and 1987 did not quite dare to speak their name. Sviatoslav Zabelin, a slim, bearded, bespectacled biologist and an environmental organizer since his Moscow University student days in the early 1960s, saw ecological protest in Estonia, Lithuania and Latvia as "a political movement from the start." Green activities, he said, were tolerated because officials did not at first identify them as threats to Communist rule.[2]

In Latvia the movement began, one founding member recalled, "as a cultural rather than an ecological" protest. Its first efforts in 1984 aimed at "restoring churches and monuments officially protected by the state but actually collapsing from neglect."[3] The environment, however, quickly became a rallying cry for those whom Zabelin termed "critically aware"[4] and who wanted an outlet to protest Soviet colonialism in the Baltics and beyond.

With petitions and demonstrations that ultimately helped stop the construction of a dam on the Daugava River, the Latvians went from being dissident artists and musicians to a role as citizen-stalwarts in a national awakening. (See chapter 1.) In January 1990 they joined with two other groups to announce the formation of a Green Party that claimed about three thousand initial adherents.[5] A few months later they won six seats in the republic's parliament.[6]

Their beliefs, the Latvians said, put them "neither on the right nor the left—merely at the front." Actually, Estonian Greens could have claimed that honor. They had founded their party five months earlier to campaign for free elections, statehood and environmental purity, and they went on to prevail in seven legislative races.[7]

From Armenia in March 1986, 350 intellectuals, with writer Zori Balayan prominent among them, sent a petition to Gorbachev "protesting environmental pollution and warning about growing health problems" in the smog-shrouded capital of Yerevan.[8] From words they moved to deeds, picketing first at the Nairit Scientific Production Association to halt its toxic emissions of chloroprene and then—weeks before Chernobyl—at the construction site of a nuclear reactor. "Although organized originally around environmental issues," wrote an American who had long studied Soviet ecological problems, "this group became the natural focus for the discussion of other issues affecting what was seen to be the well-being of Armenia. Considering that there was virtually no other non-state organization to turn to, it is not surprising that the environmental group began to express itself on non-environmental matters as well."[9] When anger over Azerbaijani treatment of Armenians in the Nagorno-Karabakh enclave brought an estimated million protesters into the streets of Yerevan for days on end in February 1988, Balayan was a leader in the small group who flew to Moscow to work out a short-lived truce with Soviet authorities.

In the Ukraine, traumatized by Chernobyl and its aftermath, "ecological consciousness became part of our national consciousness," recalled a senior leader of Rukh, the republic-wide popular front. Demonstrations against nuclear power, he added, "were part of the larger protest against the [Soviet] empire itself."[10]

Although Rukh, at its founding congress in September 1989, pushed for "measures to protect the environment" along with its calls for political and economic autonomy,[11] the Ukraine also gave birth—a year later—to its own Green Party, led by cardiologist-writer Yury Shcherbak, head of the *Zelyonny Svit* (Green World) movement in the republic and author of the first popular chronicle of the Chernobyl catastrophe.

READY FOR PRIME TIME

Shcherbak, who in 1991 became the Ukraine's environmental affairs minister, was also among the eloquent voices of ecological and social outrage that turned the Soviet Congress of People's Deputies in 1989 into something of a national group therapy session. A Gorbachev initiative in the drive for democratization and the first Soviet parliament in fifty years to contain legislators chosen through genuine electoral contests, the Congress that convened in Moscow at the end of May 1989 seemed destined at first to be a fairly tame affair.

The elections had served to discredit and defeat hosts of regional Party bosses, whose names voters struck from their ballots even where the functionaries ran unopposed. But second round polling in these cases had not always handed victory to committed reformers. Because the nominating machinery was engineered to favor the Soviet establishment, 88 percent of the 1,957 seats in the new national legislature went to Party members.[12] "Not more than 15 to 20 percent of deputies," judged an English scholar, "could be considered oppositional."[13]

The numbers, outspokenness and grit of the dissenters, as well as the contagion of their example, nonetheless proved enough to turn the Congress's May–June session and the follow-up work of the smaller Supreme Soviet into a combination of civic schoolroom and democratic revival meeting. The 1989 contests that had not been hopelessly rigged had brought to the surface a number of protest groups and leaders inside and outside the Communist Party in different parts of the country. Some of them made it to Moscow and to the wooden dais under the giant sculpture of Lenin at the front of the antiseptic cavern called the Palace of Congresses.

Among the new voices were such opposition figures as Shcherbak, who had taken their first steps into the public arena as environmentalists but had quickly become standard-bearers as well for democratic values or the rights of ethnic minorities or both. Others, who had seemed reliable enough establishmentarians to pass preelectoral screening, brought angry messages from their constituents. They walked to the podium as Party hacks only to walk away as militant reformers, if not renegades.

Televised to an avid national audience over thirteen days, the Congress sessions aired political heresies that, not long before, either had been only whispered among the closest of friends or, if openly expressed, had been promptly punished. Among the most sensational episodes at the Congress were verbal attacks on the "bloody history" of the "underground empire" of the secret police;[14] on the conduct of Soviet soldiers in Afghanistan and on the leadership's responsibility for deploying troops who had used gas, clubs and sharpened shovels to attack, injure and—in at least nineteen cases to kill—nationalist demonstrators in the Georgian capital of Tblisi in April 1989.

Environmental and health issues drummed a counterpoint to these heated debates. Regional spokesmen such as Tulepbergen Kaipbergenov lamented the death of the Aral Sea. Valentin Rasputin preached a sermon on the defense of Lake Baikal, the Volga River and all of Russia's waters. (See chapters 4 and 6.) Others spoke up for the orphans, invalids, pensioners and others in the lower depths of the welfare state. To the podium on June 2, for example, came the first secretary of the Cherkassy City Komosomol Committee. An army major when he was crippled in Afghanistan, he rose to plead the cause of his fellow veterans and his own right to decent artificial limbs to replace the ones he had lost in battle.

Introduced and applauded as "an internationalist soldier," the veteran gave a crowd-pleasing attack on Andrei Sakharov and others for their "persecution of the Soviet Army." He even pledged to fight on for "the state, the motherland and Communism," but not before launching a general indictment of Soviet mismanagement:

> It is an insult [to the state] to have rationing coupons in the 72nd year of Soviet power, an insult in the collapse of the economy, the devastated villages . . . the fishless rivers and the cities with chemical smog. . . .
>
> It is an insult [to Afghan veterans] to wait in the so-called preferential lines for a baby carriage when the child is already in school, to wait until the year 2000 for an apartment . . . [to have] our prosthetics industry . . . remain at a Stone-Age level.
>
> Comrades, I will not beat around the bush. My prostheses were manufactured on equipment at one of the two prostheses plants given to us

after the war by Churchill's wife. Yes, respected scientists, it is possible to mow with a 12th century model scythe,* and even do a good job with it, but I would not even wish it upon my enemies to have to move around with such a deformity at the end of the 20th century.[15]

In the midst of such incendiary rhetoric, the formal admissions of social, economic, political and environmental shortcomings dutifully offered by top Party spokesmen had a dry and hollow ring. Latvia's chief executive, Anatoly Gorbunov, for one, spoke of "the unjustified construction of large and super-large enterprises, often without taking into account ecological and social consequences," but he and his colleagues in the leadership put little passion into their reports.[16]

Valentin Rasputin, by contrast, could suggest with icy irony that Russia might be better off if it could shed *its* membership in a Soviet Union whose minorities "accuse [Russia] of [causing] all [their] misfortunes because its underdeveloped and cumbersome nature burden your progressive aspirations." He could also attack Prime Minister Nikolai Ryzhkov for having seemed to endorse construction work on the Katun Dam, could urge putting the question of nuclear power to a national referendum and could even ask, "What is the point of trying to build a new and just state, if, as a result of our treatment of nature, our years are numbered?"[17]

June 2 was both an explosive and an ordinary day at the Congress. Its white-hot moments came in attacks on Sakharov by soldiers, including the amputee from Cherkassy, who claimed he had slandered them. But the afternoon session gave four other speakers, two loyalists and two dissenters, their chances to lay out the ecological nightmares haunting their constituents.

The first orator in what proved to be rapid succession was a Siberian aviation plant director. He called on Moscow authorities "to eliminate the threat to human health" posed by the factories in Angarsk, Baikalsk and Bratsk that regularly exceed limits for harmful emissions "by 10, 100 and more times."[18] The head of the Moscow trade union council then offered—along with a predictable defense of the "very great gains of the October Revolution"—a surprising attack on inequities in health care.

Why, we must ask, do some people enjoying position and power have the opportunity for treatment in a sanatorium every year while others—if you take the norms for [free] travel vouchers—wait years for such an

---

*The reference was to Vassily Belov's denunciation a few minutes earlier of the state of Soviet farm technology. (See chapter 3.)

opportunity? Some people are fed in hospitals for a ruble and a half, others for three rubles. I think we should decide to redistribute social [welfare] funds in favor of the badly off.[19]

The editor of Odessa's evening paper used his allotted three minutes to warn that in "5 or 10 years, we will enter the Black Sea in the Red Book [of endangered or extinct species]. . . . It is no longer a national health resort, no longer a resort, but a deception . . . a testing ground for . . . successfully experimenting with all available means to destroy the environment."[20] And a journalist from the Ukrainian city of Zhitomir called her hometown, in the Chernobyl fallout area, "a zone of particularly heavy radiation that is being turned into a zone of particularly deep silence. . . . The Ukrainian Minister of Public Health Romanenko tells us who live in this zone that it is almost a Swiss resort. This is simply infuriating."[21]

The two journalists would be heard from again. As a candidate for the Supreme Soviet, the Odessa editor had been targeted by the Communist apparatus for demotion. But he held his post and in 1990 it was his environmental correspondent, using the paper as a powerful weapon during the campaign, who defeated Georgy Kryuchkov. The Zhitomir reporter, Alla Yaroshinskaya, defeated a city Party secretary in a race for a seat in the Ukrainian parliament in 1990. She went on to help oust the republic's health minister and to write, for the national press, an article in 1991 that blew the lid off much remaining post-Chernobyl secrecy. (See chapter 7.)

Even when the Congress adjourned to be replaced by the smaller, full-time Supreme Soviet, and when the live telecasts gave way to delayed radio transmissions, the candor continued. It prompted Health Minister Yevgeny Chazov, for instance, to defend his twenty years as head of the ministry's Fourth Main Directorate, the hush-hush service that—until it and a host of special privileges were abolished in 1990—cared for the Party elite with medical services and facilities unavailable to ordinary Soviets.

"Even during . . . what is now called the period of stagnation [the Brezhnev years]," Chazov told legislators weighing his nomination in July 1989 to the ministerial post he had actually held since early 1987, "I was always raising the issue of the bad state of the health service. . . . What we are saying today was said by Supreme Soviet deputies [twelve years ago]. . . . Unfortunately, no solutions were found. . . . I have never acted against my conscience. I always defended my principles."[22]

The difference between Chazov's role in health care before and after

Gorbachev was the difference between night and day, between debates behind closed doors and arguments in the bright light of *glasnost*. Many knowledgeable Soviets in the health field, in fact, privately credited Chazov with the instincts of a serious reformer and regretted his resignation in 1990. They felt that his position in the Fourth Main Directorate had given him valuable access to top Party figures and the opportunity to win them over to the long-delayed pay raises for medical personnel and to added investments in hospital facilities and equipment.[23] His stature as joint winner of the 1985 Nobel Peace Prize with Dr. Bernard Lown, co-chairman with Chazov of International Physicians for the Prevention of Nuclear War, also helped him mobilize foreign medical aid for the USSR.

As a publicist explaining the gravity of the Soviet health crisis to his fellow citizens, once openness was sanctioned, Chazov came into his own. He did not find solutions to the problems that had been festering for years, but he unwrapped the secrecy that had shrouded them. In that sense, he was a one-man embodiment of the spirit of the Congress of People's Deputies.

That *zeitgeist* carried over to the second round of Soviet elections, the 1990 contests for local, municipal and republican parliamentary posts. It helped put reformers in many offices. But it did not help them resolve the problem of what to do with their new powers and responsibilities.

BRUSHFIRES AT THE GRASS ROOTS

The election campaigns coincided with powerful but disconnected surges of grass-roots environmental activism. The anxiety and indignation spawned "more than 400"[24] informal nature protection groups—some solid, some fleeting—to widen and to channel the protests. And out of the hurly-burly, new leaders emerged to challenge both polluters and the politicians who backed them. The 1990 elections were a first opportunity to put Green power to a test, and the mixed results suggested that Soviet ecological crusaders, like many other new participants in the equally novel democratic process, had come a long way in a short time but still had a very long way to go.

The environmentalists started from a strong base of popular concern. Soviet and American sociologists who regarded the capital as a fair model for the entire country took a spring 1990 poll in Moscow and its suburbs. They found 98 percent of those questioned more worried about pollution than about rising crime, the threat of AIDS, international conflict or even the reality of food and consumer goods shortages.[25] A much wider June 1990 survey of 96,000 Soviet citizens in 850 cities and towns reinforced the picture of psycho-ecological distress. In the study 54 percent were recorded as unhappy about local environmental conditions, 20 percent partly content and just 8 percent fully satisfied. When asked the source of their worries, 81 percent cited air pollution, 73 percent mentioned unsafe drinking water and 71 percent said they were bothered by radiation dangers.[26]

Fifty-four percent of the Moscow sampling said they trusted the Green movement. Only the Orthodox Church (64 percent) and the armed forces (56 percent) scored higher. In this snapshot of public confidence, the Communist Party still received a 39 percent approval rating; the government, 28 percent and the police, 23 percent.[27] The nationwide inquest, by contrast, found only 11 percent who regarded ecological citizens' groups positively—still better than the 4 percent who took a trusting view of state environmental protection agencies. It also tallied almost 38 percent who said they knew nothing of the work of the Green activists.[28]

Just as indicative of ecological thinking—and a further warning to the Greens of the limits on their effectiveness—were the broader survey's findings about the antipollution measures the public endorsed. Even though roughly two-thirds of those questioned felt that air and water quality had worsened in the preceding five years, fewer than one in ten supported the idea of closing polluting enterprises either for good or for total overhauls. More than half (55 percent) opted for installing purification devices or switching production to nonpolluting activities, while nearly one-third advocated moving dirty factories far outside city limits or imposing stiff fines on polluters or doing both.[29]

One place where the issue was clear and the remedy not in dispute was the city of Semipalatinsk in Kazakhstan. Its inhabitants lived hard by a top-secret site where, from 1949 to 1962, the Soviet military conducted approximately three hundred nuclear weapons tests without telling the civilian population that fallout might result and expose them to danger. After atmospheric explosions were banned under the Soviet-Anglo-American Limited Test Ban Treaty negotiated in 1963, the blasts continued underground, still hush-hush, but supposedly engineered to preclude any dangerous releases of radioactivity.

On February 12, 1989, an experiment went wrong. Gases that vented into the atmosphere carried a load of radioactivity about 150 times the normal background level. A Soviet Air Force pilot on a routine training flight flew, unwarned, through the cloud, measured the hazard and grew alarmed for his family and friends. Five days later he telephoned a prominent writer in Alma-Ata, the republic capital, a man he knew only by reputation as an eloquent foe of ecocide. Out of their conversation, one of the largest and most effective Soviet environmental protest groups was born.

The writer was Olzhas Suleimeinov, a geologist by training, a historian by choice, and a candidate for the Congress of People's Deputies. In that role, he had been invited for the first time ever to give a live television broadcast, without submitting a script for prior censorship. On February 25 he went before the cameras and disclosed the story the pilot had told him. He invited others who shared his concern to meet with him the next day at the headquarters of the Kazakh Writers' Union.[30] Hundreds of people came, and over the succeeding days, their numbers mushroomed. Out of nowhere a popular protest erupted and became so powerful that Mikhail Gorbachev later told an American foe of nuclear testing, "If you could exert as much pressure on President Bush as the Kazakh people are putting on me, we would have a test ban."[31]

The group called itself Nevada-Semipalatinsk, sometimes adding Mururoa, to link the Soviet and American test sites to the Pacific atoll used by the French. It quickly became a republic-wide movement, easily blending Kazakhs and Russians in a common cause. By the fall of 1989 the Soviet military had been forced to accept an eighteen-month shutdown of the testing grounds. By 1990 Kazakhstan had adopted a declaration of sovereignty that barred nuclear testing entirely.

"The popular movement worked on the parliament and together the two influenced the government," explained Suleimeinov, a deep-voiced, solidly built Kazakh. "It is a fantastic result that could never have been predicted in earlier times."[32]

The group pierced the secrecy around Semipalatinsk, began to force long-hidden data on radiation exposure and health into the open, raised 1.5 million rubles in private contributions for its activities during a five-hour telethon in 1990 and began that year to widen its concerns to the issue of assuring clean air and clean water in the cities and remote villages of Kazakhstan. Nevada-Semipalatinsk activists have recruited scientists from Moscow and Leningrad to design affordable water purification equipment for small settlements. In Suleimeinov's words, "Mothers in Kazakhstan are drinking water so contaminated by mercury that their babies die. Our people can't wait any longer for the government to help them. It can destroy. Only we can create."[33]

FIGHTING CITY HALL

Protest, rather than program, was the *leitmotif* of the Green movement's electoral debut in most other parts of the Soviet Union. In Yaroslavl,

Volgograd and Odessa the political establishment by 1990 had become as much the issue as the physical environment, and ecopoliticians—though novices—were able to capitalize on a throw-the-rascals-out mood. In Turkmenistan the Party *apparat* held firm sway over an apathetic citizenry. Andrei Zatoka, a lone Green candidate and a Russian by nationality, could therefore count it a moral victory when he lost his race for an *oblast* council post by only a 45 to 55 margin.[34]

In Yaroslavl, popular discontent already ran high enough in 1989 to carry two insurgents to seats in the Congress of People's Deputies, thus paving the way for more outsiders—democrats, ecologists and others—to contest local races the following year. Three of the successful candidates were Greens, two of whom moved onto the *oblast* council and one, into the city *soviet*.

Of the former, Lydia Ivanovna Boykova was a trained hydrologist, a no-nonsense, strawberry-blond mother of three, the founder of Yaroslavl's "Green Branch" Club and a sparkplug in the local chapter of the Committee for the Salvation of the Volga. Starting her Green Branch with twenty members in June 1988, she had purposely limited its membership since then to about forty committed activists. Their strategy was "to consolidate ecological, political and scientific forces."[35]

Counting the 1990 local election results a defeat, she nevertheless could point to action on some significant, early environmental measures that Green Branch had advocated. One was a decision—temporary though it proved—to have the local oil refinery stop manufacturing leaded gasoline. Another was an order issued during the heat of the election campaign to cancel plans for the construction of a nuclear energy plant.[36]

Perhaps even more significant was the grant of authority that *oblast* authorities also made on election eve, allowing citizen groups to mount patrols against environmental hazards. To be armed with monitoring equipment financed by fees and penalties paid by polluters—an estimated 5 million rubles by the end of 1990—and under the supervision of the regional environmental protection committee, activists were, in effect, to be deputized as ecological watchdogs.

If Yaroslavl was the scene of evolution under pressure, Volgograd—some one thousand miles to the south on Russia's most famous river—was an environmental and political free-fire zone. The first Communist Party casualties were self-inflicted, high level and almost total. In what came to be called the "February revolution," the regional Party's first secretary was forced to resign early in 1990 after the public learned that he had arranged to get a city apartment for his married daughter ahead of thousands of less well connected applicants. Such nepotism had long been standard practice for the Soviet elite, but in the Gorbachev era, it brought down not just the senior Volgograd practitioner but the entire executive committee he chaired in the *oblast* Party organization.[37]

Next to fall was the chief of the regional environmental protection committee. His mistake was to be stopped by a traffic policeman late at night, perhaps a bit tipsy, driving with a lady other than his wife, a bottle of brandy and a supply of black-market caviar that had come from poachers his job required him to punish, not patronize. After the Volgograd Party paper reported the incident, he was demoted to a position as head of the water inspection service.[38]

The debacle among the Reds at the top cleared the way for Greens to surge upward from the bottom. Thanks to the Krasnoarmeisky district protests against the chemical factories' air and water pollution, environmentalists already constituted an organized presence in the city. (See chapter 1.) Alfred Pavlenko's Ecology Club was the nerve center, but the local chapter of the Committee for the Salvation of the Volga was its strong right arm.

Its founder, Lydia Ivanovna Savelyeva, a round-faced, bob-haired vocational school teacher in her early fifties, was one of two Ecology Club candidates to win seats on the *oblast* council. The other was Volodya Polosukhin, the mild-mannered astronomer whom the February 1988 protest march made into an instant radical and ecological leader.

Working closely together and easily rallying the support of other Volgograders—students, especially they targeted the Volga-Don (Transfer) Canal being excavated just north of the city as environmental Enemy Number One. The canal was yet another tentacle of the octopus-like scheme that the Kremlin had supposedly shelved in 1986 to pipe water from Siberia's rivers to the Volga and the Caspian Sea.

Speeding up the construction work, apparently in hopes of presenting officials and protesters with a *fait accompli*, Minvodkhoz engineers had sunk 130 million rubles by early 1990 into excavating 80 percent of the canal's approximately twenty-five-mile length and lining one-fourth of it with concrete. Another 100 million rubles was budgeted just for construction work and billions planned for future irrigation networks.[39]

Fighting the clock and the still-considerable clout of the deposed Volgograd Party secretary, a former Russian Republic water ministry boss who backed the canal to the bureaucratic hilt, Savelyeva and her followers mobilized technical and financial arguments, street demonstrations and imaginative political theater against the project. At a day-long mock trial in June 1990, experts from Moscow argued that the canal would do more economic harm than good, that land conservation, not wasteful irrigation, was needed to improve the region's agriculture and that the badly polluted Volga needed every drop of its own water to keep a semblance of ecological equilibrium.

The specialists' testimony was overshadowed by a dramatic disclosure that the new *oblast* Party secretary, though on record as demanding an environmental impact study of the project, had secretly endorsed the dig and a reduced-scale irrigation plan in a letter to Moscow.[40] As Savelyeva said to a local journalist, "We have to drop the stereotype we have of criminals as people who always carry a knife or a pistol. Thieves can come 'armed' with nothing but folders of papers and bulldozers and rob us as no ordinary criminal ever could."[41]

Her passion—and the revelation of the Party secretary's double-dealing—turned the tide. On July 26, 1990, the *oblast* council voted to cut off all funds for further canal construction. In order to salvage something from the investment already made, it announced a public competition for proposals on ways to put the existing installations to productive use.[42] Looking back on the fight a few months after that victory, Pavlenko spoke for many of his fellow activists. "Ours is an apocalyptic country," he said. "We have to go through enormous upheavals to change anything. In some ways, I don't think any of us has much of a chance, but faith is what matters. It is everything."[43]

The environmental faithful of Odessa had been escalating their upheavals since 1986. From a fight over the neglect of the city zoo—won when a biologist from outside Party ranks was appointed director—to mass picketing that prevented the construction of facilities to unload and process Syrian fertilizer, the trim figure of Lyudmila Sokolovskaya had been constantly in the forefront. As a crusading journalist, she became Georgy Kryuchkov's nemesis.

An Odessan almost since her birth in 1949, a student of philology, she combined marriage to a physicist and the raising of a son with a quiet professional niche on the literary pages of the city's evening paper. "But when Gorbachev came to power," she recalled, "it seemed that the time had come for normal people to take journalism seriously. Ecology was the subject that attracted me immediately."[44]

Her reporting quickly attracted a following. In 1986, using the newspaper offices as their meeting place and shelter, a group Sokolovskaya described as "specialists—biologists, chemists, engineers" founded the first environmental club in the city. One of the earliest members of what grew into a civic association called Ecopolis was Alla Shevchuk. She was Sokolovskaya's senior by seventeen years, dark where the journalist was blond, and a risk-taker since the days in the 1960s when she had typed the proscribed writings of poets such as Anna Akhmatova and Osip

Mandelstam in multiple copies for clandestine circulation to other free-thinkers.

Together, the two women were a powerhouse. They incarnated what Francine du Plessix Gray, herself of Russian extraction, has described as common traits among Soviet women: "a searing energy, an iron discipline, a formidable will to dominate."[45] Starting alone, Shevchuk had launched what became a ten-day public demonstration in 1987 against plans to cut down the chestnut trees lining the monumental steps above Odessa's downtown seafront. The trees—on a site that the baby-carriage scene in Sergei Eisenstein's film *The Battleship Potemkin* had made famous—were spared.

From a nucleus of no more than ten members, Shevchuk and Sokolovskaya built their club into a civic force that raised public awareness of Odessa's environmental hazards. By the time of the 1990 elections, air pollution, unsafe water, dirty beaches and the state of the Black Sea were all issues of widespread concern. Even Party candidates pledged to build new defenses against pollution as soon as the voters legitimized their hold on local power.

Although Rukh and other Ukrainian democratic groups were poorly organized in Odessa, Ecopolis was not. It was part of a wide protest movement, perhaps the most tightly focused part. It named its strongest candidates as the *apparatchiks'* opponents and matched Sokolovskaya against Kryuchkov in a decorous public campaign that, behind the scenes, amounted to a battle royal.

"Actually, Kryuchkov was one of the few intelligent functionaries," Sokolovskaya conceded. "He could talk to the voters and be open and persuasive. For our part, we tried to keep the campaign civilized, to keep the extremists out of things."[46] On election day, March 4, those tactics brought a partial payoff. In a field of four, Sokolovskaya and Kryuchkov got the most votes, but neither had a clear majority. A runoff poll was set for March 17.

By then, the Party was in a panic. Printed flyers appeared in voters' mailboxes, calling Sokolovskaya "a flashy loudmouth" and questioning her ability to get anything done. Shevchuk countered by going door to door commending Kryuchkov's talents while asking pointedly whether as a deputy to both the USSR and Ukrainian parliaments and a Party boss, he might not be spreading himself too thin. "I would say, 'We need Sokolovskaya here at the *oblast* level. That way we'll have two good people to represent us.' "[47]

Despite stuffing some ballot boxes and manipulating a few tallies, the Party lost overwhelmingly. Nine thousand voters went to the polls in the Malinovsky district, and 70 percent of them voted for Sokolovskaya.

Alla Shevchuk, who had been a poll-watcher from seven in the morning till eight at night and had then monitored the ballot counting until two A.M., did not get to the victory party at her friend's newspaper office until four in the morning.

There was still some champagne to drink and, she remembered, a last cheer of victory when a Radio Liberty broadcaster in Munich announced at dawn that "a journalist had beaten Kryuchkov in Odessa." The outcome was so unwelcome to officials, she added, that "our own papers didn't print the news for three days."[48]

ALL POWER TO THE SOVIETS!

The thrill of political victory wore off quickly in Odessa and Volgograd—even in Moscow and Leningrad where reformers won majority control of municipal councils, rather than just a vocal presence on them. The newly elected—articulate protesters but novice policymakers—found they had gained only a share of authority; the old *apparat* still held the executive agencies and the reins of governmental power at all levels.

Local problems, moreover, proved in many cases not to be of exclusively local origin nor firmly within local control. Soviet pollution and health care crises were symptoms of a flawed system of economic and social priorities that could be set right only by wholesale political, ideological and financial changes. The fight over those issues was centered in Moscow and, as the August 1991 *putsch* against Mikhail Gorbachev revealed, was far from resolved.

Reforms that advocates wanted to be sweeping were creeping instead. But change was in the air, and among those who had helped to put it aloft, Soviet environmentalists kept on pushing, praying and experimenting with ways to keep their cause alive and their influence effective.

Enforcement was one of the more active tracks they pursued. On paper at least, Soviet environmental laws were tough. Only their application had been toothless. While Aleksei Yablokov and other respected national figures suggested bringing the KGB into pollution-control work, partly to deflect it from its traditional role as a suppressor of dissent, local authorities in Kuibyshev, Dnepro-Dzerzhinsk, the republic of Moldova and Moscow actually moved to establish various types of ecological police forces.

Going beyond the Yaroslavl model of citizen watchdogs to put uniformed militiamen into environmental monitoring teams, the Kuibyshev city council authorized a detail of seventy officers to fine polluters, from factories with smoking stacks to drivers with smoky exhausts. In Moscow the squad was more an emergency detail to respond to citizens' complaints and, where proof of environmental violations could be determined, to hand the matter over to the courts. Moldova built the concept of an ecology police into its long-term cleanup plan as an "important step toward the creation of an integrated state mechanism for environmental protection."[49]

The key word—and the missing link—in such initiatives was "integrated." With the fundamental structure of the Soviet Union itself up for grabs in 1990 and 1991, reforms in health and ecology administration became a side show to the main event. Even the elevation of the State Committee on Environmental Protection (Goskompriroda) into a ministry in the spring of 1991 did not give it clear authority over the State Committee on Hydrometereology, the agency that actually gathered data on the condition of air and water resources in the USSR. Nor did the new ministry acquire the power in all instances to inspect, modify or overrule development plans of other state agencies.

Early in 1989 Fyodor Morgun, Goskompriroda's then chief, asked himself the question: "Is a decisive turnaround in environmental protection taking place?" He replied: "Despite a number of positive steps . . . the answer, unfortunately, must still be no. . . . The main reason is the prevailing attitude of production enterprises toward nature as a free and inexhaustible resource and toward the territory on which they operate as a spacious expanse to accommodate them."[50]

Ten months later Morgun had left the scene, and editor-ecologist Sergei Zalygin lamented that Goskompriroda, after two years in business, was a disappointment. "In our self-perpetuating system of ministries and departments, this committee has never found its place . . . [or established] what kind of authority and functions should be vested in it."[51]

By the fall of 1990, the competition for political turf in the field of the environment had become even more complex. No longer just a fight up and down Moscow's corridors of power, the contest had spread outward from the center to the self-assertive republics. A top Soviet official overseeing emergency situations, including ecological ones, argued that "mutual relations between the republics and the center will hardly develop constructively if legislators and executive organs do not recognize that nature is one and does not take administrative boundaries into consideration. Life shows, alas, that not everyone understands this."[52]

Specifically, the official noted, Latvia, Lithuania and Estonia, having proclaimed their independence, had also turned down Goskompriroda proposals for a "single monitoring service" for the Baltic Sea. The republics bordering the Caspian Sea had scuttled a similar joint over-sight agency, and at a lower level, an effort by regional authorities in Kostroma, north of Moscow, to unify protection of their fish and forest resources had run into the veto of the related national ministries. At least, the government official urged, let there be "a nationwide system to collect, process and analyze" ecological data and a "reasonable com-bination of decentralization" in using the information to set and imple-ment resource-use policy.[53]

The howling winds of change in the Gorbachev era drowned out such calls for "reasonable" accommodations of conflicting and competitive interests, whether in environmental or economic or political matters. As Moscow's hold on power weakened, almost every aspect of Soviet life was in metamorphosis, but in almost no case could the outcome or even the direction of the change be forecast confidently.

Environmentalists could point with hope to one spreading experi-ment: systems of fees and fines that could at last force manufacturers and processors to factor significant resource and pollution costs into their economic calculations. On an experimental basis in fifty cities and regions in 1989 and in sixty-four the next year, Goskompriroda man-dated stiff penalties for infringing environmental rules. The proceeds were to go "85 percent to municipal budgets, 10 percent to *oblast* accounts and 5 percent to an all-Union fund."[54] The key, said Nikolai Vorontsov, the agency's chairman, "is not just to fine polluting enter-prises . . . but to widen [the use of] resource-conservation technology and purification equipment."[55]

In Volgograd, where the experiment began in 1990, the process of determining fees was far from automatic. "It's been a tough, long process of haggling," Vladimir Loktionov, the energetic, burly, forty-two-year-old director of a silica-processing factory, told an American visitor in October 1990. "The authorities started out in July trying to charge us 45,000 rubles a year for our emissions and then a penalty of 50 rubles for every ton of waste above a set limit. We've gotten the initial charge down to 22,000 rubles, but it will take us a minimum of ten years to modernize the whole factory."[56]

Even before the regulatory pressure became a reality, Loktionov and his chief engineer, Viktor Pismenny, had been trying to find an electro-static filter the factory could use to trap dust particles from the rare, fine sand it processed for water purification systems. The hunt was hard and the wait, long.

"We saw a filter in 1987 and got the manufacturer to accept us as a customer for 1988," Pismenny recounted. "They gave us the plans in 1989," he said, "and we'll start getting the equipment in 1991 and have it operating by 1993."

After the six years spent just to get the device, "It will take fifteen years to pay off the 350,000 rubles it costs. But we have to worry about the health of the people who work and live here. You can't count just the cost of the equipment."[57]

With only five hundred employees and only one case of occupational illness among its employees in twenty-five years, Pismenny added, "We're nothing compared to the [giant Volgograd] tractor factory or the aluminum factory. But it's always easiest to beat up on the weakest guy around."[58]

By 1991 the fee-fine system was supposed to be in operation nation-wide. Listing 210 different harmful substances, the Russian Republic Goskompriroda fixed *average* fees of 3.3 rubles for each ton of atmospheric emissions within set yearly limits and a 15.8-ruble penalty for each ton in excess of the base. Water discharge rates on 129 named ingredients ran from 443.5 rubles per allowable ton to 2,346 for each one in the penalty zone. The regulations also specified that all funds collected would go to local authorities, none for national environmental protection work.[59]

These figures were only averages. The one-ton penalty for emitting a form of leaded tetraethylene into the air ran to 333,333 rubles. For ten water pollutants, including DDT and hexachlorophene, the fine was set at 20,000 rubles per ton.[60]

Moscow's reformer-led city council enthusiastically embraced the idea that the polluter should pay and that government treasuries should profit. Using statistics by Moscow University economists to calculate the costs of pollution, the council imposed charges higher than those of the Russian Republic. Inside the capital a ton of heavy metal salts put into the water system, within fixed margins, would cost 29,000 rubles and every ton above the ceiling, 70,000 rubles.[61]

THINGS FALL APART

Such widely varying charges reflected not just political competition between different levels of government but also the continuing inability of Soviet economists, denied the yardstick of free-market prices, to measure the value of the nation's natural resources and the cost of abusing them. As early as 1985, Minvodkhoz, for example, had promised it would institute a system of charging customers for the irrigation water they used. As of 1990, no fees had been set.[62]

Finally, attractive as the fee-and-penalty schemes were in theory, their application amounted to another assault on a production network already suffering, if not terminally ill, from a host of economic disorders.

Expensive ecological controls would have been hard to institute in a buoyant setting. In the midst of economic disintegration, they fed the gathering backlash against Gorbachev's reform drive in general and Green campaigners in particular.

The conflict surfaced dramatically in the fall of 1990 when the Kremlin ordered what had once been obedient subordinates in the republics, regions and cities to reverse decrees that had shut down essential production on environmental-hazard grounds. Roughly one thousand factories and firms, it was said, had been affected. In the preceding four years, by another count, "300 enterprises, one-third of them chemical, have been closed down for ecological reasons alone. . . . The [chemical] sector has lost nearly three billion rubles."[63]

Those calculations did not include short-term closures such as the three hundred that Tadjikistan's environmental control agency had imposed in 1989 on everything from small workshops to major sections of fertilizer and battery factories.[64] Nor did the number of plant closings, temporary or long-term, measure the irritation Goskompriroda had caused by trying to block fifty-seven Minvodkhoz water and land reclamation projects late in 1988 and by forbidding the Ministry of the Timber Industry to bring planned, new pulp and papermaking activities on stream.[65]

The offended institutions fought back. In Cherkassy the head of the city council admitted that he and his fellow deputies had caused "a departmental storm" by ordering a local cellophane manufacturer either to reduce pollution by cutting its output by 40 percent by the start of 1990 or to face the threat of a full shutdown in February. "[People] have charged us with attempted intimidation," he said. " 'Do you want us to cause another shortage?' they ask. 'After all, cellophane is used to wrap sausage!' "[66]

In Armenia, where the hated Nairit combine was ordered closed in June 1989, even an environmentalist contended that the politicians had done their work not wisely, but too well. The giant plant should have been reconfigured over time, he argued almost a year later. "As a result . . . of rash decisions . . . we are now on the verge of the total collapse of the republic economy without having solved any of our ecological problems to any appreciable extent."[67]

South of Moscow, Greens in the city of Tula, who managed to suspend the work of a laundry detergent factory in 1989, were criticized for worsening already acute shortages of soap in the USSR.[68] Ecological priorities hit the 225 Soviet pharmaceutical manufacturers especially hard. Each lost an average of twenty days' output during the first eight months of 1990, in large part because of environmental bottlenecks that shut off their supply of raw materials.[69]

That straightforward conflict between immediate medical needs and what ecologists argued should be long-term public health priorities was an acute instance of Green politics promoting contradictory consequences. It was not necessarily the only one. As a Leningrad paper pointed out in April 1991, local environmentalists had concentrated so much energy on preventing the discharge of 420 tons of wastes yearly from a small pulp and paper mill into a tributary of Lake Ladoga that they had done nothing about a factory across the river that put out the same volume of pollutants every day.

> The "Greens," the civic activists, it seems, simply do not understand the essence of the problem. They shout themselves hoarse and then they relax. . . . As a result of their "great victory," we have a 130,000-ton shortage of cellulose. We used to sell some for hard currency. Now we have to buy it overseas. . . . The functionaries in these [environmental] organizations act like Arctic wolves. They do not have the daring to attack strong, healthy reindeer. They only go after the sick and the weak that lag behind the herd.[70]

Vladimir Polosukhin and Lydia Savelyeva in Volgograd, like Alla Shevchuk and Lyudmila Sokolovskaya in Odessa, would not recognize themselves in that disparaging characterization. By their reckoning, they had taken on and beaten powerful foes.

They had also helped to break down many of the barriers of mistrust that Stalinist terror had taught individual Soviets to erect against one another. Under the umbrella of the 200-member, Moscow-based Socio-Ecological Union, headed by Maria Cherkasova, and through organizations such as the Committee for the Salvation of the Volga, activists in different cities and regions of the USSR came to know and respect as co-workers men and women whose existence, a few years earlier, they had hardly suspected. At the student level, a *Druzhina* movement sprang up and expanded across the country, modeling itself on the amateur nature-protection club that Sviatoslav Zabelin and Cherkasova had formed in the early 1960s at Moscow University.

Strangers at the start of their campaigns, environmentalists in many cities became allies in a shared crusade. They traded news and the newspapers that local organizations managed to print and circulate. Like the host of civic, cultural, religious and political groups that blossomed in the Gorbachev era awakening of Soviet society, the Greens constituted not just single-issue pressure groups but a collective support for progress toward a more democratic nation, more open, more balanced and more restrained in its treatment of nature and of human beings.

The attempt by Party hard-liners at the end of August 1991 to put an end to Gorbachev's rule and his political reforms brought the crisis between democratizers and centralizers to a peak of intensity. It put all the social changes in the USSR, including the steps toward environmental protection, in doubt. What it did not alter was the reality of deepening ecological crisis or the role ordinary and extraordinary Soviets had taken in confronting that crisis and trying to reverse it.

CHAPTER 12

A Time to Heal

DURING THE THREE anxious August days of the attempted hard-line revolt against Mikhail Gorbachev's reform programs, only one member of the Soviet cabinet emerged in public to condemn the coup and its plotters. Nikolai Vorontsov, whose status as chairman of Gos-kompriroda had been changed to that of USSR minister of the environment, a distinguished geneticist and the first non-Communist since 1922 elevated to such a post, showed himself a man of considerable civic courage.

At noon on the first day of the putsch, Boris Yeltsin, the most popular politician in the Soviet Union, clambered to the top of an army tank in front of the white skyscraper that housed the Russian Republic parliament. Yeltsin used that unlikely podium—a symbol of what proved to be a decisive split within the Soviet military—to rally the crowd in front of him, the city around him and the world beyond to defy what he sneeringly termed the "junta" in the Kremlin.[1]

Vorontsov was the next to speak from the tank's deck and to denounce the takeover attempt as "illegal." Having declared his defiance in public, he repeated it in private at an evening meeting of the Soviet cabinet. Even behind closed doors he was the only minister to voice uncompromising opposition to the men he later called "incorrigible conservatives." Two of his Kremlin colleagues—a deputy prime minister and the cultural affairs chief—declined to endorse the coup and its aims, but only Vorontsov truly resisted the conspiracy while the outcome was still in doubt. Reflecting two days later on the leadership errors that had led to the crisis, Vorontsov said, "Gorbachev trusted those people whom he should not have trusted, and he did not trust those who were ultimately prepared to fight for his freedom."[2]

The freedom at issue was not just Gorbachev's personal well-being but that of an entire nation. Under his leadership, the Soviet people had come to taste individual liberty and to savor the right to speak out, to protest, to elect representative men and women to official positions and to take part, as citizens instead of subjects, in guiding the work of government. The sixty-hour coup put all those gains in jeopardy and, ending in humiliation for the reactionaries, gave new impetus to the process of reform. The political showdown, however, did nothing to change the grim realities of a nation in an economic tailspin, with many of its people physically debilitated and under heavy siege from visible and invisible poisons in the air, water and land.

Fireworks of euphoria lit the Moscow sky early in the evening of the day that the leading plotters were arrested and Mikhail Gorbachev reinstated as president. The morning after, though, all the ecological threats remained undiminished.

- Dark clouds of industrial pollution still stained the air of Moscow and one hundred other Soviet cities.
- Agricultural chemicals still leached in toxic doses from millions of acres of farmland into the nation's water supply, while topsoil eroded and grew less fertile and crops continued to rot in the fields.
- Salt and sand from the dry bed of the Aral Sea still blew in violent dust storms—part of changing weather patterns—across Central Asia, adding new poisons to land and water supplies already contaminated by overloads of pesticides and herbicides.
- Fish-killing worms still infested the turgid waters of the Volga, the Don, the Dniepr and other great rivers, while choking algae spread in the waters of the Black Sea, the Sea of Azov and the Caspian.
- Construction sites for planned nuclear power stations stood idle, while badly maintained oil and gas pipelines leaked and obsolete equipment lowered the life expectancy and the productivity of coal miners deep underground.
- Thousands of hospitals and clinics remained overcrowded, poorly staffed, woefully underequipped and disastrously short of medicine.
- Dozens of mothers giving birth, hundreds of infants and thousands of men and women old and weak before their time died unnecessary deaths each day.

The attempted coup answered many questions about the political health of what had been the Union of Soviet Socialist Republics. But the quick triumph of Russian democrats sustained by what the USSR's former satellites called "people power" brought no quick relief to the lingering illnesses of a society on the edge of ecocide.

To cure those maladies would take more than individual acts of bravery by men like Nikolai Vorontsov. Full recovery would require not only his kind of civic courage, but the fortitude and initiative and imagination to sustain a long and terribly costly effort to overcome decades of environmental and medical impoverishment. It would require as well a genuine commitment to accord public health, nature and basic social needs the funds too long diverted into propping up an ossified, paranoiac regime at home and projecting its military power abroad.

No one who watched the drama of the Gorbachev era metamorphosis could fail to be impressed by the inner reserves of the people's strength and—in a moment of grave crisis—by their newfound daring. But nor could anyone, surveying the internal crises still to be met and the time and costs still to be endured, fail to recognize that the tests ahead, less dramatic than the August days of 1991, could prove even more wrenching and harder to surmount.

ENVIRONMENTAL ECONOMICS

A year before he was named Ukrainian minister of the environment, Yury Shcherbak went to the United States to take part in a parliamentarians' conference on global ecological problems. A Russian-speaking American introduced himself to Shcherbak in the lobby of a Washington hotel and, without much preamble, asked him how Soviets proposed to finance their ambitious environmental programs.

"You tell me first how we're going to feed and clothe the Soviet people," the stocky, gray-haired, onetime cardiologist replied brusquely, "and then I'll tell you when we'll start talking about the cost of cleaning up the environment." Eyes blazing behind round metal-rimmed glasses, he added, "It's rich countries that can allow themselves the luxury of comprehensive environmental protection."[3]

Shcherbak's reply was pat, simplistic and, in part, wrong. No one could dispute the USSR's urgent need to tackle its basic economic failures with changes that would put decent, sufficient and affordable food on consumers' tables and that would provide them with respectable clothing and housing. But many would argue that without cleaner air, purer water and agriculture less dependent on dangerous chemicals, advances in other measures of social and economic well-being could not be sustained.

Among those making the argument, in fact, were Soviet scholars who calculated the *annual* economic costs of environmental damage as of 1990 at 15 to 17 percent of GNP. Among big-ticket items, they counted wind and water erosion and wastage of natural resources combined as a 25-billion-ruble-a-year loss, an amount equal to earnings forgone from forestry, fisheries and fur-trapping. Additionally, they put the price paid by the Soviet economy for air and water pollution and for contaminated land at 60 billion rubles and noted that the overall economic toll of environmental abuse during the 1980s ran eleven to fifteen times above the amounts spent on environmental protection.[4] Their calculations, moreover, did not include the further 27-billion-ruble-a-year drain in sick pay and missing output due to the illnesses—many of them related to unclean air and water—that kept 4 million Soviet workers from their jobs each day.[5]

Another authority making the case for environmental protection on economic grounds was Barber Conable, president of the World Bank in 1990. Speaking in Warsaw only a few weeks before Shcherbak's visit to the United States, Conable pledged his institution's support for the work of "reform and development" in the former Soviet client states of East Europe. He specified health, education, housing and social security as areas needing urgent modernization. Then, in terms just as applicable in Moscow, Kiev, Minsk or Alma-Ata as in Warsaw, he added:

> Economic progress is a Pyrrhic victory for those who cannot breathe, or drink the water, or avoid toxic assaults on their physical well-being.
>
> Action on the environmental front cannot be postponed to some future date when the economic crisis has been overcome. . . .
>
> [It] must be part and parcel of the process of reform. Economic incentives, new investment, legislation, enforcement and public education must combine to pull Poland and other countries back from the brink of environmental disaster.[6]

Many Soviet leaders talked as if they had already assimilated that lesson. Presenting his government's program to the Congress of People's Deputies in 1989, Prime Minister Nikolai Ryzhkov called for "radical economic reform . . . simultaneously with . . . major measures for profound structural" redesign of an economy that had "concentrated 60 percent of all fixed industrial production assets" just in *producing* raw material, leaving 4 percent for light industry and 6 percent for food production.[7]

Ryzhkov claimed that health care expenditures were already 45 percent higher than in 1985. He promised that the next five years would see an additional 80 billion rubles spent on housing, health, education, culture and social welfare in general. And, to applause, he announced plans to open to the public the Health Ministry facilities previously reserved for the elite.[8]

Given the scope of the Soviet ecological crisis, he explained that "it would be extremely difficult to improve the unfavorable situation . . . over a short period of time." But over a fifteen-year period starting in 1990, he said, 135 billion rubles would have to be "allotted to . . . the long-term state nature-conservation draft program, while ensuring the necessary development of the country's production capacity."[9] The funds would amount to a tripling of previous rates of environmental spending, but, he added, "it is not just a matter of finances. To assimilate such funds, the specialized capacities of construction organizations need to be developed as well, and perhaps most important is to create ecologically clean technologies and appropriate equipment."[10]

"Specialized capacities" was jargon for the weakest links in the Soviet Union's brittle chain of environmental protection defenses. The term meant producers capable of turning out purification and emission-control devices and users with the funds, incentives and know-how to buy, install and operate the equipment. Few Soviet enterprises fit either half of the description.

In the Chuvash autonomous republic along the west bank of the Volga River, for example, a check of all 133 existing water purification installations in 1990 revealed that 30 percent of them "had never been used." As a result, 90 percent of the region's effluent went into the Volga insufficiently treated.[11]

A year before Ryzhkov announced his program, the rates at which Soviet authorities were putting environmental protection projects into commission were lagging far behind plan. The Russian Republic, Kazakhstan and Azerbaijan met only 26 percent of their targets for building water treatment facilities in the first six months of 1988. Petrochemical and timber ministries, as well, were making "virtually no provision" for installing purification systems in 1989.[12]

The government's commitments to improvement paid no quick dividends. By some measures, in fact, the situation worsened. In 1990, for want of funds and because the local railroad could not be counted on to deliver the needed equipment, two giant nickel smelters in Norilsk scaled back antipollution investments. They had planned to spend $900 million on imported technology to cut their sulfur dioxide emissions by two-thirds. Instead, they cut spending for the modernization program by at least one-third, leaving its eventual fate in doubt.[13]

THE PRICES OF CLEANUP

The most serious problem with the Ryzhkov program, however, was not that Soviet industry could not assimilate the money the state proposed to provide, but that the money was nowhere near enough. The prime minister had called the sum of 135 billion rubles a preliminary calculation and the program a draft. By the time Goskompriroda presented a detailed program worked out in an interagency negotiating process, the cost had nearly tripled.

According to the Goskompriroda study—submitted eighteen months after Ryzhkov outlined the preliminary version—the minimum fifteen-year price tag for capital investments and operations and maintenance in environmental protection stood at 240 billion rubles. The maximum was 335 billion rubles, and to either the high or low figure was added 150 billion rubles for pollution-abatement and resource-conservation hardware.[14]

Even as a minimum, the 390-billion-ruble total was an impressive sum compared to previous levels of expenditure. It amounted to doubling the proportion of Soviet GNP to be spent on clean air and water, on reducing toxic wastes and combatting erosion, on lowering environmental hazards, on recycling industrial wastes and on increasing nature conservation, environmental monitoring and ecological research.[15]

The program set ambitious targets for 1995: a 17 to 20 percent cut from 1987 levels in gross emissions of atmospheric pollutants from stationary sources and a 7 to 10 percent reduction in those from vehicles, as well as the addition of sewage treatment facilities capable of purifying 35 million cubic meters of water a day.[16] It also faced reality. Until surface water could be made safe, funds would have to go to provide bottled drinking water—an emergency expedient and a costly one—"beginning with the Central Asian republics."[17]

But the very sweep of the endeavor—realistic though it appeared—undercut its prospects for success, and nearly two years after it was presented for legislative enactment, it remained unapproved. The long-range program embraced campaigns against noise pollution and radiation dangers from unsafe nuclear power plants. It outlined measures to "stabilize" the Aral Sea and to cut runoff into the Baltic and Black seas by half. And it envisioned "restoring the environment and safe living and working conditions for the population in the Chernobyl accident zone."[18]

The gap between will and wallet was too large not to be noticed. At 9 billion rubles, Chernobyl cleanup costs were obviously understated. The so-called 500 Days program of economic reforms developed (and then shelved) in the fall of 1990 under the direction of Gorbachev's then-senior economic advisor put the price at 25 billion rubles.[19] Other unofficial but convincing calculations of the Chernobyl repair bill ranged from 40 billion to 250 billion rubles, counting—in the latter case—the extra costs of treating those who fell ill and of bringing other energy sources on stream to make up for the power that nuclear stations—never to be built—would otherwise have provided.[20]

For air pollution control, the Goskompriroda program set a fifteen-year spending goal of 39 billion rubles, 22 billion for capital investments and the rest for operations and maintenance. Those sums, by reputable unofficial projections, were at least five times too low.[21] Just to reduce sulfur dioxide emissions to meet the program's targets for that particularly hazardous ingredient in air pollution, capital investments needed to range around 50 billion rubles, not the 2.3 billion that the program established.[22] An American environmental engineer has calculated that installation of sulfur dioxide abatement technology to meet EPA clean-air standards adds 20 percent to the basic construction costs of new utility plants in the United States.[23]

For the Aral and Caspian seas together, 1991 to 2005 expenditures under the Goskompriroda design were officially projected at 16.5 billion rubles. In fact, allowing for inflation and based on expert, though incomplete, data, the allocation should have been three times higher.[24] Soviet researchers have put the cost of capital investments needed to restore the flow of the Amu and Syr Darya rivers to the Aral at anything between 20 and 100 billion rubles.[25]

Just the cost of installing new water and sewer systems on the 18,750 miles of pipes in the Russian Republic that a Soviet minister of housing and municipal services described in 1987 as "completely worn out"[26] could cost 100 billion rubles. That price represented the per-mile cost of installing new water pipes in the city of Baku, the capital of Azerbaijan, multiplied by the length of RSFSR pipes in urgent need of replacement.[27]

Since Soviet authorities traditionally installed municipal water lines without lining any of them with anticorrosive materials, all of the Russian Republic's system—not just the one-fourth designated in 1987 as "completely worn out"—should probably be overhauled by 2005. If that work were undertaken for the other half of the Soviet population, moreover, the repair bill could easily come to 800 billion rubles. That amount would be twice the total funding desired for the entire fifteen-year environmental protection program and not much less than the estimated value of total Soviet GNP in 1991.

With estimated Soviet GNP down by 4 to 5 percent in 1990 and 8 to 10 percent in the first half of 1991,[28] the Goskompriroda design for environmental recovery in the USSR, like many ambitious Gorbachev era plans, became a benchmark rather than a road sign. It amounted to a wish list, but—especially as the republics separated from the center—nothing like an operational directive for investments. It would serve, however, as an analytical basis for determining the gravest ecological threats and for helping new decision makers choose which ones to try to address first.

The Russian Republic, for instance, began the process of setting its own goals in mid-1990 with a study that refined the Goskompriroda approach into a fifteen-year program of environmental stabilization. At an estimated cost of 70 billion rubles in government funds and another 140 billion to be raised from enterprises on its territory, the republic's plan emphasized *preventing* further ecological decline, slowing the pace of erosion and pollution as a prelude to a subsequent drive toward cleanup.[29]

Like so many other Soviet statistics used in these pages, both the Goskompriroda estimates and those of the Russian Republic environment ministry can be cited only to describe, rather than to define, the financial dimensions of the ecological repair bill the Soviet Union and its component parts actually faced at the end of the Gorbachev era. Another way to measure the scope of their problem—by comparing U.S. outlays to those in the USSR—also provides only an approximate guide to reality.

Dollars have a measurable value. Rubles, as of August 1991, lacked a reliable exchange rate. Nevertheless, in considering the price that the USSR must eventually pay for its flirtation with ecocide, the nearly $1.5 trillion—measured in constant 1982 dollars—that Americans spent from 1972 to 1988 for clean air and water and solid waste disposal provides a guideline.[30] If the Soviet Union were simply to try to reach the U.S. level of 2 percent of GNP spent on pollution abatement,[31] it would have to budget at least 255 billion rubles for that aspect of environmental protection alone between 1991 and 2005.

FIRST THINGS FIRST

Economic catastrophe and political confusion made it impossible to believe that even those sums could be budgeted for the defense of nature and of human health in the immediate future. But on the eve of the attempted coup, leading environmental activists such as Aleksei Yablokov, Maria Cherkasova and Mikhail Lemeshev showed that they were not prepared to put their hopes on indefinite hold.

To bolster their case for prompt and coherent action, they made their own economic point: Ecocide was draining the nation's wealth and strength to the tune of 43 billion rubles a year, the price, as they computed it, of working days lost to illness, of cropland made unusable, of water fit neither to drink nor to use in industrial processes. "Ecological destruction," they wrote, "has become a formidable barrier on the road to the economic and social rebirth of Russia."[32]

The key point of their assessment was in the connection they made between economic and political reform and environmental progress. Representing the intellectual and scientific leadership of the Green movement and its affiliation with the relatively moderate democratizing forces in Soviet politics—in contrast to the passion, mixed with Russian nationalism, of conservative writers such as Vassily Belov and Valentin Rasputin—Yablokov, Cherkasova and their allies tried to put what they saw as first things first.

Without economic stabilization and a market framework that put measurable prices on natural resources and their use and abuse, environmentalists can expect no real improvement from the fee-and-penalty pollution regulation machinery being set in tentative and unstable motion in 1991. Without a stable political setting and a reliable judiciary as well, the strictest laws will go as unenforced in the future as they have in the past. In other words, without the radical reforms that Ryzhkov had promised in 1989 and then helped to block, the reform in ecological practices—no matter what the cost—will be stillborn.

This understanding of economic/ecological symbiosis took the movement that had begun in protest and alarm a long step toward political relevance. Led by men and women who had established working ties with Vorontsov and Yeltsin, ecologists in the Russian Republic, at least, appear well positioned to press for stronger moves toward a manageable program of environmental action in the largest and, in many respects, most polluted of the Soviet republics. With the antitank barricades and the Communist monuments both being removed from the streets of Moscow at the end of August 1991, an era of confrontation was ending and a coalition forming that might open the way to genuine progress toward cleaner air and water, more productive land and a less wasteful pattern of production.

Vast difficulties lay ahead. Just as the Soviet Union lacks simple meters to measure water and power use accurately, it is also desperately short of sophisticated environmental monitoring devices with which to assess the gravity of hazards from radiation levels to nitrate concentrations. At the level of fundamental research, it is also floundering in ignorance—as are most other nations—of the precise impact on human health of exposure to pollutants in the volumes and particularly in the combinations that so often occur in the atmosphere of Soviet cities and in the country's waterways.

Without a sounder scientific basis for decision making—the instruments to compile accurate data and the analytical skills to assess the findings—it will be hard to match financial resources and pollution reduction priorities. For at least several more perilous years, it will be easier to point to the size of the ecological danger than to define the most cost-effective ways to reduce it and to say with a hollow laugh, as the Russian Republic minister of health had in 1989: "To live longer, you must breathe less."[33]

His ironic recipe did make one valid point: the need for efficiency in the use of natural resources. Wasteful as the Soviet Union has been in the energy it consumed, the cropland and forests it contaminated and destroyed, the water it squandered in massive irrigation projects, it has an enormous potential for cost-saving conservation measures across the board. When and if incentives are put in place to fix genuine prices for land, minerals, electricity, water and labor, it will be possible, though not easy or automatic, to establish a calculus that matches environmental goals and economic growth and uses efficiency gains as a means to move toward both.

RX FOR HEALTH

If the scope of the environmental challenge and the cost of meeting it are beyond precise definition, the dimensions of Soviet health care failings are easier to ascertain but almost as complex to remedy. Aside from the tangible issues of costs and priorities, less concrete obstacles litter the road to reform.

One is ideological: the long-standing contract—honored more in the breach—that bound the state to give its citizens free and universal medical care. The promise had not been kept, but no leading political figure is ready to disown it entirely. While legislative commissions examine various proposals to shift to a system of employer-financed health insurance and while doctors and hospital administrators win more and more leeway to set and collect fees for private services, there is little certainty to any of the organizational experiments being attempted or contemplated.

The other unquantifiable obstacle to health care reform and improvement is a matter of leadership. Soviet doctors, with few exceptions, are not agitators. Unlike the environmental activists, with whom they came to side mostly in extreme situations, they had rarely built social contacts or political constituencies outside their professional ranks and had not distinguished themselves by going to the head of the civic protests that had brought so many new leaders to the fore in the tumult of the Gorbachev years.

There are exceptions. A whistle-blowing doctor in Kirishi, eventually fired for his temerity, was one of the leaders who had made the human health hazards associated with the production of protein-vitamin concentrates for animal feed a national scandal. He and the print and television journalists who promoted his cause helped put the Soviet chemical industry so deeply on the defensive that the minister of the medical and microbiology industry, formerly the director of the Kirishi plant, accused his detractors of trying "to bomb the economy with ecology."[34]

Other physicians are setting examples of involvement that some of their colleagues found the courage to follow. As elected political figures, Shcherbak and Sviatoslav Fyodorov are working to educate their colleagues and, through the press, the general public. The organizers of the Lenin Children's Fund are setting an example of charity at work in Central Asia and are pressing, as lobbyists, for the rights of orphaned and handicapped youngsters nationally. Finally, there are the activists in the streets—the Novosibirsk hunger-strikers demanding their promised clinic and the leaders of the August 1990 protests across the nation that spurred the development of independent professional medical associations.

In general, however, doctors mind their patients and keep their civic profiles low. The oath they had sworn obliged them to work not just as healers but also "for the state." The time and energy required to fulfill their professional and family responsibilities left them exhausted. And experience with a nay-saying officialdom left them cynical.

Olga Goldfarb, a pediatrician who graduated from Moscow's respected Second Medical Institute in 1975 and emigrated to America in 1989, explained that of all Soviet professions, "medicine is the least dependent on political life. Diarrhea is diarrhea whether under Stalin or Khrushchev or Brezhnev." She remembered that her training included "no environmental education" and her practice taught her the futility of protest.

"I never met anybody who struggled against the medical bureaucracy," she told an American friend. "Their rationale was that they would have to give full time to any internal, social cause and that would mean neglecting their patients. Besides, what's the point in beating your head against a wall? It's better to do the best job possible.

"Everyone knew the reasons that everything was so bad, and everyone knew that they couldn't do anything about it."[35]

That reality is not changing as fast in medicine as in other fields of Soviet life. The Ministry of Health remained the dominant dispenser of training, supplies, equipment, travel funds and money for building or repairing hospital and clinic facilities throughout the Gorbachev years. "What we've seen in medicine," commented Elena Bonner, Andrei Sakharov's widow and a former pediatrician, "is a steady progress of declining levels of education and rising levels of bureaucratization and *apparat*ization."[36]

What she also saw was hope. She talked about it late one night in Moscow with a friend who remembered her cluttered apartment as the site of her husband's stubborn, sometimes pathetic efforts to promote the cause of human rights and to publicize the individual victims of Brezhnev regime violations of human dignity. As she turned off the television set at the end of a delayed broadcast of a stormy session of the Russian Republic parliament, she reflected on the world Sakharov had died trying to remake. "The important thing," she said, "is that Russia is coming alive again."[37]

That was an important change for Soviet medicine as well, but slow to make itself felt. When Yevgeny Chazov left his post as Soviet health minister in 1990 after the three years he said he had set for himself as the limit of his assignment, he revealed a September 1987 letter he had written to the Politburo. The report, submitted after he had held his post six months, "was probably the first time they recognized just how bad the situation in the field [of health] actually was."[38]

Until then and even afterward, Soviet medical investments were determined by counting the numbers of beds, doctors, nurses and machines money could buy, but not the impact on the people's health or longevity. As a step toward reform, Chazov argued that the USSR should be spending—as Western nations did on average—roughly 7 percent of GNP on health care, not the 4 percent then allocated. In ruble terms, he estimated that outlays should rise to "80 to 90 billion rubles a year." He settled on that figure by taking the average cost of care given patients tended in the modern facilities of the ministry's disbanded Fourth (or Kremlin) Main Directorate and multiplying it for the entire Soviet population in need of treatment—a formula that failed to forecast the raging inflation that his successor in 1991 said was cutting actual expenditures by 12 to 17 percent, or between 4.2 and 5.9 billion rubles.[39]

One presumed reason for Chazov's resignation, however, was that such funds were not and would not soon be available. Even using his GNP percentage standard and estimating GNP at 800 billion rubles, it was apparent that the Soviet treasury could not provide the roughly 40-billion-ruble difference between actual 1990 health outlays and the 72 billion that a 7 percent-of-GNP norm would mandate.

Other Soviet physicians and health care analysts argued not for 72, or 80 or 90 billion rubles, but for annual expenditures of 100 billion.[40] When the USSR Supreme Soviet committee on health in November 1990 adopted its program "for the prevention of illness and the formation of a healthy way of life," it also set an annual spending level: approximately 30 billion rubles from the state budget.[41] A year earlier committee chairman Yury Borodin said 80 billion rubles was needed, but "in our country's complicated economic situation, such a sum cannot be found. We will insist, however, on adding 3–5 billion rubles" to the 1989 budget level.[42]

Chazov and his successor, Igor Denisov, both argued that financial problems were far from the only ills besetting Soviet medicine. Management and morale also figured high on their list of problems, but at the heart of the USSR's failure in the health field lay the priority given to the quantity of care rather than its quality. Hospital officials measured their success—and were financed accordingly—much the same way that steel mills measured theirs: in terms of the number of patients treated, like the volume of ingots stamped.

Until the incentives built into the system could be changed, the priorities would remain misguided. The first change to be made—and a relatively inexpensive one—would be to promote basic sanitation measures in medical settings, where, incredibly, they have been so long neglected. Simply insisting on adequate sterilization of medical equipment and facilities could save millions of people—especially infants—from avoidable, even fatal illnesses as well as tens of millions of rubles in economic losses attributable to infectious diseases.

Taking that emphasis a step further, a low-cost program of education in hygiene could also produce significant progress in lowering illness rates. A public aware of the harm caused by excessive use of agricultural chemicals would also be a public alert to the contagion spread by unsupervised trash and garbage dumps leaking their poisons into the water supply.

Going beyond elementary hygiene, cost-effective hospital and clinic administration, even without the radical changes suggested by Sviatoslav Fyodorov (see chapter 9), could help to reduce the numbers of underqualified and underpaid employees and provide decent incomes to skilled and essential personnel. If the emphasis on primary care that Health Minister Denisov advocated produced a new breed of family physicians, it could also help to catch illnesses in their early stage and bring relatively low-cost therapy into play before critical conditions set in.

Better-trained physicians, however, must have far better medical equipment than the Soviet system provides. From basic medicines to decent scalpels to readable X-ray film, the first ingredients need not be the most costly. In 1990 Western pharmaceutical manufacturers were all but beating down the doors of Soviet ministries to win contracts for joint production ventures. Considering how much capacity already existed in the Eastern European countries that had been the main suppliers of such goods to the USSR before the economic collapse, sound economic development policy might dictate investments in modernizing existing facilities outside the Soviet Union first. The size of the Soviet market, however, suggests that once the various republics set their new legal and monetary rules, they will find willing Western partners to help build a drug- and medical-equipment supply network.

Finally, combining environmental and social progress with medical reforms could dramatically improve Soviet health. Unclean water as a source of contagion does far more to lower Soviet life expectancy and the quality of life than the shortage of CAT scan machines. The absence of family planning programs, skilled and available prenatal care and inexpensive contraceptives does as much to raise infant and maternal mortality rates as the excessive presence of pesticides on the fields of Moldova, Armenia and Central Asia.

WHENCE COMETH MY HELP

Near the beginning of this book, the following sentence appeared: "The Soviet Union remained a land of vast natural resources, of strong, talented and resilient people." Those words could usefully have been repeated in every chapter, after every account of failure, error and act of inhumanity. The Soviet people have proved how tough they can be under terrible physical conditions—the violence of agricultural collectivization and of Nazi invasion—and in the face of psychological and social brutality—the terror of Stalinism, the thuggish abuse of Brezhnev era cronyism and conformity. They have survived on what Ronald Reagan once disparaged as "a diet of sawdust" and have lived to make an epochal change in their oldest political tradition—away from subservience and apathy to civic involvement and the beginnings of self-reliance.

Albert Likhanov, the charismatic writer who made the Lenin Children's Fund an emergency rescue squad for the imperiled infants of Central Asia, was eloquent in his "bow to the 2,000 doctors, especially the women, for their volunteer charity" in the eighty-day campaign in 1988 that, he said, saved "9,000 young lives."[43] His organization also pushed an idea borrowed from American Seventh-Day Adventists to manufacture additional infant formula for the 2.7 million Soviet newborns threatened by malnutrition in their first weeks of life.[44]

Maria Cherkasova, the forceful, thoughtful, somewhat schoolmarmish leader in the Socio-Ecological Union, took hope from "the one thing Gorbachev has given us: *glasnost*. All of a sudden," she said, "everywhere people started to talk and to act. It is not enough to wake up a sleeping people, as some of us thought, but it is an essential first step."[45] On a visit to the United States in May 1990 to organize what became ten months later a ground-breaking encounter between nongovernmental U.S. and Soviet environmental activists, she argued that another step was needed. "Environmental problems can't be divided into American problems and Soviet problems. They are the common problems of the whole globe.

"Your dirt is our dirt, and our dirt is your dirt. If America sends the Soviet Union polluting technology because you can make a quick profit from the sale, the wastes will return to harm you over time."[46]

At the time she was full of ideas for cooperative action in training, in monitoring, in research and analysis. "It's useless to send us new technology in our present situation," she maintained. "What we need is scientific experts."[47] At the 1991 conference in Moscow some of the research projects she had promoted came into being. More were proposed.

In health care, similar joint ventures are also getting underway, sometimes between American doctors whose families came from the Baltic Republics and physicians in the lands they left behind. Other efforts at assistance grew out of emergency calls like the summons that brought Dr. John Remensnyder, Jr., a burn specialist from the staff of Massachusetts General Hospital, to the wards of Children's Hospital Number 9 in Moscow.

The first visit was a rescue operation in the wake of the 1989 natural gas pipeline blast in the Urals that left thirty-seven children on the trains caught in the explosion critically burned.[48] His second trip to Moscow, sponsored by Project Hope, in the fall of 1990 was longer and, growing out of the first, involved helping Dr. Pyotr Prodeus modernize his burn clinic and upgrade the skills of its staff.

A short visit to Petropavlovsk on the Pacific Coast of the Soviet Union turned an Anchorage, Alaska, family practitioner into a benefactor. When Soviet sailors arrived from the other side of the Bering Straits with a few dollars they planned to use in buying single-use syringes for a children's hospital, Dr. Matison White "rounded up medical supplies" in the state's largest city and shipped them by air freight to the small port where the Soviets had landed.[49]

Charity could only be a stop-gap. And at the end of the summer of 1991, most commercial ventures with Western investors were still stalled in the political and economic upheaval. But Marco Vezzani, an Italian engineer working in Volgograd's industrial suburb of Volzhsky to finish a turnkey factory to manufacture oil-well tubes, was confident that the future lay with business cooperation.

After six years on the bleak steppes of southern Russia, surviving "terrible wind-chill in the winter" and having to jury-rig convoys of trucks to bring in essential materials and even cement when the Soviet transportation network failed him, Vezzani could compare the economy of the USSR to "a car with a steering wheel that doesn't respond." In almost the same breath, however, he spoke with optimism about getting into the business of manufacturing water purification equipment in Volgograd for the city's system and customers up and down the Volga. Then again, he cautioned a visitor that "for now, it's all talk. There's no capital to get anything started."[50]

He radiated pride, however, when he told how his immediate project was being completed in record time and under budget, because, he said, he had given Soviet workers on one essential construction job the right to take part of their pay in goods ordered from an Italian catalogue. "Practically right away the level of professionalism went up to world standards. The pay is still cheap, but it's become a Western firm. And the people who made that happen are the Soviets."[51]

The only people who really can make the Soviet Union a healthy and prospering nation are its citizens. Outsiders can assist in many ways but cannot dictate the outcome of a historic struggle with a brutal past and a menace-filled present. Late in 1991 that contest seemed to be taking a dramatic turn toward new hope.

The year before, protesters brandishing bitter slogans had filled Red Square during the May Day celebrations with chants of anger. Their open contempt drove Mikhail Gorbachev to leave the roof of the Lenin Mausoleum from which his predecessors had watched the organized demonstrations year after predictable year.

In 1990, however, the crowd carried not Gorbachev's portrait but signs that read: "70 Years on the Road to Nowhere" and, in scornful memory of Nikita Khrushchev's boasts about overtaking American standards of living: "Let us Catch Up with and Surpass Africa."

Signs are only signs. But even in 1990 some unusual and positive ones began to appear in a landscape littered with disillusionment. On top of a giant metallurgical factory in Krasnoyarsk, the source of 119,000 tons of atmospheric pollutants a year, a new slogan appeared: "To Protect Nature means to Defend the Motherland."[52]

Without actual investments in reducing emissions, the slogan was just another piece of familiar, hollow Soviet rhetoric. But members of the Krasnoyarsk city council had all but declared war on the factory's pollution. For the first time in the sad history of Soviet ecocide—and not just in Krasnoyarsk, but across the country—the elected officials had a chance of winning. The people were behind them.

Appendix

TABLE A.1
USSR *Population, 1959 to 1990**
(in millions)

Year	Population				
	Total	Urban	Rural	Males	Females
1959	208.8	100.0	108.8	94.0	114.8
1970	241.1	136.0	105.7	111.4	130.3
1979	262.4	163.6	98.8	122.3	140.1
1989	286.7	188.8	97.9	135.3	151.4
1990	288.6	190.6	98.0	136.4	152.2

SOURCE: Goskomstat SSSR, *Okhrana zdorov'ya v SSSR, statisticheskiy sbornik* (Moscow: Finansy i statistika, 1990), p. 7. Hereafter cited as *Okhrana zdor.*
*Census data for 1959 to 1989 and beginning-of-year estimate for 1990.

TABLE A.2
USSR Population by Republic, 1959 to 1990
(in thousands)

Republic	1959	1970	1979	1989	1990
USSR	208,827	241,720	262,436	286,731	288,624
RSFSR	117,534	130,079	137,551	147,400	148,041
Ukraine	41,869	47,126	49,755	51,707	51,839
Belorussia	8,056	9,002	9,560	10,200	10,259
Moldova	2,885	3,569	3,947	4,338	4,362
Estonia	1,197	1,356	1,466	1,573	1,583
Latvia	2,093	2,364	2,521	2,680	2,687
Lithuania	2,711	3,128	3,398	3,690	3,723
Armenia	1,763	2,492	3,031	3,288	3,293
Azerbaijan	3,698	5,117	6,028	7,038	7,131
Georgia	4,044	4,686	5,015	5,443	5,456
Kazakhstan	9,295	13,009	14,684	16,536	16,691
Kirghizia	2,066	2,934	3,529	4,290	4,367
Tajikistan	1,981	2,900	3,801	5,109	5,248
Turkmenistan	1,516	2,159	2,759	3,534	3,622
Uzbekistan	8,119	11,799	15,391	19,905	20,322

SOURCE: Okhrana zdor., p. 8.

TABLE A.3

Births, Deaths, Natural Population Growth and Infant Mortality in the USSR, 1950 to 1989

Year	In Thousands				Rate per 1,000 of Population			Rate of Deaths Prior to One Year of Age per 1,000 Live Births*
	Number of Births	Number of Deaths	Number of Deaths of Those Under One Year of Age	Natural Population Growth	Births	Deaths	Natural Population Growth	
1950	4,805.3	1,745.0	394.6	3,060.3	26.7	9.7	17.0	80.7
1960	5,341.0	1,528.6	187.7	3,812.4	24.9	7.1	17.8	35.3
1970	4,225.6	1,996.3	103.3	2,229.3	17.4	8.2	9.2	24.7
1980	4,851.4	2,743.8	131.9	2,107.6	18.3	10.3	8.0	27.3
1985	5,374.4	2,947.1	139.8	2,427.3	19.4	10.6	8.8	26.0
1986	5,610.8	2,737.4	140.7	2,873.4	20.0	9.8	10.2	25.4
1987	5,599.2	2,804.8	142.2	2,794.4	19.8	9.9	9.9	25.4
1988	5,381.1	2,888.8	134.0	2,492.3	18.9	10.1	8.8	24.7
1989	5,062.2	2,874.5	116.3	2,187.7	17.6	10.0	7.6	22.7

SOURCE: *Okhrana zdor.*, p. 8.
*See text for adjusted infant mortality figures.

273

TABLE A.4

Comparison of Life Expectancy at Birth: USSR and the United States
(number of years on average at birth)

Time Period	USSR			United States		
	Total Population	Males	Females	Total Population	Males	Females
1958–1959	68.6	64.4	71.7	69.9	66.8	73.2
1962–1963	69.6	65.4	72.8	69.9	66.6	73.4
1964–1965	70.4	66.1	73.8	70.2	66.8	73.8
1968–1969	69.8	64.9	73.7	70.5	66.8	74.4
1970–1971	69.4	64.5	73.5	71.1	67.4	75.0
1974–1975	68.8	63.7	73.1	72.5	68.7	76.5
1978–1979	67.9	62.5	72.6	73.9	70.0	77.8
1980–1981	67.7	62.3	72.5	74.2	70.4	77.8
1982–1983	68.2	62.8	73.0	74.6	71.0	78.1
1984–1985	68.1	62.9	72.7	74.7	71.2	78.2
1986–1987	69.8	65.0	73.8	75.0	71.5	78.4
1988	69.5	64.8	73.6	74.9	71.5	78.3

SOURCE: *Okhrana zdor.*, p. 20, and U.S. Department of Health and Human Services, Public Health Service, Centers for Disease Control, National Center for Health Statistics, *Monthly Vital Statistics Report*, 39, no. 7 (November 28, 1990), p. 16.

TABLE A.5

Morbidity: New Cases, Number and Rate in the USSR, 1960 to 1989
(per 100,000 Population)

Year	Total Population (100,000) (midyear)	Acute Poliomyelitis New Cases	Acute Poliomyelitis Per 100,000	Diphtheria New Cases	Diphtheria Per 100,000	Measles New Cases	Measles Per 100,000	Pertussis (Whooping Cough) New Cases	Pertussis (Whooping Cough) Per 100,000	Scarlet Fever New Cases	Scarlet Fever Per 100,000
1960	2,123.72	7,167	3.30	53,195	24.80	2,083,333	972.0	554,087	258.5	671,186	313.2
1961	2,162.86	3,752	1.72	31,426	14.40	1,969,975	903.1	437,981	200.8	599,277	274.7
1962	2,200.03	1,692	0.76	15,385	6.90	2,146,599	968.1	471,124	212.5	527,169	237.8
1963	2,234.57	959	0.43	8,980	4.00	1,647,104	731.8	364,722	162.1	492,911	219.0
1964	2,266.69	475	0.21	6,722	2.90	2,034,086	891.6	287,970	126.2	507,570	222.5
1965	2,296.28	303	0.13	4,691	2.00	2,128,666	921.8	190,045	82.3	530,836	229.9
1966	2,322.43	287	0.12	3,102	1.30	1,747,219	748.3	145,729	62.4	691,588	296.1
1967	2,348.23	135	0.06	2,595	1.10	1,798,116	761.9	114,709	48.6	597,280	253.1
1968	2,371.65	120	0.05	2,235	0.93	1,579,829	662.9	119,383	50.1	502,015	210.7
1969	2,394.68	194	0.08	1,710	0.71	510,440	212.2	52,709	21.9	434,887	180.8
1970	2,417.20	270	0.11	1,101	0.45	471,500	194.2	39,510	16.3	469,903	193.6
1971	2,438.91	188	0.08	765	0.31	588,445	240.1	42,561	17.4	510,220	208.2
1972	2,463.28	183	0.07	516	0.20	291,435	117.8	34,534	14.0	319,468	129.1
1973	2,486.74	183	0.07	319	0.13	286,245	114.2	30,237	12.1	318,665	127.6
1974	2,509.31	139	0.06	285	0.11	374,247	148.4	30,895	12.3	367,097	145.6

(Continued on next page)

TABLE A.5 (continued)

Year	Total Population (100,000) (midyear)	Acute Poliomyelitis		Diphtheria		Measles		Pertussis (Whooping Cough)		Scarlet Fever	
		New Cases	Per 100,000	New Cases	Per 100,000	New Cases	Per 100,000	New Cases	Per 100,000	New Cases	Per 100,000
1975	2,533.32	133	0.05	199	0.07	363,784	143.0	14,885	5.9	361,139	142.0
1976	2,556.05	106	0.04	198	0.07	320,844	125.0	33,022	12.9	383,564	149.4
1977	2,579.16	264	0.10	238	0.09	315,304	121.8	22,610	8.7	308,367	119.1
1978	2,601.42	152	0.06	270	0.10	545,392	208.9	17,180	6.6	287,242	11.0
1979	2,624.36	214	0.08	270	0.10	382,647	145.3	25,153	9.5	246,822	93.3
1980	2,644.86	165	0.06	345	0.13	255,654	133.9	13,908	5.2	230,142	86.7
1981	2,665.99	307	0.11	560	0.21	342,819	128.2	25,637	9.6	226,757	84.8
1982	2,688.44	257	0.09	917	0.34	466,210	172.8	27,481	10.0	324,686	120.4
1983	2,712.39	181	0.06	1,411	0.51	233,812	85.9	19,321	7.1	293,081	107.7
1984	2,738.41	115	0.04	1,609	0.58	252,510	91.9	25,985	9.4	261,682	95.2
1985	2,762.90	138	0.05	1,511	0.54	272,807	98.4	53,871	19.4	277,943	100.3
1986	2,787.84	170	0.06	1,160	0.41	165,000	59.0	17,700	6.3	357,000	128.0
1987	2,816.89	170	0.06	1,080	0.38	191,000	67.0	20,200	7.2	330,000	117.0
1988	2,860.60	160	0.06	870	0.30	165,000	58.0	45,000	15.9	215,000	75.0
1989	2,876.78	90	0.03	840	0.29	52,000	18.0	37,000	12.9	225,000	78.0

TABLE A.5 (*continued*)

Year	Total Population (100,000) (midyear)	Tetanus New Cases	Tetanus Per 100,000	Typhoid/Paratyphoid, ABC Total New Cases	Total Per 100,000	Typhoid New Cases	Typhoid Per 100,000	Paratyphoid, ABC New Cases	Paratyphoid Per 100,000	Infectious Hepatitis New Cases	Infectious Hepatitis Per 100,000	Influenza and Upper Respiratory Infections New Cases	Influenza Per 100,000
1960	2,123.72	2,319	1.09	47,291	22.3	40,834	19.1	6,457	3.0	513,052	239.4	19,831,029	9,337.9
1961	2,162.86	2,258	1.04	46,989	21.7	39,258	18.0	7,731	3.5	579,410	265.6	24,063,443	11,125.8
1962	2,200.03	2,172	0.99	40,763	18.5	34,391	15.5	6,372	2.9	462,054	208.4	44,451,912	20,205.1
1963	2,234.57	2,043	0.91	41,215	18.4	33,458	14.9	7,757	3.4	433,744	192.7	29,511,467	13,206.8
1964	2,266.69	1,641	0.72	31,541	13.9	25,512	11.2	6,029	2.6	517,883	227.0	23,834,272	10,515.0
1965	2,296.28	1,362	0.59	25,487	11.1	19,919	8.6	5,568	2.4	470,129	203.6	42,137,941	18,350.5
1966	2,322.43	1,305	0.56	27,489	11.8	21,925	9.4	5,564	2.4	465,222	199.2	29,771,456	12,819.1
1967	2,348.23	1,100	0.47	23,900	10.2	19,064	8.1	4,884	2.1	372,857	158.0	(NA)	(NA)
1968	2,371.65	900	0.38	23,300	9.8	17,842	7.5	5,430	2.3	371,309	155.8	(NA)	(NA)
1969	2,394.68	700	0.29	22,800	9.5	17,324	7.2	5,507	2.3	339,139	141.0	(NA)	(NA)
1970	2,417.20	652	0.27	22,462	9.3	17,808	7.3	4,654	1.9	404,224	166.5	55,841,700	23,101.8
1971	2,438.91	668	0.27	18,881	7.7	14,612	6.0	4,269	1.7	442,388	180.5	42,211,500	17,307.5
1972	2,463.28	617	0.25	19,558	7.9	14,346	5.8	5,212	2.1	480,437	194.1	41,692,100	16,925.4
1973	2,486.74	495	0.20	19,842	8.0	14,644	5.9	5,198	2.1	541,621	216.8	55,366,900	22,264.9
1974	2,509.31	539	0.21	23,332	9.3	16,658	6.6	6,674	2.7	527,038	209.0	46,747,200	18,629.5

(*Continued on next page*)

TABLE A.5 (continued)

Year	Total Population (100,000) (midyear)	Tetanus		Typhoid/Paratyphoid, ABC						Infectious Hepatitis		Influenza and Upper Respiratory Infections	
		New Cases	Per 100,000	Total New Cases	Total Per 100,000	Typhoid New Cases	Per 100,000	Paratyphoid, ABC New Cases	Per 100,000	New Cases	Per 100,000	New Cases	Per 100,000
1975	2,533.32	490	0.19	25,969	10.3	18,613	7.3	7,356	2.9	663,794	260.9	54,942,100	21,687.8
1976	2,556.05	430	0.17	21,000	8.2	14,653	5.7	6,320	2.5	606,812	236.4	(NA)	(NA)
1977	2,579.16	420	0.16	22,900	8.9	16,378	6.3	6,569	2.5	602,653	232.1	(NA)	(NA)
1978	2,601.42	360	0.14	18,100	7.0	13,049	5.0	5,073	1.9	589,204	225.5	(NA)	(NA)
1979	2,624.36	400	0.15	18,400	7.0	14,038	5.3	4,339	1.6	750,623	284.9	(NA)	(NA)
1980	2,644.86	300	0.11	16,900	6.4	12,836	4.8	4,024	1.5	801,545	301.9	60,369,000	22,761.0
1981	2,665.99	350	0.13	17,100	6.4	13,195	4.9	3,914	1.5	842,379	315.3	(NA)	(NA)
1982	2,688.44	350	0.13	17,200	6.4	13,179	4.9	3,980	1.5	951,617	352.8	(NA)	(NA)
1983	2,712.39	360	0.13	18,600	6.9	13,621	5.0	4,953	1.8	1,171,337	430.3	(NA)	(NA)
1984	2,738.41	330	0.12	18,900	6.9	13,342	4.8	5,543	2.0	885,762	322.4	(NA)	(NA)
1985	2,762.90	280	0.10	17,600	6.0	13,106	4.7	4,463	1.6	934,085	337.0	71,869,000	25,928.0
1986	2,787.84	260	0.09	13,200	5.0	(NA)	(NA)	(NA)	(NA)	842,000	301.0	76,641,000	27,383.0
1987	2,316.89	190	0.07	12,699	4.0	(NA)	(NA)	(NA)	(NA)	861,000	315.0	59,447,000	21,025.0
1988	2,360.60	200	0.07	11,500	4.0	(NA)	(NA)	(NA)	(NA)	716,000	251.0	(NA)	(NA)
1989	2,876.78	200	0.07	9,500	3.3	(NA)	(NA)	(NA)	(NA)	910,000	317.0	(NA)	(NA)

SOURCE: Murray Feshbach, A Compendium of Soviet Health Statistics (Washington, D.C.: 1985), pp. 78–81, and official Soviet statistical publications.
(NA) —Not available.

TABLE A.6

Incidence of Infectious Disease in the USSR by Republic, 1989
(number of registered illnesses per 100,000 population)

Type of Disease	USSR	RSFSR	Ukraine	Belorussia	Moldova	Estonia	Latvia	Lithuania
Typhoid and paratyphoid ABC	3.3	0.8	0.4	0.2	0.4	0.3	0.2	0.8
Other salmonella infections	54.6	70.8	25.4	38.8	115.3	85.5	125.8	31.7
Acute digestive illnesses	510.7	658.0	223.4	131.1	571.4	295.2	141.0	170.8
Bacterial dysentery	136.7	201.0	54.7	47.3	168.2	70.6	45.0	66.1
Yersinosis (diarrheal disease)	8.5	15.0	0.6	6.1	0.1	11.9	16.4	3.5
Brucellosis	1.9	0.4	0.0	—	0.1	—	—	—
Meningococcal infections	4.3	5.0	3.5	5.3	7.0	2.4	3.0	2.9
Cerebrospinal meningitis	1.6	2.1	0.8	1.1	3.7	1.0	1.7	1.3
Tetanus	0.07	0.05	0.18	0.08	0.07	0.06	0.04	—
Viral hepatitis	317.4	192.9	213.9	431.7	351.7	86.7	295.3	206.6
Serum hepatitis (hepatitis B)	43.3	25.1	31.6	21.2	65.3	8.7	24.8	35.9
Mumps	57.7	49.2	102.2	54.9	32.5	33.2	8.0	17.6
Rickettsiosis	0.6	0.9	0.2	0.3	1.0	—	—	0.1
Malaria	0.5	0.4	0.4	0.7	0.6	0.9	0.2	0.3
Influenza and other acute upper respiratory tract infections	23,761.0	28,619.0	24,550.0	26,501.0	14,986.0	20,220.0	15,725.0	12,403.0

(Continued on next page)

TABLE A.6 (continued)

Type of Disease	Armenia	Azerbaijan	Georgia	Kazakhstan	Kirghizia	Tajikistan	Turkmenistan	Uzbekistan
Typhoid and paratyphoid ABC	1.9	3.0	1.4	2.9	7.9	47.1	39.3	15.5
Other salmonella infections	32.1	25.5	19.7	41.0	38.5	40.1	37.5	43.1
Acute digestive illnesses	249.5	228.7	259.4	410.0	580.7	920.3	579.3	635.4
Bacterial dysentery	59.7	28.8	36.6	108.7	98.7	131.9	46.4	69.5
Yersinosis (diarrheal disease)	0.1	0.03	0.1	1.4	0.3	0.3	—	0.6
Brucellosis	4.4	1.9	4.0	10.6	14.3	6.4	11.6	5.9
Meningococcal infections	1.3	0.8	1.3	4.3	5.8	4.2	5.2	2.5
Cerebrospinal meningitis	0.03	—	0.2	2.2	3.4	0.5	3.0	1.0
Tetanus	0.06	0.11	0.15	0.05	0.07	0.04	0.03	0.05
Viral hepatitis	279.0	310.5	226.3	465.6	710.8	918.3	735.1	1,074.5
Serum hepatitis (hepatitis B)	23.4	23.3	41.0	30.8	50.3	94.2	100.8	217.0
Mumps	36.8	10.7	18.0	90.5	41.5	70.3	51.6	33.8
Rickettsiosis	—	—	0.1	0.9	1.1	0.1	0.1	0.7
Malaria	0.1	1.1	0.1	0.1	0.1	3.9	0.5	0.4
Influenza and other acute upper respiratory tract infections	15,941.0	11,538.0	12,037.0	18,428.0	13,274.0	14,119.0	10,276.0	10,232.0

SOURCE: *Okhrana zdor.*, p. 56.

TABLE A.7

Medical Cadres and the Network of Health Care Institutions by Ministry, Departments and Agencies in the USSR, 1989

	Total All Ministries and Departments		USSR Ministry of Health and the Republic Ministries of Health		USSR Ministry of Railways		Other Ministries, Departments and Organizations	
	In Thousands	As a Percentage of the Total	In Thousands	As a Percentage of the Total	In Thousands	As a Percentage of the Total	In Thousands	As a Percentage of the Total
Number of doctors in all specialties	1,278.0	100.0	1,130.0	89.0	42.0	3.0	106.0	8.0
Number of midlevel medical personnel	3,386.0	100.0	2,853.0	84.0	107.0	3.0	426.0	13.0
Number of hospitals	23.7	100.0	22.8	96.0	0.6	3.0	0.3	1.0
Number of hospital beds	3,822.0	100.0	3,660.0	96.0	122.0	3.0	40.0	1.0
Number of beds (medical and obstetric) for pregnant women and women giving birth	258.7	100.0	255.4	99.0	3.1	1.0	0.2	0.1
Number of medical institutions providing outpatient care*	42.8	100.0	40.3	94.0	1.3	3.0	1.2	3.0
Capacity of outpatient institutions (visits per shift)	5,442.0	100.0	5,136.0	94.0	211.0	4.0	95.0	2.0
Number of women's consultations, children's polyclinics and outpatient clinics (independent and as parts of the personnel of other institutions)	29.2	100.0	27.7	96.0	1.5	5.0	0.02	0.0
Number of midwifery points	90.0	100.0	88.1	98.0	1.9	2.0	—	—
Number of sanitary-epidemiological stations and points	4.9	100.0	4.5	92.0	0.4	8.0	0.1	0.0

SOURCE: *Okhrana zdor.*, p. 112.

*Included in the number of medical institutions providing outpatient care to the population are all medical institutions that provide clinical care (polyclinics, clinics, dispensaries, clinical departments of hospitals, medical first aid points, and others).

TABLE A.8

The State of Technology and Structures for General Health Care
Institutions in the USSR, October 1988*

(according to a sample survey of 10,800 structures in the USSR Ministry of
Health System; in percentages)

	Polyclinics	Hospitals
Total Structures	100	100
By year of construction:		
prior to 1918	10	12
1919–1940	9	11
1941–1945	1	1
1946–1950	3	3
1951–1960	13	15
1961–1970	16	20
1971–1980	19	18
1981–1985	8	8
1986–1988	6	5
not specified	15	7

TABLE A.8 (*continued*)

	Polyclinics	Hospitals
Condition of the facility:		
in a state of emergency	5	9
requiring reconstruction	14	14
requiring capital repair	30	32
requiring minor repair	34	30
requiring no repairs	17	15
Facilities lacking:		
water supply system	9	15
hot water	29	49
sewage system	15	24
central heating	12	19
bath (shower)	52	45
electrical supply	1	1
ventilation and air conditioning system	54	64

SOURCE: *Okhrana zdor.*, p. 150.

*Among hospital/outpatient facilities, 61 percent are located in structures that have been adapted for use and 39 percent are located in structures constructed on a standard model.

TABLE A.9

Supply of Medical Equipment in the USSR, October 1988*
*(according to a sample survey of doctors at 10,800 medical institutions in
the USSR Health Care System; in percentages)*

	Polyclinics	Hospitals
Experiencing shortages in equipment for:		
X-ray therapy	54	56
photo X-ray	52	48
diagnostic radiography	51	43
laboratory work	45	49
physiotherapy	42	44
electrocardiographs	38	35
dentistry	35	37

SOURCE: *Okhrana zdor.*, p. 151.
*Only 2 percent of polyclinics and 6 percent of hospitals are able to use ultrasound for examination of patients, while 5 percent and 13 percent use endoscopes. General health care facilities experience shortages in functional furnishings: 30 percent experience shortages of beds and chairs, 44 percent experience shortages of rolling beds, 86 percent experience shortages of simple mechanical tools; do not have enough linen, medicines and medical supplies.

TABLE A.10a

Maximum Allowable Concentrations (PDK) for Air Pollutants in the USSR
(in milligrams per cubic meter)

Substance	One-time Maximum	24-Hour Average	Substance	One-time Maximum	24-Hour Average
Nitrous dioxide (NO_2)	0.085	0.04	Mercury (metallic)	—	0.0003
Nitrous oxide (NO)	0.4	0.06	Soot	0.15	0.05
Acrylate	0.03	0.03	Lead and its compounds excluding tetraethyl lead ($Pb(C_2H_5)_4$)	—	0.0003
Ammonia	0.2	0.04	Hydrogen sulfide	0.008	0.005
Acetone	0.35	0.35	Hydrocarbons	0.03	0.05
Benzopyrene	—	0.1 microgram/100 m³	Sulfur dioxide (SO_2)	0.5	0.5
Benzol/benzene	1.5	0.1	Methanol	1.0	0.6
Vanadium	—	—	Toluene/methyl benzene (C_7H_8)	0.6	0.6
Particulate matter (dust)	0.5	0.15	Tricresol (phosphate) ($CH_3C_6H_4O)_3PO$	0.005	0.005
Hydrogen chloride	0.2	0.2	Carbon monoxide (CO)	5.0	3.0
Hydrogen cyanide (Prussic acid)	—	0.01	Phenol	0.01	0.003
Cadmium	—	0.001	Formaldehyde	0.035	0.003
Sulfuric acid	0.3	0.1	Fluorine compounds:		
Xylene	0.2	0.2	Hydrogen fluoride	0.02	0.005
Manganese and any of its compounds	0.01	0.001	Inorganic and insoluable fluorine	0.2	0.3
Copper	—	0.002	Furfural (C_4H_3OCHO)	0.05	0.05
Methyl mercaptan	$9*10^{-6}$	—	Chlorine	0.1	0.03
Nickel	—	0.001	Chromium (six valence as in CrO_3)	0.0015	0.0015
Ozone	0.16	0.03	Zinc oxide	—	0.05
Cement dust	0.3	0.01	Ethylbenzene	0.02	0.02

SOURCE: Yu. A. Izrael and F. Ya. Rovinsky, eds., Obzor sostoyaniya okruzhayushchey prirodnoy sredy v SSSR (Moscow: Gidrometeoizdat, 1990), p. 7. Hereafter cited as Obzor.

TABLE A.10b

Maximum Allowable Concentrations (PDK) for Surface Water Pollutants in the USSR
(in milligrams per liter)

Substance	Reservoirs for Public and Domestic Sanitation Use	Substance	Reservoirs for Public and Domestic Sanitation Use
Ammonium nitrate	2.0	Nitrate ions	10
Ammonia	0.39	Nitrite ions	1.0
Aniline	0.1	Nitric nitrogen	0.02
Benzopyrene	0.000005	Mercury	0.0005
DDT	0.1	Lead	0.03
Dithiophosphate (sulfur)	0.001	Sulfate ions	500
Xanthogenic compounds	0.001	(SPAV) Anionic	0.5
Cadmium	0.01	Phenols	0.001
Lignin	1.6	Chromium (six valent)	0.05
Manganese	0.01	Zinc	0.01
Copper	1.0	Cyclohexane (C_6H_{12})	0.1
Nickel	0.1		

SOURCE: *Obzor*, p. 111.

TABLE A.10c

Maximum Allowable Concentrations (PDK) for Soil Pollutants in the USSR
(in milligrams per kilogram)

Substance	Gross Content	Substance	Gross Content
Atrazine	0.5	Lead	30
Vanadium	150.0	Cymogene[a]	0.2
DDT	0.1	Thionate	0.1[b]
Hexachlorocyclohexane (insecticide)	0.1	Treflan[a]	0.1[b]
Manganese	1500.0	Trichloroacetic acid (CCl_3COOH) (herbicide)	0.2[b]
Metaphosphate	0.1	Phosalon[a]	0.5
Nickel	4.0	Manganese chlorate	1.0[b]
Mercury	2.1		

SOURCE: Obzor, p. 112.
[a] Of unknown chemical content.
[b] Estimated allowable concentration (PDK) for pesticides in soil.

TABLE A.10d

Maximum Allowable Concentrations (PDK) for Pollutants in Sea Water in the USSR
(in milligrams per liter)

Substance or Indicator	PDK	Substance or Indicator	PDK
Soluable oxygen solutions	>4.0 (winter)	Nickel	0.001
	>6.0 (summer)	Mercury (metallic)	0.0001
pH	6.5–8.5	SPAV anionic	0.1
Ammonia salt	2.9 at 13–34%	Lead	0.01
Cadmium	0.001	Phenols	0.001
Manganese (two valent)	0.01	Chloroorganic pesticides	none
Copper	0.005	Zinc	0.005
Petroleum products	0.05		

SOURCE: *Obzor,* p. 112.

TABLE A.11

Emissions of Harmful Substances into the Atmosphere from Stationary Sources for Specific Cities, 1989
(in thousands of tons, per annum)

City*	Total	Total Solids	Total Gases/Liquids	Gases and Liquids, by Compound:						
				Sulfur Anhydrides	Nitrous Dioxide	Carbon Monoxide	Hydrocarbons	Fluorine Compounds	Hydrogen Sulfides	Carbon Sulfides
Alma-Ata	43.0	9.1	34.0	15.0	4.4	11.0	1.03	0.0008	0.0	—
Almalyk	163.0	5.1	157.0	145.0	1.2	9.1	0.07	0.541	0.0	—
Angarsk	387.0	104.0	283.0	118.0	28.0	45.0	90.0	0.0015	0.7	—
Arkhangel'sk	80.0	19.0	61.0	41.0	6.0	12.0	0.6	0.00016	0.2	—
Astrakhan	51.0	12.0	39.0	19.0	5.5	9.2	4.5	0.0005	0.0	—
Ashkhabad	6.7	3.3	3.4	0.5	0.4	1.9	0.1	0.004	—	—
Baku	667.0	256.0	412.0	17.0	15.0	48.0	329.0	0.0008	0.03	—
Balakovo	70.0	4.3	66.0	30.0	9.5	1.1	0.9	0.219	1.4	20.0
Barnaul	178.0	61.0	117.0	49.0	19.0	35.0	4.2	0.0067	0.7	5.8
Berezniki	47.0	7.1	40.0	10.0	6.1	21.0	0.3	0.00004	0.01	0.02
Bratsk	129.0	42.0	87.0	23.0	6.0	51.0	0.8	2.626	1.2	—
Vilnius	32.0	2.0	30.0	17.0	4.4	5.1	1.4	0.0011	—	—
Volgograd	224.0	39.0	186.0	34.0	18.0	64.0	63.0	0.633	0.3	0.0
Volzhskiy	61.0	2.2	58.0	16.0	8.9	27.0	4.7	0.0005	0.2	0.0
Gomel'	35.0	4.7	31.0	8.1	4.7	11.0	0.8	0.189	—	—
Grodno	38.0	7.2	31.0	13.0	5.0	9.0	0.8	0.022	0.0	—
Grozny	268.0	4.5	263.0	23.0	15.0	18.0	201.0	0.00003	0.6	—
Gur'yev	37.0	2.6	35.0	10.0	2.9	2.7	19.0	0.0	0.0	—
Gyandzha	34.0	5.7	28.0	23.0	1.6	2.3	0.08	—	—	—
Dzhambul	100.0	28.0	72.0	50.0	13.0	2.8	0.7	0.701	—	—
Dzerzhinsk (Nizhegorod-skaya *oblast'*)	108.0	14.0	94.0	45.0	13.0	22.0	9.2	0.012	—	—
Dneprodzerzhinsk	287.0	47.0	240.0	45.0	21.0	165.0	3.4	0.019	1.2	0.2
Dnepropetrovsk	273.0	67.0	206.0	98.0	43.0	55.0	8.8	0.0072	0.3	0.04
Donetsk	169.0	24.0	145.0	31.0	6.1	99.0	2.0	0.02	3.5	—

(Continued on next page)

TABLE A.11 (continued)

City*	Total	Total Solids	Total Gases/ Liquids	Gases and Liquids, by Compound:						
				Sulfur Anhydrides	Nitrous Dioxide	Carbon Monoxide	Hydrocarbons	Fluorine Compounds	Hydrogen Sulfides	Carbon Sulfides
Dushanbe	25.0	7.8	17.0	5.1	4.1	7.1	0.3	0.0004	0.02	—
Yenakievo	118.0	16.0	101.0	9.3	3.0	82.0	4.1	—	1.4	0.06
Yerevan	46.0	4.4	41.0	9.6	11.0	9.6	7.0	0.015	—	0.3
Zaporozh'ye	253.0	63.0	190.0	25.0	14.0	141.0	4.6	0.405	0.2	—
Zestafoni	14.0	2.1	12.0	1.1	1.5	9.1	0.0	—	0.04	—
Zyryanovsk	11.0	5.8	5.0	1.5	0.3	3.2	0.01	—	—	—
Irkutsk	82.0	31.0	51.0	27.0	7.0	16.0	0.8	0.04	0.0	0.0
Kaliningrad	49.0	14.0	35.0	22.0	2.2	9.6	0.5	0.001	0.0	—
Kamensk-Ural'skiy	92.0	47.0	45.0	17.0	6.3	21.0	0.4	0.716	—	—
Karaganda	151.0	57.0	94.0	38.0	13.0	42.0	0.5	0.0002	—	—
Kemerovo	107.0	30.0	77.0	26.0	28.0	15.0	5.5	0.0003	0.08	0.03
Kiev	63.0	9.4	53.0	18.0	20.0	5.2	6.0	0.168	0.3	1.2
Kirov	90.0	36.0	55.0	28.0	11.0	10.0	1.9	0.0012	0.0	—
Kirovakan	6.0	0.4	5.8	0.1	0.5	0.3	0.1	—	—	—
Kishinev	29.0	6.1	23.0	8.5	4.4	6.2	3.5	0.0005	0.0	—
Kommunarsk	235.0	65.0	170.0	20.0	13.0	128.0	1.9	0.0041	2.9	—
Komsomol'sk-na-Amure	68.0	18.0	50.0	14.0	9.0	9.8	15.0	0.0008	0.05	—
Krasnoyarsk	246.0	70.0	176.0	38.0	13.0	112.0	2.9	2.052	1.3	2.7
Kremenchug	156.0	14.0	141.0	37.0	6.9	19.0	70.0	0.0007	0.3	—
Krivoy Rog	1,167.0	192.0	974.0	82.0	33.0	852.0	3.6	0.0003	2.5	—
Kuibyshev	137.0	16.0	121.0	36.0	16.0	27.0	37.0	0.0042	0.9	—
Kurgan	67.0	24.0	43.0	21.0	7.2	12.0	2.9	0.045	—	—
Leningrad	191.0	41.0	151.0	56.0	42.0	28.0	15.0	0.024	0.0	—
Leninogorsk	35.0	6.9	28.0	21.0	2.9	3.9	0.0	0.012	—	—
Liptsek	660.0	54.0	606.0	45.0	26.0	530.0	2.2	0.012	0.7	0.0
Lisichansk	123.0	3.6	119.0	20.0	7.0	39.0	51.0	0.019	0.5	—

TABLE A.11 (*continued*)

City*	Total	Total Solids	Total Gases/ Liquids	Gases and Liquids, by Compound:						
				Sulfur Anhydrides	Nitrous Dioxide	Carbon Monoxide	Hydrocarbons	Fluorine Compounds	Hydrogen Sulfides	Carbon Sulfides
Magnitogorsk	821.0	156.0	665.0	72.0	34.0	547.0	5.3	0.0002	2.8	0.1
Mariupol'	753.0	107.0	646.0	50.0	29.0	562.0	1.9	0.0065	1.2	0.0
Minsk	103.0	8.9	94.0	21.0	16.0	43.0	7.3	0.0091	0.01	—
Mogilev	106.0	7.3	99.0	60.0	7.2	20.0	1.3	0.0001	0.8	5.1
Moscow	294.0	28.0	266.0	52.0	99.0	32.0	56.0	0.543	0.0	—
Murmansk	32.0	5.2	26.0	23.0	1.3	1.9	0.1	0.00013	—	—
Nizhnekamsk	115.0	5.6	108.0	22.0	29.0	11.0	40.0	0.0002	0.0	—
Nizhny Novgorod	155.0	21.0	134.0	48.0	24.0	47.0	12.0	0.042	0.0	—
Nizhny Tagil	603.0	110.0	494.0	74.0	27.0	383.0	6.0	0.0073	0.5	0.1
Novokuznets	791.0	124.0	667.0	88.0	36.0	531.0	2.0	1.425	1.5	0.0
Novorossiisk	65.0	17.0	48.0	30.0	0.7	1.7	16.0	0.00013	—	—
Novosibirsk	218.0	77.0	141.0	65.0	30.0	37.0	6.0	0.359	0.02	—
Novotroitsk	224.0	40.0	184.0	19.0	15.0	147.0	1.2	—	0.5	—
Noril'sk	2,300.0	31.0	2,269.0	2,237.0	18.0	13.0	0.01	—	0.1	—
Odessa	85.0	16.0	69.0	13.0	5.3	31.0	15.0	0.287	0.0	—
Omsk	448.0	105.0	343.0	171.0	43.0	39.0	86.0	0.002	0.2	—
Osh	8.9	1.2	7.8	5.1	0.8	1.5	0.03	0.0001	—	—
Pavlodar	259.0	102.0	157.0	100.0	22.0	14.0	19.0	0.0002	0.02	—
Perm'	176.0	11.0	165.0	32.0	26.0	27.0	72.0	0.076	0.2	—
Riga	30.0	5.6	24.0	8.3	2.2	8.2	5.5	0.001	—	—
Rustavi	116.0	32.0	83.0	9.4	10.0	63.0	0.1	—	0.0	—
Ryazan'	120.0	8.2	112.0	34.0	7.9	13.0	47.0	0.0075	0.4	8.3
Saratov	114.0	7.4	107.0	17.0	12.0	14.0	60.0	0.0059	0.1	—
Sverdlovsk	76.0	21.0	55.0	3.4	11.0	23.0	17.0	0.0073	—	0.0
Severodonetsk	20.0	1.8	18.0	3.1	5.9	3.4	1.7	0.09	—	—
Stavropol'	30.0	3.5	27.0	1.1	1.4	22.0	1.1	0.0008	0.1	—
Sterlitamak	141.0	26.0	116.0	22.0	22.0	53.0	16.0	0.0001	0.1	—

(*Continued on next page*)

TABLE A.11 *(continued)*

City*	Total	Total Solids	Total Gases/ Liquids	Gases and Liquids, by Compound:						
				Sulfur Anhydrides	Nitrous Dioxide	Carbon Monoxide	Hydrocarbons	Fluorine Compounds	Hydrogen Sulfides	Carbon Sulfides
Sumgait	65.0	11.0	53.0	13.0	11.0	13.0	11.0	1.373	0.0	—
Tallinn	38.0	6.3	31.0	21.0	2.7	5.3	1.7	0.169	—	—
Tashkent	47.0	14.0	33.0	2.8	4.9	18.0	6.0	0.016	0.0	—
Tbilisi	40.0	6.7	34.0	2.3	3.8	23.0	0.9	0.0004	0.0	0.0
Tver'	34.0	6.3	27.0	8.3	5.2	4.8	3.4	0.0001	0.9	4.0
Temirtau (Kaz.)	850.0	231.0	619.0	99.0	34.0	482.0	2.2	0.00003	1.0	0.08
Tol'yatti	116.0	21.0	95.0	11.0	41.0	26.0	6.4	0.0435	0.0	—
Tyumen'	40.0	7.6	33.0	7.2	13.0	11.0	0.9	0.0036	—	—
Usol'ye-Sibirskoe	86.0	27.0	58.0	17.0	6.7	32.0	0.3	0.0001	—	—
Ust'-Kamenogorsk	128.0	22.0	105.0	62.0	14.0	29.0	0.2	0.011	—	—
Ufa	284.0	7.9	277.0	60.0	25.0	36.0	149.0	0.075	0.1	0.0
Fergana	137.0	18.0	120.0	34.0	9.6	5.2	63.0	0.0001	0.2	—
Frunze	71.0	19.0	52.0	34.0	8.1	6.9	1.8	0.0037	—	—
Khabarovsk	160.0	51.0	108.0	50.0	9.0	33.0	13.0	0.025	0.0	—
Tselinograd	96.0	43.0	53.0	32.0	9.0	10.0	0.2	0.037	—	—
Chardzhou	9.1	2.4	6.7	2.3	0.3	1.5	1.8	0.023	—	—
Chelyabinsk	392.0	102.0	290.0	46.0	28.0	209.0	5.4	0.06	0.3	0.04
Cherkassy	40.0	7.4	32.0	9.8	7.4	8.0	0.6	0.0006	0.4	3.2
Chimkent	94.0	21.0	73.0	24.0	7.8	24.0	12.0	0.096	0.06	—
Shelekhov	48.0	25.0	23.0	3.3	0.6	18.0	0.06	0.942	—	—
Ekibastuz	715.0	438.0	278.0	187.0	89.0	2.0	0.01	—	—	—
Yuzhno-Sakhalinsk	27.0	16.0	11.0	6.7	2.9	1.4	0.2	0.00003	—	—
Yaroslavl'	214.0	22.0	193.0	38.0	17.0	48.0	86.0	0.0007	0.7	0.1

SOURCE: *Okhrana zdor.*, pp. 182–87.
*Cities ranked as in original Soviet source (alphabetized according to Russian alphabet). In individual cases insignificant discrepancies in the sum of solid, gas and liquid emissions occur due to rouncing.
—Not applicable.

TABLE A.12

Emissions of Harmful Substances into the Atmosphere
from Automotive Sources for Selected Cities, 1988

(in thousands of tons, per annum)

City[a]	Total	Nitrous Dioxide	Carbon Monoxide	Hydrocarbons
			By Compound	
Alma-Ata[b]	164.8	11.2	130.8	22.8
Almalyk	12.6	1.5	9.2	1.9
Angarsk[b]	15.2	0.7	12.0	2.5
Arkhangel'sk	30.7	1.5	23.9	5.3
Astrakhan	60.7	2.9	47.7	10.1
Ashkhabad	51.6	2.5	41.3	7.8
Baku[b]	297.8	28.2	226.6	43.0
Balakovo	9.5	1.2	6.7	1.6
Barnaul[b]	80.3	3.7	63.5	13.1
Berezniki	12.3	0.7	9.5	2.1
Bratsk[b]	37.1	2.0	28.6	6.5
Vilnius	57.2	3.0	44.4	9.8
Volgograd[b]	116.2	6.0	91.3	18.9
Volzhskiy	22.6	1.3	17.5	3.8
Gomel'[b]	47.4	2.6	36.5	8.3
Grodno[b]	51.3	4.0	40.1	7.2
Grozny	73.1	3.8	57.7	11.6
Gur'yev[b]	22.7	1.0	17.8	3.9
Gryandzha[b]	38.0	2.9	29.8	5.3
Dzhambul[b]	51.7	2.7	40.0	9.0
Dzerzhinsk (Nizhegorodskaya oblast')	20.0	1.1	15.5	3.4
Dneprodze-zhinsk	20.8	1.2	16.3	3.3
Dnepropetrovsk	104.9	5.5	82.5	16.9

(Continued on next page)

TABLE A.12 (continued)

City[a]	Total	Nitrous Dioxide	Carbon Monoxide	Hydrocarbons
			By Compound	
Donetsk	127.1	7.1	99.3	20.7
Dushanbe[b]	76.4	3.5	60.1	12.8
Yerevan	174.2	8.8	138.9	26.5
Zaporozh'ye	104.8	5.3	82.1	17.4
Zestafoni	16.8	1.2	13.3	2.3
Zyryanovsk	7.3	0.4	5.7	1.2
Irkutsk[b]	62.2	3.0	48.7	10.5
Kaliningrad	36.9	2.0	28.5	6.4
Kamensk-Ural'skiy	11.0	0.6	8.6	1.8
Karaganda[b]	83.7	4.3	64.9	14.5
Kemerovo[b]	72.3	3.6	56.6	12.1
Kiev	244.2	11.9	194.0	38.3
Kirov	42.7	2.1	33.4	7.2
Kirovakan	19.8	1.2	15.7	2.9
Kishinev	100.7	5.1	79.4	16.2
Kommunarsk	11.4	0.6	8.9	1.9
Komsomol'sk-na-Amure	26.4	1.3	20.8	4.3
Krasnoyarsk	106.6	5.6	83.3	17.7
Kremenchug	21.3	1.3	16.3	3.7
Krivoy Rog	75.5	4.4	58.0	13.1
Kuibyshev	122.5	5.9	97.0	19.6
Kurgan	60.3	2.2	48.2	9.9
Leningrad[b]	371.9	21.1	290.9	59.9
Leninogorsk[b]	9.3	0.8	6.7	1.8
Lipetsk	60.8	3.2	47.1	10.5
Lisichansk	14.6	0.7	11.7	2.2

TABLE A.12 (continued)

City[a]	Total	Nitrous Dioxide	Carbon Monoxide	Hydrocarbons
			By Compound	
Magnitogorsk	24.7	1.5	18.7	4.5
Mariupol'	36.3	1.9	28.6	5.8
Minsk[b]	125.0	8.7	93.0	23.3
Mogilev[b]	39.5	1.8	31.2	6.5
Moscow	801.3	41.6	633.4	126.3
Murmansk	30.4	1.4	24.2	4.8
Nizhnekamsk	26.7	1.4	20.7	4.6
Nizhny Tagil	21.6	1.3	16.5	3.8
Nizhny Novgorod	133.7	7.1	103.8	22.8
Novokuznetsk[b]	55.8	3.2	43.4	9.2
Novorossiisk	31.9	1.5	25.4	5.0
Novosibirsk	108.7	5.6	84.6	18.5
Novotroitsk[b]	6.8	0.4	5.3	1.1
Noril'sk	24.5	1.5	19.2	3.8
Odessa	140.8	6.9	111.5	22.4
Omsk	154.4	7.9	121.1	25.4
Osh[b]	51.2	2.3	40.4	8.5
Pavlodar[b]	71.6	3.7	55.6	12.3
Perm'	79.8	4.3	62.3	13.2
Riga[1]	97.7	5.4	76.9	15.4
Rustavi	29.9	2.3	23.4	4.2
Ryazan'	62.8	3.2	48.9	10.7
Saratov[b]	54.7	7.8	37.7	9.2
Sverdlovsk	94.5	5.0	73.2	16.3
Severodonetsk	14.4	0.7	11.4	2.3
Stavropol'[1]	22.6	2.9	16.3	3.4

(Continued on next page)

TABLE A.12 (*continued*)

City[a]	Total	Nitrous Dioxide	By Compound Carbon Monoxide	Hydrocarbons
Sterlitamak	14.4	0.8	11.0	2.6
Sumgait	4.0	0.4	3.0	0.6
Tallinn	69.4	3.6	53.9	11.9
Tashkent	353.3	26.8	277.0	49.5
Tbilisi	282.2	18.7	224.6	38.9
Tver'[b]	33.9	1.8	26.3	5.8
Temirtay[b] (Kaz.)	19.0	1.0	14.6	3.4
Tol'yatti	61.6	3.4	48.0	10.2
Tula	39.9	2.4	29.9	7.6
Tyumen'	90.5	4.9	70.6	15.0
Usol'ye-Sibirskoe[b]	9.0	0.4	7.1	1.5
Ust'-Kamenogorsk[b]	40.3	1.9	31.8	6.6
Ufa	111.2	5.8	85.9	19.5
Fergana	115.3	11.0	87.6	16.7
Frunze[b]	74.7	3.6	58.9	12.2
Khabarovsk	59.2	3.0	46.5	9.7
Tselinograd[b]	35.5	1.8	27.2	6.5
Chardzhoy	34.4	1.6	28.0	5.8
Chelyabinsk	94.1	5.1	69.6	19.4
Cherkassy	42.6	2.0	33.7	6.9
Chimkent[b]	72.6	4.0	56.1	12.5
Shelekhov[b]	5.5	0.3	4.2	1.0
Ekibastuz[b]	21.2	1.2	16.4	3.6
Yuzhno-Sakhalinsk	17.9	2.2	12.9	2.8
Yaroslavl'[b]	53.7	2.9	41.6	9.2

SOURCE: *Okhrana zdor.*, pp. 188–90.
[a] Cities ranked as in the original Soviet source (alphabetized according to Russian alphabet).
[b] For 1987.

TABLE A.13

Frequency of Illness in Urban Populations with Elevated Air Pollution Levels,
by City, 1987 to 1989[a]

(number of cases per 100,000 population; standardized indicators)

City[b]	Malignant Neoplasms	Endocrine System Disorders	Skin Disorders	Respiratory Disorders
Arkhangel'sk				
1987	244	297	398	56,291
1988	278	190	434	71,725
1989	414	190	448	60,714
Berezniki				
1987	258	285	2,118	56,555
1988	360	347	2,166	75,746
1989	327	363	2,261	74,006
Krasnoyarsk				
1988	260	180	797	60,356
1989	461	98	757	58,135
Nizhny Novgorod				
1987	258	548	2,270	48,847
1988	360	374	2,248	63,063
1989	405	277	2,081	54,955
Novocherkassk				
1988	273	—	1,637	72,368
1989	463	230	1,182	63,680
Noril'sk				
1988	573	777	2,210	69,107
1989	485	990	1,194	65,060

(Continued on next page)

TABLE A.13 (continued)

City[b]	Malignant Neoplasms	Endocrine System Disorders	Skin Disorders	Respiratory Disorders
Sverdlovsk				
1987	311	201	1,595	24,862
1988	234	232	2,023	29,796
1989	502	261	1,924	35,418
Tol'yatti				
1987	282	356	1,906	51,091
1988	316	392	1,779	63,087
1989	298	530	1,961	65,592
Usol'ye-Sibirskoe				
1987	226	304	2,662	29,920
1988	157	353	2,801	49,583
1989	246	301	2,361	44,099
Lisichansk				
1987	635	201	1,817	45,235
1988	326	119	1,511	44,562
1989	197	274	3,254	42,450
Makeyevka				
1987	462	114	381	25,359
1988	647	273	338	38,768
1989	522	178	398	35,522
Cherkassy				
1987	261	526	3,040	58,608
1988	265	570	3,140	88,219
1989	227	442	2,688	63,679
Mogilev				
1987	356	461	1,743	67,281
1988	340	533	2,138	73,058
1989	347	452	2,250	73,528

TABLE A.13 (continued)

City[b]	Malignant Neoplasms	Endocrine System Disorders	Skin Disorders	Respiratory Disorders
Novopolotsk				
1987	310	216	1,804	56,055
1988	315	289	4,506	71,340
1989	462	409	5,158	50,027
Chirchik				
1987	231	539	1,435	52,646
1988	289	631	1,781	56,644
1989	278	407	1,405	53,576
Karaganda				
1987	264	354	3,567	43,296
1988	247	459	3,224	53,859
1989	215	679	2,519	51,712

SOURCE: *Okhrana zdor.*, pp. 63–65.
[a] For 1989, in 150 surveyed cities, the frequency of malignant neoplasms per 100,000 population was 225; endocrine disorders, 256; skin disorders, 1,177; respiratory disorders, 41,048.
[b] Cities ranked as in the orginal Soviet source (alphabetized according to Russian alphabet).

TABLE A.14

USSR *Cities Having the Highest Levels of Air Pollution, by Substance, Industry and Level of Pollution, 1990*
(air pollution index—see notes*)

City†	Substance	Industry Branch Responsible for the Pollution
Abakan[b]	BP, dust, formaldehyde	Heavy machine building, boilers
Alma-Ata[a]	BP, lead, dust, formaldehyde	Power industries, auto transport
Almalyk[a]	BP, hydrogen fluoride, dust, ammonia	Mineral fertilizer production, nonferrous metallurgy
Angarsk[b]	BP, dust, formaldehyde	Medical—biological, auto transport
Andizhan[b]	BP, dust, formaldehyde	Medical—biological, auto transport
Arkhangel'sk[b]	Methyl mercaptan, formaldehyde, carbon disulfide	Pulp and paper
Baku[d]	(NA)	Petrochemical, oil drilling
Barnaul	BP, formaldehyde, dust	(NA)
Berezniki[b]	Hydrocarbons, SO, NO$_2$, NO	Chemical, mineral fertilizer production
Bratsk[a]	BP, methyl mercaptan, carbon disulfide	Nonferrous metallurgy, pulp and paper, energy
Volgograd[c]	Hydrogen chloride	Chemical
Volzhskiy[b]	Methyl mercaptan, formaldehyde, carbon disulfide	Petrochemical, abrasives
Gorlovka[b]	Phenol, NO$_2$, SO	Coke ovens, coal mining, chemical
Grozny[a]	BP, formaldehyde, NO$_2$, phenol	Petrochemical
Dzerzhinsk[c]	Hydrogen chloride, ethylbenzol	Chemical, mineral fertilizer production
Dzhambul[a]	BP, dust, hydrogen fluoride	Mineral fertilizer production, energy
Dneprodzerzhinsk[a]	BP, formaldehyde, phenol, ammonia	Mineral fertilizer production, ferrous metallurgy, construction
Dnepropetrovsk[b]	BP, formaldehyde, dust, ammonia	Ferrous metallurgy, energy
Donetsk[a]	BP, dust, phenol, ammonia	Ferrous metallurgy, coal
Dushanbe[a]	BP, formaldehyde, dust, NO$_2$, NO	Construction, energy, railway transport
Yerevan[a]	Dust, lead, NO$_2$, ozone	Chemical, energy, auto transport
Zaporozh'ye[a]	BP, NO$_2$, formaldehyde, phenol	Ferrous metallurgy, nonferrous metallurgy
Zestafoni[a]	BP, manganese dioxide	Ferrous metallurgy
Zyryanovsk[a]	BP, NO$_2$, lead, manganese	Nonferrous metallurgy

TABLE A.14 (*continued*)

City†	Substance	Industry Branch Responsible for the Pollution
Irkutsk[b]	BP, formaldehyde, NO_2	Energy, heavy machine building
Kaliningrad	BP, carbon disulfide	(NA)
Kamensk-Uralskiy[b]	BP, hydrogen fluoride	Nonferrous metallurgy
Kemerovo[a]	BP, lead, formaldehyde, ammonia, NO_2, carbon disulfide	Mineral fertilizers, chemical, ferrous metallurgy
Kiev	BP, formaldehyde, NO_2, carbon disulfide	(NA)
Kirovakan	NO_2, ammonia	(NA)
Kommunarsk[a]	BP, NO_2, dust	Ferrous metallurgy
Komsomol'sk[a]	BP, lead, formaldehyde, dust, phenol	Electricity, ferrous metallurgy, energy, petrochemical
Kokand[b]	BP, formaldehyde, dust, NO_2	Energy, chemical, construction materials
Kramatorsk[b]	BP, phenol, dust, NO_2	Ferrous metallurgy, construction materials, heavy machine building
Krasnodar[b]	BP, Formaldehyde, phenol	Petrochemical, medical, construction materials
Krasnoperekopsk[c]	NO_2, dust, hydrogen chloride, hydrogen fluoride	Petrochemical
Krasnoyarsk[a]	BP, formaldehyde, dust, NO_2	Chemical, nonferrous metallurgy, construction materials, auto transport
Krivoy Rog[b]	BP, formaldehyde, dust, NO_2	Ferrous metallurgy, construction materials
Kuibyshev[a]	Formaldehyde, hydrogen fluoride, dust	Petrochemical, electricity
Kurgan[b]	BP, formaldehyde, dust	Petrochemical, metallurgy, construction materials
Kutaisi[b]	BP, dust, phenol, NO_2	Petrochemical, auto transport
Leninogorsk	BP, lead, nickel	(NA)
Lipetsk[b]	Formaldehyde, phenol, dust	Ferrous metallurgy, construction materials
Magnitogorsk[a]	BP, carbon disulfide, dust, phenol	Ferrous metallurgy
Makeyevka[b]	BP, carbon disulfide, dust, phenol	Ferrous metallurgy, coal mining
Mariupol[a]	BP, formaldehyde, hydrogen fluoride, ammonia	Ferrous metallurgy
Mogilev[c]	Carbon disulfide, hydrogen sulfide	Chemical, ferrous metallurgy
Moscow	Dust, NO_2, nitric oxide, phenol, formaldehyde, ammonia	(NA)
Nikopol[b]	Manganese dioxide, hydrogen fluoride, dust	Ferrous metallurgy
Nizhny Tagil[a]	BP, formaldehyde, phenol, ammonia	Ferrous metallurgy

(*Continued on next page*)

TABLE A.14 (*continued*)

City†	Substance	Industry Branch Responsible for the Pollution
Novokuznetsk[a]	BP, formaldehyde, dust	Ferrous metallurgy, nonferrous metallurgy, coal mining, energy
Novokuibyshev[d]	(NA)	Petrochemical
Novosibirsk[b]	BP, formaldehyde, NO_2	Auto transport, energy, construction materials
Novotroitsk	BP, phenol, dust	(NA)
Novocherkassk[b]	BP, formaldehyde, dust, NO_2	Metallurgy, petrochemical, energy
Odessa[a]	BP, formaldehyde, hydrogen fluoride, phenol	Casting, mineral fertilizers, auto transport
Omsk[b]	BP, formaldehyde, ammonia, acetaldehyde	Petrochemical, chemical
Orenburg	BP, dust, NO_2	(NA)
Osh[a]	BP, dust, NO_2	Energy, construction materials, boilers
Perm'[a]	BP, formaldehyde, hydrogen fluoride	Petrochemical
Prokopyevsk[b]	BP, formaldehyde, dust	Coal mining
Rostov-na-donu[b]	BP, formaldehyde, dust, phenol	Ferrous metallurgy
Rustavi[a]	BP, dust, ammonia, phenol	Construction materials, ferrous metallurgy, mineral fertilizers
Ryazan[a]	BP, carbon disulfide, phenol	Chemical, petrochemical
Salavat[d]	(NA)	Petrochemical, chemical
Sverdlovsk[b]	BP, formaldehyde, nitric oxide, NO_2, ammonia	Ferrous metallurgy, railway transport
Severodonetsk[b]	BP, formaldehyde, phenol, ammonia	Energy, mineral fertilizer, chemical
Selenginsk[b]	BP, formaldehyde, hydrogen disulfide	pulp and paper
Semipalatinsk	BP, dust, NO_2	(NA)
Slavyansk[b]	BP, NO_2, phenol	Chemical, construction materials, heavy machine building
Sterlimatak[c]	BP, acetaldehyde, NO_2, hydrogen sulfide, alphamethylsterol	Chemical, petrochemical
Sumgait[d]	(NA)	Petrochemical
Tashkent[b]	BP, NO_2, phenol	Energy, agricultural machine building, construction materials
Tbilisi[b]	BP, formaldehyde, phenol	Auto transport, machine tools, energy
Temirtau[b] (Kaz.)	BP, phenol, dust	Ferrous metallurgy
Tol'yatti[b]	Formaldehyde, acetaldehyde, hydrogen fluoride, benzol	Mineral fertilizers, auto transport

TABLE A.14 (continued)

City†	Substance	Industry Branch Responsible for the Pollution
Tyumen'[b]	BP, formaldehyde, dust	Pulp and paper, construction materials, energy
Ulan-Ude[b]	BP, formaldehyde, phenol, dust	Energy, construction materials, auto transport
Usolye-Sibirskoe[b]	BP, formaldehyde, NO_2, dust	Chemical, energy
Ust'-Kamenogorsk[a]	BP, lead, formaldehyde, sulfur dioxide, nickel	Nonferrous metallurgy
Ufa[d]	(NA)	Petrochemical, chemical
Fergana[a]	BP, formaldehyde, ammonia, phenol	Petrochemical, mineral fertilizer, energy
Frunze[a]	BP, formaldehyde, dust, nitric oxide	Energy, auto transport
Khabarovsk[b]	BP, formaldehyde, ammonia, NO_2	Energy, construction materials, petrochemical, railway transport
Chardzhou[a]	BP, hydrogen fluoride, dust	Mineral fertilizers, auto transport, energy
Chelyabinsk[a]	BP, formaldehyde, sulfur dioxide	Ferrous metallurgy, energy
Cherepovets	BP, carbon disulfide, formaldehyde, ammonia	(NA)
Chimkent[b]	BP, lead, dust	Nonferrous metallurgy
Chita[b]	BP, formaldehyde, dust	Energy, chemical, machine building, boilers
Shelekhov[b]	BP, hydrogen fluoride	Nonferrous metallurgy,
Yuzhno-Sakhalinsk[b]	BP, soot, NO_2	Energy, auto transport, boilers
Yaroslavl[d]	(NA)	Chemical, petrochemical

SOURCE: "Sostoyaniye zagryazhneniya atmosfery na territorii SSSR v 1990 i tendentsiya evo izmeneniya za pyatiletiye," *Meteorologiya i gidrologiya* 4 (April 1991): 118–123; and USSR State Committee for the Protection of Nature, *Report on the State of the Environment in the USSR, 1988* (Moscow, 1989), pp. 16–18.

*The Air Pollution Index (IZA) is a uniform index, determined as the sum of recorded annual concentrations of five substances, in PDK's, having the highest level, for each specific year, and classified as dangerous, containing sulfur gas.

†Cities ranked as in original Soviet sources (alphabetized according to Russian alphabet).

(NA) = not available

[a] Cities with consistently high levels of air pollution (as measured by an Air Pollution Index, IZA—each year of more than 15, for 1985 to 1989).

[b] Cities with an Air Pollution Index of more than 15 (for 1989).

[c] Cities with more than five cases per year where PDK levels have been exceeded by a factor of ten for specific pollutants, or exceeded the PDK levels of three or more pollutants by a factor of ten (IZA less than 15).

[d] Cities with an IZA less than 15, but with high levels of unidentified, specific pollutants.

TABLE A.15
Harmful Emissions from Enterprises of the Basic Industrial Ministries and Agencies, 1988
(in tons per year)

Ministries and Departments	Total	Solids	Sulfur Dioxide (SO_2)	Carbon Monoxide (CO)	Nitrous Dioxide (NO_2)	Hydrocarbons
USSR Ministry of Energy	15,364	4,943	7,549	171	2,668	9.7
USSR Ministry of Ferrous Metallurgy	10,389	2,025	1,081	6,714	455	45.8
USSR Ministry of Nonferrous Metallurgy	5,935	760	4,482	541	62	4.0
USSR Ministry of Oil Industry	5,554	233	60	988	54	4,140.0
USSR Ministry of Petrochemical Industry	3,704	110	519	677	50	2,241.0
USSR Ministry of Gas Industry	2,680	6	505	561	245	1,358.0
USSR Ministry of Construction and Machine Building	2,086	1,278	266	406	124	10.0
State Agro-Industry Committee	1,696	546	555	448	89	27.7
USSR Ministry of Coal Industry	1,401	352	393	614	24	1.6
USSR Ministry of Timber Industry	1,361	473	315	356	79	56.0
USSR Council of Ministers	1,250	633	163	373	53	18.6
USSR Ministry of Chemical Industry	857	108	124	305	26	107.0
USSR Ministry of Fertilizers	632	145	167	147	66	16.5
Council of Ministers of the Ukraine SSR	547	239	87	156	41	15.5
Other Ministries and Agencies	8,170	2,822	1,386	2,477	457	428.0
Total, USSR	61,633	14,675	17,651	14,938	4,492	8,480.0

Source: *Obzor*, p. 7.

NOTES

In THE CHAPTER source notes that follow, where we cite "interviews" or "conversations" we had with various sources, the first term denotes a formal discussion during which extensive notes were taken and the second, a more relaxed talk recollected in notes made afterward. Depending on whether one or both of us gained the information given in the text, we use the singular or plural of "author." Unlike the simplified usage in the text, Russian words here are transliterated according to the rules set by the U.S. Board of Geographic Names, so that Yury is Yuriy for example, or for Ukrainians, Iurii, and so on.

In source notes, the following abbreviations are used:

CDSP   *Current Digest of the Soviet Press*
CPSU—Communist Party of the Soviet Union
Doklad—Goskompriroda SSSR, *Gosudarstvenniy Doklad: Sostoyaniye prirodnoy sredy i prirodookhrannaya deyatelnost' v SSSR v 1989 godu,* N. A. Vorontsov, scientific editor, chairman, Goskompriroda (Moscow, Youth Institute of the Komsomol and Goskomtrud, 1990)
Environment Report—Goskompriroda SSSR, *Report on the State of the Environment in the USSR 1988,* trans. Kevin Hendzel (Moscow, Goskompriroda, 1989), typescript translation of Goskompriroda, *Sostoyaniye prirodnoy sredy v SSSR v 1988 godu: Mezhvedomstvenniy doklad,* V. G. Sokolovskiy, general editor (Moscow, Lesnaya Promyshlennost', 1990)

FBIS-SOV—Foreign Broadcast Information Service, *Daily Report, Soviet Union*
Goskomgidromet—State Committee on Meteorology
Goskompriroda—State Committee for the Protection of Nature and the Rational Use of Natural Resources
Goskomstat—State Committee on Statistics
JPRS—Joint Publications Research Service
   -TEN—*Environmental Affairs*
   -UEA—*Soviet Union. Economic Affairs*
   -ULS—*Soviet Union. Life Sciences*
   -UMA—*Soviet Union. Military Affairs*
   -UPA—*Soviet Union. Political Affairs*
MedGaz—*Meditsinskaya gazeta*
Narkhoz 1987 and 1989—Goskomstat SSSR, *Narodnoye khozyaystvo SSSR v 1987 (1989) godu, statisticheskiy yezhegodnik* (Moscow, Finansy i statistika, 1988 and 1990, respectively)
Obzor—Goskomgidromet, *Obzor sostoyaniya okruzhayushchey prirodnoy sredy v SSSR* (Moscow, Gidrometeoizdat, 1990)
RFE/RL—Radio Free Europe/Radio Liberty
RSFSR—Russian Soviet Federated Socialist Republic
SSSR—Union of Soviet Socialist Republics
SWB, SU—BBC Monitoring, *Summary of World Broadcasts, Soviet Union.*

Preface

1. Boris Komarov, pseudonym of Ze'ev Wolfson, *The Destruction of Nature in the Soviet Union* (White Plains, NY: M. E. Sharpe, 1980).
2. Murray Feshbach, *Economics of Health and Environment in the USSR*. Prepared for the Office of Net Assessment, U.S. Department of Defense (Washington, DC: forthcoming 1992).

1
Facing Facts

1. "Gosudarstvennaya programma profilaktiki zabolevanii i formirovaniya zdorovogo obraza zhizni naseleniya SSSR na period do 2000 goda," unpublished report prepared by the All-Union Scientific Research Center on Preventive Medicine of the USSR Ministry of Health and adopted by the USSR Supreme Soviet Committee on Health Protection. A précis of the report appeared under the title "Kak spasti zdorovye naroda," *MedGaz*, 23 November 1990, pp. 1–2.
2. Mark Tol'ts, "Voprosy zhizni," *Sovetskaya kultura*, 21 July 1987, p. 6.

3. Michael Ryan, *Contemporary Soviet Society: A Statistical Handbook* (London: Edward Elgar, 1990), p. 212; Alexandr Androshin, "Free Medical Services: The End of a Myth," *Business in the USSR* (December 1990): 28.

4. Christopher Davis and Murray Feshbach, *Rising Infant Mortality in the USSR in the 1970's,* Series P-25, No. 74, U.S. Bureau of the Census, Washington, D.C., September 1980.

5. Goskomstat SSSR, " soobshchaet," *Argumenty i fakty* 45 (1989): 3; M. Ya. Studenikin, "Sovremenniye problemy detskoy smertnosti," *Vestnik Akademii nauk SSSR* 12 (December 1988): 29–34; Natal'ya Paroyatnikova, "Chtobiy zhili deti . . ." *Moskovskiye novosti* 28, 12 July 1987.

6. B. Chernov, "Smert' posle rozhdeniya," *Sel'skaya novosti* 10 (October 1988): 12.

7. G. A. Yagodin, excerpts of speech to Nineteenth All-Union CPSU Conference, broadcast by Radio Moscow, 1 July 1988; *FBIS-SOV,* 5 July 1988, p. 83.

8. "Gosudarstvennaya programma. . . ."

9. Ya. Zasurskiy, "Ryadavoi Lomonosov, dva shaga vperyod!" *Komsomol'-skaya pravda,* 10 July 1991, p. 1.

10. Androshin, "Free Medical Services," p. 29.

11. Boris Prokhorov, "The Geography of Disease," *Business in the USSR* 7 (December 1990): 30–31.

12. Yevgeniy Chazov, televised press conference, 12 April 1987, "USSR Health Minister on Restructuring Medical Services," *SWB,* 14 April 1987, SU/8542, p. B/2.

13. Yevgeniy Chazov, interviewed by Zori Balayan, "Kogda bolezn' obgonyaet lekarstva," *Literaturnaya gazeta,* 8 February 1988, p. 11.

14. Androshin, "Free Medical Services," p. 28.

15. T. A. Izmukhambetov, "Perestroika—vremya deystviy," *Zdravookhraneniye Kazakhstana* 4 (April 1988): 1–9.

16. Yevgeniy Chazov, speech to Nineteenth CPSU Conference, *Pravda,* 30 June 1988, p. 4; *FBIS-SOV-88-126,* 30 June 1988, pp. 9, 11.

17. Ibid.

18. Valeriy Bykov, "Drug Imports: Supplement Not Substitute," *Business in the USSR* 7 (December 1990): 34–35.

19. Michele Kahn, "La Pharmacie en URSS," *Le Courrier des Pays de l'Est* 352 (September 1990): 71.

20. "Lekarstvennaya 'likhoradka,' " *Pravda,* 9 November 1989, p. 2; *FBIS-SOV-89-217,* 13 November 1989, p. 100.

21. V. A. Bykov, interview with V. Romanyuk, *Izvestiya,* 16 September 1990, p. 3; *FBIS-SOV-90-187,* 26 September 1990, pp. 58–60.

22. A. Nemov, "Meditsina na marshe," in P. D. Slavutskiy, compiler, *Perestroika: perviye shagi: sbornik,* Seriya "Meditsina" 20, no. 12 (December 1987) (Moscow: Znaniye, 1987), pp. 21–22.

23. Ye. Myatiyeva, "Secret Figures," *Turkmenskaya iskra,* 5 March 1989, p. 2; *JPRS-UPA-89-039,* 12 June 1989, p. 37.

24. Pavel Voshchanov, Aleksandr Bushev, "Zdes' legko obriyvayetsya detskaya zhizn'," *Komsomol'skaya pravda*, 25 April 1990, p. 2.
25. *Sovetskoye zdravookhraneniye* 9 (September 1988): 3–6; *JPRS-ULS-89-007*, 17 May 1989, pp. 49–51.
26. Elena Bonner, "Health Care in the Soviet Union," lecture delivered 23 March 1990, in Berkeley, California, reprinted in *Freedom at Issue* (November–December 1990): 10–14.
27. M. E. Mitel'man, "O normativnoy baze sanitarno-gigiyenicheskikh parametrov okruzhayushchey sredy (PDK, OBUV)," *Novoye v okhrane okruzhayushchey sredy na predpriatiyakh goroda Moskvy* (Moscow: Znaniye, 1990), pp. 33–36.
28. Tatyana Aronson, senior specialist, RSFSR Goskompriroda, "Kto, za chto i skol'ko," *Zelyonniy mir* 7–8, 21 February 1991.
29. A. Kondrusev, deputy minister of health, in interview with N. Gogol, "Poison Without Illusions: Who Will Guarantee the Right to Health?" *Pravda*, 14 November 1990, 2d ed., p. 6; *JPRS-UPA-90-066*, 4 December 1990, pp. 50–52.
30. Unsigned article, "On the Threshold of Ruin," *Pod znamenen Leninizma* (Kiev) 15 (August 1989): 37–38; *JPRS-UPA-89-066*, 12 December 1989, pp. 57–58.
31. Aleksei Yablokov, "Probuzhdyeniye ot ekologicheskoy spyachki," *Rodina* 4 (April 1990): 67.
32. Goskompriroda SSSR, *Environment Report*, p. 107.
33. M[ikhail] Lemeshev, "Economics and Ecology," *Voprosy ekonomiki* 11 (November 1990): 71; S. Karkhanin, "We Are Living on a Test Site—Notes from USSR Prosecutor's Office Collegium Sitting," *Sovetskaya Rossiya*, 7 December 1990, p. 6; *FBIS-SOV-90-243*, 18 December 1990, pp. 70–71.
34. Ibid., p. 70.
35. V. Ivanitskiy, "On the Nature Watch: From the State Committee's First Session," *Sovetskaya Rossiya*, 28 April 1987, p. 6; *JPRS-UPA-89-038*, 8 June 1989, pp. 72–73.
36. "Cough City," *The Economist*, 16 March 1991, p. 40.
37. " 'Chorniy spisok,' " *Zerkalo*, Sverdlovsk (May 1991).
38. Calculations of Dr. Grigoriy M. Barenboim, based on *Sotsialno-gigiyenicheskiy passport goroda Kemerova*, study done by the RSFSR Ministry of Health and the Kemerovo City Council of People's Deputies, published in Kemerovo, 1990.
39. Ibid.
40. Grigoriy M. Barenboim, "Ekologicheskiy risk," interview with L. N. Strelnikova, *Khimiya i zhizn* 2 (February 1990): 26.
41. Grigoriy M. Barenboim, interview with author, Moscow, 13 October 1990.
42. Ibid.
43. Dr. Robert Peter Gale and Thomas Hauser, *Final Warning: The Legacy of Chernobyl* (New York: Warner Books, 1988), p. 27.

44. Zhores Medvedev, *The Legacy of Chernobyl* (New York: W. W. Norton, 1990), p. 20.

45. E. Mokhorov, "Top Secret: Who Created the Secrecy Around the Bryansk Tragedy?" *Rabochaya tribuna,* 27 February 1990, p. 4; *JPRS-UPA-90-012,* 12 March 1990, pp. 74–75.

46. Yu. N. Shchukin, chairman, Leningrad radiation monitoring commission, in interview with Lyudmila Kaikova, "Safety Is Not Guaranteed," *Sovetskaya torgovlya,* 15–31 March 1990; *JPRS-UPA-90-030,* 4 June 1990, p. 79.

47. Medvedev, *Legacy of Chernobyl,* p. 20.

48. Astolphe, Marquis de Custine, *Empire of the Czar: A Journey Through Eternal Russia* (New York: Doubleday, 1989), pp. 267, 269, 271.

49. Medvedev, *Legacy of Chernobyl,* p. 57.

50. Quoted in Robert G. Kaiser, *Why Gorbachev Happened: His Triumphs and His Failure* (New York: Simon & Schuster, 1991), p. 127.

51. Cited in Françoise Thom, *Le moment Gorbatchev* (Paris: Hachette, 1989), p. 68.

52. Kaiser, *Why Gorbachev Happened,* pp. 128–29.

53. V. M. Kotlyakov, "The Aral Sea Basin, A Critical Environmental Zone," *Environment* 33 (January–February 1991): 4–9, 36–38.

54. Quoted in Kaiser, *Why Gorbachev Happened,* p. 129.

55. Daina S. Stukuls, "The Impact of the Environmental Protection Movement on Political Activism in Latvia." Typescript, George Washington University, 1989, pp. 18–19.

56. Valdis Abols, director, International Department, Latvian Environmental Protection Club (VAK), talk sponsored by World Wildlife Fund, Washington, D.C., 29 January 1991.

57. Ludmilla Alexeyeva and Catherine A. Fitzpatrick, *Nyeformaly, Civil Society in the USSR* (New York: Helsinki Watch Report, February 1990), p. 9. See also *Nyeformalnaya Rossiya* (Moscow: Molodaya Gvardiya, 1990), p. 115.

58. S, Razin, "Mailman Vasilyev's Bomb," *Komsomol'skaya pravda,* 15 March 1988, p. 2. In translation in Jonathan Eisen, ed., *The Glasnost Reader* (New York: New American Library, 1990), pp. 171–74.

59. Alexeyeva and Fitzpatrick, *Nyeformaly,* pp. 44, 113.

60. Alfred A. Pavlenko, interview with author, Volgograd, 14 October 1990.

61. Dr. V. I. Vinoshkin, interview with author, Volgograd, 16 October 1990.

62. Dr. Igor V. Bondarenko, deputy director, Volgograd Regional Health Services Department, interview with author, 16 October 1990.

63. "Tsifry i fakty," *MedGaz,* 3 June 1990, p. 3.

64. Barenboim interview.

65. Karkhanin, "We Are Living on a Test Site," p. 71.

66. *Narkhoz 1989,* p. 253.

67. Karkhanin, "We Are Living on a Test Site," p. 71.

68. *Doklad,* p. 317.

69. Fyodor T. Morgun, chairman of the State Committee on the Preservation

of Nature, in interview by Vasiliy Mikhailovich Peskov, "At the Start of the Journey," *Komsomol'skaya pravda,* 8 November 1988, p. 2; *JPRS-UPA-89-001,* 6 January 1989, p. 79.

70. Pavlenko interview.

71. Ibid.

72. Vladimir Aleksandrovich Polosukhin, interview with author, Volgograd, 15 October 1990.

73. Andrei Monin, "Stagnant Zones," *Noviy Mir* 7, 7 July 1988, pp. 162–72; *JPRS-UPA-88-051,* 16 November 1988, pp. 110–18.

74. Polosukhin interview.

75. Ibid.

76. Ibid.

77. William U. Chandler, Batelle Pacific Northwest Laboratories, trip report made available to authors.

78. Lieutenant General Nikolai Savenkov, chief, Sixth Directorate, Committee on State Security, "Ekologiya i razvedka," interview in *Rabochaya tribuna,* 9 February 1991, p. 3.

79. Ibid.

80. David Remnick, "Kazakhstan: A Republic Rebels, an Empire Begins to Crumble," *Washington Post,* 1 November 1990, p. A33.

81. V. Pichugin, "Kuda ni kin'—vsyudy klin," *MedGaz,* 24 April 1991, p. 2.

82. Bernard Shaw, *The Rationalization of Russia,* ed. Harry M. Geduld (Bloomington: Indiana University Press, 1964), p. 31.

83. Dr. Aleksandr V. Doroshenko, conversation with author, Odessa, 20 October 1990.

84. Professor Georgiy K. Lavrenchenko, director, Odessa Branch, Institute of New Technologies, interview with author, Odessa, 19 October 1990.

85. Warren E. Leary, "F.D.A. Approves Heart Drug Made by Soviets," *New York Times,* 27 June 1990, p. A13; John W. Kiser, "Reverse Technology Flows," *Washington Quarterly* (Winter 1985): 77–84; Dr. Vladimir P. Sidenko, lab chief, Institute of Water Transport Hygiene, Odessa, interview with author, 18 October 1991.

86. "Perestroika for Bones," *The Economist,* 25 June 1988, pp. 87–88.

87. William J. Broad, "U.S. Ready to Buy Advanced Reactor from the Soviets," *New York Times,* 7 January 1991, pp. 1, B8.

88. William J. Broad, "In the Realm of Technology, Japan Looms Ever Larger," *New York Times,* 28 May 1991, pp. C1, C8.

2

Birth of the Future

1. Mikhail Heller and Aleksandr M. Nekrich, *Utopia in Power,* trans. Phyllis B. Carlos (New York: Summit Books, 1986), p. 53.

2. George Seldes, *Witness to a Century* (New York: Ballantine Books, 1987), p. 190.

3. Vladimir Mayakovsky, from "150,000,000," 1920, translated by Joanne Turnbull with the assistance of Nikolai Formozov, cited in Andrei Sinyavsky, *Soviet Civilization: A Cultural History* (New York: Arcade Publishing/Little, Brown, 1990), p. 44.

4. Vladimir Bukovsky, "Born Again and Again," *New Republic,* 10 and 17 September 1990 (double issue), pp. 41–42.

5. Vladimir Korolenko to A. V. Lunacharsky, quoted in Hermann Fein (Andreev), "The Dimension of Soviet Diverse-Mindedness," in *The Soviet Union and the Challenge of the Future, Volume 2, Economics and Society,* ed. Alexander Shtromas and Morton A. Kaplan (New York: Paragon House, 1989), p. 675.

6. Quoted in Alec Nove, *An Economic History of the U.S.S.R.* (London: Penguin Books, 1989), p. 57.

7. Quoted in Heller and Nekrich, *Utopia in Power,* p. 118.

8. Nove, *Economic History of the U.S.S.R.,* p. 6.

9. Heller and Nekrich, *Utopia in Power,* p. 16.

10. Nove, *Economic History of the U.S.S.R.,* p. 7.

11. Heller and Nekrich, *Utopia in Power,* pp. 120 and 16.

12. Nove, *Economic History of the U.S.S.R.,* p. 58.

13. W. Bruce Lincoln, *In War's Dark Shadow* (New York: Dial Press, 1983), p. 79.

14. Merle Fainsod, *How Russia Is Ruled* (Cambridge, MA: Harvard University Press, 1959), p. 25.

15. Nove, *Economic History of the U.S.S.R.,* p. 120.

16. Leon Trotsky, *The History of the Russian Revolution* (New York: Simon & Schuster, 1936), p. 5.

17. V. I. Lenin, *Ob organizatsii sovetskoy statistiki* (Moscow: Gospolitizdat, 1959), pp. 45–46.

18. Heller and Nekrich, *Utopia in Power,* p. 141.

19. Geoffrey Hosking, *The First Socialist Society* (Cambridge, MA: Harvard University Press, 1990), p. 357.

20. Isaac Deutscher, *Stalin. A Political Biography* (New York: Vintage Books, 1960), pp. 321–22.

21. Ibid., p. 321.

22. Yuri Alexandrovich Polyakov, Valentina Borisovna Zhiromskaya, and Igor Nikolayevich Kiselev, "Polveka molchaniya," *Sotsialistichskiye issledovaniye* 6 (June 1990): 3–25.

23. Julian Huxley, *A Scientist Among the Soviets* (London: Chatto & Windus, 1932), p. 65.

24. Ibid., p. 73.

25. Ibid., pp. 72 and 69.

26. Sir Arthur Newsholme and John Adams Kingsbury, *Red Medicine: Socialized Health in Soviet Russia* (Garden City, NY: Doubleday, Doran, 1933), p. 310.

27. W. Horsley Gantt, *Russian Medicine* (New York: Paul B. Hoeber, Inc., Harper & Brothers, 1937), p. 89.

28. Henry E. Sigerist, *Medicine and Health in the Soviet Union* (New York: The Citadel Press, 1947), pp. 15–16.

29. N. A. Semashko, quoted in ibid., p. 21.

30. Newsholme and Kingsbury, *Red Medicine*, p. 219.

31. *Statisticheskiy Yezhegodnik Rossii*, 1913, part 3, pp. 5–6, cited in Harold H. Fisher, *The Famine in Soviet Russia* (Stanford, CA: Stanford University Press, 1935), p. 429.

32. Sigerist, *Medicine and Health in the Soviet Union*, p. 35.

33. Gantt, *Russian Medicine*, p. 139 (citing Semashko).

34. Ibid., p. 141.

35. Ibid., p. 183; Fisher, *Famine in Soviet Russia*, p. 386.

36. Quoted in Michael Ryan, *The Organization of Soviet Medical Care* (Oxford: Basil Blackwell, 1978), p. 7.

37. Fisher, *Famine in Soviet Russia*, pp. 427–42.

38. Ibid., p. 444.

39. Quoted in William A. Knaus, *Inside Russian Medicine* (New York: Everest House, 1981), p. 76.

40. Warren T. Reich, editor in chief, *Encyclopedia of Bioethics* (New York: Free Press, Collier Macmillan, 1978), vol. 3, pp. 1754–55.

41. L. Y. Skorokhodov, quoted in Gantt, *Russian Medicine*, p. 168.

42. Quoted in Gantt, *Russian Medicine*, p. 163.

43. Sigerist, *Medicine and Health in the Soviet Union*, p. 27.

44. Ibid., pp. 34–35.

45. Ibid., pp. 320–21.

46. Quoted in Peter Kurth, *American Cassandra: The Life of Dorothy Thompson* (Boston: Little, Brown, 1990), p. 123.

47. Sigerist, *Medicine and Health in the Soviet Union*, p. 65.

48. Quoted in Knaus, *Inside Russian Medicine*, p. 89.

49. Knaus, *Inside Russian Medicine*, p. 29.

50. Ibid., pp. 56–57.

51. V. I. Lenin, report to the Eighth Congress of the Soviets, quoted in V. A. Yaroshenko, "Partiya interesov," in *Ekologicheskaya al'ternativa*, ed. M. Ya. Lemeshev (Moscow: Progress, 1990), p. 68.

52. Marshall I. Goldman, *The Spoils of Progress, Environmental Pollution in the Soviet Union* (Cambridge, MA: MIT Press, 1972), pp. 64 and 69.

53. N. N. Podyapolskiy, "Vladimir Ilich i okhrana prirody," *Okhrana prirody* 2 (1929): 36–38, quoted in Feliks R. Shtil'mark, " 'Nasha bednoye, mnogo-stradal'noye delo . . . ,' " in *Ekologicheskaya al'ternativa*, ed. M. Ya. Lemeshev, p. 130.

54. V. Khramtsov, "Kto pomozhet?" *Zelyonniy mir* 7–8 (1991): 10.

55. D. A. Guryn, follow-up interview with Natalya Dosayeva, *Zelyonniy mir* 7–8 (1991): 10.

56. O. Kharchenko, " 'Shishki' v zapovednike," *Zelyonniy mir* 8 (1990): 2.

57. Goskompriroda SSSR, *Environment Report*, p. 103.

58. Goskomstat SSSR, *Narodnoye khozyaystvo SSSR za 70 let: yubilyeiniy*

statisticheskiy yezhegodnik (Moscow: Finansy i statistika, 1987), p. 611; Ze'ev Wolfson (Boris Komarov), "The Natural Environment and the Soviet System," in Shtromas and Kaplan, eds., *Economics and Society*, p. 343.

59. Maria Davydova and Vladimir Koshevoi, *Nature Reserves in the USSR* (Moscow: Progress, 1989), p. 22.
60. Shtil'mark, " 'Nasha bednoye . . . ," p. 132.
61. *Okhrana prirody* 8–10 (1930): 215–16, quoted in ibid., p. 133.
62. V. N. Makarov, "Nashi zadachi," *Priroda i sotsialisticheskoye khozyaystvo* 1 (1930): 2, in Shtil'mark, " 'Nasha bednoye . . . ," p. 134.
63. Heller and Nekrich, *Utopia in Power*, p. 482.
64. Nove, *Economic History of the U.S.S.R.*, p. 183.
65. Goskomstat SSSR, *Narodnoye khozyaystvo SSSR za 70 let*, p. 34.
66. Goskomgidromet, *Obzor*, p. 6.
67. Goldman, *Spoils of Progress*, pp. 27–32.
68. Ibid., p. 35.
69. Ibid., p. 32.
70. Ibid., p. 24.
71. Boris Komarov, pseudonym of Ze'ev Wolfson, *The Destruction of Nature in the Soviet Union* (White Plains, NY: M. E. Sharpe, 1980), p. 16.
72. Ibid., p. x.
73. Nikolai Vorontsov, "Zashchita Vorontsova," interview with Mikhail Dubrovskiy, *Poisk* 28, 9–15 November 1989, pp. 4–5.
74. Nikolai Vorontsov, "Disaster Caused by . . . Thoughtlessness," *Sovetskaya kultura* 47, 17 November 1990, p. 5, *JPRS-TEN-90-017*, 6 December 1990, pp. 50–51.
75. D. Kuknov, "Yevgeniy Chazov: Pochemu ya ushel iz ministrov," *Komsomol'skaya pravda*, 13 July 1990, p. 2.
76. Yevgeniy Chazov, address to Nineteenth All-Union CPSU Conference, 28 June 1989, *FBIS-SOV-88-126*, 30 June 1989, p. 9.
77. Thomas E. Gilbert, corporate secretary, James Chemical Engineering, Groton, Connecticut, telephone conversation with author, 31 July 1991.
78. Recollection of William F. McSweeny, former vice president, Occidental Petroleum Corporation, conversation with author, Washington, D.C., July 1991.

3
Harvests of Neglect

1. Nikolai Vorontsov, "Zashchita Vorontsova," interview with Mikhail Dubrovskiy, *Poisk* 28, 9–15 November 1989, pp. 4–5.
2. A. Yablokov and G. Fleurova, "Pesticides, Environment and Human Health (Soviet Experience)," paper prepared for September 1991 Pugwash Conference, Beijing, China, Table 3.

3. Geoffrey Hosking, *The First Socialist Society,* enlarged ed. (Cambridge, MA: Harvard University Press, 1990), p. 395.
4. Gabriel Schoenfeld, "Soviet Butchery Unmasked," *CSIS Report on the USSR & Eastern Europe* 3 (December 1990).
5. Yuriy Dmitriyevich Chernichenko, speech to Congress of People's Deputies, broadcast by Moscow Television Service, 1 June 1989; *FBIS-SOV,* 5 June 1989, pp. 3–4.
6. World Resources Institute, *World Resources 1990–91* (New York: Oxford University Press, 1990), Tables 18.1 and 18.2, pp. 278–81.
7. Ibid., Table 18.1, pp. 278–79.
8. V. V. Khmura, speech to Congress of People's Deputies, taken from stenographic record of 2 June 1989; *FBIS-SOV-89-137-S,* 19 July 1989, p. 19.
9. Ibid., pp. 19–20.
10. Yevgeniy Vitalyeyich Kharchenko, "Timely Interview," interview with V. Nikolaychuk, *Belorusskaya niva,* 22 March 1991, p. 3; *JPRS-TEN-91-009,* 31 May 1991, pp. 50–52.
11. Vasiliy Ivanovich Belov, speech to Congress of People's Deputies, broadcast by Moscow Television Service, 1 June 1989; *FBIS-SOV-89-105-S,* 2 June 1989, p. 12.
12. Alec Nove, *An Economic History of the U.S.S.R.* (London: Penguin Books, 1989), pp. 12, 96–98.
13. Sergei Zavorotniy and Pyotr Polozhevets, "Operatsiya Golod," *Komsomol'skaya pravda,* 2 February 1990.
14. Nikita S. Khrushchev, *Khrushchev Remembers: The Last Testament,* trans. and ed. Strobe Talbott (Boston: Little, Brown, 1974), pp. 112–13.
15. Margot Jacobs, notes on an exhibit on rural life she visited in early 1989.
16. *Narkhoz 1989,* pp. 17 and 48.
17. Goskomstat SSSR, *Vozrast i sostoyaniye v brake naseleniye SSSR* (Moscow: Finansy i statistika, 1990), pp. 59–70.
18. Michael Dobbs, "Private Soviet Farms: A Tough Row to Hoe," *Washington Post,* 8 May 1991, p. A25.
19. Quoted in David Remnick, "Soviet Farm Legacy: Dead Souls in a Dying Countryside," *Washington Post,* 21 May 1990, p. A16.
20. Yevgeniy Chazov, "Sotni voiteley stoit odin vrachevatel' iskusnyy," interview in *Ogonyok* 42 (1988): 1–3.
21. Neil B. Weissman, "Origins of Soviet Health Administration," in *Health and Society in Revolutionary Russia,* ed. Susan Gross Solomon and John F. Hutchinson (Bloomington: Indiana University Press, 1990), p. 114.
22. Goskomstat SSSR, *Narodnoye khozyaystvo SSSR za 70 let: yubileiniy statisticheskiy yezhegodnik* (Moscow: Finansy i statistika, 1987), pp. 589, 11 and 586.
23. Goskomstat SSSR, *Sotsial'noye razvitiye i uroven' zhizni naseleniya* (Moscow: Finansy i statistika, 1989), p. 173.

24. V. P. Nikonov, as quoted by Tass, "The Party's Guarantee for the Solution of Social Tasks," *Pravda,* 12 June 1988.

25. B. Bolotin, "Kto vperedi?" *Argumenty i fakty* 16 (1991): 2, citing Organization for Economic Cooperation and Development statistics.

26. Rolf H. W. Theen, "Soviet Agriculture as the Touchstone of Soviet Reform," *The Soviet Union and the Challenge of the Future, Volume 2, Economics and Society,* ed. Alexander Shtromas and Morton A. Kaplan (New York: Paragon House, 1989), pp. 126–27.

27. Goskomstat SSSR, *Statistical Press Bulletin* 3 (March 1991): 7.

28. *Doklad,* p. 116.

29. Ibid.

30. Philip R. Pryde, *Environmental Management in the Soviet Union* (Cambridge: Cambridge University Press, 1991), p. 119.

31. Ibid., p. 121.

32. *Doklad,* p. 117.

33. "Tree-lover, Spare the Woodman," *The Economist,* 22 June 1991, pp. 19–20, 23.

34. Kathleen Braden, Seattle Pacific University, quoted in Mark Cheater, "Save That Taiga," *WorldWatch* 4, no. 4 (July–August 1991): 34.

35. Pryde, *Environmental Management in the Soviet Union,* p. 121.

36. Cheater, "Save that Tiger," p. 10.

37. *Environment Report,* p. 66.

38. *Doklad,* p. 100.

39. Fyodor T. Morgun, interview with Kim Smirnov, in *Izvestiya,* 8 May 1988, p. 2, *JPRS-UPA-88-021,* 7 June 1988, p. 45.

40. Ibid.

41. *Doklad,* p. 100.

42. "Zemlyiu ne obmanesh'," *Argumenty i fakty* 48 (December 1989): 5.

43. N. Z. Milashchenko, "Solving Ecological Problems in Farming," *Zemledeliye* 5 (May 1989): 2–6; *JPRS-UPA-89-048,* 28 July 1989, p. 63.

44. "Zemlyiu ne obmanesh'."

45. Roger Strohbehn, ed., *An Economic Analysis of USDA Erosion Control Programs: A New Perspective,* Agricultural Economic Report No. 560 (Washington, D.C.: U.S. Department of Agriculture, 1986).

46. Peter Weber, "U.S. Farmers Cut Soil Erosion by One-Third," *WorldWatch* (July–August 1990): 5, and telephone conversation with author, 20 June 1991.

47. World Resources Institute, *World Resources, 1990–91,* Table 18.2, pp. 280–81.

48. Ibid.

49. Goskomstat SSSR, *Narodnoye khozyaystvo SSSR za 70 let: yubilyeiniy statisticheskiy yezhegodnik* (Moscow: Finansy i statistika, 1987), pp. 245 and 279; *Environment Report,* p. 69.

50. Geoffrey Hosking, *The Awakening of the Soviet Union,* enlarged ed. (Cambridge, MA: Harvard University Press, 1991), p. 60.

51. Valentin Rasputin, speech to USSR Writers' Union Plenum, *Literaturnaya gazeta* 4 (25 January 1989); *JPRS-UPA-89-025*, 27 April 1989, pp. 24–30.

52. Ibid.

53. Boris Stepanovich Maslov, "Improving and Not Flooding; Is the Odious River Transfer 'Project of the Century' Dead?" interview in *Pravda*, 20 September 1990, p. 3; *JPRS-UPA-90-066*, 4 December 1990, pp. 65–67.

54. *Environment Report,* p. 69.

55. V. V. Khmura speech, p. 19.

56. N. K. Shikula, "Al'ternativnaya agroekologiya," in *Ekologicheskaya al'ternativa,* ed. M. Ya. Lemeshev (Moscow: Progress, 1990), p. 481.

57. Fyodor T. Morgun, interview, "Diktatura vedomstva ili obshchenarodniy interes?" *Izvestiya,* 7 May 1988, p. 2.

58. Fyodor T. Morgun, speech to Nineteenth All-Union CPSU Conference, 1 July 1988, *Pravda,* 2 July 1988; *FBIS-SOV-88-129,* 6 July 1988, p. 13.

59. Nikolai Olshanskiy, interview with Tatyana Tubinene, *Komsomol'skaya pravda,* Vilnius ed., 8 February 1989, p. 2; *FBIS-SOV-89-061,* 31 March 1989, pp. 83–85.

60. Igor I. Altshuler and Iurii N. Golubchikov, "Ecological Semi-*Glasnost,*" *Environmental Policy Review* 4, no. 2 (July 1990): 1–12.

61. B. Grigorieva, "Kak vpisat'sya v prirodu," *Pravda,* 31 October 1989, p. 3.

62. Bronislavas Lubis, interview with Tatyana Tubinene, *Komsomol'skaya pravda,* Vilnius ed., 8 February, 1989, 2; *FBIS-SOV-89-061,* 31 March 1989, pp. 83–85.

63. *Doklad,* Table 21, p. 110.

64. Ze'ev Wolfson, " 'Nitrates'—A New Problem for the Soviet Consumer," *Report on the USSR,* 19 May 1989, pp. 6, 8, citing *Pravda,* 27 January 1989, p. 6.

65. "I opyat' s dobavkami," *Vecherniy Volgograd,* 13 October 1990, p. 4.

66. K. Barykin, "Nitrates for Dessert?" *Ogonyok* 1 (January 1989): 32–33.

67. F. Garkusha, "Putting a Question Point-Blank: 'What Are We Eating?' " *MedGaz,* 16 April 1989, p. 1; *JPRS-ULS-90-001,* 6 January 1990, p. 54.

68. A. I. Potapov, interview with B. Pipiya, "Ecological Journal: Cities in the 'Black Book,' " *Pravda,* 1 September 1989, p. 8; *CDSP* 41, no. 3 (27 September 1989): 27.

69. A. I. Kondrusev, "There'll Be No More Pampering," *Izvestiya,* 22 September 1988, p. 3.

70. Ye. Subbotina and K. Lysenko, "Cadmium under a 'Top Secret' Classification," *Moskovskaya pravda,* 16 January 1990, p. 2.

71. Barykin, "Nitrates for Dessert?"

72. Pavel Kisin, "What Do Nitrates Cost?" *Moscow News* 47 (1989): 14.

73. I. Deryugin, "Shto my yedim?" *Argumenty i fakty,* 9 March 1990, p. 6.

74. Professor Boris Borisovich Shugaev, interview with author, Yaroslavl, 23 October 1990.

75. I. Yermakov, "Za kem speshit 'skoraya'?" *Rabochaya tribuna,* 20 July 1990, pp. 1–2.

76. Alla Lipatova, "Pizza Hut byla zakriyta gorodskoy SES," *Kommersant* 38 (24 September–1 October 1990): 4; Stuart Auerbach, "Investments in U.S.S.R. Losing Fizz," *Washington Post,* 7 July 1991, pp. H1–H5.

77. O. Geraimovich, "Tot, kto pyot moloko," *Sotsialisticheskaya industriya,* 14 September 1989, p. 2.

78. S. Chugayev, "Behind Seven Triangular Seals," *Izvestiya,* 2 October 1989; abstracted in *CDSP* 41, no. 41 (1989): 27–28.

79. V. Volovich, "Radiation and Imports: How Mineral Fertilizers 'Contaminated' with Toxic Substances Ended Up in Our Country," *Trud,* 17 May 1990, p. 2; *JPRS-TEN-90-005,* 13 June 1990, pp. 40–41.

80. N. Tereshko, "Krestniye otsy," *Zelyonniy mir* 8 (1990): 6.

81. Morgun, CPSU Conference speech, p. 12.

82. N. Z. Milashchenko, "Solving Ecological Problems in Farming," pp. 63–67.

83. S. Ya. Sergin, "Vo spaseniye," *Znaniye-sila* 10 (October 1989): 1–5.

84. Keith Schneider, "Deadly Pesticide May Face U.S. Ban," *New York Times,* 26 March 1991, p. A20.

85. Aleksei V. Yablokov, "Razvitiye ekologicheskikh issledovaniy v SSSR," *Vestnik Akademii nauk SSSR* 9 (September 1989): 41.

86. Yu. F. Novikov, "Kak vnuzdat' 'troyanskogo konya?'" *Energiya* 1 (January 1990): 34.

87. O. K. Konstantinov, G. S. Borisov and S. L. Spirin, "Raspredeleniye pestitsidnykh ostatkov v vodeyomakh posle protivokleshchevykh obrabotok taigi," *Ekologiya* 3 (May–June 1989): 883–84.

88. A. Fokin, "Ecology: Look Back in Alarm," *Pravda,* 4 August 1992, p. 4, condensed in *CDSP* 40, no. 31 (1988): 22.

89. Arsen Airiyan, "Risk Factors," *Science in the USSR* 2 (1989): 91.

90. Ibid.

91. *Doklad,* Table 20, p. 107.

92. A. G. Kosenko, "Balanced Plant Protection," *Zashchita rasteniy* 10 (October 1989): 6–9; *JPRS-UEA-90-004,* 5 February 1990, p. 49.

93. Ibid.; Yu. Veretennikov, "Pestitsidy: vred ili pol'za?" *Argumenty i fakty* 11 (November 1989): 6.

94. Aleksei V. Yablokov, "Pesticides, Ecology and Agriculture," *Kommunist* 15 (October 1988): 34–42; abstracted in *CDSP* 41, no. 2 (1989): 20.

95. Veretennikov, "Pestitsidy."

96. Aleksei V. Yablokov, *Yadovitaya priprava* (Moscow: Mysl', 1990), p. 20.

97. Ibid., p. 8, including Figure 2.

98. Aleksei V. Yablokov, "The Current State of the Soviet Environment." Paper delivered to Ecology '89 conference, Goteborg, Sweden, digested in *Environmental Policy Review, The Soviet Union and Eastern Europe* 4, no. 1 (January 1990): 5.

99. Yablokov, "Pesticides, Ecology and Agriculture," *CDSP*.

100. T. V. Moshnyagi, "T. Moshnyagi's Speech," *MedGaz*, 21 October 1988; Ze'ev Wolfson, "Dangerous Levels of Pesticides and Other Chemicals in Food," *Environmental Policy Review* 3, no. 1 (January 1989): 8.

101. Goskomstat SSSR, *Press Release 358*, 20 September 1990.

102. T. Kasumov, "Poisoned Earth: The Consequences of Excessive Use of Pesticides on the Fields of Azerbaijan," *Trud*, 25 August 1988, p. 2; *JPRS-ULS-89-002*, 1 February 1989, pp. 38–39.

103. Yablokov, *Yadovitaya priprava*, p. 57.

104. Ibid., pp. 55–56.

105. *Environment Report*, p. 120.

106. Yan Khutoranskiy, Radio Moscow, Domestic Service, 19 October 1989, reported by Radio Liberty, Munich, "Students on Harvest Poisoned by Pesticides," 20 October 1989.

107. B. Pipiya, "What Happened in the Vicinity of Sverdlovsk: The Ministry of Health and the Ministry of Defense Warn: To Work in Fields Treated with Pesticides Is Not Safe," *Pravda*, 15 May 1991, p. 1; *JPRS-UPA-91-033*, 17 July 1991, p. 45.

108. B. Pipiya, "Yadovitiy 'prizrak,'" *Pravda*, 19 August 1990, p. 4 and, under identical headline, 22 August 1990, p. 2.

109. Ibid.

110. D. Oreshkin and N. Pusenkova, "Kak khimchat u nikh i u nas," *Dialog* 4 (March 1990): p. 73.

111. Michael Dobbs, "Soviet Consumer Comes a Cropper as Potatoes Rot," *Washington Post*, 30 September 1990, pp. A23 and A30.

112. I. Repin, "Everything Is Collapsing According to Plan," *Argumenty i fakty* 9 (March 1991): 3; *JPRS-UPA-91-019*, 9 April 1991, p. 95.

113. Francis X. Clines, "Soviet Party Leader Tries to Reinvent the Authentic Peasant," *New York Times*, 2 June 1991, p. 20.

114. Mikhail Pavlov, interview with author, Yaroslavl, 23 October 1990.

115. Henry Kamm, "Estonia Turns Over Land to the Tiller," *New York Times*, 30 December 1990, p. 8.

116. Ibid.

117. Philip Taubman, "Down on the Soviet Farm, A Fear of Change," *New York Times*, 9 May 1988, pp. A1 and A12.

118. Quoted in Isaac Deutscher, *Stalin: A Political Biography* (New York: Vintage Books, Random House, 1960), p. 330.

4

A Sea of Troubles

1. All quotations from Tulepbergen Kaipbergenov are taken from verbatim transcript of proceedings, Congress of People's Deputies, 30 May 1989; *Izvestiya*, 1 June 1989, p. 5.

2. Boris Z. Rumer, *Soviet Central Asia* (Boston: Unwin Hyman, 1989), p. 62.
3. *Narkhoz 1989*, pp. 17, 23–24.
4. D. B. Oreshkin, "Aral'skaya katastrofa," *Nauka o zemle* 2 (1990): 41.
5. Ibid.
6. N. G. Minashina, "Ekologicheskiye posledstviya meliorativnovodok-hozyaistvennogo stroitel'stva v basseyne Aral'skogo morya," in *Ekologicheskaya al'ternativa*, ed. M. Ya. Lemeshev (Moscow: Progress, 1990), p. 356.
7. Philip R. Pryde, *Environmental Management in the Soviet Union* (Cambridge: Cambridge University Press, 1991), pp. 224–25.
8. Lester Brown, "The Aral Sea: Going, Going . . . ," *WorldWatch* 4, no. 1 (January–February 1991): 23.
9. "Women Scientists' Appeal for Immediate Action to Save Children in the Aral Ecological Crisis Region," trans. Katya Partan, *Environment* 3, no. 1 (January–February 1991): 36.
10. Goskomgidromet, *Obzor,* p. 104.
11. James Critchlow, *Nationalism in Uzbekistan: A Soviet Republic's Road to Sovereignty* (Boulder, CO: Westview Press, 1991), pp. 84–85.
12. Dr. M. I. Zelikin and A. S. Demidov, "The Aral Crisis and Departmental Interests." Paper presented at a conference of Soviet and American grassroots and national environmental groups, Moscow, 14–19 March 1991, p. 5, made available by Ms. Eliza Klose, executive director, Institute for Soviet-American Relations, Washington, D.C.
13. Dr. N. G. Minashina, "Ecological State of the Soils in the Aral Basin: Sources and Scope of the Crisis." Paper presented at ibid., p. 3.
14. "Obrashcheniye k sovetskoy obshchestvennosty." Declaration of participants in the "Aral-88" expedition, 23 November 1988, in *Ekologicheskaya al'ternativa*, p. 371.
15. Critchlow, *Nationalism in Uzbekistan,* p. 80.
16. Boris Stepanovich Maslov, "Improving and Not Flooding; Is the Odious River Transfer 'Project of the Century' Dead?" interview, *Pravda*, 20 September 1990, p. 3; *JPRS-UPA-90-066*, 4 December 1990, pp. 65–67, esp. 65.
17. Ze'ev Wolfson, "Central Asian Environment: A Dead End," *Environmental Policy Review* 4, no. 1 (January 1990): 9.
18. V. M. Kotlyakov, "The Aral Sea Basin: A Critical Environmental Zone," *Environment* 3, no. 1 (January–February 1991): 7.
19. Khaidar Babadzhanov and Mikhail Lemeshev, "Kakova voda—takov i razum," *Zelyonniy mir* 5–6 (1991): 6.
20. D. S. Yagdarov, "Voprosy intensifikatsii i ratsional'nogo ispol'zovaniya osnovnykh fondov Karakalpakskoy ASSR," *Obshchestvenniye nauki v Uzbekistane* 3 (1987): 16, cited in Critchlow, *Nationalism in Uzbekistan,* p. 83.
21. Critchlow, *Nationalism in Uzbekistan,* p. 68.
22. Anatoliy Khazanov, "The Ecological Situation and the National Issue

in Uzbekistan," *Environmental Policy Review* 4, no. 1 (January 1990): 25.

23. Critchlow, *Nationalism in Uzbekistan,* p. 82–83.

24. Ibid., p. 68.

25. Pavel Voshchanov and Aleksandr Bushev, "Zdes' legko obriyvaetsya detskaya zhizn' . . . ," *Komsomol'skaya pravda,* 25 April 1990, p. 2.

26. Ibid.

27. I. Deryaev and N. Yagmurov, "O reservakh snizheniya detskoy smertnosty v Turkmenskoy SSR," *Zdravookhraneniye Turkmenistana* 7 (1990): 4.

28. Quoted in Rusi Nasar, "How the Soviets Murdered a Sea," *Washington Post,* 4 June 1989, p. B3.

29. Ibid.

30. Brown, "Aral Sea," p. 22.

31. V. Kuleshov, "Heated Debates in Tashauz," *Izvestiya,* 20 November 1990, p. 1; *JPRS-UPA-90-066,* 4 December 1990, pp. 71–72.

32. E. Ponarina, "Aral ugrozhaet planete," *Sotsialisticheskaya industriya,* 20 June 1989, cited in Annette Bohr, "Health Catastrophe in Karakalpakistan," *Report on the USSR,* 21 July 1989, p. 37.

33. M. R. Pashyeva, B. Khaitmetov, P. S. Bekkhanov and G. P. Sarieva, "Kompleksnoye sotsial'no-gigiyenicheskie issledovaniye zdorovya selskikh zhitelei Tashauzskoy Oblasty," *Zdravookhraneniye Turkmenistana* 8 (1990): 5–7.

34. Khazanov, *Ecological Situation,* p. 22, citing B. Rudenko, "Solenye peski Aralkum," *Nauka i Zhizn* 10 (1989): 45.

35. Ann Sheehy, "Tajik Schoolchildren Exposed to Chemical Defoliants," *Radio Liberty Research,* RL 175/84, 2 May 1984.

36. Rumer, *Soviet Central Asia,* p. 152; David Remnick, "A New Brand of Corruption," *Washington Post,* 8 July 1991, pp. A1 and A16.

37. R. N. Nishanov, speech to Nineteenth All-Union CPSU Conference, 30 June 1988, *Pravda,* 1 July 1988; *FBIS-SOV-88-128,* 5 July 1988, pp. 45–46.

38. Goskomstat SSSR, *Press Release* 263, 4 September 1987.

39. Goskomstat SSSR, *Press Release* 442, 10 December 1990.

40. A. A. Baranov, "Aktual'niye voprosy okhrany zdorovya matery i rebyonka na sovremennom etape," *Pediatriya* 7 (July 1990): 6.

41. *Izvestiya,* 2 January 1989.

42. V. Zhukov, *Kommunist Tadjikistana,* 13 July 1987.

43. Tatyana Sharaya, "Kaplya v more," *Semya* 36 (1989): 2.

44. Yu. Lavin, "Ne delat' tainy iz statistiki," *Kommunist Tadjikistana,* 26 January 1990, p. 2.

45. Nikolai Filatov, "Sistemnoye zabolevaniye," *Semya* 22 (1990).

46. Ye. Myatiyeva, "Secret Figures," *Turkmenskaya iskra,* 5 March 1989, p. 2; *JPRS-UPA-89-039,* 12 June 1989, p. 37.

47. Ibid.

48. Ibid.

49. Ibid.

50. Francis X. Clines, "In Fabled Samarkand, Newborns Fight for Life," *New York Times,* 5 July 1990, p. A10.
51. Zelikin and Demidov, "Aral Crisis and Departmental Interests," p. 3.
52. Ibid., pp. 1–2.
53. Sergei Zalygin, "What I Disagree With and Why," *Izvestiya,* 25 March 1991, p. 3; *JPRS-UPA-91-023,* 2 May 1991, p. 78.
54. I. Kalandarov, deputy chief, Amu Darya Basin Association, Khorezm *oblast,* "The Troubled Waters of the Amu Darya; Time to Take Action in the Cis-Aral Zone," *Pravda vostoka,* 24 April 1991; *JPRS-UPA-91-033,* 17 July 1991, pp. 45–46.
55. Goskomstat SSSR, *Press Release* 436, 29 November 1989, p. 2.
56. A. Prokin, "Zhdat' bol'she nel'zya," *MedGaz,* 14 July 1989, p. 1.
57. Ibid.
58. Goskomstat SSSR, *Press Release* 436.
59. RFE/RL, *Daily Report,* "Water Purification Plant in Turkmenistan Can't Function," 30 July 1991.
60. *Narkhoz 1989,* pp. 19, 26.
61. Khazanov, *Ecological Situation,* p. 25.
62. M. I. Umarkhodzhayev, rector, Andizhan State Pedagogical Institute, speech to USSR Congress of People's Deputies, 2 June 1989, *Izvestiya,* 5 June 1989, p. 4; *FBIS-SOV-89-142-S,* 26 July 1989, p. 21.
63. Murray Feshbach, *The Soviet Union: Population Trends and Dilemmas,* Population Bulletin 37, no. 3 (August 1982) (Washington, D.C.: Population Reference Bureau, Inc.), p. 5.
64. Michael Dobbs, "New Soviet Freedoms Lead to Surge of Islam," *Washington Post,* 24 October 1990, p. A12.
65. Rumer, *Soviet Central Asia,* p. 111.
66. Hedrick Smith, *The New Russians* (New York: Random House, 1990), p. 300.
67. David Remnick, "In Soviet Central Asia, Death Stalks the Children," *Washington Post,* 22 May 1990, p. A18.
68. Yuriy Izrael and F. Rovinsky, "Points to Ponder," *Science in the USSR* 5 (September–October 1989): 55.
69. Zalygin, "What I Disagree With and Why."
70. Critchlow, *Nationalism in Uzbekistan,* p. 88.
71. Timur Pulatov, "Mass Exodus Hits Central Asia," *Moscow News* 41 (1990): 7.
72. N. F. Vasilyev, *Melioratsiya zemel—vsenarodnoye delo,* p. 61, cited by Yuriy Chernichenko, address to USSR Writers' Union Plenum, *Literaturnaya gazeta* 4, 25 January 1989, pp. 3–4; *JPRS-UPA-89-025,* 27 April 1989, p. 23.
73. Rumer, *Soviet Central Asia,* p. 82.
74. Yuriy Chernichenko, "The Land, Ecology and Perestroika," *Literaturnaya gazeta* 4, 25 January 1989, pp. 3–4; *JPRS-UPA-89-025,* 27 April 1989, p. 23.
75. Wolfson, "Central Asian Environment," p. 45.

5

Dark, Satanic Mills

1. Film in author's collection, restored by the Leningrad Center for Documentary Cinema; Nikita Khrushchev discusses the murder of Mikhoels in *Khrushchev Remembers,* trans. and ed. Strobe Talbott (Boston: Little, Brown, 1971), pp. 261–62.

2. Stephen Kotkin, *Steeltown USSR* (Berkeley: University of California Press, 1991), p. 208.

3. Dina Kaminskaya, conversation with author, Washington, D.C., 27 June 1991.

4. Figures extrapolated from percentages in Kotkin, *Steeltown USSR,* p. 136.

5. David Remnick, "Stalin's Lethal Legacy of Filth, 5-Year Plans," *Washington Post,* 21 May 1991, pp. A1 and A15.

6. Kotkin, *Steeltown USSR,* pp. 56–57, citing Tatyana Leus, "How Much Does 'Free' Medical Care Cost?" *Magnitogorsk Worker,* date and page unspecified.

7. Remnick, "Stalin's Lethal Legacy."

8. Ibid.

9. Kotkin, *Steeltown USSR,* pp. xiii, 135.

10. Nikolai Vorontsov, "Zashchita Vorontsova," interview with Mikhail Dubrovskiy, *Poisk* 28, 9–15 November 1989, pp. 4–5.

11. Yu. Chirkov, deputy chairman, Krivoy Rog city council, interviewed on "Vremya" newscast, Moscow Television Service, 3 September 1990; *FBIS-SOV-90-174,* 7 September 1990, p. 40.

12. P. Kuzmin and G. Sazonov, "Pod shapkoy smoga," *Pravda,* 13 October 1990, p. 3.

13. Ibid.

14. Nikolai Vorontsov, "Disaster Caused by . . . Thoughtlessness," *Sovetskaya kultura* 46, 17 November 1990, p. 2, *JPRS-UPA-90-066,* 4 December 1990, pp. 52–54.

15. Irina P. Pletnikova, "Opyt raboty nad regionalnymi kompleksnymi programmami okhrany prirody: vliyaniye na perestroiku ekonomiki." Paper presented at Soviet-American Conference, "Will Market Economics Save the Environment or Bury It?" sponsored by the Environmental Defense Fund and AER*X, Washington, D.C., 12–14 November 1990.

16. *Doklad,* p. 13.

17. Igor I. Altshuler and Iurii N. Golubchikov, "Ecological Semi-*Glasnost,*" *Environmental Policy Review* 4, no. 2 (July 1990): 5–6.

18. Nicholas A. Robinson, "*Perestroika* and *Priroda:* Environmental Protection in the USSR," *Pace Environmental Law Review* 5, no. 2 (Spring 1988): 359.

19. *Doklad,* Table 9, pp. 47–50.

20. World Resources Institute, *World Resources 1990–91* (New York: Oxford University Press, 1991), Table 24.5, p. 351.

21. Council on Environmental Quality, *Environmental Quality 20th Annual Report* (Washington, D.C.: Author, 1990), Appendix E, Table 8, p. 431.

22. Doug Grano, Environmental Protection Agency, Air Quality Office, Washington, D.C., conversation with authors, 16 July 1991.

23. Council on Environmental Quality, *Draft U.S. National Report for Submission to the United Nations Conference on Environment and Development* (Washington, D.C.: CEQ, May 1991), chap. 5, p. 10.

24. Ibid.

25. Worldwatch Institute, *State of the World 1991* (New York: W. W. Norton, 1991), Table 6-1, p. 96.

26. *Doklad*, p. 45; and U.S. Environmental Protection Agency, Office of Air Quality Planning and Standards, Technical Support Division, *National Air Quality and Emissions Trends Report, 1989* (Research Triangle Park, NC: EPA, February 1991).

27. Ibid.

28. D. J. Peterson, "USSR—The State of the Environment, Part II," *Radio Liberty Research*, 29 January 1990.

29. Goskomgidromet, *Obzor*, p. 12.

30. Ibid.

31. *Narkhoz 1989*, p. 253; Nikolai Tereshko, "Prokuror kupil 'rodnichok,' " *Zelyonniy mir* 3–4, 24 January 1991, p. 4; L. Dunaeva, "S dorogi, chelovek!" *Zelyonniy mir* 3 (1990): 3.

32. *Vestnik ispolkoma Mossoveta* 14 (1990): 35.

33. Aleksei Yablokov, as cited in Altshuler and Golubchikov, "Ecological Semi-*Glasnost*," p. 6.

34. L. Boldyreva, "Tvortsy ne boyatsya?" *Zelyonniy mir* 11 (1990): 3.

35. Kirill V. Paremskiy, interviewed by L. Boldyreva, "Vsyo menshe okruzhayushchei prirody," *Zelyonniy Mir* 6 (1990): 7.

36. *Doklad*, p. 31.

37. Grano conversation.

38. A. Gusarov and M. Vayablum, "Davayte razberyomsya," *Sotsialisticheskaya industriya*, 7 January 1989, p. 4.

39. *Doklad*, p. 11.

40. Peterson, "USSR."

41. U.S. Bureau of the Census, *Statistical Abstract of the United States, 1989* (Washington, DC: U.S. Department of Commerce, 1989), p. 200.

42. *Doklad*, Table 1, p. 12; Council on Environmental Quality, *Environmental Quality 20th Annual Report*, Table 42, pp. 470–71.

43. Joseph Stalin, address to business executives, February 1931, cited in Isaac Deutscher, *Stalin: A Political Biography* (New York: Vintage Books, Random House, 1960), p. 328.

44. O. Kibal'chich, abstract of paper presented by P. I. Miroshnikov, *Ekologicheskiye problemy territoriy i puti ikh resheniya*, at a scientific-practical conference, 4–5 July 1989, in Irkutsk, in O7. *Geografiya* 5 (1990): 25.

45. Ibid.

46. Michael Dobbs, "Russians Fight to Save Lake Baikal," *Washington Post,* 11 October 1990, pp. A25–26.

47. Grigoriy Barenboim, interview with author, Moscow, 13 October 1990.

48. *Doklad,* Table 8, p. 46.

49. Mikhail Salop, "Norov Noril'ska," *Khimiya i zhizn* 4 (April 1990): 34–41.

50. "Serniye strasty," *Poisk,* 5–11 October 1990.

51. Salop, "Norov Noril'ska," p. 38.

52. *Doklad,* Table 8, pp. 45–46.

53. D. Zaridze, "Budyem zdorovy?" *Izvestiya,* 6 April 1990, p. 2.

54. Salop, "Norov Noril'ska," p. 39.

55. Ibid., p. 41.

56. Ibid., p. 36.

57. Goskomstat SSSR, *Statistical Press Bulletin* 2 (1990): 10–11.

58. Data provided by Grigoriy Barenboim, based on *Sotsial'nogigiyenicheskiy passport gorod Kemerovo,* RSFSR Ministry of Health and Kemerovo City Council, 1990.

59. Ibid.

60. V. Sanatin, "Smog over the City," *Komsomol'skaya pravda,* 6 April 1988, p. 4.

61. N. I. Danilov, interview, "Ecology—The Minimum Program: Draw Nizhniy Tagil Back from the Ecological Brink," *Semya* 18 (1989): 5.

62. G. Apresyan, "Nizhniy Tagil pod smogom," *Literaturnaya gazeta,* 19 October 1988, p. 2.

63. Ibid.

64. L. Yermakova, "V ognyonnom ozherelye," *Semya* 22 (1990).

65. Ibid.

66. Salop, "Norov Noril'ska," pp. 38, 36.

67. I. Zhuravleva, "I zdorovye 'do lampochki' . . . ," *NTR Tribuna* 13–14 (1990): 10.

68. "The Soviet Union's Wasted Workers," *The Economist,* 15 June 1991, p. 63, citing data from Guy Standing, ed., *In Search of Flexibility: The New Soviet Labor Market* (Geneva: International Labor Organization, 1991).

69. Remnick, "Stalin's Lethal Legacy."

70. *Narkhoz 1989,* p. 167.

71. Yu. Teplyakov, " 'Eshcho dyshish, Ural . . . ,' " *Moskovskiye novosti,* 9 (1990).

72. Fyodor Morgun, "At the Start of the Journey," interview with Vasiliy Mikhailovich Peskov, *Komsomol'skaya pravda,* 8 November 1988, p. 2; *JPRS-UPA-89-001,* 6 January 1989, pp. 77–84.

73. Teplyakov, " 'Eshcho dyshish, Ural . . .' "

74. Ibid.

75. Amy Goldstein, "Panel Targets Md.'s Title of No. 1 Cancer State," *Washington Post,* 10 July 1991, pp. B1, B8; Goskomstat SSSR, *Okhrana zdorov'ya v SSSR, statisticheskiy sbornik* (Moscow: Finansy i statistika, 1990), p. 36.

76. Teplyakov, " 'Eshcho dyshish, Ural . . .' "
77. Ibid.
78. *Doklad*, Table 2, p. 13.
79. Ibid., pp. 20–21.
80. Goskomstat SSSR, *SSSR i zarubezhniye strany 1989* (Moscow: Finansy i statistika, 1990), p. 257.
81. "Lenin's Curse," *The Economist,* 27 April 1991, p. 11.
82. Michael Dobbs, "In Moscow, Running Out of Socks," *Washington Post,* 22 June 1991, pp. A1 and A18.
83. Vorontsov, "Disaster Caused by . . . Thoughtlessness," pp. 52–54.
84. Aleksei Yablokov, interview with authors, Washington, D.C., 21 June 1991.
85. Valentin Rasputin, speech at USSR Writers' Union Plenum, *Literaturnaya gazeta* 4, 25 January 1989; *JPRS-UPA*-89-025, 27 April 1989, p. 30.
86. Yablokov interview.
87. V. Ye. Ziberov, interviewed by S. Morozov, "Let's Look at the Situation without Emotion," *Kommunist Tadjikistana,* 5 January 1990, p. 1; *JPRS-UPA*-90-012, 12 March 1990, pp. 78–79.
88. A. Yudin, "The Perfidy of the Residual Principle," *Izvestiya,* 9 November 1990, p. 1; *JPRS-UPA*-90-071, 18 December 1990, pp. 79–80.
89. Morton Kondracke, "Life in Hell," *New Republic*, 24 June 1991, p. 20.
90. Nikolai Vorontsov, introduction to *Doklad*, p. 9.

6
Water Torture

1. *Doklad*, p. 94, Table 18, p. 99.
2. Ibid.
3. G. I. Sidorenko and V. N. Krut'ko, "Sokhranit' zdorov'ye natsiy," in *Ekologicheskaya al'ternativa,* ed. M. Ya. Lemeshev (Moscow: Progress, 1990), p. 765.
4. G. Akatov, "We Live in Freedom," *MedGaz,* 4 June 1989, p. 3; *JPRS-ULS*-90-008, 27 June 1990, p. 23.
5. Aleksei Yablokov, "Probuzhdeniye ot ekologicheskoy spyachki," *Rodina* 8 (1990): 65.
6. Cited in The Global Tomorrow Coalition, *The Global Ecology Handbook* (Boston: Beacon Press, 1990), p. 163.
7. Cited in John W. Wright, gen. ed., *The Universal Almanac 1991* (Kansas City: Andrews and McMeel, 1991), p. 534.
8. Council on Environmental Quality, *Environmental Quality 20th Annual Report* (Washington, D.C.: CEQ, 1989), Table 8, p. 431.
9. *Doklad*, pp. 244–45.
10. Goskomstat SSSR, *Demograficheskiy yezhegodnik SSSR 1989* (Moscow: Finansy i statistika, 1990), pp. 7–12.
11. Yablokov, "Probuzhdeniye . . . ," p. 66.

12. *Doklad,* Table 18, p. 99.
13. "Nizhniy Tagil, Gold in River," *Moscow News* 6, 10–17 February 1991, p. 2.
14. V. Pavlovskiy, "Kto spasyot Kansk?" *Ekologiya Krasnoyar'ya* 3 (March–April 1991): 1–2.
15. "Ekologicheskiy dnevnik," *Ekologiya Krasnoyar'ya* 5 (April–May 1991): 6.
16. Pavlovskiy, "Kto spasyot Kansk?" p. 2.
17. V. I. Lukyanenko, "A Toxicological Crisis in the Bodies of Water," *Rybnoye khozyaystvo* 6 (June 1990): 45–49; *JPRS-UPA-90-053*, 13 September 1990, pp. 67–70.
18. S. Tutorskaya, "Doctors Concerned over Increase in Parasitic Diseases," *Izvestiya,* 11 November 1990; *CDSP* 42, no. 45 (1990): 26.
19. V. P. Sergiyev et al., "Status of Parasitic Diseases in the USSR," *Zhurnal mikrobiologii, epidemioligii i immunologii* 1 (January 1990): 28–32; *JPRS-ULS-90-019*, 13 November 1990, pp. 10–13.
20. A. Kaipbergenov, "Another Outbreak?" (under the rubric "Reporting Details"), *Pravda,* 3 August 1990; *FBIS-SOV-90-152*, 7 August 1990, p. 40.
21. L. Dmitriyeva, "The Quiet Don Threatens Cholera," *Izvestiya,* 23 August 1990, p. 6; *JPRS-ULS-91-009*, 18 April 1991, pp. 11–12.
22. Valentin G. Rasputin, "Baikal," in *Ekologicheskaya al'ternativa,* ed. M. Ya. Lemeshev, p. 320.
23. Peter Matthiessen, "The Blue Pearl of Siberia," *New York Review of Books,* 14 February 1991, pp. 37–47, esp. p. 37.
24. Goskomstat SSSR, *Okhrana okruzhayushchei sredy i ratsional'noe ispol'-zovanie prirodnykh resursov v SSSR* (Moscow: Finansy i statistika, 1989), p. 133.
25. Matthiesen, "Blue Pearl of Siberia," p. 38.
26. Quoted in Boris Komarov (Ze'ev Wolfson), *The Destruction of Nature in the Soviet Union,* (White Plains, NY: M. E. Sharpe, 1980), p. 16.
27. Komarov, *Destruction of Nature,* p. 5.
28. Ibid., p. 7.
29. Rasputin, "Baikal," p. 309.
30. Quoted in Komarov, *Destruction of Nature,* p. 5.
31. Komarov, *Destruction of Nature,* pp. 8–9.
32. Goskomstat SSSR, *Narodnoye khozyaystvo SSSR za 70 let: yubileiniy statisticheskiy yezhegodnik* (Moscow: Finansy i statistika, 1987), p. 616.
33. N. Tereshko, "Baikal: K zhivoy vode," *Zelyonniy mir* 1 (1990): 7.
34. G. I. Galaziy, "Ugroza ekosisteme Baikala," in *Ekologicheskaya al'ternativa,* ed. M. Ya. Lemeshev, p. 328.
35. Komarov, *Destruction of Nature,* p. 9.
36. Michael Dobbs, "Russians Fight to Save Lake Baikal," *Washington Post,* 11 October 1990, pp. A25–26.
37. *Obzor,* p. 89.

38. Galaziy, "Ugroza ekosisteme Baikala," p. 326.
39. Komarov, *Destruction of Nature,* p. 11.
40. Galaziy, "Ugroza ekosisteme Baikala," p. 329.
41. Dobbs, "Russians Fight to Save Lake Baikal," p. A26.
42. Galaziy, "Ugroza ekosisteme Baikala," p. 329.
43. Viktor Drobotov, "Stony Volgi," in *Stony Volgi,* ed. A. V. Kokshilov (Volgograd: Nizhne-Volzhskoye knizhnoye izdatel'stvo, 1990), p. 8.
44. F. Ya. Shipunov, "Stony Volgi," *Sovetskaya Rossiya,* 18 November 1987, p. 4.
45. Drobotov, "Stony Volgi," p. 7.
46. Ibid., p. 34.
47. *Stony Volgi,* ed. A. V. Kokshilov, pp. 35, 40, citing *Volgogradskaya pravda,* 2 March 1989.
48. *Doklad,* p. 70.
49. Lukyanenko, "Toxicological Crisis," p. 68.
50. Ibid.
51. A[rif Enverovich] Mansurov, chairman, ASSR Committee for the Protection of Nature, "Caspian Alarm," interview with Ali Naibov, *Rabochaya gazeta,* 14 June 1991; *JPRS-UPA*-91-033, 17 July 1991, pp. 46–47.
52. *Doklad,* p. 135.
53. "The Dead Zone," Moscow Television Service, 11 May 1989; *FBIS-SOV*-89-091, 12 May 1989, p. 60.
54. Soviet television broadcasts, 10 July and 18 October 1989, reported in "Sumgait Refraction Plant Closed," *Radio Liberty Research,* 30 October 1989, SU/0600 C/6.
55. Ibid.
56. Islam Kuliev, "V Baku prokhodit pervaya mezhdunarodnaya konferent siya po problemam Kaspiyskogo Morya," Soviet radio broadcast, 16 June 1991, *Radio Liberty Research.*
57. Yablokov, "Probuzhdeniye . . . ," p. 67.
58. Ibid.
59. K. Sergienko, "Ladno li na Ladogye," *Sovetskaya kultura,* 27 January 1990, p. 2.
60. Ibid.
61. Vera Kondratenko, "Sevastopol Is Short of Water," *Nezavisimaya gazeta,* 24 October 1991, p. 6; *JPRS-USR*-91-050, 19 November 1991, p. 89.
62. Valentin Smaga, head of the Green World Club, "Only the Free Will Survive," *Komsomol'skaya znamya,* 5 April 1991, p. 4; *JPRS-UPS*-91-031, 14 June 1991, pp. 47–49, esp. p. 48.
63. Ibid., esp. p. 49.
64. Vladimir Kalita, "Nineteen Tons of Cadmium for Your Table," *Literaturnaya Rossiya* 6, 8 February 1991, p. 7; *JPRS-UPA*-91-031, 14 June 1991, p. 47.
65. Irena Slutsky, former arbiter and technical advisor, Kharkov Suburban

Sanitary Commission, interview with authors, Washington, D.C., 12 September 1990.

66. Ibid.

67. Goskomstat SSSR, *Zdravookhraneniye v SSSR, statisticheskiy sbornik* (Moscow: Finansy i statistika, 1989), Table 2.2, p. 9.

68. Ibid.

69. Goskomstat SSSR, *Okhrana zdorov'ya v SSSR, statisticheskiy sbornik* (Moscow: Finansy i statistika, 1990), pp. 178–79 and 25.

70. Aleksei V. Yablokov, "The Current State of the Soviet Environment." Paper delivered to Ecology '89 conference, Goteborg, Sweden, August 1989.

71. Goskomstat SSSR, *Okhrana zdorov'ya v SSSR*, pp. 178–79.

72. Goskomstat SSSR, *Zdravookhraneniye v SSSR*. Table 2.2, p. 9.

73. Tatyana V. Strikalenko, chief, Water-supply Hygiene Department, Water Transport Hygiene Research Institute, USSR Ministry of Public Health, interview with author, Odessa, 18 October 1990.

74. *Doklad,* p. 170.

75. Data from report prepared for Odessa *oblast* Council of Deputies' Subcommittee on Environmental Protection, made available to authors by subcommittee chairman, Professor Alfred Tsykalo, 19 October 1990.

76. Anatoliy M. Voitenko, M.D., director, Water Transport Hygiene Research Institute, USSR Ministry of Public Health, interview with author, Odessa, 18 October 1990.

77. Professor B. Ya. Reznik, statement to January 1990 Odessa *oblast* Party committee plenum, cited in Oleg Mel'nikov, "Yesli my grazhdanye Odessiy . . . ," *Vechernaya Odessa,* 19 January 1990, p. 4.

78. Lenin Children's Fund, *Polozheniye detey v SSSR 1990 god. Sostoyaniye. Problemy. Perspektivy* (Moscow: Dom, 1990), Table 20, p. 63.

79. Voitenko interview.

80. Alla I. Shevchuk, letter to author, Odessa, 14 May 1991.

81. S. Fateyev, "Expedition to Monitor Black Sea Pollution," broadcast on "Vremya," Moscow Television Service, 4 October 1990; *FBIS-SOV-90-195,* 9 October 1990, p. 83.

82. *Environment Report,* p. 113.

83. *Doklad,* p. 179.

84. Goskompriroda SSSR, *Environment Report,* pp. 113–14.

85. *Doklad,* pp. 66–67.

86. Ibid., pp. 177–78.

87. Ibid., p. 179.

88. Associated Press, "27 Dead in Black Sea Flooding," *Washington Post,* 9 August 1991, p. A27.

89. Sidorenko and Krut'ko, "Sokhranit' zdorov'ye natsiy," p. 769.

90. V. Romanenko, chief sanitary doctor, Yalta, "Zhdut li nas morskiye plyazhi?" *MedGaz,* 3 June 1990, p. 3.

91. Author's recollection.

92. Lukyanenko, "Toxicological Crisis," p. 67.

93. *Doklad,* p. 134.

94. "Natsional'niy doklad o sostoyanii prirodnoy sredy v SSSR," *Svet* 12 (December 1990): 55, an abridged version of the *Doklad* in the full text of which, however, the data on specific tonnages of Baltic Sea pollution could not be located.

95. D. J. Peterson, "USSR—Medicines, Newspapers, and the Dilemmas of Protecting the Environment," *Radio Liberty Research,* 6 March 1990.

96. Juris Eksteins, interview with author, Moscow, 11 October 1990.

97. Grigoriy Barenboim, interview with author, Moscow, 13 October 1990.

98. A. Umbras, "A Zone of Special Attention," *Sovetskaya molodezh,* 17 August 1988; pp. 1–3, *JPRS-UPA-89-013,* 15 February 1989, pp. 75–80.

99. "Chemical Spill Contaminates the Daugava, US Government Acts Swiftly to Help," *VAK American Open Letter #11,* Environmental Protection Club of Latvia, 2 December 1990, pp. 1–3.

100. Dzintars Medenis, *Diena,* 24 May 1991, translated as "Riga's Sewage Treatment Plant—In the Home Stretch?" *VAK USA Open Letter 13,* 30 July 1991, p. 1.

101. Umbras, "Zone of Special Attention," pp. 76–77.

102. Barenboim interview.

103. Author's recollection from visit to Lake Sevan, May 1975.

104. Alexander Mishchenko, "Experience from an Independent Examination of the Design in Flood-Control Works in Leningrad." Paper presented at Joint US-USSR NGO Conference on the Environment, Moscow, 14–19 March 1991, made available by Ms. Eliza Klose, Institute for Soviet-American Relations.

105. "Leningrad's Barrier, Shield or Sword," *Novosti,* 21 August 1990, in *SWB* 31 August 1990, SU/W0143, pp. A/12–13.

106. Vladimir Nevel'skiy, "Stroitel'stvo damby priostanovit'," *Pravda,* 18 October 1990.

107. Arkadiy Sosnov, "Bitter Medicine for the Neva," *Ogonyok* 42, 13–20 October 1990, pp. 9–11; *JPRS-TEN-91-001,* 4 January 1991, pp. 69–72.

108. Ibid., p. 70.

109. Ze'ev Wolfson, "Some Environmental and Social Aspects of Nuclear Power Development in the USSR," Research Paper 63, The Marjorie Mayrock Center for Soviet and East European Research, Hebrew University, Jerusalem, March 1987, pp. 2–4.

110. Zhores Medvedev, *The Legacy of Chernobyl* (New York: W. W. Norton, 1990), p. 12.

111. Ibid., p. 18.

7

". . . Plus Electrification"

1. Jonathan P. Stern, "Soviet Oil and Gas Production and Exports to the West: A Framework for Analysis and Forecasting," in *Gorbachev's Economic Plans,* Study Papers submitted to the Joint Economic Committee,

Congress of the United States (Washington, D.C.: U.S. Government Printing Office, 1987), vol. 1, pp. 500–13.

2. *Narkhoz 1989*, pp. 377, 644.

3. Stern, "Soviet Oil and Gas Production," p. 503.

4. Elena Bonner, "For Whom the Bell Tolls," *New York Review of Books*, 16 August 1990, p. 7.

5. Michael Dobbs, "Chernobyl: Symbol of Soviet Failure," *Washington Post*, 26 April 1991, pp. A1, A38.

6. "Powerless," *The Economist*, 13 April 1991, pp. 67–68.

7. Dobbs, "Chernobyl."

8. Judith Thornton, "Soviet Electric Power in the Wake of the Chernobyl Accident," in *Gorbachev's Economic Plans*, vol. 1, pp. 514–532, Table 1, p. 516.

9. *Narkhoz 1989*, p. 375.

10. Lev Baranov, chief, USSR Prosecutor's Office for the Administration and Supervision of the Execution of Laws in Economic Activity, "Guarantee for Disaster," interview with Nataliya Gevorkyan, *Moskovskiye novosti* 48, 2 December 1990, p. 4; FBIS-SOV-90-243, 18 December 1990, p. 76; Professor A. Andryushchenko, "When You Live Next Door to an AES [Nuclear Power Station] . . . The AES Failed the Ecological Examination," interviewed by A. Vorotnikov, *Pravda*, 3 January 1991; FBIS-SOV-91-003, 4 January 1991, p. 27.

11. Anatoliy Fyodorovich D'yakov, Deputy Minister of Energy and Electrification, interview with Mark Borozin, *Zelyonniy mir* 3–4 (1991): 7.

12. V. A. Dzhangirov, USSR Ministry of Energy, "The New USSR Energy Program to the Year 2010," *Energetik* 4 (April 1991): 2–6, esp. 3.

13. Valentin Rasputin, speech to USSR Writers' Union plenum, *Literaturnaya gazeta* 4, 25 January 1989; p. 5, JPRS-UPA-89-025, pp. 24–30, esp. p. 25.

14. Central Intelligence Agency (CIA), Directorate of Intelligence, *Soviet Energy Data Resource Handbook* (Washington, DC: U.S. Government Printing Office, May 1990), pp. 19, 23, 27.

15. CIA, Directorate of Intelligence, *Handbook of Economic Statistics 1988*, (Washington, DC: U.S. Government Printing Office, 1988), p. 74.

16. "On the Brink," *The Economist*, 16 March 1991, pp. 72–73.

17. CIA, *Soviet Energy Data Resource Handbook*, pp. 19 and 23.

18. *Narkhoz 1989*, p. 377; D'yakov interview.

19. Stuart Auerbach, "Investments in U.S.S.R. Losing Fizz," *Washington Post*, 7 July 1991, pp. H1, H5.

20. Francis X. Clines, "Soviet-Chevron Oil Venture Mired in Fears of Capitalist Exploitation," *New York Times*, 16 August 1991, pp. A1, A2.

21. Quentin Peel, "Sticky Time for a Valuable Resource," *Financial Times*, 26 October 1990, p. 18.

22. "Powerless," *The Economist*.

23. Valentin Katasonov, "Tyumenskiy apokalipsis," pt. 1, *Zelyonniy mir* 4 (1990): 6.

24. "Powerless," *The Economist.*
25. " 'Serious' Pipeline Accidents Result in Gas Leak, Oil Spill," Mikhail Prutkin, TASS news service, 16 July 1990; *JPRS-TEN-90-008,* 31 July 1990, p. 63.
26. Katasonov, "Tyumenskiy apokalipsis."
27. *Doklad,* Table 18, p. 99.
28. "Powerless," *The Economist.*
29. Ibid.
30. Pyotr Petrovich Borodavkin, Moscow Oil and Gas Institute, "Gaso-provody tayat syurprizy," interviewed by B. Konovalov, *Izvestiya,* 25 January 1990, p. 2.
31. John P. Remensnyder, M.D., "Pipeline Disaster: Treating Soviet Burn Victims," *Harvard Medical Journal* (Summer 1990): 33–36.
32. M. Chemaltindov, "Pro byelovo bychka," *MedGaz,* 3 June 1990, p. 3.
33. *Doklad,* Table 2, p. 13; Nikolai I. Ryzhkov, USSR Prime Minister, closing report to Congress of People's Deputies, 9 June 1989, *Pravda,* 10 June 1989, p. 3; *FBIS-SOV-89-112,* 13 June 1989, pp. 39–42, esp. p. 41.
34. L. G. Mel'nik, N. S. Vladimirova et al., "Ekologicheskaya tsena energii," *Energiya: Ekonomika. Tekhnika. Ekologiya* 3 (March 1991): 47–52.
35. Ibid., Table 3, p. 50.
36. Thornton, "Soviet Electric Power," p. 521.
37. Mel'nik, Vladimirova et al., "Ekologicheskaya tsena energii," Table 3, p. 50.
38. D'yakov interview.
39. Rasputin speech, p. 26.
40. Ibid.
41. Ibid., p. 25.
42. Ibid., p. 26.
43. Georgiy Alekseyevich Kopchinskiy, "We Do Not Want to Live Worse than Today?!" interview with G. Lomanov, *Pravitel'stvennyy vestnik* 37 (September 1990): 6–7; *JPRS-UEA-90-040,* 30 November 1990, pp. 84–88.
44. Ibid.
45. Yevgeniy Ivanovich Petrayev, "The Atomic Energy Industry: Arguments and Facts," Radio Moscow Domestic Service, 28 November 1990; *JPRS-TEN-90-017,* 6 December 1990, pp. 61–63.
46. Albina Tretyakova, "Fuel and Energy in the U.S. and USSR." Paper for conference held at Airlie House, Virginia, sponsored by the American Enterprise Institute for Public Policy Research, 19–22 April 1990, Table 2, p. 8.
47. Ibid.
48. Dzhangirov, "The New USSR Energy Program," p. 39.
49. Nikolai Vorontsov, quoted in Michael Lohmeyer, " 'Monocultures Are Dangerous Everywhere'; Soviet Minister Advocates Variety," *Die Presse,* 21 May 1990, p. 13; *JPRS-TEN-90-003,* 30 May 1990, p. 42.
50. Sergei Stankevich, First Deputy Chairman, Moscow City Soviet, "What

Should Be Done," interview (on subject of urban destitution) with N. Asadulloyev et al., *Literaturnaya Gazeta* 23, 12 June 1991, p. 7; *JPRS-UPA-91-032*, 2 July 1991, p. 54.

51. Yu. N. Kogan, "Electrification of the USSR. Perspectives and Features," *Energetik* 9 (September 1989): 3–5; *JPRS-UEA-89-038*, 20 November 1989, pp. 48–52.

52. Valentin Semyonovich Sheplev, "The Tragedy of Wastefulness—A Siberian Scientist Reflects on Power-Engineering Strategy," interview with Vladimir Denisov, *Sovetskaya Rossiya,* 12 September 1989, p. 2; *JPRS-UEA-89-036*, 3 November 1989, pp. 60–63.

53. Ibid.

54. Ibid.

55. Kogan, "Electrification of the USSR," p. 49.

56. A. Pavlov, "Nikopol Is Against the AES," *Pravda Ukrainy,* 7 June 1990, p. 1; *JPRS-TEN-90-009*, 2 August 1990, pp. 34–35.

57. L. Ilchenko, "Vremya" television broadcast, 19 July 1990; *JPRS-TEN-90-009*, 2 August 1990, p. 35.

58. Pavlov, "Nikopol Is Against the AES," p. 35.

59. Ibid.

60. Radio Moscow Domestic Service, 3 August 1990; *FBIS-SOV-90-151*, 6 August 1990.

61. Ze'ev Wolfson, "Some Environmental and Social Aspects of Nuclear Power Development in the USSR," Research Paper 63, The Marjorie Mayrock Center for Soviet and East European Research, Hebrew University of Jerusalem, March 1987, pp. 7–8.

62. A. Mazalov, chief, Main Administration for Industry, interview with A. Rogozhin, "The State Inspection for Nuclear Energy in Industry Reports," *Izvestiya,* 30 July 1990; *FBIS-SOV-90-151*, 6 August 1990, pp. 59–60.

63. Tanjug, citing INTERFAX, 9 December 1990; *FBIS-SOV-90-237*, 10 December 1990, p. 73.

64. "Powerless," *The Economist,* p. 68.

65. *Narkhoz 1989,* p. 377; Goskomstat SSSR, *Ekonomika SSSR v 1990 godu* (Moscow: Goskomstat Informtsentr, 1991), p. 25.

66. "Oil Output Continues to Decline," *RFE/RL USSR This Week,* 30 June 1991.

67. Anatoliy Pokrovskiy, "Nuclear Winter," *Pravda,* 19 July 1990, p. 2; *FBIS-SOV-90-140*, 20 July 1990, pp. 69–70.

68. *Narkhoz 1989,* p. 375.

69. Mazalov interview.

70. Pokrovskiy, "Nuclear Winter," p. 70.

71. Letter of appeal of collectives of enterprises of nuclear power and industry, "Radiophobia Is Fear of the Unknown," *Pravitel'stvennyy vestnik* 37 (September 1990): 6–7; *JPRS-UEA-90-040*, 30 November 1990, pp. 88–89.

72. Kopchinskiy, "We Do Not Want to Live Worse than Today?!" p. 85.

73. Ibid.

74. Cited in Iurii Shcherbak, *Chernobyl: A Documentary Story*, trans. Ian Press (London: Macmillan, 1989), p. 67.
75. Reuter, "Wider Chernobyl Evacuation Ordered," *Washington Post*, 24 April 1990, p. A21.
76. Veronika Romanenkova, TASS (in English), 16 April 1991; *JPRS-TEN-91-009*, 31 May 1991, p. 58.
77. Vladimir Yavorivskiy, interview, *Der Morgen*, 26 April 1991, summarized by German News Agency (ADN), Berlin, 25 April 1991; *JPRS-TEN-91-009*, 31 May 1991, pp. 58–59.
78. A. Illesh, "On the Outside and the Inside of the Sarcophagus—Five Years After the Chernobyl Catastrophe," *Izvestiya*, 26 April 1991, p. 8; *JPRS-TEN-91-013*, 5 July 1991, pp. 78–82, esp. p. 81.
79. Elizabeth Shogren, "4 Years Later, Chernobyl's Ills Widen," *Washington Post*, 27 April 1990, pp. A1, A36.
80. David R. Marples, "Revelations of a Chernobyl Insider," *Bulletin of the Atomic Scientists* (December 1990): 16–21.
81. Yuriy Risovannyy, in ibid., p. 21.
82. Charles Oulton, "USSR—Dying Scientist Says Chernobyl Killed 7,000," *Independent on Sunday*, 14 April 1991.
83. Author's calculations.
84. Victor Gubanov, chairman, State Commission for Emergencies, USSR Council of Ministers, Radio Moscow World Service (in English), 18 April 1991; *JPRS-TEN-91-009*, 31 May 1991, pp. 57–58.
85. Yuriy Koryakin, chief economist, Research and Development Institute of Power Engineering, "200 milliardov," *Energiya: Ekonomika. Tekhnika. Ekologiya* 8 (August 1990): 3–6, also cited in Richard L. Hudson, "Cost of Chernobyl Nuclear Disaster Soars in New Study," *Wall Street Journal*, 29 March 1990, p. A8.
86. Ibid.
87. Yuriy P. Spizhenko, minister of health, Ukrainian SSSR, speech as reported in *Robitnycha hazeta*, 20 February 1990, cited in David Marples, "USSR—One Million Ukrainians Suffering from Chernobyl," *Radio Liberty Reports*, 6 March 1990.
88. Ibid.
89. Yu. P. Spizhenko, "There Is No Prescription for Lies," interview with S. Prokopchuk, *Trud*, 25 April 1991, pp. 1–2; *JPRS-TEN-91-013*, 5 July 1991, pp. 82–85, esp. p. 83.
90. Felicity Barringer, "Chernobyl, Five Years Later the Danger Persists," *New York Times Magazine*, 14 April 1991, pp. 28ff., 32.
91. Ibid., pp. 30–31.
92. Ibid., p. 39.
93. Thomas W. Lippman, "Chernobyl Contamination Still Spreading," *Washington Post*, 5 July 1991, p. A8.
94. Knight Ridder News Service, "Stress May Have Boosted Cancer Rates Near Damaged Nuclear Plant, Study Shows," *Washington Post*, 27 May 1991, p. A24.

95. Steve Wing, University of North Carolina, quoted in Thomas W. Lippman, "Risk Found in Low Levels of Radiation," *Washington Post,* 20 March 1991, p. A3.

96. Professor Yelena Burlakova, chairman, USSR Academy of Sciences, Scientific Society on Radiobiology, cited by Andrei Surzhanskiy, TASS (in English), 27 April 1990; *FBIS-SOV-90-086,* 3 May 1990, p. 60.

97. Michael Z. Wise, "U.N. Report Blames Stress, Not Radiation, for Chernobyl Illnesses," *Washington Post,* 22 May 1991, p. A24.

98. Ibid.

99. O. M. Kalechits and V. A. Alkhimovich, "Tuberkulez i Chernobylskaya tragediya: sostoyaniye i prognoz," *Problemy tuberkuleza* 11 (November 1990): 14–16.

100. Francis X. Clines, "A New Arena for Nationalism: Chernobyl," *New York Times,* 30 December 1990, pp. 1, 8.

101. Professors I. G. Zhakov, Ye. P. Ivanov, A. K. Ustinovich et al., "Chernobyl and Health," letter to the editor, *Sovetskaya Belorussiya,* 6 May 1990, p. 2; *JPRS-ULS-90-019,* 13 November 1990, pp. 41–44, esp. p. 42.

102. "Belorussian Cancer Cases Increase Following Chernobyl," Vilnius Radio, in Belorussian, 19 June 1991; *JPRS-TEN-91-014,* 9 July 1991, p. 58.

103. S. Ulashchik, "Health Care of Belorussian Population in Connection with Accident at Chernobyl Nuclear Power Plant," *Zdravookhraneniye Belorussiy* 6 (June 1990): 3–8; *JPRS-ULS-90-020,* 10 December 1990, pp. 39–44, esp. p. 43.

104. Yukiko Shimizu, DMSc, William J. Schull, Ph.D., and Hiroo Kato, M.D., "Cancer Risk Among Atomic Bomb Survivors; The RERF Life Span Study," *Journal of the American Medical Association* 264, no. 5, 1 August 1990, p. 601.

105. William Boly, "Life in the Wasteland, Chernobyl Five Years After," *In Health* (May–June 1991): 60–70, esp. p. 70.

106. Vladimir Lupandin, speech at the Institute of Soviet-American Relations, Washington, D.C., 15 May 1991.

107. Ibid.

108. Conversation with authors.

109. Yuriy Izrael, "The Past and the Prognosis for the Future," *Pravda,* 20 March 1989, p. 4; *FBIS-SOV-89-055,* 23 March 1989, pp. 65–70.

110. Ibid., p. 70.

111. Yuriy Izrael, speech to USSR Supreme Soviet, 25 April 1990, *SWB* "Special Supplement, 2. Debate on Chernobyl," 5 May 1990, pp. SU/0756 C2/1–3.

112. E. Mokhorov, "Top Secret: Who Created the Secrecy Around the Bryansk Tragedy?" *Rabochaya tribuna,* 27 February 1990, p. 4; *JPRS-UEA-90-009,* 14 March 1990, p. 54.

113. Ibid.

114. Unattributed, "Radiation in the Class Register," *Rabochaya tribuna,* 18 January 1990, p. 4; *JPRS-ULS-90-008,* 27 June 1990, p. 65.

115. Ye. Shulzheno, "You Ask, We Answer: The Third Main Directorate

Reveals Secrets," *Gudok,* 29 December 1989, p. 4; *JPRS-ULS-90-006,* 18 June 1990, p. 39.

116. A. Yaroshinskaya, "The Truth Stamped Secret," *Komsomol'skaya pravda,* 26 April 1991; *CDSP* 43, no. 17, 1991, pp. 13–14.

117. "Not Just a Nuclear Explosion," *The Economist,* 27 April 1991, pp. 19–21.

118. Anton A. Romanovskiy, quoted in S. Pastukhov, "Nightingale Hell," *Pravda,* 24 April 1990, pp. 1, 3; *JPRS-TEN-90-003,* 30 May 1990, pp. 58–59.

119. O. Yegorova, "Dyelo o Chernobyl'skikh vrachakh," *Komsomol'skaya pravda,* 15 September 1990, p. 2.

120. Vladimir Shilov, "Ya, Vladimir Shilov, Chernobylets," *Komsomol'-skaya pravda,* 2 February 1990, p. 1.

121. Ibid.

122. A. Gotovchits, "Chernobyl Football," *Sovetskaya Belorussiya,* 27 July 1990, p. 1; *FBIS-SOV-90-169,* 30 August 1990, p. 66.

123. David Remnick, "Communists in the Red, Paper Says," *Washington Post,* 9 August 1991, pp. A23, A27.

124. D. Pavlov, "Are We Looking in the Right Place," letter to the editor, *Sovetskaya Belorussiya,* 12 June 1990, p. 1; *JPRS-UPA-90-046,* 31 July 1990.

125. TASS (in English), 28 August 1990; *FBIS-SOV-90-168,* 29 August 1990, p. 80.

126. Aleksei Petrunya, TASS (in English), 11 July 1990; *FBIS-SOV-90-134,* 12 July 1990, pp. 67–68.

127. "Wages Increased in Radioactive Ukrainian Areas," Radio Kiev, International Service (in English), 14 August 1990; *FBIS-SOV-90-159,* 16 August 1990, p. 82.

128. Spizhenko interview, p. 85.

129. V. Varvarskiy and S. Trofimov, "Kto podmetyot nebo nad gorodom?" *Zelyonniy mir* 5–6 (1991): 4.

130. Ibid.

131. Author's free translation.

132. Ibid.

133. Aleksandr I. Solzhenitsyn, *The First Circle,* Thomas P. Whitney, trans. (New York: Harper & Row, 1968).

134. Rasputin, speech, p. 25.

8
Crippled Giant

1. David Remnick, "Soviet Army Salutes Itself on Anniversary of War's End," *Washington Post,* 10 May 1990, pp. A41, A42.

2. Vassily Selyunin, Soviet economist, cited by Michael Dobbs, "Gorbachev Aides Target Military-Industrial Complex," *Washington Post,* 29 July 1991, pp. A1, A17.

3. Senator Charles McC. Mathias, "Habitual Hatred—Unsound Policy," *Foreign Affairs*, 61, no. 5 (1983): 1017–30; p. 1022: "We should not fear the giant we face so much as the deformities which cripple all but his sword-bearing arm."

4. Robert G. Kaiser, *Why Gorbachev Happened: His Triumphs and His Failures* (New York: Simon & Schuster, 1991), pp. 166–67.

5. Ibid., p. 435.

6. Valentin Pavlov, USSR minister of finance, speech to USSR Supreme Soviet, Radio Moscow, Domestic Service, 25 September 1989; *FBIS-SOV-89-185*, 26 September 1989, p. 50.

7. Rick Atkinson and Gary Lee, "Soviet Army Coming Apart at the Seams," *Washington Post*, 18 November 1990, pp. A1, A28–29.

8. Ibid.

9. Kaiser, *Why Gorbachev Happened*, pp. 115–16; Hedrick Smith, *The New Russians* (New York: Random House, 1990), p. 523.

10. Selyunin, cited by Dobbs, "Gorbachev Aides Target Military-Industrial Complex."

11. *Le Figaro*, 23 December 1990, cited in "And You Can Quote Me On That . . . ," *Arms Control Today* 21, no. 1 (January–February 1991): 28.

12. Cited in "And You Can Quote Me On That . . . ," *Arms Control Today* 21, no. 2 (March 1991): p. 30.

13. George Lardner, Jr., "Draft Dodging Rises Dramatically in Soviet Union," *Washington Post*, 3 March 1991, p. A23.

14. Rick Atkinson and Gary Lee, "The Struggle to Fill the Ranks," *Washington Post*, 19 November 1990, p. A28.

15. Marshal Dmitri Yazov, Radio Moscow, Domestic Service, 6 March 1991; *FBIS-SOV-91-045*, 7 March 1991, pp. 57–58.

16. Colonel General G. Krivosheyev, "Military Expenditure: What Is It Really?" *Krasnaya zvezda*, 18 April 1991, p. 4; *FBIS-SOV-91-080*, 25 April 1991, p. 46.

17. Colonel V. Zolotov, director, Central Military-Medical Commission, USSR Ministry of Defense, "Bud' zdorov, soldat," interview with Yevgeniy Tipikin, *Nedelya* 20, 13–19 May 1991, p. 6.

18. Anatoly Verbin, "Yazov Says Soviet Army Falling Apart through Lack of Conscripts," Reuter News Service, 27 June 1991, citing *Sovetskaya Rossiya*.

19. Oleg Moskovskiy, "Moiseyev Welcomes McDonalds to Garrisons," TASS (Russian), 24 June 1991; *FBIS-SOV-91-122*, 25 June 1991, p. 59.

20. "Powell in Moscow for 7-Day Tour," *Washington Post*, 23 July 1991, p. A17.

21. Eleanor Randolph, "Powell: Soviet Military 'Oversized,' " *Washington Post*, 25 July 1991, p. A35.

22. David Remnick, "Hard-Liners Appeal to Military to Prevent Soviet 'Humiliation,' " *Washington Post*, 24 July 1991, p. A23.

23. Michael Dobbs, "Crowds in Capital Protest Power Seizure; Yeltsin Defiant," *Washington Post*, 20 August 1991, pp. A17, A20.

24. Lieutenant General I. Matveyev, quoted in Ya. Zasurskiy, "Ryadovoy Lomonosov, dva shaga vperyod!" *Komsomol'skaya pravda*, 10 July 1991, p. 1.
25. G. A. Yagodin, excerpts of speech to Nineteenth All-Union CPSU Conference, Radio Moscow, 1 July 1988; *FBIS-SOV-88-128*, 5 July 1988, p. 83.
26. Major General V. Khrobostov and Major General V. Chevyrev, "Boleviye tochki i programma 'Zdorov'ye,' " *Tyl vooruzhonnykh sil* 9 (September 1990): 50–53, esp. p. 50; also, Zolotov interview.
27. Major General E. A. Nechayev, "Osnovnyye napravleniya deyatel'nosti voyenno-meditsinskoy sluzhby v 1991 godu," *Voyenno-meditsinskiy zhurnal* 1 (January 1991): 4–15, esp. p. 7.
28. RFE/RL, *Daily Report*, 8 September 1989.
29. Khrobostov and Chevyrev, "Boleviye tochki i programma 'Zdorov'ye,' " p. 50.
30. Colonel Yu. Deryugin, ". . . A problemy otstayutsya," interview with Z. Filatova, *Argumenty i fakty* 35, 25 August–2 September 1988, p. 1.
31. Karim Bakhiryev, People's Deputy, Uzbek SSR, "Load 200: Why Are Soldiers Not at War Dying?" *Komsomol'skaya pravda*, 1 August 1990, p. 1; *JPRS-UMA-90-023*, 15 October 1990, pp. 43–45.
32. Ibid., p. 44.
33. Goskomstat SSSR, *Narkhoz 1989*, p. 30.
34. Ibid., p. 188.
35. RFE/RL, *Daily Report*, 27 November 1987, citing *Sovetskiy patriot*, 15 November 1987.
36. Esther B. Fein, "Reactors to Cartons: Soviets Make a Factory Less Military," *New York Times*, 27 July 1991, pp. 1, 5.
37. Colonel O. Belkov, "Not All Questions Are Clear," *Krasnaya zvezda*, 15 September 1988, p. 1.
38. V. Dan'shin, "Soldat lechitsya, sluzhba idyot? . . . ," *Krasnaya zvezda*, 29 October 1989, p. 2.
39. S. Brish, "Sound the Alarm," *Voyenniye znaniya*, 2 (February 1989): 9–10; *JPRS-UMA-89-014*, 3 June 1989, p. 48.
40. Conversation with author.
41. Aleksei Dubrovskiy, Radio Moscow, April 1989, cited in *Radio Liberty Report*.
42. Major General V. Perepelin, chief epidemiologist, USSR Ministry of Defense, "Etogo nam tol'ko ne khvatalo," *Krasnaya zvezda*, 13 September 1990, p. 4.
43. Ibid.
44. V. V. Strizhak and V. A. Tatarin, "Immunologicheskaya effektivnost' revaktsinatsii protiv difteriy," *Voyenno-meditsinskiy zhurnal* 11 (November 1990): 44.
45. John Barron, *MiG Pilot, The Final Escape of Lt. Belenko* (New York: Avon, 1981), esp. pp. 82–83, 97–98.
46. N. P. Bychikhin, "Some Social and Hygiene Features of Alcohol Abuse

among Sailors," *Zdravookhraneniya Rossiskoy Federatsiy* 7 (July 1986): 29–33.

47. Boris Kalachev, "Narkomany v forme," *Sobytiya i vremya* 2 (January 1990): 24.
48. Boris Kalachev, "There's No Place for This in the Ranks," *Literaturnaya gazeta,* 26 October 1988, p. 12; *CDSP* 41, no. 5, 1 March 1989, p. 17.
49. Bakhiryev, "Load 200," p. 43.
50. Lieutenant General A. Muranov, director, Administration of Military Tribunals, interviewed by V. Litovkin, "Hazing on Trial," *Izvestiya,* 9 August 1990, p. 6; *CDSP* 42, no. 32, 12 September 1990, 24.
51. For official use, "Rekomendatsii komandiram, politrabotnikam, partiynym i komsomol'skim aktivistam po borbe s glumleniyami i izdevatel'stvami na flote" (Politupravleniye TOF, 1987), 39 pages, made available to authors by Soviet acquaintance.
52. Ibid.
53. Rick Atkinson and Gary Lee, "Brutality Stalks Soviet Conscripts," *Washington Post,* 19 November 1990, pp. A1, A28.
54. N. Panyukov, "O chem umolchal begliy soldat," *Rabochaya tribuna,* 17 October 1990.
55. Smith, *The New Russians,* p. 374.
56. Alexander Kharlamov, "Killed in Peacetime," *Kuranty* 67 (1991), reported by *Ian Press Release,* Moscow, 24 April 1991; *FBIS-SOV-91-045,* 25 April 1991, p. 46.
57. Gennadiy Zhavoronkov, "Save and Protect," *Moscow News* 30 (1990): 11.
58. Ibid.
59. Esther B. Fein, "Soviet Military's High Death Rate Draws Scrutiny," *New York Times,* 10 February 1991, p. A12.
60. Conversation with author, Mons, Belgium, 1987.
61. "V interesakh zdorov'ya voinov," *Krasnaya zvezda,* 7 January 1984, p. 1.
62. Major General V. Chevyrev, chief hygienist, USSR Ministry of Defense, "Zadachi sanitarnogo nadzora," *Tyl i snabzheniye Sovetskogo vooruzhennogo sila* 5 (May 1984): 44.
63. Goskomstat SSSR, *Zdravookhraneniye v SSSR, statisticheskiy sbornik* (Moscow: Finansy i statistika, 1989), Table 2.1, p. 8.
64. "Itogi raboty meditsinskoy sluzhby vooruzhennykh sil v 1988 godu i zadachi na noviy uchebniy god," *Voyenno-meditsinskiy zhurnal* 1 (January 1989): 5.
65. Colonel General F. Komarov, "If the Hippocratic Oath Is Broken," interview with Ye. Agapova, *Krasnaya zvezda,* 4 February 1988, p. 1; *FBIS-SOV-88-029,* 12 February 1988, pp. 61–62.
66. *Voyenno-meditsinskiy zhurnal* 8 (August 1983): 31; 1 (January 1983): 16; 8 (August 1984): 56.
67. Ibid. 5 (May 1983): 57; 6 (June 1984): 36; 8 (August 1983): 31; 11 (November 1982): 35.

68. Nechayev, "Osnovnyye napravleniya deyatel'nosti . . . ," p. 12.

69. Major General G. I. Ramodin, director, Military Medical Service, USSR Strategic Rocket Forces, "Za dal'neysheye povysheniye effektivnosti i kachestva meditsinskogo obespecheniya voysk," *Voyenno-meditsinskiy zhurnal* 11 (November 1988): 11; Colonel I. K. Adnonin, head, Cadre Department, Central Military Medical Administration, "Rabota s voyenno-meditsinskimi kadrami—demokratizatsiyu i glasnost'," interview with Colonel L. L. Galin, *Voyenno-meditsinskiy zhurnal* 1 (January 1989): 12.

70. Adnonin, "Rabota s voyenno-meditsinskimi kadrami," p. 10.

71. Nechayev, "Osnovnyye napravleniya deyatel'nosti . . . ," p. 7.

72. Ibid., p. 8.

73. Major General V. Tyurin, "Vnedryat' i ratsional'no ispol'zovat' meditsinskiye sredstva," *Tyl i snabzheniya Sovetskikh vooruzhennykh sil* 1 (January 1988): 6.

74. Captain V. Kondriyanenko, "Medicine and 'Dedovshchina,' " *Krasnaya zvezda,* 16 December 1989, p. 2.

75. Colonel A. Polyakov, "Special Medical Detachment, or Who Helps in an Emergency?" *Krasnaya zvezda,* 20 June 1991, p. 1; *JPRS UMA-91-019,* 17 July 1991, pp. 23–24.

76. A. A. Baranov, deputy minister of health USSR, "From the Peace Fund's Money," *MedGaz,* 25 May 1988, p. 1.

77. Nechayev, "Osnovnyye napravleniya deyatel'nosti . . . ," p. 10.

78. Major General V. Zheglov, chief, Fleet Medical Service, "Flotskaya meditsina poka ne bessil'na," interview with Captain V. Maryukha, *Krasnaya zvezda,* 16 April 1991, p. 4.

79. V. M. Arkhipov, "Ekonomika armii—ispytaniye reformoy," *Ekonomika i zhizn'* 5 (January 1991): 2–3.

80. Nechayev, "Osnovnyye napravleniya . . . ," p. 8.

81. Barron, *MiG Pilot,* p. 97.

82. Lieutenant Colonel Yu. A. Sorokin, "Armiya i ekologiya," interview with A. Plotnikov, *Krasnaya zvezda,* 8 January 1989, p. 2.

83. General V. M. Arkhipov, "The Soldier's Diet," interview with Colonel L. Nechayuk, *Krasnaya zvezda,* 14 April 1989, p. 2; *JPRS-UMA-89-015,* 15 June 1989, p. 48.

84. Anne Garrels, Moscow correspondent, ABC Television and National Public Radio, conversation with author, Washington, D.C., 25 July 1991.

85. Zheglov interview.

86. "The Defense Ministry Loses Its Privileges," *Moscow News* 4 (1991): 15.

87. Yu. M. Sinitsyn, deputy minister, USSR Ministry of Defense Industry, "*Pravda* Roundtable: Let's Feed Our Children," *Pravda,* 3 June 1991, p. 3; *JPRS-UPA-91-032,* 2 July 1991, pp. 48–52, esp. p. 50.

88. Michael G. Renner, "War on Nature," *WorldWatch* 4, no. 3 (May–June 1991): 18–25, 21.

89. Ibid., p. 19.

90. Keith Schneider, "Military Has New Strategic Goal in Cleanup of Toxic Waste," *New York Times,* 5 August 1991, pp. A1, D3.

91. "The Lords of Misrule," *The Economist,* 6 April 1991, pp. 17–20.

92. Lieutenant Colonel Yu. A. Sorokin, director, Environmental Protection Inspection Service, USSR Ministry of Defense, "View at the Problem," under rubric "The Inertia of the Old Approach," interview with Lieutenant Colonel O. Sedykh, *Agitator Armii i Flota* 21 (November 1988): 21.

93. Lieutenant Colonel Yu. A. Sorokin, "Armiya i ekologiya," interview with Lieutenant Colonel A. Plotnikov, *Krasnaya zvezda,* 8 January 1989, p. 2.

94. V. Onishchenko, "Secrets Are Revealed," *Trud,* 17 October 1990, p. 1; *JPRS-TEN-90-017,* 6 December 1990, p. 101.

95. Oleg Stefashin, "Collecting Space 'Debris,' " *Izvestiya,* 25 September 1990, p. 2; *JPRS-TEN-90-014,* 2 November 1990, p. 54. Stefashin, "Suit Against Glavkosmos," *Izvestiya,* 9 December 1990, p. 2; *JPRS-TEN-91-001,* 4 January 1991, pp. 92–93.

96. Stefashin, "Suit Against Glavkosmos," p. 93.

97. N. Tereshko, "A more khranit svoyu tainu," *Zelyonniy mir* 5 (1990): 1, 6. Professors A. Alimov and V. Khlebovich, "Shto zhe proizoshlo na Belom More?" *Pravda,* 16 August 1990, p. 6. Larisa Mironova, "There Are No Guilty Parties, So the Matter Is Ended?" *Tekhnika-Molodezhi* 12 (December 1990): 2–5. "Prestupleniya bez nakazanii," *Volna* (Arkhangel'sk *oblast*), 3 October 1991, pp. 1, 5, citing report by People's Deputy Andrei Zolotkov to Greenpeace Nuclear Free Seas Seminar, September 23–24, Moscow.

98. Mironova, "There Are No Guilty Parties," p. 5.

99. Aleksei Yablokov, remarks, Institute of Soviet-American Relations, Washington, D.C., 21 June 1991.

100. IAN news service, "Atomnaya verf' naznachayet srok," *Rabochaya tribuna,* 17 October 1990.

101. See Zhores A. Medvedev, *Nuclear Disaster in the Urals* (New York: W. W. Norton, 1979).

102. Thomas B. Cochran and Robert Standish Norris, "Soviet Nuclear Warhead Production," *Nuclear Weapons Databook, Working Papers,* 3d rev. (Washington, D.C.: Natural Resources Defense Council, 14 February 1991), esp. pp. 21–26.

103. Ibid.

104. A. Penyagin, Yu. Shcherbak and A. Yablokov, "Kyshymskuyu tragediyu rano sdavat' v arkhiv," *Zelyonniy mir* 10 (1990): 2.

105. Aleksei Yablokov, conversation with author, Moscow, October, 1991.

106. Aleksandr Nikolaievich Penyagin, deputy from Chelyabinsk, USSR Supreme Soviet, "Committee Views Nuclear Pollution," interviewed by Andrei Nikiforov, Radio Moscow, Domestic Service, 5 October 1990; *FBIS-SOV-90-195,* 9 October 1990, pp. 35–36.

107. Cochran and Norris, "Soviet Nuclear Warhead Production," p. 20.

108. Boris Yeltsin, 6 June 1991, broadcast by Leonid Varebus, Radio Rossii Network; *FBIS-SOV-91-110*, 7 June 1991, p. 70.

109. Ibid.

110. Pyotr Ivanovich Somin, Moscow Radio, Domestic Service, "People's Deputy on Chelyabinsk Radioactive Contamination Threat," 10 December 1990; *JPRS-TEN-91-001*, 4 January 1991, pp. 89–90.

111. Ibid., p. 90.

112. Colonel L. Nechayuk, "V gorode, u kotorogo nyet imeni," *Krasnaya zvezda*, 19 October 1990.

113. Ibid.

114. Aleksandr Penyagin, "Supreme Soviet Ecology Committee Studying Chelyabinsk Nuclear Contamination," interview with Andrei Nikiforov, Moscow Radio, Domestic Service, 5 October 1990; *JPRS-TEN-90-014*, 2 November 1990, p. 48.

115. Cochran and Norris, "Soviet Nuclear Warhead Production," p. 31.

116. V. Mirolevich, "Since the Beryllium Attack," *Izvestiya*, 4 November 1990, p. 2; *CDSP* 42, no. 44 (1990): 12, 32. P. Shchuplov, "We Don't Want to Breathe Smog. Emergency Situation," *Pravda*, 11 October 1990, p. 8; *JPRS-TEN-90-014*, 2 November 1990, p. 49.

117. Mirolevich, "Since the Beryllium Attack," p. 12.

118. Gennadiy Medvedev, "A Silent Chernobyl, or the Confession of a Man from Room Six," *Kazakhstanskya pravda*, 22 September 1990, p. 2; *JPRS-TEN-90-014*, 2 November 1990, pp. 49–64.

119. Ibid., p. 50.

120. Ibid.

121. Ibid., p. 53.

122. Ibid., pp. 53–54.

123. A. Akava, "Polezniye vstrechi," *Kazakhstanskaya pravda*, 22 November 1990.

124. Gennadiy Yanayev, acting president, USSR, "Excerpts from the New Leader's Remarks," *New York Times*, 20 August 1991, p. A12.

9
Gathering Ills

1. Cited in V[ladimir] Umnov, "A. Kashpirovskiy: Ya znayu, kak upravlyat' tolpoy," *Komsomol'skaya pravda*, 22 November 1990, p. 4, from *Argumenty i fakty*, 49 (1989).

2. O. Leonidova, "Kashpiroskiy protiv SPIDa?" *MedGaz* 14 October 1990, p. 4.

3. Umnov, "A. Kashpirovskiy."

4. TASS news service, citing report in *Tsinya*, published as "Persony non grata," *Volgogradskaya pravda*, 17 October 1990, p. 1, and *Sovetskaya Rossiya*, same headline and date.

5. Umnov, "A. Kashpirovskiy."

6. Keith Bush, "The Glass that Cheers—and Cures?" RL/RFE *Daily Report,* 26 July 1991, citing *Komsomol'skaya Pravda,* 25 July 1991; Kooperativ Volgogradskiy Bishofit, ". . . Eto Volgogradskiy Bishofit," full-page advertisement, *Zhivoye slovo,* Volgograd (September 1990): 8.

7. Julian Huxley, *A Scientist Among the Soviets* (London, Chatto & Windus, 1932), p. 73.

8. Goskomstat SSSR, "Zabolevaemost' naseleniya v nekotorikh gorodakh s povyshennym zagryazneniyem okhruzhayushchey sredy," *Statistical Press Bulletin* 2 (1990).

9. Ibid.

10. Dr. Haris Yakubov, "The Health of the Population and the State of the Environment, Certain Aspects of the Problem in Moscow." 1990 paper made available to authors; Academician Vyacheslav Tabolin, "Yest" li u nashikh detyey shans vyzhit'?" *Soverschenno sekretno* 9 (1991): 31.

11. N. Leontyeva, "To Breathe or Not to Breathe: Ecology and Economics," *Leninskoye znamya,* 29 October 1988, p. 3; *JPRS-UPA-89-013,* 15 February 1989, pp. 83–86.

12. N. Vavilova, chief pediatrician, Magnitogorsk, "Ob etom nye prinyato bylo govorit' " *Magnitogorskiy rabochiy,* 28 March 1990.

13. Goskomstat SSR, *Demograficheskiy yezhegodnik SSSR. 1990* (Moscow: Finansy i statistika, 1990), p. 491.

14. T. Sharaya, " 'Promyshlenniye deti'," *Sem'ya* 43, 23–29 October 1989, p. 7.

15. Professor Boris B. Shugayev, "Vymirayem," *Zolotoye koltso,* 26 April 1991, p. 5.

16. V. Krutko, "Zdorov'ye naroda—bogatstvo strany?" interview with B. Polukhin, *NTR Tribuna* 5–6 (1990): 7.

17. I[gor] I. Denisov, USSR minister of health, "Strategiya i taktika bor'by s infektsiyami," *MedGaz,* 5 April 1991, p. 8.

18. Ibid.

19. Ibid.

20. Robert Berkow, M.D., ed., "Recommended Schedule for Active Immunization of Normal Infants and Children," *Merck Manual of Diagnosis and Therapy, 15th Edition,* (Rahway, NJ: Merck & Co., 1987), Table 182-2, p. 1825.

21. Denisov, "Strategiya i taktika bor'by s infektsiyami"; I. Denisov, " 'Akhillesova pyata' zdravookhraneniya," *Vrach* 6 (1991): 39.

22. V[ladimir] Umnov, "Nu podumaesh'—ukol . . . ," *Komsomol'skaya pravda,* 1988.

23. V[ladimir] Umnov, "Gazetnaya bolezn', ili kak zhurnalisty raznosili po strane infektsiyu," *Komsomol'skaya pravda,* 24 October 1990.

24. Conversations with author, Moscow, January 1990.

25. Conversation with author, Moscow, 21 October 1990.

26. S. Chugayev, "Trezvo o trezvosti," *Izvestiya,* 30 October 1989, p. 1.

27. Ibid.; "Russia's Anti-Drink Campaign: Veni, vidi, vodka," *The Economist,* 23 December 1989, pp. 50–54, esp. p. 53; see also Vladimir G. Treml,

Alcohol in the USSR: A Statistical Study (Durham, NC: Duke University Press, 1982).

28. "Russia's Anti-Drink Campaign," esp. pp. 51, 52.

29. K. Trubilin, cited in Chugayev, "Trezvo o trezvosti."

30. Chugayev, "Trezvo o trezvosti."

31. Goskomstat SSSR, "Zabolevaemost' naseleniya zlokachestvennymi novoobrazovaniyami," *Press Release* 152, 20 May 1991, p. 2.

32. A. A. Gabiani, *Na krayu propasti: narkomania i narkomany* (Moscow: Mysl, 1990), p. 9; Boris Levin, USSR Institute of Sociology, conversation with author, Moscow, January 1990.

33. Paul Quinn-Judge, "Absolut Hell," *New Republic,* 31 December 1990, pp. 12–13.

34. Ibid., p. 13.

35. Figures for 1970 from *Narodnoye khozyaistvo v SSSR za 70 let, yubileiniy statisticheskiy yezhegodnik* (Moscow: Finansy i statistika, 1987), p. 408; figures for 1986–87 from *Narkhoz 1987,* p. 357; figures for 1989 from *Narkhoz 1989,* p. 40.

36. I. M. Virganskaya and V. I. Dmitriev, "The Main Problems of Medico-Demographic Development in the USSR." Paper prepared for the International Research Conference on Demographic Trends, Aging and other Non-Communicable Diseases, held at the All-Union Cardiology Center, Moscow, USSR, 1–3 October 1991, co-sponsored by the Laboratory on Medical Demography of the All-Union Cardiology Center of the USSR Academy of Medical Sciences, the National Institute of Aging, U.S. Department of Health and Human Services and the World Health Organization, p. 29.

37. Goskomstat SSSR, "Smertnost' naseleniya po prichinam smerti" [standardized indicators for 1989, weighted to correspond to population age groups], *Press Release* 181, 17 June 1991.

38. Goskomstat SSSR, "Zabolevaemost' naseleniya . . . ," *Press Release* 152, 20 May 1991; Academician N. Trapeznikov, director, All-Union Cancer Research Center, ". . . Lyudi prodolzhayut umirat'," *Argumenty i fakty* 44 (November 1990): 6.

39. Radio Kiev, International Service (in Ukrainian), 29 July 1990, "Ukraine Releases Statistics on Health"; *FBIS-SOV-90-149,* 2 August 1990, p. 81.

40. Goskomstat RSFSR, "O prichinakh smertnosti naseleniya v trudosposobnom vozraste," *Statistical Press Bulletin* 1 (1991): pp. 21–22.

41. Ibid., p. 18; USSR Ministry of Social Welfare, "Number of Workers and Employees Certified for the First Time as Invalids in Connection with Tuberculosis," *Osnovnyye pokazateli invalidnost' i deyatel'nosti VTEK v SSSR za 1986 god* (Moscow: 1987), Table 7, p. 26; Denisov, " 'Akhillesova pyata' zdravookhraneniye," p. 40.

42. Goskomstat SSSR, *Press Release* 398, 6 September 1989, "Number of Workers, Employees and Collective Farmers First Certified as Invalids"; USSR Ministry of Social Welfare, "Number of Workers and Employees Certified for the First Time as Invalids in Connection with Cancer,"

Osnovnyye pokazateli, Table 8, p. 27; USSR Ministry of Social Welfare, "Number of Workers and Employees Certified for the First Time as Invalids in Connection with Circulatory System Ailments," *Osnovnyye pokazateli,* Table 10, p. 29.

43. A. Vishnevsky, S. Vasin and V. Shkolnikov, "Epidemiological Transition in the USSR." Paper presented at International Conference on Health, Disease and Mortality Causes in the European States and the Soviet Union, 3–7 December 1990, Vilnius, Lithuania.

44. Ibid., pp. 5, 9.

45. Radio Moscow, World Service (in English), 12 February 1990; "1.5 Million AIDS [sic] Cases Predicted by 2000," *FBIS-SOV-90-049,* 13 March 1990, p. 86.

46. Gina Kolata, "Experts Debate If AIDS Epidemic Has at Last Crested in U.S.," *New York Times,* 18 June 1991, pp. C1, C9.

47. Goskomstat SSSR, "Zabolevaemost' naseleniya . . . ," *Press Release* 152, 20 May 1991, p. 3.

48. RFE/RL, *Daily Report* 144, "Too Many False Positives in AIDS Testing," 1 August 1990, citing *Eesti Arst* 3 (1990).

49. Vishnevsky, Vasin and Shkolnikov, "Epidemiological Transition in the USSR," Table 2, p. 12.

50. Ibid., Table 3, p. 13.

51. Ibid., Table 4, p. 14.

52. Y[evgeniy] I. Chazov, "Our Dialogue: The Science of Health," interview in *Sovetskaya Rossiya,* 5 July 1987, p. 1.

53. National Center for Health Statistics, "Operations for Inpatients Discharged from Non-Federal Short-stay Hospitals, According to Sex, Age and Surgical Category: U.S., 1980, 1985 and 1987," *Health, US, 1988* (Hyattsville, MD: U.S. Department of Health and Human Services, 1989), p. 118.

54. N. Kharitonova, "Status serdtsa," *Sovetskaya Rossiya,* 18 June 1988, p. 4.

55. Chazov, "Our Dialogue."

56. I. Boytko, "Gore gorkoe . . . ," *Pravda,* 1 June 1991, p. 3.

57. L. Ivchenko, "The Return on a Government Guest House: A Former Sanatorium for High-Ranking Officials Is Now Being Used Inefficiently," *Izvestiya,* 21 June 1991, p. 7; *JPRS-UPA-91-033,* 17 July 1991, pp. 53–54.

58. O. Chegodayeva, "We Continue to Die of Leukemia: For Our Country, Treatment of the Disease Has Become a Serious Economic Problem," *Komsomol'skaya pravda,* 14 November 1990, p. 2; *JPRS-ULS-91-012,* 3 June 1991, p. 40.

59. Andrei Semyonov, " 'Eto tol'ko nachalo,' " *MedGaz,* 12 October 1990, p. 1.

60. Leon Aron, "Past as Prologue in Soviet Tinderbox," *Christian Science Monitor,* 2 May 1989, p. 18.

61. Nadezhda Yefimova, "Bolit u cheloveka pochka . . . a rushitsya vsya zhizn'," *MedGaz,* 8 June 1990, p. 3.

62. Jack L. Gosnell, counsellor for Scientific Affairs, U.S. Embassy, conversation with authors, Moscow, October 1990.
63. Conversation with author, Moscow, 10 October 1990.
64. TASS News Service (in English), "Criminal Abuses Discussed," 30 August 1990; FBIS-SOV-90-170, 31 August 1990, p. 26.
65. A[leksandra] P. Biryukova, text of report to Twenty-eighth CPSU Congress, Pravda, 9 July 1990, p. 6.
66. V. Romanenko, "Minzdrav budyet likvidirovan?" Argumenty i fakty, 31 March–6 April 1990, p. 6.
67. A. Potapov, "Zdorovye—element blagosostayaniya obshchestva," Argumenty i fakty, 26 May–1 June 1990, p. 6.
68. Ibid.
69. Victor Cohn, "Less Income, Fewer Trips to the Doctor," Washington Post, Health Weekly, 31 July 1990, p. 8.
70. Pravda, 14 April 1976, p. 3.
71. Planovoye khozyaistvo 2 (February 1978): 18–23.
72. "No Paper for EKGs," MedGaz, 13 October 1982; MedGaz, 23 March 1984, p. 3.
73. Biryukova, report to CPSU Congress.
74. Goskomstat SSSR, "On Supplying Medicines and Medical Supplies," Statistical Press Bulletin 3 (1991).
75. "Can Business Cure a Sick Society?" Business in the USSR (December 1990): 35.
76. Z. Makhsumov, deputy chief doctor, treatment section, Hospital Number 1, Shakhrinau region, "Krivaya polzet vniz," letter to editor, under headline "Nikto ne dast nam izbavleniya . . . ot defitsita," MedGaz, 3 June 1990, p. 2.
77. "Spravka: O merakh po ustraneniyu nedostatkov v rabote otrasli, otmechennikh postanovleniyem KNK SSSR ot 31.03.89, kriticheskimi publikatsiyami v gazetakh 'Pravda' ot 12.04.89 i 'Izvestiya' ot 10.04. 89." Document prepared for the joint meeting of the Collegia of the USSR Ministries of Health and of the Medical and Microbiological Industry, 27 April 1989.
78. Goskomstat SSSR, Statistical Press Bulletin 3 (1991).
79. Yulia Klimovskaya, "Minzdrav preduprezhdaet . . . ," Zelyonniy mir 12 (December 1990): 4; M. Aleksandrova, "Labirint lekarstvennogo defitsita," Vrach 7 (1991): 25.
80. S. Tutorskaya, "Tabletok nyet i ne budyet . . . ," Izvestiya, 9 January 1991, p. 3.
81. Ibid.
82. V. Belitskiy, "Unprotected Against Disease . . . ," Trud, 6 December 1990, p. 2; JPRS-ULS-91-013, 17 June 1991, pp. 29–31, esp. p. 29.
83. Ibid.
84. Tom Waters, "Ecoglasnost," Discover (April 1990): 51–53, esp. p. 52.
85. Yu. Stepanov, "Turn-Key or Turn-Down? (Why the Government Deci-

sions Remained on Paper)," *Rabochaya tribuna,* 11 November 1990, p. 2; *FBIS-SOV-90-229,* 28 November 1990.

86. Klimovskaya, "Minzdrav preduprezhdaet. . . ."

87. Associated Press, *"Pravda:* Soviet Lack of Drugs Imperils the Ill," *Washington Post,* 15 August 1991, p. A41.

88. Yuriy Stepanov, "Zavody pushcheny. Nadolgo li?" *MedGaz,* 18 November 1990, p. 2.

89. Tutorskaya, "Tabletok nyet i ne budyet. . . ."

90. Ye. Seleznev, [Ph.D.] candidate in pharmaceutical sciences, Ryazan', "Vsegda li preparat po blago," letter to editor, under headline "Nikto ne dast nam izbavleniya . . . ," *MedGaz,* 3 June 1990, p. 2.

91. Ibid.

92. I. Ognev, "Doroga pod yarmo," *Izvestiya,* 28 January 1991; I. Ognev, "Kak izgonyali avtorov unikal'nikh lekarstv," *Izvestiya,* 12 May 1991, p. 2.

93. Ognev, "Kak izgnoyali avtorov. . . ."

94. Ibid.

95. Ibid.

96. G. S., "A lekarstv bol'she stanet?" *Radikal* 24, 25 June 1991, p. 1.

97. Tutorskaya, "Tabletok nyet i ne budyet . . ."; Aleksandrova, "Labirint lekarstvennogo defitsita."

98. G. Onishchenko, specialist, USSR Ministry of Health, cited in S. Tutorskaya, "Kak spravit'sya s gepatitom," *Izvestiya,* 15 August 1990, p. 3.

99. M. I. Shapiro and A. A. Degtaryev, *Profilaktika kishechnikh infektsii v krupnom gorode* (Leningrad: Meditsina, 1990), p. 108.

100. V. Chiburayev, chief, Sanitary Prophylactic Main Administration, USSR Ministry of Health, "Delay May Mean Death," interview with I. Tsarev, *Trud,* 15 May 1991, p. 4; *JPRS-TEN-91-013,* 5 July 1991, pp. 68–69, esp. p. 69.

101. Shapiro and Degtaryev, *Profilaktika kishechnikh infektsii,* p. 108.

102. Nikita Bogoslovskiy, "Zametki na polyakh shlyapy," *Sovetskaya kultura,* 14 October 1989, p. 12.

103. Conversation with author, Yaroslavl, 22 October 1990.

10

Cradle to Grave

1. G. Ginzburg, artist, printed by Planeta publishers, Moscow, 1973, in the collection of Margaret S. Nalle, Washington, D.C.

2. Goskomstat SSSR, *Okhrana zdorov'ya v SSSR, statisticheskiy sbornik* (Moscow: Finansy i statistika, 1990), p. 8.

3. I. Leshkevich, chief, Main Directorate, Mother and Child Care, USSR Ministry of Health, "Foreign Countries Will Not Help, If We Fail to Treat Our Children on Our Own," interview with I. Yefremova, *Rabochaya*

tribuna, 11 October 1990, p. 3; *JPRS-UPA-90-065,* 3 December 1990, pp. 85–87, esp. p. 86; Professor Vladimir I. Kulakov director, All-Union Scientific Research Center of Health Protection of Mothers and Children, USSR Ministry of Health, "Two Watermelons in One Hand," interview, *Pravda,* 16 December 1988; *JPRS-ULS-89-007,* 17 May 1989, pp. 69–73, esp. p. 69.

4. Vladimir Viktorovich Schmidt, "Uidi, Presidentu Gorbachevu!" *Svobodnoe slovo* 36, 9 October 1990, p. 6.

5. Ibid.

6. Alexander Baranov, USSR deputy minister of health, "First and Foremost," interview with Victoria Kramova, *Science in the USSR* 1 (January–February 1990): 63–71, esp. p. 65.

7. Cf. Shawn Dorman, master's degree candidate, Russian Area Studies Program, Georgetown University, "Abortion in the Soviet Union: A Survey of Leningrad Women," 13 February 1990, citing her own research, and a study by E. A. Sadvokasova, reported in Gordon Hyde, "Abortion and the Birth Rate in the USSR," *Journal of Biosocial Science* 2 (1970): 288.

8. Andrei Popov, "Kogda vybor nyet," *Ogonyok* (August 1988): 18–19, esp. p. 19.

9. Professor Vladimir I. Kulakov, director, All-Union Research Center for the Protection of the Health of Mother and Child, USSR Ministry of Health, "Two Melons in One Hand," interview with V. Kramova, *Pravda,* 16 December 1988, p. 3, excerpt, *CDSP* 40, no. 50 (1988): 23–24.

10. Dr. Archil Khomassuridze, quoted in Francine du Plessix Gray, *Soviet Women: Walking the Tightrope* (New York: Anchor Books, Doubleday, 1990), p. 15.

11. *Narkhoz 1989,* pp. 230, 226.

12. Dorman, "Abortion in the Soviet Union," citing her own research, and Murray Feshbach, "Health in Russia: Statistics and Reality," *Wall Street Journal,* 14 September 1981; Jodi Jacobson, "Choice at Any Cost," *WorldWatch* no. 2 (March–April 1988); N. Vladina, "Izdevat'sya nad soboi," *Sem'ya* 8 (1989); and Christopher Tietze, *Induced Abortion: A World Review,* 5th ed. (New York: The Population Council, 1983).

13. David Remnick, "Vast 'Shadow Economy' Permeates Soviet Life," *Washington Post,* 21 September 1990, pp. A1, A19.

14. Yevgeniya Albats, staff reporter, *Moscow News,* conversation with author, Washington, D.C., 18 June 1991.

15. Dorman, "Abortion in the Soviet Union," citing S. L. Polchanova, "Present-Day Anti-Abortion Propaganda," *Feldsher i akusherka* 8 (August 1984); *CDSP* 35, no. 45 (1984).

16. Goskomstat SSSR, "Materinskaya smertnost' po soyuznym respublikam," *Press Release* 263, 20 June 1989; World Resources Institute, *World Resources 1990–91* (New York: Oxford University Press, 1990), Table 16.3, pp. 258–59.

17. Leshkevich, "Foreign Countries Will Not Help."

18. A. A. Baranov, USSR deputy minister of health, "Aktual'nyye voprosy okhrany zdorov'ya materi i rebyonka na sovremennom etape," *Pediatriya* 7 (July 1990): 8.

19. Sonya Shmatova, interview with authors, Washington, D.C., 14 September 1990.

20. Dmitri Shevarov, "SPID [AIDS]," *Komsomol'skaya pravda*, 24 May 1990; V. Kornev, "Cause of Infection—A Dirty Syringe," *Izvestiya*, 5 May 1990, p. 2; condensed, *CDSP*, 41, no. 18 (1989): p. 30.

21. Shevarov, "SPID."

22. Shmatova interview.

23. "Reglamenty kazarmy?" *Akvarium*, independent newspaper of the Ecology and Health Society of Berezniki, 3 October 1990.

24. Goskomstat SSSR, *Demograficheskiy yezhegodnik. 1990* (Moscow: Finansy i statistika, 1990), p. 384.

25. Goskomstat SSSR, *Okhrana zdorov'ya*, pp. 8 and 10–12.

26. Goskomstat SSSR, *Zhenshchiny v SSSR 1989, statisticheskiye materialy* (Moscow: Finansy i statistika, 1989), p. 34.

27. Ibid., p. 5.

28. Ibid., p. 6.

29. G. Bilyalitdinova, "Takoy vot rasklad," *Pravda*, 11 February 1991, p. 4.

30. Aksoltan Atayeva, minister of health, Turkmenistan, "Okhrannaya gramota zhenshchine-materi," interview with Natalya Charukhcheva, *MedGaz*, 15 February 1991, p. 4.

31. Mukharam Il'yasova, "O zhenshchine—prozoy zhizni . . . ," interview with Anna Ambartsumyants, *Kommunist Uzbekistan*, 11 March 1990.

32. Ibid.

33. Author unnamed, extracts from letter published in T. Leus, "Mat' i ditya," *Magnitogorskiy rabochiy*, 22 July 1989, p. 2.

34. T. Mayboroda, "The Decision to Become a Mother," *Pravda Ukrainy*, 23 October 1987, p. 4; *JPRS-UPA-88-007*, 10 February 1988, pp. 108–11, esp. p. 109.

35. Leus, "Mat' i ditya."

36. Ibid.

37. Ibid.

38. Bilyalitdinova, "Takoy vot rasklad."

39. Albats conversation.

40. Atayeva interview.

41. Bilyalitdinova, "Takoy vot rasklad."

42. Goskomstat SSSR, *Zhenshchiny v SSSR 1989*, pp. 3–4.

43. Ibid.; Albats conversation.

44. *Narkhoz 1989*, p. 230.

45. T. Surkov, chairman, medical workers' collective, Zelenograd City Hospital Number 3, "Rabotat' tak dal'she ne mozhem," letter to editor, *MedGaz*, 30 March 1990, p. 1.

46. M. Sonin, *Literaturnaya gazeta,* 16 April 1969, cited in Michael Ryan, *The Organization of Soviet Medical Care* (Oxford: Basil Blackwell, 1978), p. 42.

47. N. Amosov, "Lekarstvo dlya meditsiny," *Literaturnaya gazeta* 45, 8 November 1989, p. 12.

48. "Ot otdela sotsial' niykh problem," *Trud,* 18 May 1991.

49. A. Telyukov, "Perestroika ekonomiki i organizatsii v zdravookhranenii," *Voprosy ekonomiki* 7 (July 1987): 33.

50. R. Talyshinskiy and T. Khudyakova, "Perestroika zdravookhraneniya—vsenarodnoye obsuzhdenie: Nado li platit' za lecheniye?" *Izvestiya,* 24 September 1987, p. 2, cited in Daniel S. Schultz, M.D., and Michael P. Rafferty, M.D., "Soviet Health Care and Perestroika," *American Journal of Public Health* 80, no. 2 (February 1990): 193–97, esp. pp. 193–94.

51. ". . . A tam, gdye berut," *Slovo molodyozhi,* 18 May 1991.

52. Poll conducted by All-Union Central Institute of Public Opinion, results made available to author in Moscow, January 1990.

53. "Zhizn' Rossii: Mnenie naseleniya RSFSR," *Argumenty i fakty,* 19–25 May 1990, p. 4.

54. Avishai Margalit, "The Great White Hope," *New York Review of Books,* 27 June 1991, pp. 19–25, esp. p. 20.

55. Nadezhda Melnik, quoted by Svetlana Sarasova, "Dosage," *Poisk* 15, 14–20 April 1990, pp. 4–5; *JPRS-TEN-90-005,* 13 June 1990, pp. 44–47, esp. p. 46.

56. Ye. I. Chazov, USSR minister of health, "Tasks of the Health Care Agencies and Institutions in Terms of Carrying Out the 'Basic Guidelines for the Development of Public Health Protection and the Restructuring of Health Care in the 12th Five-Year Plan and in the Period up to the Year 2000,' " *Sovetskoye zdravookhraneniye* 2 (February 1989): 3–22, excerpt *JPRS-ULS-90-012,* 16 July 1990, p. 36.

57. Dr. Andrei Petrovich Volosatov, "Chto bolit, doktor?" interview with O. Chegodayeva, *Komsomol'skaya pravda,* 17 April 1990, p. 1.

58. M. Mamonov, Vishnevskiy Institute of Surgery, USSR Academy of Medical Sciences, "Restructuring Healthcare: A Nationwide Discussion," *Izvestiya,* 1 October 1987, p. 4; *JPRS-ULS-88-002,* 26 February 1988.

59. P. V. Berlinskiy and F. N. Tsyrdya, Kishinev Medical Institute, "Data Processing for Medical and Health Care Services," *Zdravookhraneniye (Kishinev)* 3 (May–June 1990): 3–7; excerpt *JPRS-ULS-90-006,* 18 June 1990, pp. 36–37.

60. Murray Feshbach and Ann Rubin, "Health Care in the USSR," in *Economic Reforms and Welfare Systems,* ed. Jan Adam (London: Macmillan, 1991), p. 73.

61. V. Z. Kucherenko, E. G. Fyodorova and V. M. Borisov, "Otsenka metodik analiza diagnosticheskikh oshibok," *Sovetskoye zdravookhraneniye,* 9 (September 1990): 32–37, esp. Table 2, p. 34.

62. A. M. Ubaidullaev, Sh. U. Ismailov and I. V. Liberko, "Diagnosticheskiye

oshibki na dogospital'nom etape pri raznikh formakh organizatsii pul'-monologicheskoy pomoshchi," *Meditsinskiy zhurnal Uzbekistana* 7 (July 1990): 3–4, esp. p. 3.

63. L. Ivchenko, "Yesli nachat' s immuniteta . . . ," *Izvestiya*, 23 October 1990, p. 3.

64. V. S. Savel'ev, "Puti sovershenstvovaniya khirurgicheskoy pomoshchi naseleniyu RSFSR," *Sovetskaya meditsina* 10 (October 1990): 3–10, esp. p. 7.

65. Ibid., p. 8.

66. William Jarosz, Center for International Affairs, Harvard University, November 1990 trip notes made available to authors.

67. Ibid.

68. Yuriy Levin, "Kak zdorov'ye, zemlyaki?" *Leningradskaya panorama*, 9 September 1990, pp. 7–9, esp. p. 8.

69. A. Lavrushenko, "Glavvrach ob'yavlyet golodovku," *Sotsialisticheskaya industriya*, 12 January 1989, p. 7.

70. RFE/RL, *Daily Report*, "Donbass Miners Strike over Pollution Problems"; Alexander Zinoviev, "Rabotaet pravitel'stvennaya kommissiya," *Izvestiya*, 13 April 1990, p. 2, and "Ekologicheskaya aktsiya," *Izvestiya*, 14 May 1990, p. 2.

71. S. Tutorskaya, "Only Ambulance Service Not on Strike," *Izvestiya*, 9 February 1991, p. 2; *FBIS-SOV-91-031*, 14 February 1991, p. 24.

72. Anatoliy Solov'yev, "Operatsiya bez scalpelya," interview with Irina Krasnopol'skaya, *Soyuz* 18 (May 1991): 8.

73. Jarosz trip notes.

74. Nancy Shute, "From Unalaska to Petropavlovsk: Warm Welcomes Amid Geysers and Snow," *Smithsonian* 22, no. 5 (August 1991): 30–39, esp. p. 37.

75. L. Relin, deputy director, Main Directorate, USSR Cotton-Textile Production, response to letter from reader in Volgograd, *Argumenty i fakty* 1 (1990).

76. Savel'ev, "Puti sovershenstvovaniya . . . ," p. 9.

77. Ye. I. Chazov, USSR minister of health, "Na chto zhaluyetes' doktor," interview with Z. Yeroshok and S. Leskov, *Komsomol'skaya pravda*, 18 June 1988, p. 2.

78. A. P. Krasil'nikov and A. A. Adarchenko, "Current Problems of Nosocomial Infections and the Medicinal Stability of Microorganisms," *Zdravookhraneniye Belorussii* (November 1988): 73.

79. Liliya Serdobol'skaya and Valeriy Milyutin, "Auknulos' snizu—otkliknulos' sverkhu," *MedGaz*, 8 June 1990, p. 1.

80. M. Kuz'menko, chairman, RSFSR health workers' trade union, "Vosemnadtsatogo Avgusta luchshe ne bolyet'," interview with I. Isakova, FNPR press service, *Trud*, 11 August 1990, p. 2.

81. *Ekspress khronika* (in English), 34, 21 August 1990.

82. Goskomstat SSSR, *Ekspress Informatsiya*, 1 June 1989, citing USSR Health Minister Chazov.

83. Chazov interview.

84. Goskomstat RSFSR, *Statistical Press Bulletin* 4 (1991): 73.

85. A. Bukhtoyarov, V. Zhuravlev, Ye. Smirnova et al., "Kak istratit' milliard," *MedGaz,* 13 April 1990, p. 2.

86. N. K. Deryugo, "Republic Meeting of the Party-Economic Aktiv to Discuss the TsK and SovMin Plan for Restructuring Health Care," *Zdravookhraneniye Belorussii* 11 (November 1987): 71–72.

87. T. A. Izmukhambetov, minister of health, Kazakhstan, "Perestroika—A Time of Action," *Zdravookhraneniye Kazakhstana* 4 (April 1988): 1.

88. A. G. Alzhanov, V. I. Larionov and L. Ye. Karkoshkina, Department of Disinfection, Kazakh SSR, Ministry of Health, "Tasks and Problems in Centralized Sterilization Departments," *Zdravookhraneniye Kazakhstana* 2 (February 1989): 13–14.

89. Leus, "Mat' i ditya."

90. Conversation with author, Yaroslavl, 24 October 1990.

91. S. Inyushkin and V. Shishkin, "Vremya" broadcast, Moscow Television, 3 September 1990; *FBIS-SOV-90-174,* 7 September 1990, pp. 44–45.

92. N. Nazarovich, TASS, "Pulse: Physicists under Contract to the Medical Profession," *MedGaz,* 9 July 1989, p. 1; *JPRS-ULS-90-012,* 16 July 1990, p. 17.

93. V. Shustov, director, Scientific and Practical Association of Occupational Pathology and Hematology, Saratov Medical Institute, "The Times Dictate the Choice," *MedGaz,* 23 June 1989, p. 1; *JPRS-ULS-90-006,* 18 June 1990.

94. "InterMedTest," half-page advertisement, *Moscow News* 34, 2–9 September 1990, p. 13.

95. " 'Diagnoz'—na zdorov'ye," *Komsomol'skaya pravda,* 27 October 1990, p. 2.

96. Alexander Pevzner, "Medical Cooperatives: An Hour of Trial," *Business in the USSR* 7 (December 1990): 38.

97. Author's notes, visit to Fyodorov's institute, May 1991.

98. Sviatoslav Fyodorov, "Chetyre goda svobody," interview with Tomas Kolesnichenko, *Pravda* (Union Edition), 18 October 1990.

99. Dr. Pyotr Prodeus, chief surgeon, Children's Hospital No. 9, Moscow, conversation with author, Moscow, 21 October 1990.

100. Igor N. Denisov, USSR minister of health, "New Minister Prepared to Begin Reform of Soviet Health Care: District Doctors May Disappear, But Family Doctors Will Appear," interview with Marina Goncharenko, *Chas pik* 20, 20 May 1991, p. 6; *JPRS-UPA-91-033,* 17 July 1991, pp. 51–52.

101. Ibid.

102. Prodeus conversation.

11
The People Speak

1. Ilya Zaslavskiy, chairman, Oktyabrskoy *rayon* council, Moscow, talk at the National Endowment for Democracy, Washington, D.C., 13 July 1990.

2. Sviatoslav Zabelin, presentation at Natural Resources Defense Council offices, Washington, D.C., 22 April 1991, organized by Institute for Soviet-American Relations.

3. Valdis Abols, director, international affairs, Environmental Protection Club of Latvia (VAK), speech presented to the Environmental Law Institute, Washington, D.C., 29 January 1991.

4. Zabelin presentation.

5. " 'Green Party' Set Up in Latvia," Radio Moscow, Domestic Service, 18 January 1990; *FBIS-SOV-90-015*, 23 January 1990, p. 66.

6. Hilary F. French, "Green Revolutions: Environmental Reconstruction in Eastern Europe and the Soviet Union," *Worldwatch Paper 99* (November 1990): 33.

7. "Estonian Green Party Formed 10 Aug.," Radio Tallinn, Domestic Service, 10 August 1989; *FBIS-SOV-89-164*, 25 August 1989, pp. 43–44. French, "Green Revolutions."

8. Professor Marshall I. Goldman, associate director, Russian Research Center, Harvard University, "The USSR's New Class Struggle," *World Monitor* (February 1989): 46–50, esp. p. 48.

9. Ibid.

10. Mykhailo Horyn, secretariat chairman, Popular Movement of the Ukraine for Perebudova, (Rukh), talk at the National Endowment for Democracy, Washington, D.C., 11 September 1990.

11. Michael Dobbs, "Ukraine Stirs; Kremlin Shudders," *Washington Post,* 1 September 1989, pp. A1, A18.

12. V. Mavin, "Dialog pered s'yezdom," *Pravda,* 25 May 1989, p. 3.

13. Geoffrey Hosking, *The Awakening of the Soviet Union* (Cambridge, MA: Harvard University Press, 1991), p. 165.

14. Yuriy Petrovich Vlasov, Moscow city deputy, speech to Congress of People's Deputies, 31 May 1989, Moscow Television; *FBIS-SOV-89-104-S*, 1 June 1989, pp. 31–34, esp. pp. 33–34.

15. S. V. Chervonopiskiy, first secretary, city Komsomol committee, Cherkassy, speech to Congress of People's Deputies, 2 June 1989, *Izvestiya,* 5 June 1989, p. 1; *FBIS-SOV-89-142-S*, 26 July 1989, p. 1.

16. Anatoliy Valerianovich Gorbunov, chairman of the presidium, Supreme Soviet, Latvian SSR, speech to Congress of People's Deputies, 31 May 1989, Moscow Television; *FBIS-SOV-89-104-S*, 1 June 1989, pp. 19–21, esp. p. 20.

17. Valentin G. Rasputin, speech to Congress of People's Deputies, Moscow Television, 6 June 1989; *FBIS-SOV-89-108*, 7 June 1989, pp. 20–23, esp. pp. 22–23.

18. G. N. Gorbunov, director, "60-letiye SSSR" Aviation Plant, Irkutsk, speech to Congress of People's Deputies, Moscow Television, 2 June 1989; *FBIS-SOV-89-142-S*, 26 July 1989, pp. 5–7.

19. V. P. Shcherbakov, chairman, Moscow City Trade Unions Council, speech to Congress of People's Deputies, Moscow Television, 2 June 1989; *FBIS-SOV-89-142-S*, 26 July 1989, pp. 13–15.

20. V. P. Derevyanko, editor, *Vechernyaya Odessa,* speech to Congress of People's Deputies, Moscow Television, 2 June 1989; *FBIS-SOV-89-142-S*, 26 July 1989, pp. 19–20.

21. A. A. Zgerskaya (Yaroshinskaya), correspondent, *Radyanskaya Zhito-mirshchina,* speech to Congress of People's Deputies, Moscow Television, 2 June 1989; *FBIS-SOV-89-142-S*, 26 July 1989, p. 21.

22. Yevgeniy Chazov, minister of health, debate in USSR Supreme Soviet, Moscow Radio, Domestic Service, 10 July 1989; *FBIS-SOV-89-131*, 11 July 1989, pp. 54–55.

23. Various conversations with author, Moscow and elsewhere, 1989, 1990.

24. "Vsegda li pravy 'zelyonniye'?" *Zelyonniy mir* 11 (1990): 4.

25. *Doklad,* p. 336.

26. Goskomstat SSSR, *Press Release* 7, 27 February 1991, p. 1.

27. Vladimir Lupandin and Gennadiy Denisovsky, "The 'Greens' Coming to the Fore," *Moscow News* 22, 10–17 June 1990, p. 7.

28. Goskomstat SSSR, *Press Release* 7, p. 2.

29. Ibid., p. 3.

30. Olzhas Suleimeinov, speech sponsored by Russian Area Studies Program, Georgetown University, Washington, D.C., 18 March 1991.

31. Mikhail Gorbachev to Dr. Bernard Lown, co-chairman, International Physicians for the Prevention of Nuclear War, *Nuclear Times* (Autumn 1990), reprinted in "And You Can Quote Me On That . . . ," *Arms Control Today* 20, no. 9 (November 1990): 30.

32. Suleimeinov speech.

33. Ibid.

34. Andrei Zatoka, summary of speech to Joint US-USSR NGO Conference on the Environment, Moscow, 14 March 1991, in *Proceedings* (Institute for Soviet-American Relations and Socio-Ecological Union, Washington, D.C., and Moscow, 1991), p. 24.

35. Lydiya I. Boykova, deputy, *oblast* council, interview with author, Yaro-slavl, 23 October 1990.

36. Z. Bystrova, "Fact and Commentary: A Dissenting Opinion," *Pravda,* 21 May 1990, p. 8; *JPRS-TEN-90-006*, 27 June 1990, p. 59.

37. "Volgograd *Oblast* Party Buro Resigns," *SWB,* 2 February 1990, SU/0678 i.

38. Natalya V. Abramovich, associate editor, *Molodoy Leninets,* conversation with author, Volgograd, 15 October 1990.

39. Gosplan SSSR, "Postanovleniye ob ekspertize proyekta stroitelstva per-voy ocheredi Kanala Volgo-Don-P i vodokhozyaistvennomu balansu reki

Volgi na 1995 god," Expert State Commission of Inquiry, 14 March 1990, text of findings made available to author by Lydia Savel'yeva, Volgograd, October 1990.

40. Ibid.

41. Lydiya I. Savel'yeva, "Imenem dvizheniya za spaseniye Volgi . . . ," interview with N[ina] Baturina, *Volgogradskaya pravda,* 3 June 1990.

42. "Construction of Volga-Don No. 2 Canal Stopped," *SWB,* 3 August 1990, SU/WO139, p. A/11.

43. Alfred Pavlenko, interview with author, Volgograd, 14 October 1990.

44. Lyudmila Sokolovskaya, deputy, Odessa *oblast* council, interview with author, Odessa, 19 October 1990.

45. Francine du Plessix Gray, *Soviet Women: Walking the Tightrope* (New York: Anchor Books, Doubleday, 1991), p. 3.

46. Sokolovskaya interview.

47. Alla Shevchuk, interview with author, Odessa, 19 October 1990.

48. Ibid.

49. Sergei Zhigalov, "Ecological Militia Established," datelined Kuibyshev, *Izvestiya,* 10 September 1990, p. 2; *FBIS-SOV-90-177,* 12 September 1990, p. 63. "Dnepro-Dzerzhinsk Doctor-Militiamen," *Moscow News* 7 (1991): 2. "Ecology Police? Yes," *Sovetskaya Moldaviya,* 28 March 1990, p. 4; *JPRS-TEN-90-005,* 13 June 1990; pp. 38–40. "Pomoshch' prirodye," *Trud,* 5 May 1990, p. 4.

50. Fyodor T. Morgun, "Economics and Ecology: The Ecology in the System of Planning," *Planovoye khozyaystvo* 2 (February 1989): 53–63; *JPRS-UEA-89-017,* 23 June 1989, pp. 15–22, esp. p. 15.

51. Sergei Zalygin, chairman, Ecology and Peace Association, "The State and Ecology: Reflections of a People's Deputy," *Pravda,* 23 October 1989, p. 4; *JPRS-UPA-89-068,* 19 December 1989, pp. 130–35, esp. p. 130.

52. A. Tsygankov, deputy chairman, State Committee for Emergency Situations, USSR Council of Ministers, "Nature Is Still Hoping," *Pravitel'stvennyy vestnik* 38 (September 1990): 10–11; *JPRS-UPA-90-066,* 4 December 1990, pp. 49–50.

53. Ibid.

54. Nikolai Vorontsov, chairman, Goskompriroda, "Vremya ekologicheskoy bezopasnosti," interview with F. Vladov, *NTR tribuna* 23–24, 15 December 1989, p. 3.

55. Ibid.

56. Vladimir V. Loktionov, director, Volgograd Factory for Special Petroleum-Based Materials, interview with author, Volgograd, 14 October 1990.

57. Viktor Pismenny, chief engineer, Volgograd Factory for Special Petroleum-Based Materials, interview with author, Volgograd, 14 October 1990.

58. Ibid.

59. Tatyana Aronson, senior specialist RSFSR Goskompriroda, "Kto, za chto i skol'ko," *Zelyonniy mir* 7–8, 21 February 1991.

60. Goskompriroda RSFSR, *Ekologicheskiy vestnik Rossii* (July 1990): 10–29.

61. A. Kudin, chairman, Moskompriroda, "Ekologiya i ekonomika: vperviye vmeste," interview, *Vechernyaya Moskva,* 4 June 1991, p. 2.

62. S[ergei] Zalygin, A[leksei] Yablokov et al., "Water in the Nets of Minvodkhoz," *Izvestiya,* 7 February 1990, p. 3; *JPRS-UEA-90-010,* 21 March, 1990, pp. 48–51, esp. p. 49.

63. V. Antonov, "Are the Greens Always Right?" *Izvestiya,* 18 September 1990, p. 54; *JPRS-TEN-91-001,* 4 January 1991, pp. 54–55.

64. M. Nazriyev, chairman, Tadjik SSSR, Goskompriroda, "Defending the Ecology Is Everybody's Cause," *Kommunist Tadjikistana,* 6 April 1990, p. 3; *JPRS-TEN-90-006,* 27 June 1990, pp. 83–84.

65. TASS, International Service, "Projects Stopped on Environmental Grounds," 7 January 1989; *FBIS-SOV-89-006,* 10 January 1989, pp. 77–78.

66. G. Sasko, chairman, Executive Committee, Cherkassy City Soviet of People's Deputies, "Lessons in Democracy: Verbal Promissory Notes," *Pravda Ukrainy,* 31 December 1989; *JPRS-UPA-90-012,* 12 March 1990, pp. 79–80.

67. A. Matnishyan, member, Public Ecology Council, Armenian SSR Goskompriroda, "Look Before You . . . ," *Kommunist* (Yerevan), 4 May 1990; *JPRS-TEN-90-009,* 2 August 1990, pp. 49–50.

68. Francis X. Clines, "New Candor Transfixes a Soviet City," *New York Times,* 8 June 1989, p. A18.

69. Lyudmila Dunayeva, "Klubok dlya prokurora," *Zelyonniy mir* 12 (1990): 4–5.

70. L. O., "Extremisty 'zelyonniye' tak zhe opasny, kak krasniye ili korichneviye," *Chas pik* 15, 15 April 1991, p. 6.

12
A Time to Heal

1. Michael Dobbs, "Crowds in Capital Protest Power Seizure; Yeltsin Defiant," *Washington Post,* 20 August 1991, pp. A17, A20.

2. Michael Dobbs, " 'Yeltsin Magic' Turns the Tide," *Washington Post,* 22 August 1991, pp. A1, A29.

3. Iurii N. Shcherbak, conversation with author, Washington, D.C., 30 April 1990.

4. *Izvestiya Akademii nauk SSSR, Seriya ekonomicheskaya* 3 (May–June 1990): 22–30; *JPRS-TEN-90-009,* 2 August 1990, pp. 21–27.

5. Alexander Androshin, "Free Medical Services: The End of a Myth," *Business in the USSR* 7 (December 1990): 28.

6. Barber B. Conable, president, The World Bank Group, address as prepared for delivery, Warsaw, Poland, 22 February 1990 (Washington, D.C.: World Bank, 1990).

7. Nikolai Ivanovich Ryzhkov, report of the government's program, delivered to the USSR Congress of People's Deputies, 7 June 1989, Soviet television broadcast; SWB, 9 June 1989, SU/0478, pp. C/7–C/20, esp. p. C/10.

8. Ibid., pp. C/11, C/12.

9. Ibid., p. C/17.

10. Ibid.

11. F. Kh. Agisher, section head, Chuvash ASSR, State Committee for Environmental Protection, quoted on "Vremya" broadcast, Moscow Television, 6 August 1990; FBIS-SOV-90-154, 9 August 1990, p. 46.

12. I. Mosin, "Notes from a Session of a USSR Supreme Soviet Commission," Sotsialisticheskaya industriya, 23 September 1988, SWB, C. Special Supplement, 15 October 1988, SU/0283, pp. C1–C2.

13. RFE/RL, Daily Report, "Pollution Abatement Plan Scaled Down," 28 March 1991.

14. Doklad, pp. 244–45.

15. "State Program for the Protection of the Environment and the Intelligent Use of the Natural Resources of the USSR in 1991–95 and Over the Long Range Up to 2005," Ekonomika i zhizn 41 (October 1990), Supplement: 1–8; JPRS-TEN-90-015, 14 November 1990, pp. 32–69.

16. Ibid., p. 36.

17. Ibid.

18. Ibid., pp. 37, 39, 41, 43, 42, and 38.

19. S. Shatalin et al., "Programma stabilizatsii ekonomiki i perekhoda k rynku (proyekt)." Typescript, Moscow, 1990, pp. 140–41.

20. Yuriy Koryakin, chief economist, Research and Development Institute of Power Engineering, "200 milliardov," Energiya: Ekonomika. Tekhnika. Ekologiya 8 (August 1990): 3–6.

21. Based on Yu. Ya. Ol'sevich, Sotsial'naya pereoriyentatsiya ekonomiki, Seriya ekonomika, no. 1 (Moscow: Znaniye, 1990), p. 42.

22. V. Gsovskiy, "Sotsial'nyye problemy okhrany okruzhayushchey sredy v stranakh SEV," Voprosy ekonomiki, 12 (December 1985): 101.

23. Thomas E. Gilbert, corporate secretary, James Chemical Engineering, Inc., Groton, Connecticut, telephone conversation with author, 31 July 1991.

24. Author's calculations.

25. V. Korbanov, Kontseptsii operativnoy stabilizatsii urovnya, sokhraneniya i vosstanovleniya Aral'skogo morya i biosfery Priaral'ya (Tashkent: n. p., 1990), p. 13.

26. V. Popov, USSR minister of housing and municipal services, Soviet television, 18 November 1987, SWB, 4 December 1987, SU/W0003.

27. Gina Despres, counsel to U.S. Senator Bill Bradley, letter to author, 2 March 1988, recounting talks with Baku city officials.

28. J. Paul Horne, "Gorby's Back: Lessons of a Failed Coup," *Smith Barney International Research,* 23 August 1991, p. 6, citing estimates by the OECD, IMF, World Bank and European Bank for Reconstruction and Development.

29. A. M. Koval'chuk, RSFSR minister of the environment, "Kompleks mer po ozdrovleniyu prirody v Rossii," *Zhilishchnoye i kommunal'noye khozyaistvo,* 6 (June 1990): 5–8.

30. Council on Environmental Quality, *Environmental Quality 21st Annual Report* (Washington, D.C.: CEQ, 1991), Table 9, p. 271.

31. Ibid., p. 267.

32. Aleksei Yablokov, Sviatoslav Zabelin, Mikhail Lemeshev, Maria Cherkasova et al., "Russia: Gasping for Breath, Choking in Waste, Dying Young," trans. Eliza Klose, *Washington Post,* 18 August 1991, p. C3.

33. A. I. Potapov, RSFSR minister of health, "Ecological Journal: Cities in the 'Black Book' interview with B. Pipia", *Pravda,* 1 September 1989, p. 8; *CDSP* 41, no. 3, 27 September 1989, p. 27.

34. Mosin, "Notes from a Session of a USSR Supreme Soviet Commission," p. C/2.

35. Dr. Olga Goldfarb, interview with author, Stamford, Connecticut, 9 September 1990,

36. Elena Bonner, interview with author, Moscow, 10 October 1990.

37. Ibid.

38. Yevgeniy Chazov, "Pochemu ya ushel iz ministrov," interview with D. Kukunov, *Komsomol'skaya pravda,* 13 July 1990, p. 2.

39. Ibid.; I. Denisov, "Kak vyyti iz krizisa," *Vrach* 9 (1991): 13.

40. Conversations with author at Semashko Public Health Institute, Moscow, January 1990.

41. Sergei Pospelov, "Kak spasti zdorov'ye naroda," *MedGaz,* 23 November 1990, pp. 1, 2.

42. Yu. I. Borodin, chairman, USSR Supreme Soviet Committee for the Protection of the People's Health, interview to TASS, "At the USSR Supreme Soviet Committees and Commissions: There Are No Unequivocal Answers," *Sel'skaya zhizn,* 30 September 1989, p. 1; *FBIS-SOV-89-192,* 5 October 1989, p. 38.

43. Albert Anatol'yevich Likhanov, "Deti—eto nashe nastoyashcheye. Budushchim oni smogut stat', lish' yesli my pomozhem im segodnya. Zavtra budyet pozdno." Speech to USSR Congress of People's Deputies, 1 June 1989, *Sem'ya,* 5 June 1989, p. 3.

44. Albert Likhanov, "The Cries of Hungry Infants: A Response to *Pravda*'s Initiative," *Pravda,* 20 May 1991, p. 3; *JPRS-UPA-91-032,* 2 July 1991, pp. 46–48. Albert Likhanov quoted in V. Lyubitskiy and L. Pyatiletova, "*Pravda* Roundtable: Let's Feed our Children!" *Pravda,* 3 June 1991, p. 3; *JPRS-UPA-91-032,* 2 July 1991, pp. 48–52, esp. p. 48.

45. Maria Cherkasova, interview with authors, Washington, D.C., 24 May 1990.

46. Maria Cherkasova, speech at Institute of Soviet-American Relations, Washington, D.C., 29 May 1990.

47. Ibid.

48. John P. Remensnyder, Jr., M.D., "Pipeline Disaster: Treating Soviet Burn Victims," *Harvard Medical Journal* (Summer 1990): 33–36.

49. Nancy Shute, "From Unalaska to Petropavlovsk: Warm Welcomes Amid Geysers and Snow," *Smithsonian* 22, no. 5 (August 1991): 30–39, esp. p. 38.

50. Marco Vezzani, Volzhsky project manager for Italimpianti, interview with author, Volgograd, 17 October 1991.

51. Ibid.

52. A. Yerashova and T. Shevchenko, "KrAZ: Pora pred'yavit' schot," *Ekologiya Krasnoyariya* 3 (April 1990): 4.

SELECTED
BIBLIOGRAPHY

WE LIST HERE only those books, journals and other periodicals that constitute major sources of our information and that are among the basic reference works we recommend to others seeking to understand questions of ecology and health in the Soviet Union. The listing purposefully does not include either the standard, sometimes classic, studies of Russian and Soviet history, economics and current affairs that we also consulted or mass-circulation Soviet newspapers and magazines. This concise bibliography is meant to serve as a guide to the specialized subjects that have been our particular concern.

Books

ALEXEYEVA, LUDMILLA, and CATHERINE A. FITZPATRICK. *Nyeformaly. Civil Society in the USSR*. New York: Helsinki Watch Report, February 1990.

BALZER, HARLEY. *Soviet Science on the Edge of Reform*. Boulder, CO: Westview Press, 1989.

BEZUGLAYA, E. YU., G. P. RASTORGUYEVA and I. V. SMIRNOVA. *Chem dyshit promyshlennyy gorod*. Leningrad: Gidrometeoizdat, 1991.

CENTRAL INTELLIGENCE AGENCY, DIRECTORATE OF INTELLIGENCE. *Soviet Energy Data Resource Handbook*. Washington, DC: U.S. Government Printing Office, May 1990.

CRITCHLOW, JAMES. *Nationalism in Uzbekistan: A Soviet Republic's Road to Sovereignty*. Boulder, CO: Westview Press, 1991.

DAVIS, CHRISTOPHER, and MURRAY FESHBACH. *Rising Infant Mortality in the*

USSR in the 1970s. Series P-25, no. 74. Washington, DC: U.S. Bureau of the Census, September 1980.

DAVYDOVA, MARI, and VLADIMIR KOSHEVOI. *Nature Reserves in the USSR.* Moscow: Progress, 1989.

FESHBACH, MURRAY. *Economics of Health and Environment in the USSR.* Prepared for the Office of Net Assessment, U.S. Department of Defense. Washington, DC: forthcoming.

FESHBACH, MURRAY. *The Soviet Union: Population Trends and Dilemmas.* *Population Bulletin,* 37, no. 3. Washington, DC: Population Reference Bureau, August 1982.

GABIANI, A. A. *Na krayu propasti: narkomaniya i narkomy.* Moscow: Mysl', 1990.

GANTT, W. HORSLEY. *Russian Medicine.* New York: Paul B. Hoeber, Harper & Brothers, 1937.

THE GLOBAL TOMORROW COALITION. *The Global Ecology Handbook.* Boston: Beacon Press, 1990.

GOLDMAN, MARSHALL I. *The Spoils of Progress: Environmental Pollution in the Soviet Union.* Cambridge, MA: MIT Press, 1972.

GOSKOMGIDROMET SSSR. *Obzor sostoyaniya okruzhayushchey prirodnoy sredy v SSSR.* Moscow: Gidrometeoizdat, 1990.

GOSKOMPRIRODA SSSR. *Gosudarstvennyy doklad: Sostoyaniye prirodnoy sredy i prirodookhrannaya deyatel'nost' v SSSR v 1989 godu.* Typescript. N. A. Vorontsov, scientific ed., chairman Goskompriroda. Moscow: Goskompriroda, 1990.

GOSKOMPRIRODA SSSR. *Sostoyaniya prirodnoy sredy v SSSR v 1988 godu: mezhvedomstvennyy doklad.* V. G. Sokolovskiy, general ed., Moscow: Lesnaya promyshlennost', 1988.

GOSKOMPRIRODA SSSR. *Report on the State of the Environment in the USSR 1988.* Kevin Hendzel, trans. Typescript. Moscow: Goskompriroda, 1989.

GOSKOMSTAT SSSR. *Demograficheskiy sbornik SSSR 1989.* Moscow: Finansy i statistika, 1990.

GOSKOMSTAT SSSR. *Narodnoye khozyaystvo SSSR v 19— godu. Statisticheskiy yezhegodnik.* Moscow: Finansy i statistika, 19—. Various years.

GOSKOMSTAT SSSR. *Okhrana okruzhayushchey sredy i ratsional'noye ispol'-zovaniye prirodnykh resursov v SSSR.* Moscow: Finansy i statistika, 1989.

GOSKOMSTAT SSSR. *Okhrana zdorov'ya v SSSR. Statisticheskiy sbornik.* Moscow: Finansy i statistika, 1990.

GOSKOMSTAT SSSR. *Sotsial'noye razvitiye i uroven' zhizni naseleniya.* Moscow: Finansy i statistika, 1989.

GOSKOMSTAT SSSR. *Vozrast i sostoyaniye v brake naseleniya SSSR.* Moscow: Finansy i statistika, 1990.

GOSKOMSTAT SSSR. *Zdravookhraneniya v SSSR.* Moscow: Finansy i statistika, 1989.

GUSTAFSON, THANE. *Crisis Amid Plenty: The Politics of Soviet Energy Under Brezhnev and Gorbachev.* Princeton: Princeton University Press, 1991.

JANCAR, BARBARA. *Environmental Management in the Soviet Union and Yugoslavia*. Durham, NC: Duke University Press, 1987.

JONES, ANTHONY, WALTER D. CONNOR and DAVID E. POWELL, EDS. *Soviet Social Problems*. Boulder, CO: Westview Press, 1991.

KOKSHILOV, A. V., ED. *Stony Volgi*. Volgograd: Nizhne-Volzhskoye knizhnoye izdatel'stvo, 1990.

KOMAROV, BORIS. *The Destruction of Nature in the Soviet Union*. White Plains, NY: M.E. Sharpe, 1980.

KOTKIN, STEPHEN. *Steeltown, USSR: Soviet Society in the Gorbachev Era*. Berkeley: University of California Press, 1991.

LEMESHEV, M. YA., CHIEF ED. *Ekologicheskaya al'ternativa*. Moscow: Progress, 1990.

LENIN CHILDREN'S FUND. *Polozheniye detey v SSSR 1990 god. Sostoyaniye. Problemy. Perspektivy*. Moscow: Dom, 1990.

MARPLES, DAVID R. *The Social Impact of the Chernobyl Disaster*. London: Macmillan, 1988.

MEDVEDEV, GRIGORY. *The Truth About Chernobyl*. New York: Basic Books, 1991.

MEDVEDEV, ZHORES A. *The Nuclear Disaster in the Urals*. New York: W. W. Norton, 1990.

MEDVEDEV, ZHORES A. *The Legacy of Chernobyl*. New York: W. W. Norton, 1990.

MILLAR, JAMES R., ED. *Politics, Work, and Daily Life in the USSR: A Survey of Former Soviet Citizens*. Cambridge: Cambridge University Press, 1987.

NEWSHOLME, ARTHUR, and JOHN ADAMS KINGSBURY. *Red Medicine: Socialized Health in Soviet Russia*. Garden City, NY: Doubleday, Doran, 1933.

ORGANIZATION FOR ECONOMIC CO-OPERATION AND DEVELOPMENT. *OECD Environmental Data. Compendium 1989*. Paris: OECD, 1989.

PRYDE, PHILIP R. *Environmental Management in the Soviet Union*. Cambridge: Cambridge University Press, 1991.

Rekomendatsii komandiram, politrabotnikam, partiynym i komsomol'skim aktivistam po bor'be s glumleniyam i isdevatel'stvami na flote. Polituprav-leniye TOF, 1987.

REICH, WARREN T., EDITOR-IN-CHIEF. *Encyclopedia of Bioethics*. New York and London: The Free Press, Collier Macmillan, 1978.

RUMER, BORIS Z. *Soviet Central Asia*. Boston: Unwin, Hyman, 1989.

RYAN, MICHAEL. *The Organization of Soviet Medical Care*. Oxford: Basil Blackwell, 1978.

SHAPIRO, M. I., and A. A. DEGTLARYEV. *Profilaktika kishechnykh infektsii v krupnom gorode*. Leningrad: Meditsina, 1990.

SHCHERBAK, IURII. *Chernobyl: A Documentary Story*. Translated by Ian Press. London: Macmillan, 1989.

SHTROMAS, ALEXANDER, and MORTON A. KAPLAN, EDS. *The Soviet Union and the Challenge of the Future. Vol. 2: Economics and Society*. New York: Paragon House, 1989.

SIGERIST, HENRY E. *Medicine and Health in the Soviet Union*. New York: Citadel, 1947.

SOLOMON, SUSAN GROSS, and JOHN F. HUTCHINSON, EDS. *Health and Society in Revolutionary Russia*. Bloomington: Indiana University Press, 1990.

STITES, RICHARD. *Utopia and Experiment in the Russian Revolution: Some Preliminary Thoughts*. Washington, DC: Kennan Institute, 1981.

TREML, VLADIMIR G. *Alcohol in the USSR: A Statistical Study*. Durham, NC: Duke University Press, 1982.

UNITED NATIONS ENVIRONMENT PROGRAMME. *Environmental Data Report*. 3rd Ed. 1991/1992. Prepared for UNEP by the Global Environmental Monitoring System's Monitoring and Research Assessment Research Centre, London, in cooperation with the World Resources Institute, Washington, D.C., and the UK Department of the Environment, London. Oxford: Basil Blackwell, 1991.

U.S. CONGRESS. Joint Economic Committee. All compendia on the Soviet economy during the period 1962 to 1987, contain articles by Murray Feshbach on Soviet population, manpower, migration, science and technology and civilian and military health issues.

USSR MINISTRY OF SOCIAL WELFARE. *Osnovnyye pokazateli invalidnost' i deyatel'nosti VTEK v SSSR za 1986 god*. Moscow: MSW, 1987.

WEINER, DOUGLAS R. *Models of Nature: Ecology, Conservation, and Cultural Revolution in Soviet Russia*. Bloomington: Indiana University Press, 1988.

WORLD RESOURCES INSTITUTE. *World Resources 1990–1991*. New York and Oxford: Oxford University Press, 1990.

YABLOKOV, ALEKSEI V. *Yadovitaya priprava*. Moscow: Mysl', 1990.

Soviet Journals and Newspapers

Agitator Armii i Flota
Byulleten' Mosgorispolkoma
Ekologicheskiy vestnik Rossii
Ekologiya
Ekologiya Krasnoyar'ya
Energiya: Ekonomika. Tekhnika. Ekologiya
Gigiyeniya i sanitoriya
Meditsinskaya gazeta
Meditsinskiy zhurnal Uzbekistana
Nauka o zemle
Pediatriya
Planovoye khozyaystvo
Press vypusk (Goskomstat SSSR)
Science in the USSR
Sem'ya
Sovetskaya meditsina

Sovetskoye zdravookhraneniye
Statisticheskiy press-byulleten' (Goskomstat SSSR)
Tyl i snabzheniya Sovetskikh vooruzhenykh sil
Vestnik Akademii nauk SSSR
Voprosy ekonomiki
Voyenno-meditskinskiy zhurnal
Vrach
Zdravookhraneniye Belorussii
Zdravookhraneniye Kazakhstana
Zdravookhraneniye Turkmenistana
Zdravookhraneniye RSFSR
Zelyonniy mir
Zhilishchnoye i kommunal'noye khozyaystvo
Zhurnal mikrobiologii, epidemiologii i immunologii

Western Periodicals

American Journal of Public Health
Business in the USSR (joint venture)
Current Digest of the Soviet Press
Environmental Policy Review
Journal of the American Medical Association
Le Courrier des Pays de l'Est
Pace Environmental Law Review
Radio Liberty Research
WorldWatch

INDEX

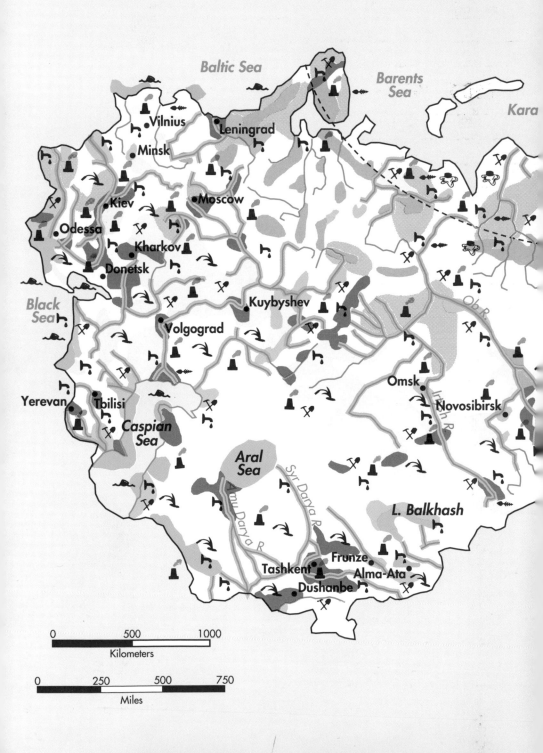

Baltic Sea

Barents Sea

Kara

Vilnius

Leningrad

Minsk

Moscow

Kiev

Odessa

Kharkov

Donetsk

Ob R.

Kuybyshev

Black Sea

Volgograd

Omsk

Yerevan

Tbilisi

Novosibirsk

Caspian Sea

Irtysh R.

Aral Sea

L. Balkhash

Amu Darya R.

Syr Darya R.

Frunze

Tashkent

Alma-Ata

Dushanbe

0   500   1000
Kilometers

0   250   500   750
Miles